TOWARDS SUSTAINABLE WELL-BEING

Moving beyond GDP in Canada and the World

Edited by Anders Hayden, Céofride Gaudet, and Jeffrey Wilson

Towards Sustainable Well-Being examines existing efforts and emerging possibilities to improve upon gross domestic product as the dominant indicator of economic and social performance. Contributions from leading international and Canadian researchers in the field of beyond-GDP measurement offer a rich range of perspectives on alternative ways to measure well-being and sustainability, along with lessons from around the world on how to bring those metrics into the policy process.

Key topics include the policy and political impacts of major beyond-GDP measurement initiatives; the most promising possibilities and policy applications for beyond-GDP measurement; key barriers to introducing beyond-GDP metrics; and complementary measures to ensure new measurements are not merely calculated but taken into account in policymaking.

The book highlights a distinction between a reformist beyond-GDP vision, which seeks to improve policymaking and quality of life within existing political and economic institutions, and a transformative vision aiming for more fundamental change including a move beyond economic growth. Illustrating the many advances that have occurred in Canada and internationally, *Towards Sustainable Well-Being* proposes next steps for both the reformist and transformative visions, as well as possible common ground between them in the pursuit of sustainable well-being.

ANDERS HAYDEN is an associate professor in the Department of Political Science at Dalhousie University.

CÉOFRIDE GAUDET, a retired federal government economist and policy analyst, was the public servant in residence at Dalhousie University's School for Resource and Environmental Studies from 2017–2019.

JEFFREY WILSON is an assistant professor in the School of Environment, Enterprise, and Development at the University of Waterloo.

Towards Sustainable Well-Being

Moving beyond GDP in Canada and the World

EDITED BY ANDERS HAYDEN,
CÉOFRIDE GAUDET, AND JEFFREY WILSON

UNIVERSITY OF TORONTO PRESS
Toronto Buffalo London

© University of Toronto Press 2022
Toronto Buffalo London
utorontopress.com

ISBN 978-1-4875-0784-8 (cloth)   ISBN 978-1-4875-3707-4 (EPUB)
ISBN 978-1-4875-2541-5 (paper)   ISBN 978-1-4875-3706-7 (PDF)

Library and Archives Canada Cataloguing in Publication

Title: Towards sustainable well-being : moving beyond GDP in Canada and the world / edited by
    Anders Hayden, Céofride Gaudet, and Jeffrey Wilson.
Names: Hayden, Anders, 1969– editor. | Gaudet, Céofride, editor. | Wilson, Jeffrey, editor.
Description: Chapters examine international and Canadian experiences with moving "beyond
    GDP" and bringing new metrics into decisions about policy and societal priorities. | Includes
    bibliographical references and index.
Identifiers: Canadiana (print) 20220159327 | Canadiana (ebook) 20220159432 | ISBN
    9781487507848 (cloth) | ISBN 9781487525415 (paper) | ISBN 9781487537074 (EPUB) |
    ISBN 9781487537067 (PDF)
Subjects: LCSH: Well-being – Measurement. | LCSH: Sustainable development – Measurement. |
    LCSH: Economic indicators. | LCSH: Social indicators.
Classification: LCC HN25 .T69 2022 | DDC 306 – dc23

We wish to acknowledge the land on which the University of Toronto Press operates. This land is
the traditional territory of the Wendat, the Anishnaabeg, the Haudenosaunee, the Métis, and the
Mississaugas of the Credit First Nation.

This book has been published with the help of a grant from the Federation for the Humanities
and Social Sciences, through the Awards to Scholarly Publications Program, using funds provided
by the Social Sciences and Humanities Research Council of Canada.

University of Toronto Press acknowledges the financial support of the Government of Canada,
the Canada Council for the Arts, and the Ontario Arts Council, an agency of the Government of
Ontario, for its publishing activities.

Canada Council   **Conseil des Arts**
for the Arts   **du Canada**

ONTARIO ARTS COUNCIL
CONSEIL DES ARTS DE L'ONTARIO
an Ontario government agency
un organisme du gouvernement de l'Ontario

Funded by the   Financé par le
Government   gouvernement
of Canada   du Canada | **Canadä**

Contents

Preface

This book can be traced back to September 2017, when I was introduced to Céo Gaudet, who had just arrived at Dalhousie University's School for Resource and Environmental Studies as its public servant in residence. After a career in Ottawa, most recently at Environment and Climate Change Canada, he was teaching a course on well-being indicators, a topic I had been working on with Jeff Wilson since 2014. Céo and I began to meet regularly for lunch, and at one such meeting we did some blue-sky thinking about bringing together some of the leading figures working on these issues in Canada and around the world. Our hope was to learn from the growing number of "beyond-GDP" measurement initiatives that have proliferated internationally since 2009, when the Commission on the Measurement of Economic Performance and Social Progress called on world governments to find better ways to measure well-being and sustainability and to contribute to the debate about how Canada can take the next steps forward in this area.

With contributions from a diverse team of partners, some good fortune, and a Connections Grant from the Social Sciences and Humanities Research Council (SSHRC), we were able to welcome 22 speakers and 65 other participants to a workshop on "Beyond GDP: International Experiences, Canada's Options" at Dalhousie in May 2019. The event was hosted by the Centre for the Study of Security and Development and the Department of Political Science at Dalhousie, in collaboration with Engage Nova Scotia, a non-profit organization that is leading the Nova Scotia Quality of Life Initiative. The workshop was co-sponsored by Green Analytics (an ecological economic consultancy), the Canadian International Council (which promotes discussion of Canada's role in international affairs), and the Sustainable Consumption Research and Action Initiative (an international network of researchers and practitioners seeking alternatives to current consumption patterns). The diversity of partners reflects the wide-ranging interest in the search for better measures of well-being and sustainability. So, too, does the interdisciplinarity of the speakers at that event and contributors to this book, with backgrounds in fields including economics (macroeconomics, economics of happiness/well-being, environmental and ecological economics), statistics, environmental studies, political science, political economy, and public policy.

This book, like the workshop, aims to reach an interdisciplinary audience with an interest in moving beyond GDP as the main indicator of prosperity and well-being. It includes contributions not only from Canadian and international academics but also practitioners working in government, non-governmental organizations, and international agencies. Many chapters build on presentations at that workshop, along with some chapters that grew out of discussions at the event and some additional contributions.

The book addresses a range of questions similar[1] to those we asked presenters to reflect on and examine at the workshop:

- What have been the policy and other impacts of key beyond-GDP measurement initiatives so far?
- What are the most promising possibilities and policy applications for beyond-GDP measurement?
- Which approach to well-being measurement should guide construction of indicators if governments – whether the Government of Canada, provincial governments, or governments elsewhere – create an official beyond-GDP indicator or indicator dashboard?
- What complementary measures and related policy tools can help ensure that new measurements are not merely calculated and published but are taken into account in policymaking?
- What are they key barriers to introducing beyond-GDP metrics and using them in decision-making?
- What are the key next steps for beyond-GDP measurement?

Each chapter addresses a number (and in some cases, all) of these questions, with authors drawing on their research and experience to address those issues most relevant to their work. Some suggestions on where to look for answers to specific questions are provided in the Introduction.

After work on the book was underway, the COVID-19 crisis erupted. Although most chapters do not explicitly address that crisis, they all have something to offer in thinking about the meaning of well-being or sustainability, how to measure them, and how to take action to promote them, which will be centrally important issues as we work to build back better.

Anders Hayden

NOTE

1   The questions listed here are a slightly revised and streamlined version of the original workshop questions. For the original questions and more information about the workshop, see the event website: https://www.beyondgdpindicators.com /workshop-1.

Abbreviations

ANDI	Australian National Development Index
APPGWE	All-Party Parliamentary Group on Wellbeing Economics (UK)
BLI	Better Life Initiative (OECD)
CBA	Cost–Benefit Analysis
CCHS	Canadian Community Health Survey
CEIP	Community Employment Innovation Project
CES	Conference of European Statisticians
CIW	Canadian Index of Wellbeing
CPRA	Child Poverty Reduction Act (New Zealand)
CSO	Civil Society Organizations
CW	Comprehensive Wealth
DoHC	Database of Happiness Coefficients
EC	European Commission
ECB	European Central Bank
EEA	European Environment Agency
EI	Employment Insurance
ESRC	Economic and Social Research Council
ESSC	European Statistical System Committee
EU	European Union
GDP	Gross Domestic Product
GHG	Greenhouse Gas
GNH	Gross National Happiness
GNI	Gross National Income
GNP	Gross National Product
GPI	Genuine Progress Indicator (international usage)
	Genuine Progress Index (Nova Scotia)
GVA	Gross Value Added
HDI	Human Development Index
HKI	Humankind Index (Oxfam Scotland)

HLEG	High-Level Expert Group on the Measurement of Economic Performance and Social Progress
HPI	Happy Planet Index
HRSDC	Human Resources and Social Development Canada
IAPTs	Improving Access to Psychological Therapies
ICSE	Independent Commission on Sustainable Equality
ICU	Intensive Care Unit
IEA	International Energy Agency
IIP	International Investment Position
IISD	International Institute for Sustainable Development
ILO	International Labour Organization
IPCC	Intergovernmental Panel on Climate Change
ISEW	Index of Sustainable Economic Welfare
LDC	Least Developed Country
LMIC	Lower Middle-Income Country
LSF	Living Standards Framework (New Zealand)
MEP	Member of European Parliament
MEW	Measure of Economic Welfare
MNW	Measuring National Wellbeing
MP	Member of Parliament
NAEC	New Approaches to Economic Challenges
NCWI	National Comprehensive Wealth Index
NDP	New Democratic Party (Canada)
	New Development Paradigm (Bhutan)
NEF	New Economics Foundation (UK)
NGO	Non-Governmental Organization
NICE	National Institute for Health and Care Excellence (UK)
NPF	National Performance Framework (Scotland)
NPV+	Net Present Value Plus
NS	Nova Scotia
NSOs	National Statistics Offices
OECD	Organisation for Economic Co-operation and Development
OneNS	One Nova Scotia
ONS	Office for National Statistics (UK)
ONS4	Office for National Statistics' four subjective wellbeing questions
OSM	Office of Strategy Management (Nova Scotia)
QALYs	Quality Adjusted Life Years
PISA	Programme for International Students Assessment
PMPs	Participatory Measures of Progress
R&D	Research and Development
RGOB	Royal Government of Bhutan
RIAs	Regulatory Impact Assessments

SA	Social Assistance
SDGs	Sustainable Development Goals
SDIs	Sustainable Development Indicators
SEEA	System of Economic and Environmental Accounts
SNA	System of National Accounts
SRDC	Social Research and Demonstration Corporation
SSF	Stiglitz-Sen-Fitoussi
SWB	Subjective Wellbeing
SWL	Satisfaction with Life
UN	United Nations
UNDP	United Nations Development Programme
UNECE	United Nations Economic Commission for Europe
UNODC	United Nations Office on Drugs and Crime
WALYs / WELLBYs	Wellbeing Adjusted Life Years
WEAll	Wellbeing Economy Alliance
WEGo	Wellbeing Economy Governments
WEMWBS	Warwick-Edinburgh Mental Wellbeing Scale
WHO	World Health Organization
WWCW	What Works Centre for Wellbeing

Acknowledgments

From the initial inspiration to the final publication of this volume, many people have made contributions that deserve thanks.

The Beyond GDP workshop that ultimately led to this book would not have been possible without the support of numerous individuals and organizations. At Dalhousie University, the event was hosted by the Centre for the Study of Security and Development (CSSD) and the Department of Political Science, with important contributions from David Black, Brian Bow, Mary Okwese, and Tracy Powell. The support of Engage Nova Scotia – and from Danny Graham, Nancy Watson, Michael Flood, and other staff – was key to the workshop's success. Adam MacDonald, the CSSD's deputy director, earned eternal gratitude for reliably putting out fires as they emerged, while graduate research assistants Jill Hatcher and Amy MacKenzie also made essential contributions before, during, and after the workshop. In addition to the presenters who authored chapters in this volume, the conversation at the workshop benefited from presentations by Mark Anielski, Anita Chandra, Grant Schellenberg, Bryan Smale (who also provided valuable support with chapter ten), John Talberth, and Ugo Therien. Support for the event also came from the Social Sciences and Humanities Research Council (SSHRC), Dalhousie's Faculty of Arts & Social Sciences, Green Analytics, the Canadian International Council, and the Sustainable Consumption Research and Action Initiative.

We are grateful to Environment and Climate Change Canada and the Canada School of Public Service for their support via the Public Servant in Residence program, which provided Céofride Gaudet with the latitude and opportunity for creativity that helped lead to the workshop and book.

Thanks also to Nafisa Abdulhamid, Haruka Aoyama, Valerie Bachynsky, Chris Beckett, Scott Burbidge, Brendan Haley, Andrea Lane, Linda Pannozzo, Rosa Poirier-McKiggan, and Peter Tyedmers, who made important contributions at various points along the way.

We are grateful to the two anonymous reviewers for their valuable suggestions that strengthened the book and to Daniel Quinlan, Stephanie Mazza, Deborah Kopka, and the rest of the team at University of Toronto Press.

There were some challenging moments along the way. Thanks to Bob Huish for his sage advice about how to navigate those challenges. Special thanks to Fran Farrell for her support that carried me through to the finish line.

Apologies to those whose contributions I have overlooked.

One of the attendees at the Beyond GDP workshop was Silver Donald Cameron, whose writing and commitment to social justice and environmental sustainability has been a great inspiration. His presence will be greatly missed as the work towards sustainable well-being continues.

Anders Hayden

TOWARDS SUSTAINABLE WELL-BEING

Introduction

ANDERS HAYDEN, CÉOFRIDE GAUDET, AND JEFFREY WILSON

How well are we doing as a society? What would it mean to be doing better? What matters most? How do we measure it? How do we go beyond merely measuring success and use the results to inform government policy and actions by other social actors? Such questions have long been asked, but they are increasingly urgent now in a context of overlapping crises that pose serious threats to well-being and its sustainability over time.

The later stages of writing this book have taken place during a deadly pandemic that has curtailed much social activity and many opportunities for connection; a related economic downturn that has left many struggling to get by and with great uncertainty about their livelihoods; widespread social protest over violent acts of racial injustice and a broader legacy of systemic inequality; profound social and political divisions, and – in some jurisdictions and corners of the social world – distrust of governments and institutions; and awareness that only a short time remains to decarbonize the global energy system to avoid catastrophic disruption to the climate system. The Gross Domestic Product (GDP) – long considered by many to be the main overall measure of economic performance and social progress – can tell us something useful about a part of these challenges. It tracks the monetary value of economic output – and its increase is the indicator of economic growth that has become such a central political priority. GDP remains valuable, for example, for governments to understand how their fiscal position may evolve and the degree of difficulty their citizens may experience in finding jobs.[1] That said, even as a measure of the state of the economy, GDP does not fully express the depth of related problems, such as the economic insecurity people experience during recessions (Hacker 2018; Stiglitz, Fitoussi, and Durand 2018, 81–7).

Due to its limited scope, GDP not only ignores many of costs of the multiple crises faced today, it also misses some bright spots. Although many commentators spoke of the economy shutting down in the early stages of the pandemic, many of the most valuable activities never stopped – and not only the essential work of courageous front-line doctors and nurses, supermarket employees, truckers, bus drivers, and many others. As one Internet meme pointed out at the height of the first lockdown period, "The economy is not 'closed.' Everyone is cooking, cleaning, and taking care of their loved ones." That unpaid work – most of which is still done by women – does not count as a contribution to GDP. Nor does GDP capture the degree of social cooperation – often referred to as "social capital" – evident in the widespread acceptance of measures to halt the coronavirus's spread and protect the vulnerable in a massive act of solidarity (even if challenges in maintaining high levels of cooperation became more evident as the pandemic wore on). Although a pandemic-driven scaling back of many forms of production is no way to achieve long-term environmental solutions, temporary reductions in air pollution, greenhouse gas emissions, congestion, and noise provided some short-term respite. If ways are found to make some of these gains permanent – and many creative ideas have emerged to try to do so – it will not be directly evident in increases in GDP; indeed, it is entirely possible that their effects may be to dampen GDP growth, even as they improve well-being or environmental sustainability. Meanwhile, if recent protests and demands for change do lead to real and lasting reduction of racial inequities, there is no line item for it in the calculation of the GDP.

This book is not mainly about what is wrong with GDP as an indicator of well-being – a role for which it was not originally intended. That case has been made many times before (e.g., Cobb, Halstead, and Rowe 1995; Kennedy 1968; Kuznets 1934; Stiglitz, Sen, and Fitoussi 2009; Waring 1988) – and it is widely, although not universally, accepted by now, even among mainstream economists and bodies that reflect dominant economic ideas, such as the Organisation for Economic Co-operation and Development (OECD) and the World Economic Forum. Still, to provide background to the debates in the book, critiques of GDP – including its failure to account for inequality in distribution, the value of non-market activities in communities and households, and environmental costs, among other issues – are discussed at various points.

The book's main focus is on alternative or complementary metrics that could allow a move beyond GDP as the single, dominant indicator of economic and social performance. It examines a wide range of ways to measure well-being and the important related issue of sustainability, as well as lessons from the growing number of efforts around the world to measure well-being differently and bring those measurements into the policy process through complementary actions and new policy tools. Rather than assuming these efforts have had or will have the significant impact their proponents have hoped for, the book examines what those impacts have been and highlights some promising examples of applications while also considering barriers to the use of alternative well-being indicators. We hope the book will help advance the debate about what to do in Canada – a country where many individuals and organizations have made impressive contributions to the global beyond-GDP debate, but government action at federal and provincial levels has, until recently, been limited. With the release in 2021 of Canada's preliminary quality-of-life measurement framework, and the likelihood of further steps to come, this volume can contribute to informing ongoing public discussion of the issues related to the country's still-evolving approach. Finally, we also hope the book will contribute to the wider international debate about the next steps for beyond-GDP measurement.

In the remainder of this introductory chapter, we outline some key distinctions in terminology and hopes people have for moving beyond GDP, potential uses of new metrics, and main categories of measurement alternatives. We conclude with an overview of the chapters that follow.

Beyond GDP or Beyond Growth? Reformist and Transformative Goals, Varying Uses

What do we mean by "beyond GDP"? Our usage of the term is similar to that in many prominent works in the field (e.g., Costanza et al. 2009; Fleurbaey and Blanchet 2013; Stiglitz, Fitoussi, and Durand 2018). "Beyond GDP" is about the quest for alternatives (or, for some observers, complements) to the GDP as the dominant indicator of societal well-being, prosperity, or national success; it is essentially about measurement, or measuring what matters. All chapters in the book are about "beyond GDP" in this sense; they all address, in their own way, efforts to improve the measurement of well-being and/or related questions of sustainability. That said, the beyond-GDP debate spills over into two other key areas. One issue, touched on above, is that it is not enough merely to produce new metrics; a key question is how to bring the information from those measurements into policymaking. Many chapters in this book also address that question. In addition, some proponents of new measurement frameworks, including some contributors to this volume, see a need not merely to move beyond GDP as an indicator but also to move "beyond growth," i.e., beyond the pursuit of economic growth as a societal priority.[2]

Indeed, for many ecologically minded participants in this debate, critique of GDP as a prosperity indicator is part of a wider post-growth project (e.g., Anderson 1991; Daly and Cobb 1989; Jackson 2017; Meadows 1998), with some seeing a need for new indicators to guide "degrowth" towards a sustainable, steady-state economy (O'Neill 2012). For example, Britain's New Economics Foundation, which launched a Wellbeing Manifesto in 2004 (Shah and Marks 2004) and became a key player in that country's beyond-GDP debate, argued that alternatives to GDP were needed, in part, because "ever-more economic growth is incompatible with the planetary limits we are up against" (Jeffrey, Wheatley, and Abdallah 2016, 2). Similarly, in the US, the growth critique has been "central to all the practitioners that work on the GPI," i.e., the Genuine Progress Indicator, a main challenger to GDP.[3]

These issues relate to a distinction, evident in this book's various chapters and in the beyond-GDP debate more generally, between transformative and reformist visions (Hayden and Wilson 2016; 2017; 2018). Viewed through a transformative lens, indicators can have a "challenge function" in seeking to destabilize dominant practices and thought frameworks (Lehtonen, Sébastien, and Bauler 2016, 6). Some observers have argued that a shift to new prosperity indicators could have transformative impacts, directing societies towards sustainability, less consumption-intensive sources of well-being, and greater equity – amounting to a "short, sharp statistical shock to the system" in the words of Jonathan Porritt (2007, 255), then-chair of the UK Sustainable Development Commission. In addition to those seeking to move beyond the growth paradigm mainly for ecological reasons, some see the transformative potential of new indicators largely in social terms, contributing to efforts to redistribute power and resources or prioritize poverty reduction. Others have emphasized the goal of creating a "new economy" – one that needs new measures of success (Zencey 2018, 80) – or proposed a "Republic of Wellbeing" that highlights "human and ecosystem wellbeing as the ultimate objective of progress" (Fioramonti et al. 2015). As Bleys and Thiry (this volume) note, some "see Beyond GDP initiatives as a window of opportunity for a more radical debate on the organization of society."

In contrast, advocates of a reformist perspective have put forward a less radical vision of alternative indicators as a tool for better policymaking without challenging the overall growth paradigm or other core features of existing economic structures (e.g., O'Donnell et al. 2014; Stiglitz, Fitoussi, and Durand 2018). As the beyond-GDP message has moved into the political mainstream and been adopted by some governments and international organizations (chapter one), it has typically been in this less provocative form – with the goal, as expressed in the OECD's slogan, of "better policies for better lives" (Stiglitz, Fitoussi, and Durand 2018, 7, see also 104–7). A reformist approach to beyond-GDP measurement is often linked to goals of more "sustainable," "green," or "inclusive" growth,[4] while some of its proponents state explicitly that the beyond-GDP measurement agenda should not be seen as "anti-growth" (Stiglitz, Fitoussi, and Durand 2018, 14; see also Department of Finance 2021a, 410).

Goals related to the reformist perspective – which proponents of a transformative vision often share, although they aim to go further – that we have encountered in our research include: gaining a more balanced and complete picture of well-being; making better evidence-based decisions in light of more comprehensive well-being and sustainability data; more quickly identifying issues and sources of discontent requiring a policy response; informing the budget-making process and making more effective use of public spending;

improving the experience of public services; overcoming policy silos and enabling different departments to work towards shared goals; analysing the impacts of public policies in more comprehensive ways; and offering members of the public new ways to evaluate the effectiveness of their elected representatives (Department of Finance 2021b, 10; Hayden and Wilson 2016; 2017; 2018). Proponents of a reformist perspective will argue that the potential benefits can be substantial (and may even use the word "transformative"). As will become clear in the pages that follow, some chapters in the book are clearly in the reformist or transformative camp, while others straddle a boundary that can become blurred.[5]

In addition to these differing visions, there are different potential uses for well-being and sustainability indicators. The direct influence of indicators as inputs into specific policy and decision outcomes has been categorized as "instrumental use" – a goal of many indicator initiatives that has not always been achieved (chapter one). There are also possible indirect pathways of influence over a longer term through "conceptual use" – by introducing new ideas and reshaping frameworks of thought and mental models (Hezri 2004; Lehtonen, Sébastien, and Bauler 2016; Rinne, Lyytimäki, and Kautto 2013; Sébastien, Bauler, and Lehtonen 2014). For example, alternative metrics could play a role over time in eroding the primacy of short-term economic growth over other societal goals that GDP reflects.

Another key category is "political use," in which indicators serve as "ammunition" to support users' positions and persuade others to see problems in a particular way – e.g., using the data from beyond-GDP metrics to make a case for different policy choices. Variations on political use can include "tactical" use of indicators as a "delaying tactic, as a substitute for action or to deflect criticisms," while "symbolic use" gives "ritualistic assurances that those who make the decisions hold appropriate attitudes towards decision-making" (Hezri 2004, 366; see also Rinne, Lyytimäki, and Kautto 2013; Sébastien, Bauler, and Lehtonen 2014). We will draw on the concepts of instrumental, conceptual, and political use at various points in the book, including the Conclusion.

Competing Measurement Alternatives

Important distinctions also exist among the proposed alternatives that have proliferated with the growing awareness of GDP's limitations as a well-being measure (for more detailed reviews, see, e.g., Barrington-Leigh and Escande 2018; Bleys 2012; Costanza et al. 2009; Fleurbaey and Blanchet 2013; van den Bergh and Antal 2014; see also wikiprogress.org). The number of options is almost overwhelming – Hoekstra (2019) refers to "hundreds of alternatives." In fact, one key challenge facing the beyond-GDP movement has been the lack of consensus on an alternative approach to unify around. As Bleys and Thiry (this volume) note, there can be a "certain dog-eat-dog" feel to the struggle among proponents to gain attention for their particular approach. Indeed, we have experienced forceful arguments for and against differing approaches while putting together this book. Although it is impossible to discuss all the options here – we have chosen to highlight some of the most prominent international and Canadian examples – one can identify four major categories of options, each with their own pros and cons.

One main category involves adjusting GDP (or GNP) – adding the value of benefits and subtracting costs that it ignores – to provide a more accurate or comprehensive monetary indicator. Nordhaus and Tobin (1972) took this approach with one of the first beyond-GDP indicators, the Measure of Economic Welfare (MEW).[6] Daly and Cobb's Index of Sustainable Economic Welfare (ISEW) and its later iteration, the Genuine Progress Indicator (GPI), went further in this direction, making still more adjustments, e.g., for inequality in distribution and the cost of various forms of pollution and environmental degradation (Berik, this volume; Hayden and Wilson 2018; Talberth, Cobb, and Slattery 2006; Talberth and Weisdorf 2017).[7] Monetary adjustments to GDP have the advantage of generating a single number that is easy to communicate and contrast with GDP, while showing trends over time – for instance, many GPI calculations show a significant gap as "genuine progress" trails GDP or even declines (e.g., Kubiszewski et al. 2013). Monetary indicators are also familiar to policymakers and others accustomed to GDP and, with all values measured in comparable monetary units, enable policy simulations and assessment of costs and benefits of different policy options (Berik, this volume). Critics raise concerns about whether it is appropriate to measure or estimate all relevant values in monetary terms, or possible to do so accurately, while there are inevitable questions about the judgments involved in choosing which specific adjustments to make to GDP and whether there is a coherent theoretical basis to justify those choices.

Composite indices that aggregate multiple social, economic, and/or ecological indicators into a single number represent another major approach. Among the most globally prominent is the Human Development Index (HDI) – a composite of per-capita income, life expectancy, and education (see Berik, this volume) – which both reflects and has contributed to awareness that "development" is about more than increasing incomes. However, critics note that the HDI, like GDP, does not acknowledge the dependence of human development on ecological sustainability (e.g., Hickel 2020). Numerous other examples of indices range from the Sustainable Development Index[8] (according to which Cuba ranked number one) to the conservative Heritage Foundation's Index of Economic Freedom (Cuba ranked 178 out of 180).[9] These examples highlight the fact that although the various metrics typically aim to provide objective data on socio-economic conditions, they also inevitably reflect different normative and political stances about what matters most (McGregor 2015). Like GDP and other monetary indicators, composite indices have the advantage of being able to communicate a complex reality in a single number, but questions inevitably arise about the choices involved in selecting and weighting an index's various components. Particular concerns arise if indices add up measures of conceptually distinct matters of well being and sustainability to produce one overall number (Stiglitz, Sen, and Fitoussi 2009, 17). Composite indices discussed in this book include Bhutan's Gross National Happiness (GNH) Index (Kim and MacKenzie), Oxfam Scotland's Humankind Index and Australia's National Development Index (Rodgers and Trebeck), the Happy Planet Index (Berik), and the Canadian Index of Wellbeing (DaSilva and Hayden).

Some participants in the debate instead emphasize surveying individuals about their subjective well-being (SWB), a.k.a. "happiness" (Helliwell et al. 2020; Layard 2020; O'Donnell et al. 2014). There are multiple ways to assess SWB, including the level of satisfaction with life overall, feelings that one's life has meaning or purpose, and the presence of positive or negative emotions at a particular time. In this book, the chapters by Helliwell et al. and Barrington-Leigh[10] are based on a primary role for happiness, specifically life satisfaction. Proponents argue that SWB, notably life satisfaction, has the potential to serve as the main measure of social success and that relying on people's own accounts of how well they are doing sidesteps the need for index-creators to impose their own subjective judgments about what matters most. A long-standing philosophical debate exists about whether happiness ought to be society's overriding goal. Critics argue that relatively high SWB could reflect limited aspirations and adaptation to marginalization, poverty, or other problematic circumstances. High SWB today might also come at the cost of eroding the ecological foundations for future well-being (indeed, that is a fair summary of the situation today in high-income nations).[11] For such reasons, some observers see a need to complement SWB measurement with sustainability indicators and related policies (Barrington-Leigh, this volume), or other objective measures. In Britain, SWB measures, which are part of a larger indicator set, have played a high-profile role in efforts to measure national well-being, contributed to the growing evidence base on the determinants of SWB, and seen some policy application (Bache), while examples of policy application are growing elsewhere (Helliwell et al., this volume).

Other prominent voices in the debate emphasize the need for dashboards of multiple measures covering a range of phenomena relevant to well-being and sustainability (Stiglitz, Fitoussi, and Durand 2018; Stiglitz, Sen, and Fitoussi 2009). Several dashboards are discussed in the book, including the OECD's Better Life Initiative (Durand and Mira d'Ercole; Berik); New Zealand's Living Standards Framework (Ng); Britain's Measuring National Wellbeing Programme indicator set and varying dashboards in Scotland, Wales, and Northern

Ireland (Bache); and dashboards in France, Slovenia, and the EU (Laurent). Also of note are dashboards that have emerged to measure progress towards the UN's Sustainable Development Goals and local-level dashboards, such as the Vital Signs program of the Community Foundations of Canada. Composite indices, such as the Canadian Index of Wellbeing, are also built upon an underlying dashboard, whose individual components may in fact provide the most useful information (Dasilva and Hayden). Dashboards can provide a wide range of information of potential interest to the public and policymakers and avoid the problem of combining incommensurate measures into a composite index. However, they have communication disadvantages as they lack a single headline number that can capture public attention and show a clear summary trend. Large dashboards can become particularly unwieldy, with a risk that, rather than informing public policy and priorities, they amount to little more than "data clearinghouses" (Barrington-Leigh and Escande 2018, 904).

Chapter Overview

With those background concepts and distinctions established, we can now turn to the content of the chapters in the book. Critique of GDP as a measure of wellbeing goes back many decades. In chapter one, Anders Hayden and Jeffrey Wilson trace the long road beyond GDP, including evolution of the critique of GDP and major steps in the development of alternatives, internationally and in Canada. They also identify major currents of thought that have contributed to beyond-GDP thinking. The latter part of the chapter draws on the authors' research into cases in Canada, Britain, the United States, and Bhutan to examine possibilities for measurement alternatives to reform and transform policy and public priorities, as well as obstacles and challenges that often limit the impacts. Hayden and Wilson raise a question to reflect on when considering the subsequent chapters: have we arrived at a point of breakthrough into the beyond-GDP world or is it time to acknowledge the profound obstacles faced and adopt new strategies? Or perhaps some mix of the two?

Publication of the report of the Commission on the Measurement of Economic Performance and Social Progress (Stiglitz, Sen, and Fitoussi 2009) was a watershed moment in the evolution of the beyond-GDP thinking. In chapter two, Martine Durand and Marco Mira d'Ercole from the OECD, an organization playing a leading international role in this field, take stock of progress since then and outline a measurement agenda for the years ahead. They draw on two recent reports by the OECD-hosted High Level Expert Group (HLEG), whose recommendations include use of a dashboard of indicators rather than a single metric of a country's well-being, improved measures of inequality and sustainability, and the use of well-being metrics at all stages of the policy process. New areas of focus include measurements of economic insecurity, trust, and inequality of opportunity. The chapter also examines actions in various countries to anchor such measurements in the policy process.

What role can participatory processes play in the creation of new measures of progress? In chapter three, Julia Rodgers and Kathrerine Trebeck emphasize the transformative potential of such processes in allowing communities and the public, especially the most disadvantaged, to highlight their priorities and shape new measurement frameworks. They examine two specific cases: Oxfam's Humankind Index in Scotland and Australia's National Development Index. Many beyond-GDP initiatives pay insufficient attention to citizen participation, according to Rodgers and Trebeck, but those based on meaningful participation can help "prefigure" a new well-being economy, providing a model of the type of shift in power needed "to address the crisis of democracy that sits alongside and exacerbates social and environmental crises."

With its concept of GNH, Bhutan helped pique the world's curiosity about what beyond-GDP approaches could achieve. In chapter four, Julia Kim and Amy MacKenzie discuss this small Himalayan nation's journey towards GNH, which involves more than an alternative set of numbers to measure well-being. While the GNH Index measures the conditions for Bhutan's distinct Buddhist-oriented conception of happiness, the idea of GNH has applications at many other levels: international promotion of a new development paradigm, national-level policies to achieve environmentally sustainable and equitable development while preserving cultural traditions, and even the personal level. Cautioning against seeing Bhutan as a Shangri-La, Kim and MacKenzie discuss challenges including finding balance between GNH and economic growth, adjustment to new democratic practices, encouraging a GNH orientation in the growing private sector, and a cultural identity crisis linked to openness to globalization. They conclude with thoughts on how Bhutan's experience could contribute to a global well-being economy, including the need to balance material and intangible aspects of well-being and embrace notions of sufficiency, equity, and sustainability.

Among high-income nations, the UK has seen some of the most significant exploration of beyond-GDP approaches. In chapter five, Ian Bache examines the rise of well-being in British politics and policy since the 1990s, related policy initiatives, and the recent focus on accumulating evidence on how policies impact well-being. The UK's Measuring National Well-being program includes a broad indicator dashboard, with measurement of subjective well-being the most prominent element, while Scotland, Wales, and Northern Ireland have their own differing initiatives. While well-being has been taken seriously in Britain, Bache cautions that its overall impact on policy has been limited, and it has not displaced conventional economic concerns. Although the accumulation of robust evidence on the drivers of well-being is important, Bache notes that evidence alone is rarely decisive in politics and policy and that political will is key. Some recent political developments nevertheless suggest possibilities for a greater prioritization of well-being in the years ahead.

A key way to bring well-being indicators into policy is through their use in shaping government budgets. In chapter six, Éloi Laurent examines four such cases in Europe: France, Slovenia, the EU, and Finland. Laurent argues that we have entered the third age of critique of economic growth, having advanced from early philosophical critique to development of alternative indicators that prioritize human well-being rather than economic growth to institutionalization of those indicators. However, he adds a note of caution, showing that their integration into policymaking has involved varying "degrees of sincerity" in different jurisdictions, ranging from manipulation of indicators by governments for political gain to integration in ways that promote sustainable well-being. In addition to going beyond changing indicators to changing policies, Laurent calls for indicators to be embedded in a new narrative that links sustainability and justice.

The hopes generated by beyond-GDP initiatives have not always been fulfilled, prompting questions about the barriers faced and possibilities for different strategies. The "rise and fall" of Beyond GDP in the EU, from initial transformative ambitions to the restoration of a conventional economic agenda in the 2010s, is the subject of chapter seven by Brent Bleys and Géraldine Thiry. EU efforts came to focus on producing new statistics, with little change in actual policy or overriding objectives, which remained focused on economic growth. Obstacles have included the inherent complexity of a multidimensional beyond-GDP agenda, the lack of a coherent political or policy agenda for the use of alternative indicators, and the existence of many disparate initiatives rather than a unified, comprehensive endeavour. The authors conclude by looking beyond "Beyond GDP," and see opportunities in the growing momentum behind "post-growth" economic ideas, which focus less on the indicator (GDP) and more on a new policy agenda and supporting narrative, and related advances in ecological macroeconomics.

One of the most contentious issues in the beyond-GDP debate, noted above, has been whether to use a single, composite measure, such as the Genuine Progress Indicator (GPI). In chapter eight, Günseli Berik examines the case for using the GPI by comparing it to other prominent international beyond-GDP options. The GPI stands out for its ability to measure what matters and guide policy, she argues. Among the main options, Berik sees it as the most responsive to GDP's shortcomings, as it counts key non-market contributors to and detractors from well-being, including income inequality, environmental damage, unpaid care work, underwork, and overwork. Berik also emphasizes the GPI's value as a monetary measure to evaluate the welfare impact of policy proposals. The chapter acknowledges criticisms of the GPI, which have led to efforts to reformulate it as an indicator of current welfare rather than sustainability and to standardize the methodology to enable cross-country comparability. Berik clearly positions the GPI as an indicator in the transformative camp, with the goal of challenging what she calls the "growth-mindset."

New Zealand is one of the countries that has gone furthest in adopting well-being as an overriding objective and integrating its measurement into policy-making, offering an important case study. In chapter nine, Tim Ng from the New Zealand Treasury discusses the country's Living Standards Framework – a multidimensional indicator dashboard that complements conventional economic performance measures – and its application in diagnosing issues requiring government attention and assessing intervention proposals. The LSF provides a common "language" for all government departments and enables comparison of initiatives in terms of well-being outcomes. Most notable has been its use in developing a "well-being budget" – an example that may have important lessons for other countries, including Canada, where government interest in a similar initiative is evident.

The scene shifts, in chapter ten, from international experiences and perspectives to Canada, which is home to a pioneering example of national well-being measurement, the Canadian Index of Wellbeing (CIW). Clay Dasilva and Anders Hayden examine the CIW framework, its development, and its applications, followed by a more detailed examination of its use in the Nova Scotia Quality of Life Initiative, one of the most significant provincial-level beyond-GDP efforts. The Initiative, which has included its own Nova Scotia Quality of Life Index and a subsequent Quality of Life Survey, emerged in a context of debate about how Nova Scotia could address longstanding economic challenges and spur economic growth. While acknowledging the importance of strengthening the province's economy, the Initiative's leaders have promoted the engagement of Nova Scotians in pursuit of a broader vision of prosperity that goes beyond financial or material concerns. The authors provide an initial assessment of the Initiative's impacts and prospects, as well as obstacles to a full embrace of a quality-of-life orientation in the province.

Measurement of happiness and understanding of its determinants has played a key role in the evolution of beyond-GDP thinking. In chapter eleven, John F. Helliwell, David Gyarmati, Craig Joyce, and Heather Orpana propose a further step: an "epidemiology of happiness" that seeks to understand not only the sources and consequences of disease but more broadly, and positively, the sources and consequences of healthy and happy lives. While a case has long existed for a broader epidemiology of this kind, the authors argue, the opportunities and need have never been greater. Opportunities have grown with advances in the science of well-being, which, in addition to providing growing evidence on the determinants of well-being, can now be used to design and rank policy options, and evaluate policy interventions. The chapter highlights Canadian examples of life-satisfaction research and policy analysis, including the use of impacts on subjective well-being in cost–benefit analyses and comparisons of return on investment. Turning their attention to the COVID-19 crisis, the authors argue that the need for such an approach has grown more urgent since policy decisions have required a broader approach than that offered by more typical policy evaluations.

An emphasis on happiness or life satisfaction can face tensions with the issue of sustainability. In chapter twelve, Christopher Barrington-Leigh emphasizes the importance of life satisfaction as a measure of well-being, arguing that it can serve as a core goal to reorient policymaking, but he acknowledges the possibility that high life satisfaction today could come at the expense of future generations by exhausting key resources. He proposes addressing well-being and environmental sustainability separately rather than conflating them conceptually or combining them in the same measurements. His approach combines a system of material constraints on activity to address sustainability, within which life satisfaction could be maximized. The chapter includes discussion of the institutional changes that would be required to achieve this vision – among them a "database of happiness coefficients" with the best available knowledge about how differing life circumstances affect life satisfaction.

How best to measure sustainability – and assess tradeoffs between current and future welfare – is a complex and contentious question. In chapter thirteen, Robert Smith, Kieran McDougal, and Livia Bizikova outline one major approach: measuring comprehensive wealth, which is "the value of all the assets a nation has at its disposal," including produced, financial, natural, human, and social "capital." While the overall measured value of comprehensive wealth in Canada has increased since 1980, trends in some areas – e.g., declining value of market natural capital (and signs of decline in non-monetary indicators of ecosystem health and the climate system) – are less promising. Smith, McDougal, and Bizikova characterize the sustainability of Canadian development as fragile at best since 2008. While acknowledging some challenges in measuring comprehensive wealth, the authors argue that it provides an important complement to GDP that decision-makers should pay attention to.

In a provocative argument bridging international and Canadian experiences, Ronald Colman says it is "Time for a Reality Check" in chapter fourteen. As a leading figure in Canada's beyond-GDP movement, who worked closely for many years with Bhutan's former prime minister and contributed to related work in New Zealand, Colman has had a first-hand view of key developments since the 1990s. Early hopes that more and better information – such as documenting the true costs and benefits of the full range of economic activity – would transform policymaking and public priorities were naïve, he concludes. Colman calls for a clear-eyed assessment of how a new economic paradigm based on ecological sustainability, fair distribution, and efficient resource use has been thwarted by powerful vested interests committed to "business as usual," bureaucratic inertia, and the nature of capitalism itself. Only then, he argues, can a constructive path forward be found, in which indicator aficionados and analysts gear their findings to an entirely different audience. The chapter also provides a critical account of the limits of the GNH experience in Bhutan that contrasts with Kim and Mackenzie's chapter four.

In the concluding chapter, the editors provide an overview of the responses given by the chapter authors, along with some answers of their own, to the questions introduced in the preface. These questions relate to the impacts of beyond-GDP measurement initiatives to date, their promising possibilities and applications, the merits of competing measurement frameworks, complementary measures and related policy tools to bring new metrics into policymaking, barriers to introducing beyond-GDP metrics and using them in decision-making, and next steps. Regarding the latter, the editors offer thoughts on potential common ground between reformist and transformative perspectives around the idea of a well-being economy. For readers looking for more guidance about where particular questions are addressed, we provide additional details in the appendix to this introduction.

As noted in the preface, the issue of beyond-GDP measurement attracts people from many sectors and disciplinary backgrounds with varying interests. Although we encourage readers to engage with all the chapters to gain new insights and understandings, we offer some suggestions for those with particular interests: historical background on the critique of GDP and emergence of alternatives to it (chapters one and two); public policy (chapters two, four, six, nine, eleven, twelve, and fourteen); politics and political economy of well-being and sustainability measurement (chapters one, five, six, seven, ten, and fourteen); ecological economics (chapters seven, eight, twelve, thirteen, and fourteen); economics of happiness and well-being (chapters eleven and twelve); and the role of civil society and non-governmental organizations (chapters three, four, and ten). We note that the book's anonymous reviewers encourage readers to read chapter fourteen, which we have placed towards the end of the book so that readers can engage with its challenges to the beyond-GDP movement after first gaining or expanding familiarity with the range of initiatives and approaches.

Next, we turn to tracing the journey that has already been travelled on the road beyond GDP.

Appendix 0.1: Core Questions and Chapters Addressing Them

What have been the policy and other impacts of key beyond-GDP measurement initiatives so far? Many chapters discuss impacts of specific initiatives or measurement approaches (chapters four through 10) or provide a more general assessment (chapters one, two, and fourteen).

What are the most promising possibilities and policy applications for beyond-GDP measurement? Examples are found throughout the book, including an overview of potentially transformative possibilities (chapter one), options to use well-being metrics at every stage of the policy cycle (chapter two) including budgeting (chapters six and nine), use of related participatory processes to deepen democratic engagement (chapters three and ten), policy applications of the GPI (chapter eight) and life-satisfaction measurement (chapters eleven and twelve), and other innovations evident in national initiatives (chapters four, five, and nine).

Competing answers to the question of which well-being measurement approach should guide construction of a beyond-GDP indicator or indicator dashboard are implicit in chapters that make a case for the GPI (chapter eight), life satisfaction (chapters eleven and twelve), and comprehensive wealth measurement (chapter thirteen). Another major option, the Canadian Index of Wellbeing, and its underlying indicator dashboard, is examined in chapter ten. Chapter two includes the OECD's recommendation of an indicator dashboard rather than any single indicator. Readers may also find value in drawing on insights from the experience of other international initiatives chapters (three through seven and nine) to determine their own position on the approach that governments in Canada – or indeed other countries – ought to take.

What complementary measures and related policy tools can help ensure that new measurements are not merely calculated and published but are taken into account in policymaking? The importance of such measures is introduced in chapter one, followed by a discussion of ways countries have started to move "from measurement to policy" in chapter two. Among the key complementary measures are new cost–benefit analysis tools that integrate beyond-GDP indicators – touched on briefly in chapters one, two, and five and in more detail in chapters nine and eleven – and the development of a solid evidence base on the determinants of well-being (chapters five, eleven, and twelve). Case studies of international (chapters three through six and nine) and Canadian (chapter ten) initiatives include discussion of various other complementary measures. Meanwhile, chapter fourteen highlights a different area for complementary action: acknowledging the fundamental obstacles that have prevented a shift to post-growth policymaking and developing strategies to overcome them.

What are the key barriers to introducing beyond-GDP metrics and using them in decision-making? These themes are prominent in chapter one and especially chapters seven and fourteen, which emphasize obstacles to the transformative goals of those with wider aspirations to move beyond the growth paradigm; meanwhile, other chapters (four, five, six, eight, nine, ten, and thirteen) identify barriers facing particular initiatives or measurement approaches.

What are the key next steps for beyond-GDP measurement? All chapters make points relevant to this question, with some addressing it more explicitly.

Some chapters (eight, nine, eleven, twelve, and thirteen) refer to next steps for particular measurement approaches, while others highlight needs such as continued development of evidence on the determinants of well-being and the political will to act on it (chapter five), and further embedding of beyond-GDP indicators into policymaking and into a new narrative of justice and sustainability (chapter six). While chapter two outlines the OECD's forward-looking agenda for well-being measurement in line with a reformist approach to beyond-GDP measurement, chapters seven and fourteen highlight next steps for a transformative vision that seeks to move not only beyond GDP as the dominant prosperity indicator but beyond the growth paradigm more generally.

NOTES

1 GDP can also be used, for example, as part of an effort to estimate the economic cost to society of action, or inaction, in response to the climate crisis (e.g., Stern 2006) and the economic cost of the COVID-19 crisis.

2 A further distinction will be evident later in the book between those in the "beyond growth" camp who seek to move beyond economic (GDP) growth as the dominant societal and political priority, even if it remains a key means to achieve other more important ends, and others who argue for an end to the pursuit of GDP growth and the embrace of a post-growth or degrowth economy.

3 Interview with ecological economist John Talberth, 2017. See Hayden and Wilson (2018).

4 See, e.g., Bleys and Thiry's examination of the evolution of beyond-GDP ideas in the EU, Bache's discussion of Scotland's National Performance Framework, Ng's discussion of the New Zealand's Living Standards Framework that complements market-oriented policies to increase incomes, and DaSilva and Hayden's analysis of the Nova Scotia Quality of Life Initiative in this volume.

5 While this book emphasizes reformist and transformative perspectives, those with more politically conservative leanings have also engaged with the beyond-GDP debate, for example, through "economic freedom" indices (e.g., Heritage Foundation 2020). Canada's Fraser Institute (2015), a right-wing think tank, argued that its Economic Freedom Index, which reflects a particular neoliberal conception of freedom, has a stronger relationship with average life satisfaction than does per-capita income or whether a country has a democratic political system. However, the fact that Scandinavian social democracies dominate the *World Happiness Report's* upper rankings, year after year (Martela et al. 2020), casts doubt on the assertion that a neoliberal, minimal-state agenda is the path to widespread life satisfaction.

6 The MEW starts with personal consumption expenditure (GDP's largest component) and adds the estimated value of benefits, such as leisure time and

unpaid work, while subtracting costs such as negative externalities associated with urbanization and commuting.

7 Another variation on monetary adjustment to GDP is calculation of a "green GDP," which subtracts the costs of environmental damage (e.g., Li and Lang 2010).

8 The Sustainable Development Index aims to measure the "ecological efficiency of human development." It divides each nation's HDI score by the extent to which consumption-based CO_2 emissions and material footprint exceed "per-capita shares of planetary boundaries" (i.e., the degree of "ecological overshoot") (Sustainable Development Index 2020; see also Hickel 2020).

9 The Heritage Foundation (2020), which produces the index, defines economic freedom as "the fundamental right of every human to control his or her own labor and property." It measures economic freedom with twelve indicators grouped under four main pillars: rule of law, government size, regulatory efficiency, and open markets.

10 Barrington-Leigh offers a hybrid approach, proposing a composite well-being index with the weighting of each component reflecting empirical evidence about its relative contribution to life satisfaction (see also Barrington-Leigh and Escande 2018).

11 O'Neill et al. (2018) show that countries that have done well in surpassing the social thresholds to provide good lives for their people, including high levels of life satisfaction, are also the ones that have transgressed the greatest numbers of biophysical boundaries, indicating ecological unsustainability.

REFERENCES

Anderson, Victor. 1991. *Alternative Economic Indicators*. London: Routledge.

Barrington-Leigh, Christopher, and Alice Escande. 2018. "Measuring Progress and Well-Being: A Comparative Review of Indicators." *Social Indicators Research* 135, no. 3: 893–925. https://doi.org/10.1007/s11205-016-1505-0.

Bergh, Jeroen van den, and Miklos Antal. 2014. "Evaluating Alternatives to GDP as Measures of Social Welfare/Progress." Working Paper no 56. Vienna: Welfare, Wealth and Work for Europe. http://www.foreurope.eu/fileadmin/documents/pdf/Workingpapers/WWWforEurope_WPS_no056_MS211.pdf.

Bleys, Brent. 2012. "Beyond GDP: Classifying Alternative Measures for Progress." *Social Indicators Research* 109, no. 3: 355–76. https://doi.org/10.1007/s11205-011-9906-6.

Cobb, Clifford, Ted Halstead, and Jonathan Rowe. 1995. "If the GDP Is Up, Why Is America Down?" *Atlantic Monthly*, October 1995.

Costanza, Robert, Maureen Hart, Stephen Posner, and John Talberth. 2009. "Beyond GDP: The Need for New Measures of Progress." Pardee Papers 4. Boston: Frederick S. Pardee Center for the Study of the Longer-Range Future, Boston University.

Daly, Herman E., and John B. Cobb. 1989. *For the Common Good*. Boston: Beacon Press.

Department of Finance. 2021a. "A Recovery Plan for Jobs, Growth, and Resilience: Budget 2021." Ottawa: Department of Finance Canada. https://www.budget .gc.ca/2021/home-accueil-en.html.

– 2021b. "Toward a Quality of Life Strategy for Canada." Ottawa: Department of Finance Canada.

Fioramonti, Lorenzo, Enrico Giovannini, Robert Costanza, Ida Kubiszewski, Kate Pickett, Kristín Vala Ragnarsdóttir, Roberto De Vogli, and Richard Wilkinson. 2015. "Say Goodbye to Capitalism: Welcome to the Republic of Wellbeing." *The Guardian*, 2 September 2015. http://www.theguardian.com /sustainable-business/2015/sep/02/say-goodbye-to-capitalism-welcome-to-the -republic-of-wellbeing.

Fleurbaey, Marc, and Didier Blanchet. 2013. *Beyond GDP: Measuring Welfare and Assessing Sustainability*. Oxford: Oxford University Press.

Fraser Institute. 2015. "Economic Freedom of the World: 2015 Annual Report." Vancouver: Fraser Institute.

Hacker, Jacob S. 2018. "Economic Security." In *For Good Measure: Advancing Research on Well-Being Metrics Beyond GDP*, edited by Joseph E. Stiglitz, Jean-Paul Fitoussi, and Martine Durand, 203–42. Paris: OECD.

Hayden, Anders, and Jeffrey Wilson. 2016. "Is It What You Measure That Really Matters? The Struggle to Move beyond GDP in Canada." *Sustainability* 8, no. 7: 623.

– 2017. "'Beyond GDP' Indicators: Changing the Economic Narrative for a Post-Consumerist Society?" In *Social Change and the Coming of Post-Consumer Society: Theoretical Advances and Policy Implications*, edited by Maurie J. Cohen, Halina S. Brown, and Philip J. Vergragt, 170–91. New York: Routledge.

– 2018. "Taking the First Steps beyond GDP: Maryland's Experience in Measuring 'Genuine Progress.'" *Sustainability* 10, no. 2: 462. https://doi.org/10.3390 /su10020462.

Helliwell, John F., Richard Layard, Jeffrey Sachs, and Jan-Emmanuel De Neve, eds. 2020. *World Happiness Report 2020*. New York: Sustainable Development Solutions Network.

Heritage Foundation. 2020. "2020 Index of Economic Freedom: About the Index." http://www.heritage.org/index/about.

Hezri, Adnan A. 2004. "Sustainability Indicator System and Policy Processes in Malaysia: A Framework for Utilisation and Learning." *Journal of Environmental Management* 73, no. 4: 357–71. https://doi.org/10.1016/j.jenvman.2004.07.010.

Hickel, Jason. 2020. "The Sustainable Development Index: Measuring the Ecological Efficiency of Human Development in the Anthropocene." *Ecological Economics* 167 (January): 106331. https://doi.org/10.1016/j.ecolecon.2019.05.011.

Hoekstra, Rutger. 2019. *Replacing GDP by 2030*. Cambridge: Cambridge University Press.

Jackson, Tim. 2017. *Prosperity Without Growth*. 2nd ed. Abingdon, UK: Routledge.

Jeffrey, Karen, Hanna Wheatley, and Saamah Abdallah. 2016. "The Happy Planet Index 2016." London: New Economics Foundation. https://static1 .squarespace.com/static/5735c421e321402778ee0ce9/t/57e0052d440243730fdf 03f3/1474299185121/Briefing+paper+-+HPI+2016.pdf.

Kennedy, Robert F. 1968. "Remarks at the University of Kansas." http://www .jfklibrary.org/Research/Research-Aids/Ready-Reference/RFK-Speeches/Remarks -of-Robert-F-Kennedy-at-the-University-of-Kansas-March-18–1968.aspx.

Kubiszewski, Ida, Robert Costanza, Carol Franco, Philip Lawn, John Talberth, Tim Jackson, and Camille Aylmer. 2013. "Beyond GDP: Measuring and Achieving Global Genuine Progress." *Ecological Economics* 93 (September): 57–68. https:// doi.org/10.1016/j.ecolecon.2013.04.019.

Kuznets, Simon. 1934. "National Income, 1929–1932." Senate Document No. 124, 73rd Congress. 2nd Session. Washington, DC: US Government Printing Office.

Layard, Richard. 2020. *Can We Be Happier? Evidence and Ethics*. London: Pelican.

Lehtonen, Markku, Léa Sébastien, and Tom Bauler. 2016. "The Multiple Roles of Sustainability Indicators in Informational Governance: Between Intended Use and Unanticipated Influence." *Current Opinion in Environmental Sustainability* 18 (February): 1–9. https://doi.org/10.1016/j.cosust.2015.05.009.

Li, Vic, and Graeme Lang. 2010. "China's 'Green GDP' Experiment and the Struggle for Ecological Modernisation." *Journal of Contemporary Asia* 40, no. 1: 44–62. https://doi.org/10.1080/00472330903270346.

Martela, Frank, Bent Greve, Bo Rothstein, and Juho Saari. 2020. "The Nordic Exceptionalism: What Explains Why the Nordic Countries Are Constantly Among the Happiest in the World." In *World Happiness Report 2020*, edited by John Helliwell, Richard Layard, Jeffrey Sachs, and Jan-Emmanuel De Neve, 129– 46. New York: Sustainable Development Solutions Network.

McGregor, J. Allister. 2015. "Global Initiatives in Measuring Human Wellbeing: Convergence and Divergence." CWiPP Working Paper Series No. 2. Sheffield, UK: Centre for Wellbeing in Public Policy, University of Sheffield. https://www .sheffield.ac.uk/polopoly_fs/1.522118!/file/CWiPP_WP_201502_McGregor.pdf.

Meadows, Donella H. 1998. "Indicators and Information Systems for Sustainable Development." Hartland Four Corners VT: The Sustainability Institute. http:// www.iisd.org/pdf/s_ind_2.pdf.

Nordhaus, William, and James Tobin. 1972. "Is Growth Obsolete?" In *Economic Research: Retrospect and Prospect, Volume 5, Economic Growth*. Washington, DC: National Bureau of Economic Research. http://www.nber.org/chapters/c7620.

O'Donnell, Gus, Angus Deaton, Martine Durand, David Halpern, and Richard Layard. 2014. "Wellbeing and Policy." London: Legatum Institute.

O'Neill, Daniel W. 2012. "Measuring Progress in the Degrowth Transition to a Steady State Economy." *Ecological Economics* 84 (December): 221–31. https://doi .org/10.1016/j.ecolecon.2011.05.020.

O'Neill, Daniel W., Andrew L. Fanning, William F. Lamb, and Julia K. Steinberger. 2018. "A Good Life for All within Planetary Boundaries." *Nature Sustainability* 1, no. 2: 88–95. https://doi.org/10.1038/s41893-018-0021-4.

Porritt, Jonathon. 2007. *Capitalism as If the World Matters*. London: Earthscan.

Rinne, Janne, Jari Lyytimäki, and Petrus Kautto. 2013. "From Sustainability to Well-Being: Lessons Learned from the Use of Sustainable Development Indicators at National and EU Level." *Ecological Indicators* 35 (December): 35–42. https://doi.org/10.1016/j.ecolind.2012.09.023.

Sébastien, Léa, Tom Bauler, and Markku Lehtonen. 2014. "Can Indicators Bridge the Gap between Science and Policy? An Exploration into the (Non) Use and (Non) Influence of Indicators in EU and UK Policy Making." *Nature + Culture; New York* 9, no. 3: 316–43.

Shah, Hetan, and Nic Marks. 2004. "A Well-Being Manifesto for a Flourishing Society." London: New Economics Foundation. http://www.neweconomics.org/gen/uploads/21xv5yytotlxxu322pmyada205102004103948.pdf.

Stern, Nicholas. 2006. "Stern Review: The Economics of Climate Change." London: HM Treasury. http://www.hm-treasury.gov.uk/stern_review_report.htm.

Stiglitz, Joseph E., Jean-Paul Fitoussi, and Martine Durand. 2018. "Beyond GDP – Measuring What Counts for Economic and Social Performance." Paris: OECD. http://www.oecd.org/corruption/beyond-gdp-9789264307292-en.htm.

Stiglitz, Joseph E., Amartya Sen, and Jean-Paul Fitoussi. 2009. "Report by the Commission on the Measurement of Economic Performance and Social Progress." Paris. http://www.stiglitz-sen-fitoussi.fr/documents/rapport_anglais.pdf.

Sustainable Development Index (SDI). 2020. "Sustainable Development Index." https://www.sustainabledevelopmentindex.org.

Talberth, John, Clifford Cobb, and Noah Slattery. 2006. "The Genuine Progress Indicator 2006: A Tool for Sustainable Development." Oakland, CA: Redefining Progress. http://issuu.com/genuine-progress/docs/indicator-2006/1?e=7627340/1756730.

Talberth, John, and Michael Weisdorf. 2017. "Genuine Progress Indicator 2.0: Pilot Accounts for the US, Maryland, and City of Baltimore 2012–2014." *Ecological Economics* 142 (December): 1–11. https://doi.org/10.1016/j.ecolecon.2017.06.012.

Waring, Marilyn. 1988. *If Women Counted: A New Feminist Economics*. San Francisco: Harper & Row.

Zencey, Eric. 2018. "The 2018 Vermont Genuine Progress Indicator Report." Burlington, VT: The Vermont Genuine Progress Indicator Project, University of Vermont.

PART ONE

Background and Visions

1 The Long Road beyond GDP: Have We Finally Reached a Time for Breakthroughs?

ANDERS HAYDEN AND JEFFREY WILSON

Introduction

The need to move beyond GDP as the primary indicator of well-being or prosperity is increasingly widely recognized. In the words of a senior Nova Scotia public official, it is "almost now the orthodoxy that GDP is not the way to measure progress and success."[1] Whatever one makes of the word "almost" in that statement, and however much further there still is to travel, a substantial distance has been covered to get to this point.

This chapter begins with an overview of the evolution of the critique of GDP and major steps in the development of alternatives, internationally and in Canada. In addition to providing historical background to recent developments covered in later chapters, these sections highlight main currents of thought that have contributed to beyond-GDP thinking. In the latter part of the chapter, we draw on our research in Canada, Britain, the United States, and Bhutan to highlight some promising possibilities for those seeking to reform or transform policy and public priorities, the relatively limited impacts that have (so far) fallen short of many of the hopes, and some considerations about why new measurements – on their own – are insufficient. We conclude with a question about where things stand after decades of travel on the road beyond GDP: have these efforts finally reached the point of major breakthroughs, or is it time to adopt new approaches that acknowledge fundamental obstacles on the path?

A Brief History of the Long Road Beyond GDP

One can trace the critique of GDP – and related measures, such as Gross National Product (GNP), which was more commonly used until recently[2] – back to the birth of national income accounting. The key figure behind this innovation, economist Simon Kuznets (1934, 7), famously warned that "the welfare of a nation can … scarcely be inferred from a measurement of national income." That said, national income accounting was a useful tool to confront the challenges of the Great Depression. If government was to intervene to boost economic output – and the employment and tax revenues that went with it – estimates of the market value of that output were valuable to assess the success of New Deal and Keynesian policies (Fioramonti 2013; Philipsen 2015). Even more important was national income accounting's role as a planning tool during the Second World War, as it enabled policymakers to estimate potential revenues, identify unused capacity, maximize production, and allocate additional resources for the war effort (Anderson 1991; Cobb, Halstead, and Rowe 1995; Fioramonti 2013).

Equating increases in production, and the consumption it enabled, with progress – and even a national purpose that countries could unite around – became more entrenched during the post-war economic boom (Yarrow 2010). During this "golden age" of capitalism, leading capitalist nations experienced rapid economic growth, mostly low unemployment, and income growth distributed broadly enough to boost middle- and working-class consumption – although class, racial, and gender inequities remained (Cohen 2004). Despite significant successes linked to rapid GNP growth, critical voices soon became audible. Among them was John Kenneth Galbraith (1958), who suggested in *The Affluent Society* that the drive for an ever-larger GNP no longer had the same urgency as in times of greater scarcity. "To furnish a barren room is one thing," he wrote. "To continue to crowd in furniture until the foundation buckles is quite another." He also highlighted the "poor use of our affluence," contrasting America's "private opulence and public squalor."

The First Wave of Political Interest in a Wider Conception of Well-being

By the 1960s, critique of excessive focus on production and consumption growth was voiced not only by the burgeoning counterculture but also some political leaders. US President Lyndon Johnson (1964) questioned "unbridled growth" in his call to construct a "Great Society," in which the challenge was no longer to "create an order of plenty," but rather "to use that wealth to enrich and elevate our national life, and to advance the quality of our American civilization." His Great Society was "concerned not with how much, but with how good – not with the quantity of goods but with the quality of our lives."[3]

Robert Kennedy (1968) also targeted the over-emphasis on the quantity of production in a well-known speech two days after launching his presidential campaign:

The Gross National Product … counts special locks for our doors and the jails for the people who break them. It counts the destruction of the redwood and the loss of our natural wonder in chaotic sprawl. It counts napalm and counts nuclear warheads and armored cars for the police to fight the riots in our cities. ... Yet the gross national product does not allow for the health of our children, the quality of their education or the joy of their play. It does not include the beauty of our poetry or the strength of our marriages, the intelligence of our public debate or the integrity of our public officials. It measures neither our wit nor our courage, neither our wisdom nor our learning, neither our compassion nor our devotion to our country, it measures everything in short, except that which makes life worthwhile.

The post-materialist current of the time is evident in Kennedy's speech: "Too much and for too long, we seemed to have surrendered personal excellence and community values in the mere accumulation of material things." But he also highlighted continued material deprivation, within an economy of plenty, experienced by groups including African Americans, Native Americans, and Appalachia's white working class. Also noteworthy from today's vantage point is Kennedy's concern for the "growing division between Americans" and the fact that "we confront our fellow citizen across impossible barriers of hostility and mistrust" – a problem that would in later years be understood in terms of "social capital" or lack thereof.

Awareness of GNP's limits as an indicator of societal well-being was widespread enough at this time that even the arch-conservative Richard Nixon acknowledged the issue. In his 1970 State of the Union address, he stated: "In the next 10 years we will increase our wealth by 50 percent. The profound question is, does this mean that we will be 50 percent richer in any real sense, 50 percent better off, 50 percent happier?" (quoted in Campbell 1981, 4). Economist Richard Easterlin (1974) soon showed that, despite substantial economic growth in previous decades, happiness levels remained practically unchanged over time, sparking a debate on the precise relationship between these variables that continues to this day.

This first wave of political interest in well-being measurement and its application to policy in the 1960s and early 1970s was associated with a social indicators movement, which sought wider quality-of-life measures in many countries (Allin and Hand 2014, 53–5; Bache and Reardon 2016, 39–44). Proposals included a system of "social accounts" to provide a more comprehensive assessment of costs and benefits to society than that provided by market-based accounts. The US federal government established a Panel on Social Indicators (1969, xii–xiii; Bache and Reardon 2016, 40), which recognized the limits of economic indicators in measuring national well-being and assessing the effects of public programs. In 1970, Britain's Central Statistical Office began publishing *Social Trends*, an annual compilation of economic, social, and environmental statistics that gave a more complete picture of British life than did GNP/GDP (Allin and Hand 2014, 218, 221).

Growing environmental concerns – illustrated by the first Earth Day in 1970, the first global conference on the human environment in Stockholm in 1972, and the Club of Rome's *Limits to Growth* report (Meadows et al. 1972) – also affected the measurement debate. Noted environmentalist Paul Ehrlich "speaks for a multitude when he says, 'We must acquire a life style which has as its goal maximum freedom and happiness for the individual, not a maximum Gross National Product,'" wrote economists William Nordhaus and James Tobin (1972, 1). Although they rejected environmental arguments about limits to growth, Nordhaus and Tobin acknowledged that "GNP is not a measure of economic welfare" and that "maximization of GNP is not a proper objective of policy" (4). They took an important early step beyond GDP by making numerous additions to, and subtractions from, personal consumption expenditures to calculate their Measure of Economic Welfare (MEW).

While many governments in the Global South aimed at this time to throw off the constraints of tradition to allow economic "take off" towards the heights of "mass consumption" (Rostow 1960), interest in alternative paths for "developing" countries was emerging. The Himalayan nation of Bhutan brought a critical perspective on GNP to that issue. In the 1970s, journalists in India asked Bhutan's Fourth King about his country's GNP. "We are not concerned about Gross National Product, we care about Gross National Happiness," or GNH, he reportedly replied (Dorji 2012).[4] Bhutan's alternative understanding of well-being and development – focused on GNH – preceded adoption of a different measurement framework; it did not begin to calculate a GNH Index until much later, in 2008.

While developments differed from country to country, the first wave of political interest in well-being measurement had modest impacts overall – and failed to dethrone GNP from its primacy in politics and policy (Allin and Hand 2014; Bache and Reardon 2016). With an oil shock–induced recession in 1973, and another in 1979, political focus centred on restoring GNP growth and combatting unemployment and inflation. The growing prominence of market-oriented neoliberal ideas also helped to elevate supply-side concern for business profitability over a wider conception of well-being.

Renewed Interest and a Second Wave

A key contribution, which helped expand awareness of the misuse of GNP/GDP as measures of economic "progress" and revive debate on these issues, came from feminist economist Marilyn Waring (1988) in her book *If Women Counted*. She highlighted the failure of the System of National Accounts to consider the value of unpaid work and care in households and communities, as well as the value of nature, in determining what counts as productive.

Another key step was Herman Daly and John Cobb's (1989) Index of Sustainable Economic Welfare (ISEW), which built on Nordhaus and Tobin's MEW but reflected ecological concerns about the unsustainability of economic growth by, among other adjustments, subtracting the costs of environmental degradation and natural-capital depletion. Later revisions to the ISEW led to the Genuine Progress Indicator (GPI), which gained prominence with an influential 1995 article in the *Atlantic Monthly* entitled "If GDP is Up, Why is America Down?" (Cobb, Halstead, and Rowe 1995) and has generated several national and subnational offshoots (see Berik, this volume).

By roughly the mid-1990s, the second wave of political interest in well-being measurement was building, with further growth of environmental concern a key driver (Bache and Reardon 2016, 44; see also Allin and Hand 2014). Following the Brundtland Report on "sustainable development" and the 1992 Rio Earth Summit, many countries looked to adopt environment and sustainability indicators, while interest grew in linking well-being and sustainability measurement – with the ISEW/GPI being one example (Costanza et al. 2009). Growing interest in, and acceptance of, the measurement of subjective well-being/happiness, and the related growth of the academic literature on their determinants (e.g., Layard 2005), have been other key developments (Bache and Reardon 2016, 47–8). The second wave of interest has also featured a significant role for international organizations and coordinated international efforts in this area (Bache and Reardon 2016, 48–60).

Growing mainstream interest in alternative well-being measures was evident in the 2007 Istanbul Declaration, in which the Organisation for Economic Co-operation and Development (OECD) and other international organizations acknowledged an "emerging consensus" on the importance of "going beyond conventional measures such as GDP per capita" (OECD 2007). That same year, the European Union launched its "beyond GDP" program (Bleys and Thiry, this volume). A particularly important step was former French president Sarkozy's establishment of the Commission on the Measurement of Economic Performance and Social Progress, led by Joseph Stiglitz, Amartya Sen, and Jean-Paul Fitoussi. The Commission's report gave a major boost to international awareness of GDP's limitations in assessing economic performance, which its authors described as "mismeasuring our lives" (Stiglitz, Sen, and Fitoussi 2010; see also Durand and Mira d'Ercole, this volume).

National beyond-GDP initiatives also began to proliferate in this period. China's experimentation with a "green GDP," which incorporated environmental damage costs, in 2006 and 2007 was an early, albeit short-lived, example – one that generated "fierce opposition from local officials eager to maintain growth" (Buckley 2007; see also Li and Lang 2010). More enduring has been British Prime Minister David Cameron's (2010) instruction to the UK's Office for National Statistics to develop new well-being measures to complement (but not replace) GDP – an initiative that, in his words, "reaffirms the fact that our success as a country is about more than economic growth" (see also Bache, this volume). The UK initiative is noteworthy not only because it had a high-level political champion, at least for a time, or because that backing came from a conservative leader,[5] but also because it has led to considerable data gathering about "what works" for well-being, which has helped expand possibilities for using well-being data in policy (What Works Centre for Wellbeing 2020). Beyond-GDP initiatives have also been launched in many EU countries (Bleys and Thiry, this volume; Laurent, this volume).

In the United States, state- and local-level initiatives have stood out. Governor Martin O'Malley announced in 2010 that Maryland would begin calculating the GPI (Hayden and Wilson 2018). Vermont followed with its GPI Act of 2012, which established a GPI for the state, and several other states saw efforts to launch GPI initiatives, part of a wider "Genuine Progress in the States" (2014) campaign. Meanwhile, local well-being measurement initiatives were introduced in communities such as Santa Monica (California) and Somerville (Massachusetts).

Bhutan also contributed to the growing international prominence of these issues during the latest wave of interest (Colman, this volume; Kim and MacKenzie, this volume; Hayden 2015). It was the main force behind a UN General Assembly (2011) resolution on "happiness," which recognized GDP's inadequacy as a well-being indicator, the dangers of "unsustainable patterns of production and consumption," and the need for "a more inclusive, equitable and balanced approach to economic growth." Bhutan hosted a high-level UN meeting in 2012 on "Happiness and Well-Being: Defining a New Economic Paradigm," where Prime Minister Jigmi Thinley (2012) told assembled delegates: "The GDP led development model that compels boundless growth on a planet with limited resources no longer makes economic sense." This fundamental challenge to the dominant economic model – which went beyond merely proposing new measurement frameworks – was more than many powerful interests were ready to hear, as Colman (this volume) describes.

At the 2012 UN event sponsored by Bhutan, the now-annual *World Happiness Report* was launched (Helliwell, Layard, and Sachs 2012). Growing international interest in happiness measurement and related policies was also evident in the 2016 announcement of a National Program for Happiness and Wellbeing, including a happiness ministry, in the United Arab Emirates, which went on to host the launch of two reports by the new Global Happiness Council (2018).

Ongoing efforts to promote sustainable development have remained an important driver of recent beyond-GDP activity. At the 2012 Rio+20 sustainable development conference, heads of state and government acknowledged "the need for broader measures of progress to complement gross domestic product" (UN 2012, para. 38). Meanwhile, agreement in 2015 on the UN's 17 Sustainable Development Goals (SDGs), which include 169 targets, has generated considerable debate on how to best measure progress towards these goals and boosted efforts to establish SDG indicator dashboards and composite SDG indices (Bertlesmann Stiftung and SDSN 2019).

A final international development of note has been the emergence of the Wellbeing Economy Governments (WEGo), which at the time of writing consist of New Zealand, Iceland, Scotland, Wales, and Finland. Jacinda Ardern's government in New Zealand made international headlines with its 2019 "wellbeing budget," discussed in detail by Ng (this volume). Iceland approved a new well-being indicator framework of its own (Ćirić 2020), while Prime Minister Katrín Jakobsdóttir (2020), echoing Bhutan's message to the world in 2012, wrote of the need to "develop a new economic model, which is centred on wellbeing rather than on production and consumption" and to "change the way we live" to address climate change. Meanwhile, Scottish First Minister Nicola Sturgeon (2020) stated that Scotland was "redefining" what it means to be a "successful country," and "putting wellbeing at the heart of what we are doing."

This overview of international developments illustrates the varied currents of thought that have informed the desire to move beyond GDP, including: social critique of the divergence between growing economic production and quality of life, and related questioning of the connection between GDP and happiness; environmental critique by ecological economists and others of over-consumption and the costs of pursuing infinite economic growth; critique of income inequality and related inequities of race, class, and gender that GDP does not consider; feminist critique of the failure to value unpaid work; the search for alternative development paths in the Global South, whether variations on "sustainable development" or more radical calls for a "new economic paradigm"; interest among international organizations in finding better economic, social, and environmental performance measures; and recognition among many conventional economists of GDP's flaws as a well-being measure. This multiplicity of currents feeding into the beyond-GDP movement makes it a rich intellectual terrain but also creates challenges in establishing a unified approach to move forward.

What about Canada?

Canadians have played a surprisingly large role in these issues – dating back to the Ontario-born Galbraith's "affluent society" critique. Canadian researchers, including John Helliwell and Alex Michalos have played key roles in advancing the study of happiness and well-being (e.g., Helliwell 2019; Helliwell et al., this volume; Michalos 2014), while Helliwell has been lead author of the *World Happiness Report* since its launch (Helliwell, Layard, and Sachs 2012).

In the late 1990s, Canadian economists Lars Osberg and Andrew Sharpe (2010) developed an Index of Economic Wellbeing that expressed many of the principles that the Stiglitz-Sen-Fitoussi (2010) Commission later highlighted. Innovations in GPI calculations were first applied in Alberta by the Pembina Institute and ecological economist Mark Anielski (Anielski et al. 2001). Work on the GPI took a different direction in Nova Scotia, where rather than producing a single composite indicator, GPI Atlantic (2007) produced a range of pioneering studies of the "real costs and benefits of economic activity." Its founder, Ron Colman, contributed to related work in New Zealand and played a key role in Bhutan's efforts to measure Gross National Happiness (GNH) and promote a "new economic paradigm" (Colman, this volume; Colman 2021). Michael Pennock also contributed to Bhutan's efforts through work on a GNH policy screening tool and the survey underlying the GNH Index – as has Julia Kim as program director of the GNH Centre (Kim and MacKenzie, this volume). Meanwhile, with the Canadian Index of Wellbeing's 2011 launch (Dasilva and Hayden, this volume), Canada became one of the first countries with a composite well-being index, although it was neither produced nor adopted by the federal government.

At the workshop that was a step towards this book, one invited guest from Europe asked, "Why is it that Canadians have contributed so much in this area, but Canadian governments have done so little?" We do not have a full answer, but we have certainly been aware of this contrast between Canadian contributions and limited government action, at least until recently. That said, there have been hopes for a breakthrough at various points, which have recently re-emerged, and some significant activity behind the scenes that is worth acknowledging.

In the late 1990s, a grassroots campaign for a Canada Wellbeing Measurement Act was initiated by sustainability activist Mike Nickerson (2009) and Peter Bevan-Baker (who went on to lead the Green Party and official opposition in Prince Edward Island). Liberal MP Joe Jordan took up the cause and introduced a private member's bill in 2000 to require the federal government to produce new economic, social, and environmental well-being indicators. The House of Commons approved a related, non-binding motion in 2003, with substantial cross-party support, but the bill itself never made its way through Parliament.

In 2000, federal finance minister Paul Martin provided $9 million to the National Round Table on the Environment and Economy to develop environmental and sustainable development indicators. Martin (2000) optimistically proclaimed: "In the years ahead, these environmental indicators could well have a greater impact on public policy than any other single measure we might introduce." Martin himself favoured a "Green GDP" adjusted for environmental depletion costs, but the idea did not become a priority while he was finance minister or prime minister. Nor is there any indication that the environmental and sustainable development indicators ever had the hoped-for policy impact (Hayden and Wilson 2016).

At the provincial level, considerable hope for a breakthrough existed in Nova Scotia, where prior to taking power in 2009, the New Democratic Party (NDP) promised "to incorporate Genuine Progress accounting into provincial policy analysis" (GPI Atlantic 2009); however, after forming a government, the NDP did not act on this promise (Colman, this volume).

The 2011 launch of the non-governmental CIW – the result of a decade-long effort by leading Canadians working in this field, funded by the Atkinson Charitable Foundation (Dasilva and Hayden, this volume) – came at an unfavourable time for those hoping the new data would inform evidence-based policy or stimulate a comparable federal-government measurement initiative. The Conservative Harper government's well-known disregard for evidence that challenged its political priorities was visible, for example, in its silencing of federal environmental scientists and closure of the National Round Table on Environment and Economy, prompting protests by scientists against the "death of evidence" (Hayden and Wilson 2016). That said, during these years Statistics Canada was a leader in gathering life-satisfaction data and examining influences on it, among other innovative work below the political radar within the federal public service (see Helliwell et al., this volume).

Renewed interest in wider well-being measures has been evident under the Trudeau Liberals. The prime minister's mandate letter (Trudeau 2019) to the minister of middle-class prosperity and associate minister of finance directed her to lead work to "better incorporate quality of life measurements into government decision-making and budgeting, drawing on lessons from other jurisdictions such as New Zealand and Scotland." By early 2020, the federal government was considering and consulting on its own well-being budget, following New Zealand's example (Ng, this volume; Tumilty 2020), although the COVID-19 crisis became the more immediate priority. The July 2020 "economic and fiscal snapshot" acknowledged the need to look beyond GDP,[6] a theme also present in the 2021 budget (Government of Canada 2021, 46, 410). Although the terms "well-being" and "quality of life" did not appear in either the finance minister's budget speech nor the government's media release[7] – suggesting the government was not ready for a high-profile well-being budget, as in New Zealand – the budget did include significant spending to address gaps in Statistics Canada's quality-of-life measurement capacity (313), a statement outlining work on "measuring what matters" (410–12), and initial steps towards assessing the impact of spending initiatives on a draft set of quality-of-life indicators (Annex 5). At the same time, the Department of Finance (2021) released *Toward a Quality of Life Strategy for Canada*, which outlined the government's proposed quality-of-life measurement framework – a dashboard approach, influenced by the OECD's well-being work, built around five domains of prosperity, health, environment, society, and good governance – as a basis for further public consultation. Meanwhile, a separate initiative, led by Employment and Social Development Canada, has been establishing an indicator set to measure Canada's progress towards the UN SDGs.

Considerable activity has also taken place below the federal level. The CIW has turned much of its attention to provincial and local-level work, including a Saskatchewan Index of Wellbeing and Nova Scotia Quality of Life Initiative, and its community-level measurement of well-being (Dasilva and Hayden, this volume). Numerous municipal dashboards also exist in cities across the country, which are providing a local testing ground for more comprehensive ways to measure well-being.

Possibilities, Impacts, and Challenges

As indicated by the previous discussion, there is now a wealth of initiatives to learn from both inside and beyond Canada's borders, which illustrate many interesting possibilities but also provide some reasons for caution about whether the hoped-for impacts will be achieved. In this section, we draw on our research into the policy and political impacts of work in Canada leading to the Canadian Index of Wellbeing, Britain's Measuring National Well-being Programme, and state-level GPIs in Maryland and Vermont (Hayden and Wilson 2016; 2017a; 2017b; 2018; Wilson and Hayden, in progress)[8] – and also make reference to earlier, complementary work on Bhutan (Hayden 2015). These cases are, of course, not comprehensive nor are they necessarily representative of the full range of beyond-GDP experiences, but they do highlight some themes that we believe are worthy of consideration as Canadians, and others, consider options to move forward in this area.

Possibilities of Reformed/Transformed Policy and Priorities

The introductory chapter outlined a distinction between a transformative vision – which sees beyond-GDP measurement as part of a project to build a new economy that is more equitable, sustainable, and no longer focused on the pursuit of economic growth – and a less expansive, reformist vision aiming to use new well-being measurements to improve policymaking. Existing cases reveal intriguing possibilities if Canada or other nations were to move beyond a focus on GDP growth, which are in line with a transformative vision, but might in some cases also be supported by those with reformist goals.

Starting with overall goals, economic strategy could be geared towards ends other than GDP growth. For example, Vermont's Comprehensive Economic

Development Strategy of 2014 and 2016 includes conventional goals such as increasing investment, jobs, wages, and GDP, but its "overarching goal" is to increase the state's GPI (Agency of Commerce and Community Development 2016, 1). Alternatively, that overarching goal could be defined in terms of "happiness" or "well-being," as in the emerging framing of the "well-being economies" group – or, in Bhutan's case, GNH – with economic growth reduced to one possible means among others towards achieving that end (and, we would emphasize, with strong measures to ensure sustainability over time). A shift in end goals could, if truly used to drive the policy agenda, bring with it profound shifts in priorities, such as giving greater weight to ensuring stable employment levels (avoiding boom-bust cycles) and reducing poverty and inequality even if it means lower average growth of national income. These were among the recommendations of the All-Party Parliamentary Group on Wellbeing Economics in Britain, in light of evidence about what matters most for well-being (APPGWE 2014, 4, 20).

A more comprehensive understanding of well-being and greater appreciation for sustainability could lead to policy proposals and spending initiatives being appraised and evaluated in new ways, going beyond narrow, conventional economic costs and benefits. Bhutan's GNH policy-screening tool, for example, assesses proposed projects' effects on some two dozen variables reflecting GNH's nine domains, with low-scoring proposals needing improvement before they can be approved (Centre for Bhutan & GNH Studies n.d.; Kim and MacKenzie, this volume).

Among the offshoots of Maryland's GPI initiative was exploration of Net Present Value Plus (NPV+) analysis, which goes beyond conventional "incomplete cost-benefit analyses" that ignores key social and environmental considerations to "count the uncounted" (GFN 2015, 4, 8).[9] Pilot NPV+ analysis of state investment options showed, for example, that there was more value to the state in purchasing wetlands and forests and protecting them – and the ecological services they provide – than in allowing suburban development on those lands (14).[10] Alternatively, policies and programs could be judged based on the degree to which they improve subjective well-being (life satisfaction) rather than through conventional cost–benefit analysis. In the UK, techniques have been developed to use life satisfaction as the benefit measure in cost–benefit analysis (Bache, this volume) – with some initial exploration in Canada as well (Helliwell et al., this volume; Shi et al. 2019).

Beyond-GDP measurement could also support, and be supported by, a new societal narrative. For example, rather than prioritizing per-capita GDP and dismissing lower-GDP regions as economically backward, a new narrative could celebrate high levels of life satisfaction, environmental quality, and the way in which people take care of each other in communities. An attempt to shift the social narrative in this direction, albeit without rejecting the need for economic growth, has been evident in messaging from the Nova Scotia Quality of Life Initiative (Dasilva and Hayden, this volume).

Impacts Have Often Been Limited in Practice

The impacts of new approaches of this kind are potentially very substantial. For example, Bhutan's use of its GNH Policy Screening Tool led most of its policy planners, in 2008, to reverse their previous support for joining the World Trade Organization and instead oppose membership (Colman 2021; Hayden 2015). That said, such examples are not the norm – arguably even in Bhutan, which has generated contrasting evaluations in this volume.[11]

In other cases that we researched (Canada, Britain, Maryland, and Vermont), we struggled to find evidence (or even plausible claims) of any impact on policy decisions – with Britain being a partial exception. That country's debate on well-being measurement and policy has, for example, contributed to initiatives to improve mental health service provision and address the well-being-damaging effects of loneliness and isolation, particularly among the elderly (see Bache, this volume, for additional examples). Still, the overall impact so far has been modest, as Bache notes. Well-being has not yet become an overriding state priority. Nor has well-being politics yet become the transformative force that early proponents, such as the New Economics Foundation, had hoped for (Quick 2019), with one interviewee expressing disappointment that, rather than broad changes in economic and social policy such as income redistribution justified by well-being evidence, the agenda in the UK had been reduced to "let's do things a bit better."[12]

Direct impacts on policy – or "instrumental use," as explained in the introductory chapter – have often been elusive, as other researchers have also found for recent beyond-GDP well-being measurement initiatives (e.g., Bache and Reardon 2016; Bleys and Whitby 2015; Whitby et al. 2014), as well as for the sustainable-development indicators that proliferated globally after the 1992 Earth Summit (e.g., Bell and Morse 2011; Rinne, Lyytimäki, and Kautto 2013). In Vermont, for example, we could find no evidence that existence of a state GPI affected any policy choices, despite the significant "symbolic boost," as one interviewee put it, of the state defining its development goals in terms of increasing the GPI. Meanwhile, in Maryland, despite experimentation with new policy tools, such as pilot NPV+ studies mentioned above, the analysis was not actually used to inform any policy decisions before a Republican governor, with little interest in the GPI, took office (Hayden and Wilson 2018).

Much more evident than instrumental use with a direct impact on policy is "political use" – i.e., use of well-being indicators and the knowledge they generate by political actors as "ammunition" to defend and advocate policy positions.

We encountered many such examples, including: use of the GPI in Maryland and Vermont by politicians, academics, NGO leaders, and ordinary citizens to support their calls for investments in public transit, protection of waterways, and action to reduce income inequality (Hayden and Wilson 2018; Zencey 2018); use of well-being evidence in Britain to call for a range of changes from greater provision of psychological therapies (Layard and Clark 2014) to a reduction in working hours (APPGWE 2014); and use of the CIW in Canada to critique the contrast between rising GDP and declining environmental conditions and leisure time – and, more generally, the failures of "trickle down" economics (Romanow 2016).

The possibility also remains of indirect influence over a longer term by introducing new ideas and reshaping frameworks of thought – or "conceptual use." Although such impacts are uncertain, several interviewees in different jurisdictions expressed optimism to us about the possibilities over time. In Vermont, interviewees referred to the way that new prosperity measurements can "help change the narrative" about economic progress and prosperity and "provide the basis for different conversations." An interviewee in Maryland said, "I see it more as a way of changing the thinking and then that thinking itself – rather than the number of the GPI – needs to drive the policy" (Hayden and Wilson 2018). Meanwhile in Canada, interviewees expressed hopes for impacts over time via the spread of the idea that "well-being is not exclusively about the scale or scope of the Canadian economy," a development that "opens up a possibility for the future" (Hayden and Wilson 2016).

Questioning the Assumption That Measurement Always Matters

From challenges with timely data availability to inertia and resistance of various kinds, a long list of obstacles and challenges exists to the use of new well-being measurements to improve policymaking – and an even longer list faces a transformative vision. A full review of these obstacles is beyond the scope of this chapter (see, e.g., Bleys and Whitby 2015; Bleys and Thiry, this volume; Hayden and Wilson 2017a; Whitby et al. 2014), but we highlight a few main issues here.

It is frequently assumed that simply producing new measurements alone will result in policy impacts and, even more optimistically, transformative change – what some have called the "indicators fantasy."[13] According to Scott (2012, 19), well-being and sustainability indicators have long suffered from a "vain expectation that data in itself would inform policy and the more data the better." In fact, policymaking in practice rarely lives up to the rationalist-positivist vision of indicators serving as tools that lead directly to "evidence-based policymaking" and better decisions (Lehtonen, Sébastien, and Bauler 2016; Rinne, Lyytimäki, and Kautto 2013; Scott 2012). Influences on policymakers include ideology, interests, information, and institutional constraints – information being only one of four "I's" (Bell and Morse 2011), and frequently not the most important one.

One step towards addressing the "indicators fantasy" is the realization that a need exists not only to calculate new indicators but also to take active steps to integrate them into the policy process (Stiglitz, Fitoussi, and Durand 2018, 14; Whitby et al. 2014). Indeed, we encountered awareness of this need in our research in Britain and Maryland, for example, and the options for addressing it have become a key topic within international beyond-GDP debates. As Durand and Exton (2019, 142, 158) of the OECD state, "it is not sufficient to rely on the adage 'what gets measured gets done.'" Acknowledging that several national efforts to measure well-being have remained "largely disconnected from policy practice," they emphasize the importance of "bringing well-being into the heart of decision-making, not just the heart of national statistics."

Beyond that task, a bigger set of challenges remains for those who see beyond-GDP measurement as part of a transformative move beyond growth. The economic-growth paradigm's continued dominance of mainstream politics creates strong obstacles to the extent that beyond-GDP measurement is seen as a challenge to that paradigm (Bell and Morse 2011; Hayden and Wilson 2017a; Whitby et al. 2014, 20). In Vermont, we found that GPI proponents had to downplay the growth critique that was a key element of their original motivations in order to "sell" their idea to policymakers. Other advocates of beyond-GDP measurement, as noted in the introductory chapter, go out of their way to say their agenda is not "anti-growth" (Stiglitz, Fitoussi, and Durand 2018, 14). Adoption of new prosperity measures in a way that challenges GDP growth as a top priority confronts the daunting problem of modern economies' structural dependency on growth (Schneidewind and Zahrnt 2014, 40) and related systemic imperatives for growth (Richters and Simoneit 2019; Wiedmann et al. 2020) – leading to challenging questions about how to overcome that dependency, which we will return to in the conclusion of the book (see also Colman, this volume).

Where Do We Stand? A Time of Breakthroughs or a Need for New Approaches?

We have come a long way from Kuznets's 1934 warning against using a measure of a nation's income to assess its welfare to today's emergence of countries that declare themselves well-being economies intent on redefining national success. Or have we? In light of the advances in well-being measurement, proliferation of new measurement initiatives, and growing number of efforts to integrate them with policymaking, one could conclude, as did the former Cabinet Secretary (top civil servant) in Britain, that we have already reached "the end of the

GDP-only world" (O'Donnell et al. 2014, 16). Yet other observers see the limits of existing initiatives, the lack of consensus on the alternative(s), and maintain that the "goal of replacing GDP does not seem to be coming any closer. The number of alternatives is expanding at a staggering rate, but the societal impact is not" (Hoekstra 2019, 21).

The chapters that follow include many other examples of recent initiatives in the beyond-GDP field, which, for some observers, indicate that the time of breakthroughs has arrived – perhaps representing a third wave, where policies and priorities actually change. A very different view is put forward by some contributors who see a need to look beyond recent beyond-GDP efforts, recognize the powerful resistance and structural obstacles to the substantial change that many working in this area have long sought, and find new strategies, whether that involves greater efforts to develop a unified approach to well-being and sustainability measurement or shifting the focus beyond measurement to post-growth policies and political activism. Meanwhile, other chapters balance a sense of possibility with caution about the limits of what has been achieved so far and recognition of substantial obstacles – a balance we have tried to convey here.

We will return to this question of whether we are already entering the beyond-GDP era or are still a long way from it in the conclusion of the book, after considering the various perspectives on it in other chapters. For now, suffice it to say that one can make a case for both views. Indeed, it is possible that both positions could be correct in their own way based on different expectations of the degree of transformation that movement beyond GDP ought to achieve.

We now turn to two chapters which approach the beyond-GDP agenda from different perspectives: one a view from the leading international organization working in this area, the OECD, and the other a bottom-up perspective that emphasizes the participation and empowerment of the most disadvantaged in new measurement initiatives.

NOTES

1 Interview, 2 July 2020. See Dasilva and Hayden (this volume).
2 GDP estimates the value of goods and services produced within a country's borders (by both citizens and non-citizens), while GNP estimates the value of goods and services produced by a country's citizens, both domestically and abroad. In 1986, Canada switched from reporting GNP to GDP, which was by then the international standard.
3 The quotation is sometimes attributed to Johnson himself (e.g., Nevarez 2011, 29), but the earliest source we found in the chain of quotations (Campbell 1981, 4) attributes it to an "early spokesman for Lyndon Johnson's Great Society."

4 According to other accounts, the king said, "Gross National Happiness is more important than Gross National Product" – wording that is somewhat less dismissive of GNP. Accounts also differ on the exact timing of the king's statement (Hayden 2015).

5 For explanations of Cameron's interest in the issue, see Bache and Reardon (2016, 76, 90) and Hayden and Wilson (2017b, 16).

6 It noted that: "Traditional economic measurements such as Gross Domestic Product (GDP) alone do not give a full picture of Canadians' quality of life, and the pandemic has further exposed this fact. The government is working on incorporating quality of life measurements into decision-making, including in the development and implementation of Canada's COVID-19 Economic Response Plan" (Department of Finance 2020, 35).

7 See https://www.canada.ca/en/department-finance/news/2021/04/budget-2021-a-recovery-plan-for-jobs-growth-and-resilience.html.

8 In each of these cases we conducted research using semi-structured interviews with individuals – political leaders, senior public servants, academics, NGO researchers, and activists – involved in developing and applying new indicators or advocating their use, along with analysis of relevant documents.

9 There has been considerable work in recent years in bringing previously uncounted costs and benefits into cost-benefit analysis. What is noteworthy in this case is the impetus Maryland's GPI initiative gave to bringing a wider lens of that kind to decisions about state investments, at least on a pilot basis.

10 Also in Maryland, NGO researchers developed prototype "GPI notes" to analyse the impacts of policy proposals on the state GPI – a more comprehensive alternative to the standard fiscal notes that only examine impacts on state and local government finances. These GPI notes showed the value of policies that, for example, reduce inequality, such as a minimum wage increase, or which improve environmental outcomes (e.g., Talberth 2014).

11 Colman (2021) argues that high-level political will to act did exist in Bhutan at least from 2008 to 2013, but he sees little discernible influence of GNH on recent policy choices (see also Colman, this volume). However, Kim and MacKenzie (this volume) see continuing impacts of a GNH approach. We return to this issue in the concluding chapter.

12 Interview, Juliet Michaelson, NEF, 6 July 2015.

13 We first encountered this idea in an interview with Charles Seaford of NEF in July 2014.

REFERENCES

Agency of Commerce and Community Development. 2016. "Vermont 2020: Comprehensive Economic Development Strategy." Montpelier, Vermont: Agency of Commerce and Community Development.

Allin, Paul, and David J. Hand. 2014. *The Wellbeing of Nations: Meaning, Motive and Measurement*. Hoboken, NJ: Wiley.

Anderson, Victor. 1991. *Alternative Economic Indicators*. London: Routledge.

Anielski, Mark, Mary Griffiths, David Pollock, Amy Taylor, Jeff Wilson, and Sara Wilson. 2001. "Alberta Sustainability Trends 2000: The Genuine Progress Indicators Report 1961 to 1999." Drayton Valley, AB: Pembina Institute. http://www.pembina.org/reports/gpi-ab2000-trends.pdf.

APPGWE. 2014. "Wellbeing in Four Policy Areas: Report by the All-Party Parliamentary Group on Wellbeing Economics." London: All-Party Parliamentary Group on Wellbeing Economics.

Bache, Ian, and Louise Reardon. 2016. *The Politics and Policy of Wellbeing*. Cheltenham, UK: Edward Elgar.

Bell, Simon, and Stephen Morse. 2011. "An Analysis of the Factors Influencing the Use of Indicators in the European Union." *Local Environment* 16, no. 3: 281–302. https://doi.org/10.1080/13549839.2011.566851.

Bertlesmann Stiftung, and SDSN. 2019. "Sustainable Development Report 2019." Gütersloh, Germany/New York: Bertlesmann Stiftung and Sustainable Development Solutions Network.

Bleys, Brent, and Alistair Whitby. 2015. "Barriers and Opportunities for Alternative Measures of Economic Welfare." *Ecological Economics* 117 (September): 162–72. https://doi.org/10.1016/j.ecolecon.2015.06.021.

Buckley, Chris. 2007. "China Silences Green GDP Study, Report Says." *Reuters*, 23 July 2007. https://www.reuters.com/article/environment-china-environment-dc-idUSPEK21998120070723.

Cameron, David. 2010. "PM Speech on Wellbeing." 25 November 2010. https://www.gov.uk/government/speeches/pm-speech-on-wellbeing.

Campbell, Angus. 1981. *The Sense of Well-Being in America*. New York: McGraw-Hill. Secondary title: *Recent Patterns and Trends*.

Centre for Bhutan & GNH Studies. n.d. "GNH Policy & Project Screening Tools." http://www.grossnationalhappiness.com/gnh-policy-and-project-screening-tools/.

Ćirić, Jelena. 2020. "Iceland to Measure Social and Environmental Prosperity." *Iceland Review*, 27 April 2020. https://www.icelandreview.com/politics/iceland-to-measure-social-and-environmental-prosperity/.

Cobb, Clifford, Ted Halstead, and Jonathan Rowe. 1995. "If the GDP Is Up, Why Is America Down?" *Atlantic Monthly*, October 1995.

Cohen, Lizabeth. 2004. *A Consumers' Republic: The Politics of Mass Consumption in Postwar America*. New York: Vintage.

Colman, Ronald. 2021. *What Really Counts: The Case for a Sustainable and Equitable Economy*. New York: Columbia University Press.

Costanza, Robert, Maureen Hart, Stephen Posner, and John Talberth. 2009. "Beyond GDP: The Need for New Measures of Progress." Pardee Papers 4. Boston: Frederick S. Pardee Center for the Study of the Longer-Range Future, Boston University.

Daly, Herman E., and John B. Cobb. 1989. *For the Common Good*. Boston: Beacon Press.

Department of Finance. 2020. "Economic and Fiscal Snapshot 2020." Ottawa: Department of Finance Canada. https://www.canada.ca/content/dam/fin /publications/efs-peb/homepage/EFS2020-eng.pdf.

– 2021. "Toward a Quality of Life Strategy for Canada." Ottawa: Department of Finance Canada.

Dorji, Kinley. 2012. "Why Bhutan? A GNH Perspective." *Kuensel*, 29 December 2012. www.kuenselonline.com/why-bhutan-a-gnh-perspective/.

Durand, Martine, and Carrie Exton. 2019. "Adopting a Well-Being Approach in Central Government: Policy Mechanisms and Practical Tools." In *Global Happiness and Wellbeing Policy Report 2019*, edited by Global Council for Happiness and Wellbeing, 140–62. New York: Sustainable Development Solutions Network.

Easterlin, Richard A. 1974. "Does Economic Growth Improve the Human Lot? Some Empirical Evidence." In *Nations and Households in Economic Growth: Essays in Honor of Moses Abramovitz*, edited by Paul A. David and Melvin W. Reder, 89–125. New York: Academic Press.

Fioramonti, Lorenzo. 2013. *Gross Domestic Problem: The Politics Behind the World's Most Powerful Number*. London: Zed Books.

Galbraith, John Kenneth. 1958. *The Affluent Society*. New York: The New American Library.

Genuine Progress in the States. 2014. "Genuine Progress in the States." http://www .gpiinthestates.org/.

GFN. 2015. "Making the Economic Case for Sustainable Investments in Maryland." Oakland, CA: Global Footprint Network.

Global Happiness Council. 2018. "Global Happiness Policy Report." New York: Sustainable Development Solutions Network.

Government of Canada. 2021. "A Recovery Plan for Jobs, Growth, and Resilience: Budget 2021." Ottawa: Department of Finance Canada. https://www.budget .gc.ca/2021/home-accueil-en.html.

GPI Atlantic. 2007. "About Us." GPI Atlantic: Genuine Progress Index for Atlantic Canada. http://www.gpiatlantic.org/about.htm.

– 2009. "'New Policy Directions' Urged for Nova Scotia; NDP Will Bring 'Genuine Progress Accounting into Policy Analysis.'" Glen Haven, NS: GPI Atlantic. http:// www.gpiatlantic.org/releases/pr_manual.htm.

Hayden, Anders. 2015. "Bhutan: Blazing a Trail to a Postgrowth Future? Or Stepping on the Treadmill of Production?" *The Journal of Environment & Development* 24 (April): 161–86. https://doi.org/10.1177/1070496515579199.

Hayden, Anders, and Jeffrey Wilson. 2016. "Is It What You Measure That Really Matters? The Struggle to Move beyond GDP in Canada." *Sustainability* 8, no. 7: 623.

– 2017a. "'Beyond GDP' Indicators: Changing the Economic Narrative for a Post-Consumerist Society?" In *Social Change and the Coming of Post-Consumer Society: Theoretical Advances and Policy Implications*, edited by Maurie J. Cohen, Halina S. Brown, and Philip J. Vergragt, 170–91. New York: Routledge.

– 2017b. "'The End of the GDP-Only World' in Britain: A Step Toward a Green State and Beyond the Growth Paradigm." Working Paper. www.beyondgdpindicators .com.

– 2018. "Taking the First Steps beyond GDP: Maryland's Experience in Measuring 'Genuine Progress.'" *Sustainability* 10, no. 2: 462. https://doi.org/10.3390 /su10020462.

Helliwell, John. 2019. "Measuring and Using Happiness to Support Public Policies." NBER Working Paper No. 26529. Cambridge, MA: National Bureau of Economic Research.

Helliwell, John, Richard Layard, and Jeffrey Sachs. 2012. "World Happiness Report." New York: Earth Institute, Columbia University.

Hoekstra, Rutger. 2019. *Replacing GDP by 2030*. Cambridge: Cambridge University Press.

Jakobsdóttir, Katrín. 2020. "In Iceland, Well-Being Is the Measure of Our Success." *Evening Standard*, 2 January 2020. https://www.standard.co.uk/comment /comment/iceland-wellbeing-measure-success-katr-n-jakobsd-ttir-a4324791.html.

Johnson, Lyndon B. 1964. "The Great Society." Speech delivered at Ann Arbor, Michigan. http://www.emersonkent.com/speeches/the_great_society.htm.

Kennedy, Robert F. 1968. "Remarks at the University of Kansas." http://www .jfklibrary.org/Research/Research-Aids/Ready-Reference/RFK-Speeches /Remarks-of-Robert-F-Kennedy-at-the-University-of-Kansas-March-18–1968.aspx.

Kuznets, Simon. 1934. "National Income, 1929–1932." Senate Document No. 124, 73rd Congress. 2nd Session. Washington, DC: US Government Printing Office.

Layard, Richard. 2005. *Happiness: Lessons from a New Science*. New York: Penguin Press.

Layard, Richard, and David M. Clark. 2014. *Thrive: The Power of Evidence-Based Psychological Therapies*. London: Allen Lane.

Lehtonen, Markku, Léa Sébastien, and Tom Bauler. 2016. "The Multiple Roles of Sustainability Indicators in Informational Governance: Between Intended Use and Unanticipated Influence." *Current Opinion in Environmental Sustainability* 18 (February): 1–9. https://doi.org/10.1016/j.cosust.2015.05.009.

Li, Vic, and Graeme Lang. 2010. "China's 'Green GDP' Experiment and the Struggle for Ecological Modernisation." *Journal of Contemporary Asia* 40, no. 1: 44–62. https://doi.org/10.1080/00472330903270346.

Martin, Paul. 2000. "The Budget Speech 2000: Better Finances, Better Lives." Ottawa: Department of Finance. http://fin.gc.ca/budget00/pdf/speeche.pdf.

Meadows, Donella H., Dennis L. Meadows, Jørgen Randers, and William W. Behrens III. 1972. *Limits to Growth*. New York: Universe Books.

Michalos, Alex, ed. 2014. *Encyclopedia of Quality of Life and Well-Being Research*. 2014 edition. New York: Springer.

Nevarez, Leonard. 2011. *Pursuing Quality of Life*. London: Routledge.

Nickerson, Mike. 2009. *Life, Money, and Illusion*. Lanark, ON/Gabriola Island, BC: Seven Generations Publishing/New Society Publishers.

Nordhaus, William, and James Tobin. 1972. "Is Growth Obsolete?" In *Economic Research: Retrospect and Prospect*, Volume 5, *Economic Growth*. Washington, DC: National Bureau of Economic Research. http://www.nber.org/chapters/c7620.

O'Donnell, Gus, Angus Deaton, Martine Durand, David Halpern, and Richard Layard. 2014. "Wellbeing and Policy." London: Legatum Institute.

OECD. 2007. "Istanbul Declaration." Paris: OECD. https://www.oecd.org/newsroom/38883774.pdf.

Osberg, Lars, and Andrew Sharpe. 2010. "The Index of Economic Well-Being." *Challenge* 53, no. 4: 25–42.

Panel on Social Indicators. 1969. "Toward a Social Report." Washington, DC: Government Publishing Office.

Philipsen, Dirk. 2015. *The Little Big Number: How GDP Came to Rule the World and What to Do about It*. Princeton, NJ: Princeton University Press.

Quick, Annie. 2019. "Does New Economics Need Wellbeing?" *New Economics Foundation* (blog). 20 March 2019. https://neweconomics.org/2019/03/does-new-economics-need-wellbeing?mc_cid=c5a6dde7e7&mc_eid=863939ed46.

Richters, Oliver, and Andreas Simoneit. 2019. "Growth Imperatives: Substantiating a Contested Concept." *Structural Change and Economic Dynamics* 51 (December): 126–37. https://doi.org/10.1016/j.strueco.2019.07.012.

Rinne, Janne, Jari Lyytimäki, and Petrus Kautto. 2013. "From Sustainability to Well-Being: Lessons Learned from the Use of Sustainable Development Indicators at National and EU Level." *Ecological Indicators* 35 (December): 35–42. https://doi.org/10.1016/j.ecolind.2012.09.023.

Romanow, Roy. 2016. "Pursuit of Economic Growth Leaving Millions of Canadians Behind." *Toronto Star*, 22 November 2016. https://www.thestar.com/opinion/commentary/2016/11/22/pursuit-of-economic-growth-leaving-millions-of-canadians-behind.html.

Rostow, W.W. 1960. *The Stages of Economic Growth: A Non-Communist Manifesto*. Cambridge: Cambridge University Press.

Schneidewind, Uwe, and Angelika Zahrnt. 2014. *The Politics of Sufficiency: Making It Easier to Live the Good Life*. Munich: Oekom. http://epub.wupperinst.org/frontdoor/index/index/docId/5550.

Scott, Karen. 2012. *Measuring Wellbeing: Towards Sustainability?* London: Routledge.

Shi, Yipu, Craig Joyce, Ron Wall, Heather Orpana, and Christina Bancej. 2019. "A Life Satisfaction Approach to Valuing the Impact of Health Behaviours on

Subjective Well-Being." *BMC Public Health* 19, no. 1: 1547. https://doi.org/10.1186/s12889-019-7896-5.

Stiglitz, Joseph E., Jean-Paul Fitoussi, and Martine Durand. 2018. "Beyond GDP - Measuring What Counts for Economic and Social Performance." Paris: OECD. http://www.oecd.org/corruption/beyond-gdp-9789264307292-en.htm.

Stiglitz, Joseph E., Amartya Sen, and Jean-Paul Fitoussi. 2010. *Mismeasuring Our Lives: Why GDP Doesn't Add Up.* New York: The New Press.

Sturgeon, Nicola. 2020. "Wellbeing Economy Alliance Conference: First Minister's Speech." Keynote address, Edinburgh. https://www.gov.scot/publications/wellbeing-economy-alliance-conference/.

Talberth, John. 2014. "HB 295: Maryland Minimum Wage Act of 2014." Washington, DC: Center for Sustainable Economy. http://sustainable-economy.org/wp-content/uploads/2014/06/GPI-Note-Minimum-Wage-Act-of-2014.pdf.

Thinley, Jigmi. 2012. "Address by the Hon'ble Prime Minister on Well Being and Happiness at the UN Head Quarters, New York." 2 April 2012. Thimphu: Cabinet Secretariat, Royal Government of Bhutan. http://www.cabinet.gov.bt/?page_id=207.

Trudeau, Pierre. 2019. "Minister of Middle Class Prosperity and Associate Minister of Finance Mandate Letter." 12 December 2019. https://pm.gc.ca/en/mandate-letters/2019/12/13/minister-middle-class-prosperity-and-associate-minister-finance-mandate.

Tumilty, Ryan. 2020. "Liberal Budget Could Focus More on Personal Happiness, Less on Country's Financial Condition." *National Post*, 29 January 2020. https://nationalpost.com/news/politics/liberal-budget-could-focus-more-on-personal-happiness-less-on-countrys-financial-condition.

UN. 2012. "The Future We Want." Outcome Document of the United Nations Conference on Sustainable Development in Rio de Janeiro. New York: United Nations. http://www.unep.org/rio20/portals/24180/Docs/727The%20Future%20We%20Want%2019%20June%201230pm.pdf.

UN General Assembly. 2011. "Resolution Adopted by the General Assembly. 65/309. Happiness: Towards a Holistic Approach to Development." New York: United Nations. https://digitallibrary.un.org/record/715187?ln=en.

Waring, Marilyn. 1988. *If Women Counted: A New Feminist Economics.* San Francisco: Harper & Row.

What Works Centre for Wellbeing. 2020. "What Works Wellbeing." https://whatworkswellbeing.org/.

Whitby, Alistair, et al. 2014. "BRAINPOoL Project Final Report: Beyond GDP – From Measurement to Politics and Policy." Hamburg: World Future Council. https://www.worldfuturecouncil.org/wp-content/uploads/2016/01/BRAINPOoL_2014_Beyond-GDP_From_Measurement_to_Politics_and_Policy.pdf.

Wiedmann, Thomas, Manfred Lenzen, Lorenz T. Keyßer, and Julia K. Steinberger. 2020. "Scientists' Warning on Affluence." *Nature Communications* 11, no. 1: 1–10. https://doi.org/10.1038/s41467-020-16941-y.

Yarrow, Andrew L. 2010. *Measuring America: How Economic Growth Came to Define American Greatness in the Late Twentieth Century.* Amherst: University of Massachusetts Press.

Zencey, Eric. 2018. "The 2018 Vermont Genuine Progress Indicator Report." Burlington, VT: The Vermont Genuine Progress Indicator Project, University of Vermont.

2 Ten Years After: From SSF to HLEG – An Agenda for Well-Being Measurement in the Next Decade

MARTINE DURAND AND MARCO MIRA D'ERCOLE[1]

1. Introduction

The 2009 report of the Commission on the Measurement of Economic Performance and Social Progress (also known as SSF, from the names of Joe Stiglitz, Amartya Sen, and Jean-Paul Fitoussi, its chairs and coordinator) was a milestone for statistical work on "Beyond GDP." The report, to which the OECD contributed in significant ways, gave visibility to a range of considerations that, while well recognized by economists and statisticians, are typically ignored in policy discussions.

The considerations put forward by the SSF report were not meant to detract from the usefulness of GDP, which remains a critical metric for assessing macro-economic conditions and a range of policies, but to highlight the distortions that come to the fore when GDP is used for purposes that it was not designed to meet, i.e., as an overall metric of countries' "success." As argued by SSF, GDP – a measure of the volume of goods and services produced by a country over a given period[2] – is not a measure of people's well-being, neither of their economic well-being (i.e., what economists describe as people's consumption possibilities) nor of their quality of life more generally. On one side, more suitable measures of (average) economic welfare than GDP are available within the System of National Accounts (SNA), such as measures of household adjusted disposable income.[3] More importantly, no SNA (average) measures can reflect the experience of a "typical" household or individual, in particular when inequalities are rising. Macro-economic statistics also don't account for the many non-market factors that contribute to people's lived experiences (from health to skills, from political voice to subjective evaluations of their life), as well as for those factors that shape the characteristics of the communities where people live, from inequalities in all life dimensions to the resources that shape the sustainability of well-being over time.

A decade after the release of the SSF report, two reports by the OECD-hosted High Level Expert Group on the Measurement of Economic Performance and Social Progress (HLEG) allow us to take stock of progress achieved since 2009, as well as to outline the measurement agenda that lays ahead.[4] The first report (*For Good Measure*, Stiglitz et al. 2018a) is a collection of chapters authored by some of the HLEG's members, dealing with topics that either already figured in the SSF report or where new research provides guidance on the type of metrics that could be developed by the statistical community in the future. The second report (*Beyond GDP – Measuring What Counts*, Stiglitz et al. 2018b) is an overview of the HLEG work done by its co-chairs, providing a broad perspective on the issues that fall under the Beyond-GDP agenda, as well as twelve recommendations (presented in Box 2.1) to move the measurement agenda forward.

BOX 2.1. RECOMMENDATIONS BY THE CHAIRS OF THE HLEG

1. No single metric will ever provide a good measure of the health of a country, even when the focus is limited to the functioning of the economic system. Policies need to be guided by a dashboard of indicators informing about people's material conditions and the quality of their lives, inequalities thereof, and sustainability. This dashboard should include indicators that allow us to assess people's conditions over the economic cycle. Arguably, policy responses to the Great Recession might have been different had such a dashboard been used.

2. Developing better metrics of people's well-being is important for all countries, whatever their level of development. National Statistical Offices should be given the resources and independence needed to pursue this task in effective ways, including through harnessing the potential of big data. The international community should invest more in upgrading the statistical capacities of poorer countries.

3. The quality and comparability of existing metrics of economic inequality related to income and, particularly, wealth should be further improved, including by allowing Statistical Offices to use tax records to capture developments at the top end of the distribution, and by developing measures of the joint distribution of household income, consumption and wealth.

4. Data should be disaggregated by age, gender, disability status, sexual orientation, education and other markers of social status in order to describe group differences in well-being outcomes; and metrics to describe within-household

inequalities, such as those related to asset ownership and the sharing of resources and financial decisions within the household, should be developed.

5. Efforts to integrate information on economic inequalities within the System of National Accounts should be pursued, in the perspective of achieving convergence between micro- and macro-approaches, and of understanding how the benefits of GDP growth are shared in society.

6. Assessing equality of opportunity is important. Measures of a broad range of people's circumstances should be developed, including by linking administrative records across generations and by including retrospective questions on parental conditions in household surveys, so as to allow comparison of measures of inequality of opportunity across countries and over time.

7. Regular, frequent and standardised collection of both evaluative and experiential measures of subjective well-being should be pursued, based on large representative samples with a view to shedding light on their drivers and on the directions of causality.

8. Policies should be routinely assessed for their effects on people's economic insecurity, measured through a dashboard of indicators that inform about people's experiences in the face of economic shocks, the buffers that are available to them, the adequacy of social insurance against key risks, and subjective evaluations of insecurity.

9. Better measures of sustainability are needed. This requires developing full balance sheets for various institutional sectors, covering all their assets and liabilities, measuring the rents implicit in asset valuations, as well as improved metrics of human and environmental capital and of the vulnerability and resilience of systems.

10. The measurement of trust and other social norms should be improved, through both general and specialised household surveys as well as more experimental tools administered to representative samples of respondents that rely on insights from psychology and behavioural economics.

11. Access to statistical data and administrative records by academics and policy analysts should be facilitated, in ways that preserve the confidentiality of the information disseminated and that ensure a level playing field across different research teams and theoretical perspectives.

12. To deliver "better policies for better lives," well-being metrics should be used to inform decisions at all stages of the policy process, from identifying priorities for action and aligning program objectives to investigating the benefits and costs of different policy options; from making budgeting and financing decisions to monitoring policies, program implementation and evaluation.

This chapter provides a high-level perspective on some of the key themes featured in these two reports. This perspective is inevitably subjective and reflects our specific standpoint, which is informed by the role the OECD has played in moving the Beyond-GDP agenda forward since the SSF report was released in 2009.

The chapter is organized as follows. Following a brief overview of the key measurement initiatives undertaken in this field since 2009 (Section 2), we highlight some of the key themes featured in the HLEG reports that have a claim to shape the measurement agenda that should be pursued in the next decade (Section 3). Section 4 notes some of the ways in which new well-being metrics are starting to be used in policy, while Section 5 concludes.

2. Progress in the "Beyond GDP" Measurement Agenda since 2009

Official statisticians are often described as "guardians of the temple," keener to preserve existing practices than to venture into uncharted territories. This characterization has proven to be wrong when it comes to the follow-up of the SSF report. Since its release in 2009, the SSF report had a large resonance within the statistical community, spurring a large number of measurement initiatives worldwide. The SSF report has also acted as a catalyst for research and for communicating the Beyond-GDP agenda to the public.

Progress in this field has mainly resulted from national initiatives, with frameworks and indicator dashboards now published and updated regularly by several countries around the world.[5] While the motivations underlying the development of well-being frameworks and indicator dashboards differed across countries, some features are common. These include an understanding of people's well-being as multidimensional, combining data about people's economic circumstances alongside a wider range of quality-of-life factors, and the use of consultations with large audiences to bring "legitimacy" to the indicator sets and ensure longevity of the reporting.

At the international level, the OECD Better Life Initiative, launched in 2011, reflects some of the common features of these national projects. The key element of the OECD Better Life Initiative is the regular monitoring of OECD countries' performance in several dimensions of people's life, based on the framework shown in Figure 2.1 and around twenty-five indicators included in the OECD How's Life? reports (OECD 2017), alongside a communication tool (the OECD Better Life Index) aiming to reach the wider public.[6]

Beyond these initiatives to develop dashboards of existing indicators, the statistical community has devoted significant efforts to creating the basis for improved well-being statistics in the future, with a focus on those areas that currently lack a foundation within official statistics. On the environment side, a milestone was the adoption in 2012 by the UN Statistical Commission of the "Core Accounts" of the System of Economic and Environmental Accounts (SEEA; UN et al., "Central Framework," 2014) as an "international statistical standard,"[7] with a companion set of ecosystem accounts recognized as "experimental" (UN et al., "Experimental Ecosystem Accounting," 2014). While the SEEA process pre-dated the SSF report, it tapped into one of its key areas of focus, i.e., sustainability. On the economic side, G-20 Finance Ministers and Central Bank Governors mandated international statistical agencies to address some of the glaring data gaps that were highlighted by the 2008 financial crisis, leading to initiatives to monitor risks in the financial sector; to analyse vulnerabilities, inter-connections, and spill-overs (including across borders); and to introduce information on economic inequalities within macro-economic statistics. On labour statistics, the 2013 revision of the international standards governing the compilation of labour force surveys referred to the SSF recommendations to justify the need to broaden existing standards to measure people's engagement in different forms of work, paid and unpaid, as well as to develop broader measures of labour force underutilization (ILO 2013).

More generally, several international organizations undertook methodological work in areas identified by SSF. The OECD developed statistical guidelines to produce more comparable measures of subjective well-being (OECD 2013a), wealth inequalities (OECD 2013b), the working environment (OECD 2017a), and trust (OECD 2017b), as well as a framework to allow joint analysis and coincident measurement of household income, consumption, and wealth (OECD 2013c). Within the UN system, initiatives undertaken by various UN agencies referred to the SSF report as part of the motivation for improving the quality and comparability of existing statistics on time use (UNECE 2013), victimization (UNODC 2015), sustainable development (UNECE 2014), and governance (Praia Group 2020). Overall, take up of the SSF recommendations by the statistical community has been significant. Our hope is that the two HLEG reports will have the same success over the next decade.

3. An Agenda for Well-Being Measurement in the Next Decade

The two HLEG reports did not have the same breadth as the SSF report. The goal was not to revisit in a systematic way all the facets of well-being measurement addressed by the SSF report, but rather to focus on specific issues where, in the views of its members, progress in research and economic theory warranted a similar evolution in statistical practices. Some of the key areas for future work featuring in the two HLEG reports are highlighted below, distinguishing between those that already featured in the SSF report but required further development and those that are new.

Areas That Are Already Featured in the SSF Report

Improving measures on the distribution of household economic resources was one of the key recommendations of SSF,[8] and one where greater advances have been achieved since 2009 – also reflecting seminal contributions by several SSF and HLEG members who put inequalities at the centre of policy discussions (Stiglitz 2012; Deaton 2013; Piketty 2014; Atkinson 2015). Statistical standards for measuring income distribution were revised in 2011 (UNECE 2011), while guidelines for measuring wealth distribution were developed by the OECD in 2013 (OECD 2013b), with more systematic reporting on them starting to be undertaken by researchers, statistical offices, and international organizations (Balestra and Tonkin 2018). Growing awareness of higher income inequalities has also made people and policymakers aware that, when these inequalities are rising (and the labour share in GDP is falling), changes in GDP will not reflect what is happening to most people.[9] A new focus on "global income inequality" (Milanovich 2016), i.e., what would be observed if all people in the world were considered as citizens of the same country, has also drawn attention to the statistics available in less developed countries, prompting researchers to find ways to make the best use of the available information to provide such global perspective.

At the same time, increasing awareness that countries differ in the extent to which different types of economic resources are correlated with each other (and that these correlations change over time), has prompted research to assess the joint distribution of all types of resources (Fisher et al. 2019).

This sprout of interest, however, has also made clear that the existing statistics in this field still fall short of what is needed. There are large differences across countries in the availability and timeliness of data, as well as in their comparability – in particular between developing countries (where most statistics on economic inequalities refer to the distribution of consumption expenditures) and developed countries (where income is the common metric).[10] Some types of economic resources (such as transfers in kind, in the case of income, or pension wealth, in the case of assets) are also not routinely covered by existing data.

Nora Lustig (2018) recommended taking steps in a number of directions. Her recommendations (which are also reflected in Stiglitz et al. 2018b) include defining a more comprehensive income concept (including benefits in kind and consumption taxes), to be used as "experimental statistics" alongside more established concepts; correcting for the underreporting and non-coverage of the rich in household surveys, which requires allowing national statistical offices (NSOs) to link (anonymized) tax records to survey records; mobilizing the full range of data sources available on wealth distribution (e.g., surveys, censuses, lists of large wealth-holders, administrative data on people's estate at death, annual wealth taxes); and addressing inconsistencies among the (secondary) datasets that are currently used for research on the global income distribution. Steps are also needed to improve the consistency and coherence of data on the distribution of household consumption expenditure (an area where little international guidance exists) and to incorporate distributional data within macro-economic statistics, to allow assessment of who benefits from GDP growth.[11]

While most of the available measures on the distribution of household economic resources refer to "vertical" inequalities (between individuals with, say, high and low income), Carmen Diana Deere, Ravi Kanbur, and Frances Stewart (2018) draw attention to the importance of "horizontal" inequalities, i.e., differences in average outcomes among groups sharing similar characteristics, as well as to inequalities in non-economic aspects (e.g., in longevity or skills). Horizontal inequalities matter because shared experiences (based on people's place of living, disability, ethnicity, or sexual orientation) are often more important as a source of people's identity and collective mobilization than vertical inequalities. While the criteria that matter for measuring horizontal inequalities are many, some of them (e.g., disability or ethnicity) don't have standard definitions that are consistently used throughout the statistical system. Even when these definitions do exist, as in the case of gender, Deere et al. stressed that the assumptions commonly used in research and statistical reporting (e.g., that all household members fully pool and equally share what is earned by each member) hide some of the most important inequalities within societies (e.g., those between women and men). This situation calls for new approaches, such as greater use of individual-level data or introducing supplementary questions on within-household inequalities in surveys.

Another key recommendation of the SSF report was that statistical offices should incorporate in their household surveys questions to capture people's life evaluations, hedonic experiences, and priorities in their own life. This has been another area of significant uptake by both researchers and statistical offices, in particular since the release of OECD measurement guidelines on subjective well-being (OECD 2013a). While only a few statistical offices included these questions in their surveys in 2010, most OECD NSOs do so today, with these measures also starting to be used to assess a range of public policies and programs. Greater data availability has, in turn, generated new knowledge on both substantive issues (e.g., on the relation between different aspects of subjective well-being and income/GDP, or on age patterns in these measures) and methodological ones (such as the impact of memory and recall periods on survey responses, or how people's valuation of the trade-offs between competing goals affect their behaviour).

Arthur Stone and Alan Krueger (2018) recommend that the regular data collection based on the standardized survey questions recommended by the

OECD Guidelines should continue in the future. In the present juncture, the priority for data producers should be to collect quality data on the joint distribution of subjective well-being and other variables, such as household income, a step that some NSOs (e.g., the statistical office of the European Union) have taken by including subjective well-being questions in their income surveys. It is also important to look beyond life satisfaction to other aspects of subjective well-being, such as hedonic experiences, to better understand how these relate to each other. More research is also needed to resolve methodological issues, such as systemic interpersonal differences in people's response styles, and to understand how different subjective well-being measures predict (and are affected by) other variables.

Beyond inequalities and subjective well-being, much of the drive to develop measures that look beyond GDP has historically come from concerns about the sustainability of current development patterns. The SSF report argued that sustainability should be understood in broader terms than simply the environment, by looking at all aspects where today's decisions are putting at risk the resources needed for development to last; and that these intertemporal aspects can be described by looking at changes in different types of "capital," e.g., stocks/flows of economic, natural, human, and social capital. The statistical community has taken some significant initiatives to improve available metrics in this field. We have already mentioned some of the work undertaken (in the context of the G20 Data Gap Initiative) to improve the measurement of economic capital, by developing balance sheets for all institutional sectors, extending the range of assets and liabilities covered, measuring cross-border and cross-sectoral links as well as currency and maturity mismatches of different sectors; and, on natural capital, through the adoption of the SEEA Central Framework as a statistical standard, which several NSOs are currently implementing in different areas (e.g., asset accounts for land and sub-soil assets in many non-EU countries; flow-accounts of emissions to air and water in several EU countries). Progress has also been achieved on measuring human capital by measuring a range of cognitive skills through instruments such as the OECD Programme for International Students Assessment (PISA) and the Survey of Adult Skills (PIAAC) and through the development by some NSOs of monetized satellite accounts, typically limited to formal education.

Overall, however, our view is that progress in developing sustainability metrics has lagged behind both other aspects of the Beyond-GDP agenda and the ambition of the SSF report. Marleen De Smedt, Enrico Giovannini, and Walter J. Radermacher (2018) stress that the measurement agenda on sustainability remains huge. On economic capital, full and timely balance sheets for all institutional sectors, with a broad coverage of assets and liabilities and distinguishing between changes in values and volumes, remain a distant goal in many countries. More fundamentally, progress in compiling balance sheets extended to non-market assets has not yet led economists and statisticians to reconsider our traditional distinctions between consumption and investment, e.g., by recognizing the long-term benefits of environmental protection expenditures or of spending on education and training. On natural capital, steps will need to be taken to fully implement the SEEA, to improve its timeliness and communication, and to start reflecting the scientific consensus on planetary boundaries for different types of natural assets (Rockström et al. 2009). On human capital, progress is needed to improve individual-level measures of non-cognitive skills, to increase the frequency of skills assessments, and to extend these measures to preschool children. More fundamentally, research needs to look beyond each type of capital, to understand the relation between assets and well-being outcomes, as well as among these assets and how they interact with each other in the context of the systems where they operate, i.e., focusing on new risks and threats to their resilience. Dialogue and cooperation across different disciplines are required to move forward.

New Areas of Focus in the HLEG Reports

Other issues addressed in the HLEG reports featured only in a marginal way in the SSF report. One of these is the concept of economic insecurity, which Jacob Hacker (2018) defined as "vulnerability to economic losses," with the qualifier "economic" used to describe the consequence of a shock (e.g., an income loss) rather than its causes (e.g., sickness, unemployment, or family breakdown). The concept of economic vulnerability is an important one for policies, as many of the reforms introduced over the past few decades (e.g., the move from "defined benefits" to "defined contributions" pension systems) have implicitly shifted risks from firms/governments towards households, i.e., those less capable to edge against these risks. To some extent, this development has reflected a situation where no measure of economic insecurity (either based on people's self-reports or on more objective metrics) is currently accepted by the statistical community and widely used. At the same time, as noted by Hacker, some measures exist that are consistent with both economic theory and empirical evidence. Some of these measures could be easily produced with existing data and should be used in policy to reduce economic insecurity.

What could be done? Hacker pleads for encouraging multidisciplinary research on concepts (e.g., salient risks and available buffers) and measures (to identify causality and confounders). Second, he argues for improving the evidence base available, through the development of internationally comparable panel data (which could allow computing measures of the share of people experiencing a large income loss from one year to the next), linking panel and administrative data on benefit use, and incorporating a small set of "security" questions (e.g., on the likelihood of losing one's job) in surveys. Finally, Hacker stresses the importance of identifying a small number of core metrics (e.g., of income losses, available buffers, perceived insecurity, or risks in terms of unemployment or disability), not aggregated into a single index.

Another new issue addressed by the HLEG reports is that of trust. While SSF had focused on social connections, trust is one of the outcomes of social connections and social capital more generally. The *OECD Guidelines on Measuring Trust* defined trust as "a person's belief that another person or institution will act consistently with their expectations of positive behaviour" (OECD 2017a) and proposed questions that NSOs could include in their surveys to measure its key aspects (i.e., people's trust in others and in different institutions). Yann Algan (2018) takes stock of the extensive evidence from research showing that measures of trust are significantly correlated with a broad range of economic (i.e., GDP per capita) and social outcomes (e.g., life satisfaction, longevity, and income inequality). He also argues that trust is affected by countries' institutional features and policies, while Stiglitz et al. (2018b) note that the response to the 2008 crisis might have reduced people's trust in governments, contributing to the weaker recovery and the political crisis that now affects so many countries across the world.

Despite this, the evidence base on trust remains very limited. What exists is a limited range of measures, typically based on small-scale, often one-off, unofficial household surveys that use different questions and response scales, and that question respondents about their trust in a different range of people (e.g., strangers, people they know personally) or institutions (e.g., government, the judicial system, the army, the press). To overcome this situation, NSOs should include trust questions in their official surveys based on the approach put forward in the OECD Guidelines and pursue research on the properties and validity of these measures. The HLEG reports also stress the importance of developing quasi-behavioural measures of different types of trust based on experimental games and psychological tests administered to representative samples of the population, as in the Trustlab platform developed by the OECD and researchers in several OECD countries.

A final topic addressed by the HLEG reports is that of inequality of opportunity, a term used by François Bourguignon (2018) to refer to those circumstances involuntarily inherited or faced by people that shape their achievements later in life. These circumstances are among the key drivers of outcome inequalities and, because they are typically associated with discrimination and other factors limiting the full use of available talents, also imply lower economic efficiency.[12] But, as noted by Bourguignon, inequality of opportunity is inherently difficult to measure in a comprehensive way, as many circumstances cannot be observed and other factors beyond efforts (a variable that, anyway, is hard to measure) shape the relation between circumstances and outcomes (e.g., preferences or luck). While data shining light on specific facets of inequality of opportunity exist, and are sometimes reported in comparative research (OECD 2018), very few metrics allow comparison of *changes* in inequality of opportunity over time and across countries, a gap that represents a significant obstacle for policy.

The measurement agenda in this field is huge. It ranges from developing long-term panels to measure individual circumstances from childhood to adulthood to linking administrative data for parents and children when such data are available (as is the case in Nordic countries) to introducing recall questions on past family circumstances in cross-sectional surveys to having questions on bequests in wealth surveys to developing instruments to measure the cognitive and non-cognitive skills of preschool children (in which case outcomes and opportunities coincide). While these investments will require time and resources to generate the required evidence, some statistics could be routinely computed based on existing data. These include measures of inequality in students' test scores by family background (and of the share of total inequality in students' scores that is explained by these background factors) and measures of gender pay gaps adjusted for differences in workers' background characteristics (such as education, age, occupation, and job experience). As noted by Bourguignon, while "unadjusted" measures of gender pay gaps convey the reassuring message that most OECD countries have made progress in reducing them, much of these gains reflect women's higher education and job experience, implying no progress in reducing gender discrimination in the workplace.

4. From Measurement to Policy

While better measures of "progress" are surely needed, they are also not enough. What matters even more is to anchor these measures in the policy process in ways that survive the vagaries of electoral cycles. Stiglitz et al. (2018b) take stock of country experiences in using well-being indicators in the different phases of the policymaking process. These experiences range from identifying policy priorities to assessing the pros and cons of different strategies to achieve a given goal, allocate the resources needed to implement the selected strategy, monitor interventions, and audit and assess the results achieved (Figure 2.1). While recent, these experiences show that innovations can deliver policies that, by going beyond traditional silos, are more effective in achieving their goals and in improving people's lives.

Countries' experiences in the policy use of well-being metrics typically rest on five key mechanisms. The first is to shape the national budget, which in all countries is a major lever for delivering policy objectives. This can take the form of monitoring a dashboard of well-being indicators (used as complements to standard economic and fiscal measures) to frame the parliamentary discussion that accompanies the budget (as in the case of France since 2015 and of Italy and Sweden since 2017); but also to identify a few whole-of-government

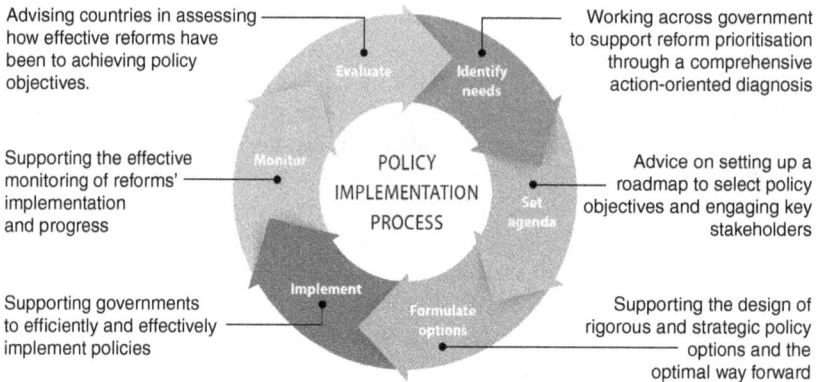

Advising countries in assessing how effective reforms have been to achieving policy objectives.

Working across government to support reform prioritisation through a comprehensive action-oriented diagnosis

Supporting the effective monitoring of reforms' implementation and progress

Advice on setting up a roadmap to select policy objectives and engaging key stakeholders

POLICY IMPLEMENTATION PROCESS

Evaluate — Identify needs — Set agenda — Formulate options — Implement — Monitor

Supporting governments to efficiently and effectively implement policies

Supporting the design of rigorous and strategic policy options and the optimal way forward

Figure 2.1. Well-being metrics can be used at every step of the policy cycle

priorities (as in New Zealand's experience with its 2019 "Wellbeing Budget") and adapt the cost–benefit template used for departmental submissions of spending proposals to include well-being considerations.

The second form has been to use legislation to "lock in" certain aspects of well-being. In Scotland, for example, the 2015 Community Empowerment Act places a duty on Scottish Ministers to consult on, develop, and publish a set of outcomes measures and to review them at least every five years. In New Zealand, the government is now revising the country's Public Finance Act to require the government of the day to set well-being objectives and to report on them annually. In Wales, the 2015 Well-being of Future Generations Act requires all public bodies to place seven high-level well-being goals at the centre of their decisions, with implementation overseen by the auditor general and the future generations commissioner.

A third form has been the development of well-being dashboards to reflect how the government thinks about progress. While strategic development plans are often used to set out specific priorities for national progress in the medium and long term, countries such as Colombia, Slovenia, Ecuador, and Latvia have explicitly introduced well-being frameworks into their planning strategies, often aligned to the UN Sustainable Development Goals. The Scottish National Performance Framework, for example, relies on a broad set of well-being indicators to spell out the government's long-term strategic objectives.

A fourth form has been the creation of new institutional positions or structures to promote the use of well-being evidence in government. Examples range from creating specific high-level roles (e.g., ministerial positions in the United Arab Emirates) to establishing new accountability mechanisms (Wales), creating new government departments (Ecuador), or forming a separate agency (the

What Works Centre in the United Kingdom). New responsibilities can also be assigned to existing structures, as in New Zealand, where the Treasury now has cross-cutting responsibility for well-being and sustainability.

The last path has been that of using well-being frameworks to think about interdependencies among outcomes, or to assess specific policy challenges from a multidimensional perspective. For example, while regulatory impact assessments (RIAs) are now a formal requirement when developing both primary laws and subordinate regulations in most OECD countries, some countries have now expanded the number of outcomes (and population groups) on which impacts of regulations are explicitly assessed, going well beyond traditional economic concerns. In twenty-three OECD countries, RIAs routinely assess effects on the environment, while in fourteen countries they also assess impacts on income inequality. Other countries, such as New Zealand, have used subjective well-being metrics in the context of their cost-benefit analysis, while in the United Kingdom, Treasury Guidance of cost–benefit analysis highlights several steps for using well-being as a lens for policymaking.

5. Conclusion

For several years now, the OECD has argued that governments need a new compass to gauge "progress," moving beyond "economic efficiency" as the sole criteria to assess their policies. The experience of OECD countries since the late 1970s shows that the traditional "efficiency first" approach has both failed to deliver GDP growth[13] and has led to an ecological, social, and political crisis that will weigh heavily on the prospects of future generations. Developing a better "compass" will require improvements in statistical practice along all the areas discussed in the HLEG reports. At the same time, it would be naïve to think that statistics will be the only factor at play. As noted by J.M. Keynes, "The real difficulty in changing any enterprise lies not in developing new ideas, but in escaping from old ones." To which, one might add, quoting Max Plank, that "scientific truth does not triumph by convincing its opponents and making them see the light, but rather because its opponents eventually die, and a new generation grows up that is familiar with it."

NOTES

1 At the time of writing, the authors were, respectively, OECD chief statistician and director of the OECD Statistics and Data Directorate and head of household statistics in the same OECD Directorate. Martine Durand chaired, alongside Joseph Stiglitz and Jean-Paul Fitoussi, the OECD-hosted High-Level Expert Group on the Measurement of Economic Performance and Social Progress (HLEG), an independent group that met from 2013 to 2018 and whose two reports (Stiglitz et

al. 2018a and 2018b) were recently published by the OECD. Marco Mira d'Ercole acted as rapporteur of the HLEG.

2 To be more precise, GDP should be calculated by adding all "economic production within the SNA production boundary," a boundary that excludes unpaid work devoted to producing housing services (e.g., care of children and frail elderly), volunteering, or contributing to Wikipedia.

3 Household disposable income, as defined in the SNA, is the sum of all income flows received by the household sector over a given period, net of the direct taxes and social security contributions paid by households. Household "adjusted" disposable income adds to household disposable income the value of the in-kind services (such as education and health care) that households receive for free or at subsidized prices from governments and non-profit institutions.

4 The HLEG included members of the SSF Commission (Joseph Stiglitz, Jean-Paul Fitoussi, Angus Deaton, François Bourguignon, Enrico Giovannini, Jeffrey Heal, Alan Krueger) alongside new members (Martine Durand, Yann Algan, Nora Lustig, Jacob Hacker, Ravi Kanbur, Jil Matheson, Thomas Piketty, Walter Radermacher, Chiara Saraceno, Arthur Stone, and Yang Yao).

5 Table A.1 in Stiglitz et al. (2018a), summarizes the key features of national initiatives on measuring well-being undertaken in twelve countries (or subnational jurisdictions) since 2009 (Austria, Belgium, Ecuador, Germany, Italy, Israel, Japan, Luxembourg, the Netherlands, Scotland, Slovenia, and the United Kingdom).

6 The Better Life Index (available at http://www.oecdbetterlifeindex.org/) allows users to construct an overall measure of countries' average well-being performance based on the dashboard of OECD indicators and on users' own choices on the weight to be attributed to each life dimension.

7 UN statistical standards create a reporting obligation for national statistical offices (NSOs).

8 Some of the key recommendations by SSF were about giving "prominence to the distribution of income, consumption and wealth," "considering income and consumption jointly with wealth," and focusing on "the household perspective," to be achieved through measures referring to households rather than to the economic system as a whole.

9 Since February 2018, the OECD has been releasing quarterly data on changes in (SNA) average household adjusted disposable income, which highlight how household income and GDP move at a different pace. For example, by the second quarter of 2019, GDP growth in the Euro area had exceeded growth in household disposable income by almost six points (cumulative since early 2010); the gap was only 0.2 per cent in the case of Canada (OECD 2019b).

10 Inequality comparisons between developing and developed countries based on the two sets of metrics implicitly assume that savings rates are zero, an assumption that, while plausible when the focus is on measuring extreme poverty, is less so when the focus is on measuring inequalities across a broad range of countries.

Deininger and Squire (1996) suggested that, across a range of developing countries, Gini indexes based on consumption expenditures are some 6.6 points lower than when based on income. Within countries, inequality measures for household income and for household consumption can also change at different paces, when not in different directions, as evidenced by the experience of the United States in the years preceding the 2008 financial crisis.

11 Both researchers and NSOs are currently active in this field, although with significant differences in approaches. For example, while the "Distributional National Accounts" discussed by Alvaredo et al. (2018) take national income, i.e., the economy as a whole, as a reference point, the work pursued by the OECD, Eurostat, and several NSOs targets the income of the household sector, e.g., without assuming that business profits translate into higher income for resident households in the same year in which they are generated.

12 For this reason, several economists are more at ease with the concept of inequality of opportunity than with the broader one of inequality of outcomes. As argued above, the distinction between the two is blurred, as inequalities in outcomes for one generation translate into inequality of opportunity for the generation that follows.

13 In "old Europe," the annual growth rate of GDP per capita since the 1970s has been less than half that achieved over the previous thirty years. While this decline in GDP growth is typically attributed to the exhaustion of the gains from "catching up" relative to the United States, even the United States (the technology leader) has experienced a decline of its GDP growth rate since the 1970s of around one-fourth, relative to what was experienced in the previous thirty-year period.

REFERENCES

Algan, Yann. 2018. "Trust and Social Capital." In *For Good Measure: Advancing Research on Well-Being Metrics beyond GDP*, edited by Joseph E. Stiglitz, Jean-Paul Fitoussi, and Martine Durand, 285–322. Paris: OECD.

Alvaredo, Facundo, Lucas Chancel, Thomas Piketty, Emmanuel Saez, and Gabriel Zucman. 2018. "Distributional National Accounts." In *For Good Measure: Advancing Research on Well-Being Metrics beyond GDP*, edited by Joseph E. Stiglitz, Jean-Paul Fitoussi, and Martine Durand, 143–62. Paris: OECD.

Atkinson, Anthony. 2015. *Inequality – What Can Be Done?* Cambridge, MA: Harvard University Press.

Balestra, Carlotta, and Richard Tonkin. 2018. "Inequalities in Household Wealth across OECD Countries – Evidence from the OECD Wealth Distribution Database." Paris: OECD Publishing. https://www.oecd-ilibrary.org/economics /inequalities-in-household-wealth-across-oecd-countries_7e1bf673-en.

Bourguignon, François. 2018. "Inequality of Opportunity." In *For Good Measure: Advancing Research on Well-Being Metrics beyond GDP*, edited by

Joseph E. Stiglitz, Jean-Paul Fitoussi, and Martine Durand, 101–42. Paris: OECD.

Deaton, Angus. 2013. *The Great Escape: Health, Wealth and the Origins of Inequality*. Princeton, NJ: Princeton University Press.

Deere, Carmen Diana, Ravi Kanbur, and Frances Stewart. 2018. "Horizontal Inequalities." In *For Good Measure: Advancing Research on Well-Being Metrics beyond GDP*, edited by Joseph E. Stiglitz, Jean-Paul Fitoussi, and Martine Durand, 85–100. Paris: OECD.

Deininger, Klaus, and Lyn Squire. 1996. "A New Data Set Measuring Income Inequality." *World Bank Economic Review* 10, no. 3: 565–91.

Fisher, Jonathan, David Johnson, Timothy Smeeding, and Jeffrey Thompson. 2018. "Inequality in 3-D: Income, Consumption, and Wealth." FEDS Working Paper No. 2018–001. https://ssrn.com/abstract=3097391.

Hacker, Jacob S. 2018. "Economic Security." In *For Good Measure: Advancing Research on Well-Being Metrics beyond GDP*, edited by Joseph E. Stiglitz, Jean-Paul Fitoussi, and Martine Durand, 203–42. Paris: OECD.

ILO. 2013. Resolution Concerning Statistics of Work, Employment and Labour Underutilization, Adopted by the Nineteenth International Conference of Labour Statisticians, October 2013. www.ilo.org/global/statistics-and-databases /standards-and-guidelines/resolutions-adopted-by-international-conferences-of -labour-statisticians/WCMS_230304/lang--en/index.htm.

Lustig, Nora. 2018. "Measuring the Distribution of Household Income, Consumption and Wealth." In *For Good Measure: Advancing Research on Well-Being Metrics beyond GDP*, edited by Joseph E. Stiglitz, Jean-Paul Fitoussi, and Martine Durand, 49–84. Paris: OECD.

Milanovic, Branko. 2016. *Global Inequality: A New Approach for the Age of Globalization*. Cambridge, MA: Harvard University Press.

OECD. 2013a. *OECD Guidelines on Measuring Subjective Well-being*. Paris: OECD Publishing. http://dx.doi.org/10.1787/9789264191655-en.

– 2013b. *OECD Guidelines for Micro Statistics on Household Wealth*. Paris: OECD Publishing. https://doi.org/10.1787/9789264194878-en.

– 2013c. *OECD Framework for Statistics on the Distribution of Household Income, Consumption and Wealth*. Paris: OECD Publishing. https://www.oecd.org /statistics/framework-for-statistics-on-the-distribution-of-household-income -consumption-and-wealth-9789264194830-en.htm.

– 2017a. *How's Life? Measuring Well-being*. Paris: OECD Publishing. https://doi .org/10.1787/how_life-2017-en.

– 2017b. *OECD Guidelines on Measuring Trust*. Paris: OECD Publishing. http:// dx.doi.org/10.1787/9789264278219-en.

– 2017c. *OECD Guidelines on Measuring the Quality of the Working Environment*. Paris: OECD Publishing. https://www.oecd.org/social

/oecd-guidelines-on-measuring-the-quality-of-the-working-environment
-9789264278240-en.htm.

– 2018. *A Broken Social Elevator? How to Promote Social Mobility*. Paris: OECD
Publishing. https://doi.org/10.1787/9789264301085-en.

– 2019a. *Economic Review of New Zealand*. Paris: OECD Publishing.

– 2019b. "Growth and Economic Well-being: OECD Household Income Growth
Continued to Outpace GDP Growth in the Second Quarter of 2019." News
Release, 7 November 2019. Paris: OECD. http://www.oecd.org/sdd/na/Growth
-and-economic-well-being-oecd-11-2019.pdf.

Piketty, Thomas. 2014. *Capital in the 21st Century*. Cambridge, MA: Harvard
University Press.

Praia Group. 2020. *Handbook on Governance Statistics*. Praia, Cabo Verde: Praia
Group on Governance Statistics.

Rockström, Johan, Will Steffen, Kevin Noone, Asa Persson, F Stuart III Chapin, Eric
Lambin, Timothy M. Lenton, et al. 2009. "Planetary Boundaries: Exploring the
Safe Operating Space for Humanity." *Ecology and Society* 14, no. 2: 32.

Smedt, Marleen De, Enrico Giovannini, and Walter J. Radermacher. 2018.
"Measuring Sustainability." In *For Good Measure: Advancing Research on Well-
Being Metrics beyond GDP*, edited by Joseph E. Stiglitz, Jean-Paul Fitoussi, and
Martine Durand, 243–84. Paris: OECD.

Stiglitz, Joseph. 2012. *The Price of Inequality: How Today's Divided Society Endangers
Our Future*. New York: W.W. Norton and Company.

Stiglitz, Joseph, Jean-Paul Fitoussi, and Martine Durand, eds. 2018a. *For Good
Measure: Advancing Research on Well-being Metrics beyond GDP*. Paris: OECD
Publishing.

–, eds. 2018b. *Beyond GDP: Measuring What Counts for Economic and Social
Performance*. Paris: OECD Publishing.

Stone, Arthur A., and Alan B. Krueger. 2018. "Understanding Subjective Well-being."
In *For Good Measure: Advancing Research on Well-Being Metrics beyond GDP*,
edited by Joseph E. Stiglitz, Jean-Paul Fitoussi, and Martine Durand, 163–202.
Paris: OECD.

UN, EC, FAO, IMF, OECD, and World Bank. 2014. *System of Environmental-
Economic Accounting 2012 – Central Framework*, United Nations. https://unstats
.un.org/unsd/envaccounting/seearev/seea_cf_final_en.pdf.

UN, EC, FAO, OECD, and World Bank. 2014. *System of Environmental-Economic
Accounting 2012 – Experimental Ecosystem Accounting*. United Nations. https://
unstats.un.org/unsd/envaccounting/seeaRev/eea_final_en.pdf.

UNECE. 2011. *The Canberra Group Handbook on Household Income Statistics,
Second Edition*. Geneva: United Nations Economic Commission for Europe.
\www.unece.org/fileadmin/DAM/stats/groups/cgh/Canbera_Handbook_2011
_WEB.pdf.

– 2013. *Guidelines for Harmonizing Time-use Surveys*. New York and Geneva: United Nations Economic Commission for Europe. www.unece.org/fileadmin/DAM/stats/publications/2013/TimeUseSurvey_Guidelines.pdf.

– 2014. *Conference of European Statisticians Recommendations on Measuring Sustainable Development*. New York and Geneva: United Nations Economic Commission for Europe. www.unece.org/fileadmin/DAM/stats/publications/2013/CES_SD_web.pdf.

UNODC. 2015. "International Classification of Crime for Statistical Purposes." Vienna: United Nations Office on Drugs and Crime. www.unodc.org/documents/data-and-analysis/statistics/crime/ICCS/ICCS_English_2016_web.pdf.

3   Measures for a New Economy: Shifting Power via Public Participation

JULIA RODGERS AND KATHERINE TREBECK[1]

Introduction

Our economic and political systems are producing outcomes that are misaligned with what people need and what the planet requires to be sustainable. This misalignment has created multiple social, environmental, and financial crises. One root cause of this misalignment is how we measure success – and in response, an emerging suite of initiatives seek to create "beyond Gross Domestic Product (GDP)" measures to ascertain a country's success and well-being and drive a more holistic focus. To the extent they are adopted and go on to shape public policy, these initiatives have the potential to represent a *repurposing* of the economic system – away from growth *per se* to a more direct focus on social progress, sustainability, and quality of life.

Yet, how do these initiatives respond to another crisis facing the world: that of democracy and imbalances of power? "Political capture," or the confluence between wealth and power that enables those with resources to configure the economic system in their interests, continues to accentuate inequality in many dimensions, including political inequality. The widening gaps preserve privilege and further marginalize those already disempowered. How do – or can – beyond-GDP measures help address such inequalities?

With some notable exceptions, not least the formulation of the Sustainable Development Goals (SDGs) and many of Canada's quality-of-life initiatives, the beyond-GDP field often neglects the question of the democratic nature of initiatives. This chapter warns against replacing problematic practices and measures (such as GDP) with a system that, although more focused on sustainability and human needs, is nonetheless a product of decisions by those with greater resources. It suggests that while all initiatives have their merit, beyond-GDP measures must not be remote from the communities they seek to benefit, lest they reinforce power imbalances and insufficiently attend to democratic deficits. Thus, this chapter argues that the beyond-GDP movement – and the wider new economy agenda, of which beyond-GDP initiatives are invariably a key pillar – need to attend to the importance of power shifts. It suggests a need to ensure that alternatives to GDP *embody* efforts to rebalance power and influence by ensuring that the voices and views of those currently ill-served by the economy are at the fore of redefining progress.

This chapter considers how a new economic system will be attainable only with a new measure of progress that signals a shift in the purpose of the economy. It situates participatory measures of progress (hereafter PMPs) in an effort to transform the economic system, reflecting on their scope to close the misalignment between what people and the planet need and the economic model. Two illustrations of participatory measures of progress are briefly shared: Oxfam's Humankind Index for Scotland and Australia's National Development Index. It concludes by reflecting on the potential of PMPs to have added importance as "prefiguring" a redressing of current power imbalances.

Today's GDP-Shaped Economy

As other chapters in this book have set out, the current economic model adopted in many countries seems unable to deliver flourishing lives for all, despite their GDP growth of recent decades. No national economy meets the basic requirements for its citizens at a globally sustainable level of resource use (O'Neill et al. 2018). This failure intensifies the demands for new measures of progress (Stiglitz, Sen, and Fitoussi 2009). Many diverse organizations continue to call for better measures of economic progress that reconcile the interests of people and the planet with the objectives and outcomes of the economic system.

Conflating GDP and well-being, be it social, environmental, or economic well-being, can skew policymaking because decision-makers receive only a partial view of how people are faring (see, for example, Sachs 2019). Aware of such potential misuse, Simon Kuznets (the architect of what became GDP) himself warned that "welfare of a nation can, therefore, scarcely be inferred from a measurement of national income" (Kuznets 1934). These words were echoed by the Stiglitz-Sen-Fitoussi Commission, established by then French president Sarkozy, which stated that "conflating the two [GDP and economic well-being] can lead to misleading indications about how well-off people are and entail the wrong policy decisions" (Stiglitz, Sen, and Fitoussi 2009, 169). This is evident in that the GDP ledger can rise – unilaterally deemed a positive occurrence – regardless of the societal or environmental harms. Consequently, continued pursuit of GDP as a national and hence policy goal exacerbates misalignment between the outcomes of the economic system and what people and the planet need.

Yet, GDP has become the dominant measure of national progress and success. In the decades following the Second World War, GDP growth came to be seen as the solution to poverty and class struggle, and the very essence of development (Michaelson et al. 2009). As stated by the Organisation for Economic Co-operation and Development (OECD), much twentieth-century policymaking hinged on an implicit assumption that economic growth was synonymous with progress or an assumption that growing GDP meant the improvement of general well-being (Stiglitz, Fitoussi, and Durand 2018). The media and mainstream politicians define a small reduction in GDP growth as a "crisis," with the former holding the latter to account for GDP growth. Whereas Kuznets designed GDP as an instrument to indicate levels of economic activity, nowadays rankings of countries are often based on economic size, with power in global politics and access to global governance institutions (for example, groupings like the G7 or G20) defined according to GDP (Fioramonti 2013).

These dynamics prevent people from looking beyond growth (as measured by GDP) for solutions: political decision-makers are driven to increase GDP as a fix-all response. The political imagination is closed down, confined to construing merely surviving the current system as "progress." Accordingly, efforts that seek to address the root causes of inequality, precariousness, insecurity, despair, and ecological degradation rarely encroach on prevailing economic models (Otero et al. 2020). In other words, efforts to forge a new system confront a "hegemony of the common sense" (Gramsci 1971).

The Power Imbalances in GDP-Based Economies

The critiques of a growth-based economy and the flaws of GDP as a measure of progress are well known, but often absent from the critiques of growth and beyond-GDP literature is explicit reference to a telling body of work about the crisis of democracy. Our current conceptualization of GDP critique tends to miss the issue of "political capture," a process that both results from and causes inequality since inequalities of income and wealth translate into inequalities of power and vice versa (Callahan and Mijin Cha 2013; Fuentes-Nieva and Galasso 2014; Stoddart 2014). Kevin Watkins (2016) points to evidence that a "recent surge in inequality has been accompanied by the rise of vested interests, the decline of a political system capable of advancing the interests of the poor, and the emergence of social attitudes inimical to fair distribution" (1451). One exacerbates the other as the richest can donate to political parties and hire lobbyists to promote their interests, leading to under-representation of lower income groups in government. The threat of moving business abroad, playing governments against each other, or influence in public institutions via the "revolving door" of politics and business employment are further examples of democracy being undermined.

As a consequence, the economy becomes configured in the interests of the richest, as they benefit from institutional arrangements that shift rents to those at the top (Bivens and Mishel 2015). For example, the returns to wealth are often taxed more favourably than earned income (the UK's increases in wealth often escape National Insurance contributions that fund state benefits, often have preferential tax rates levied upon them, reaping the benefits from generous deductions) (Nicholas 2013). Inheritance tax and capital gains tax only impinge on wealth a little, and they are themselves subject to avoidance and exemptions (raising as little as 1 per cent of tax revenue in the UK) (Nicholas 2013). Moreover, some actors are able to reap shares of financial rewards from the innovation process disproportionate to their contribution; they do so by positioning themselves at the point where innovative efforts to date begin to generate financial returns (Lazonick and Mazzucato 2013). Lazonick and Mazzucato (2013) found that a "major source of inequality is the ability of economic actors to appropriate returns from the innovation processes that are not warranted by their investments of capital and/or labour in it."

When the wealthiest are able to bend the rules in their favour, democracy is eroded. At the very least, it seems the economic model is governed only by a "thin" form of representative democracy (Barber 1984), which is often captured by entities wielding disproportionate influence on the basis of their economic strength (Fuentes-Nieva and Galasso 2014). Repurposing the economy to focus on social justice and sustainability necessitates addressing this. It necessitates positioning people currently ill-served by the economic system in the forefront of determining its purpose.

Power, Prefiguration, and Participatory Measures of Progress

Transformative Economies

An economy which is better aligned with what people and the planet need (what growing numbers are referring to as a "well-being economy") demands a profound shift in the very purpose of the economy (WEAll 2019). It is from the very goal of the economy that much policy and many decisions about trade-offs follow. To significantly change the system, then, there needs to be a repurposing – what Maja Gopel (2014) and others describe as a "paradigm shift." This echoes the findings of a leading systems thinker, the late Donella Meadows. In her list of twelve ways to shift a system, Meadows highlights *goals* (the purpose or function of the system, root issues) and *paradigms* (the mindset out of which the system – its goals, structure, rules, parameters – arise) as penultimate and ultimate leverage points (Meadows 2010).

A growing movement is forming around this goal of transforming the economy. It is supported by the Wellbeing Economy Alliance (WEAll) – a newly formed collaboration of a range of actors that bring diverse emphases and strategies to the common objective of building an economy in service of people and the planet. WEAll has played a catalytic role in the formation of the Wellbeing Economy Governments partnership (WEGo). At the time of writing, WEGo comprised the New Zealand, Icelandic, Scottish, Welsh, and Finnish governments, their partnership borne of a shared interest to exchange experience and lessons regarding putting collective well-being at the heart of economic policymaking (Sturgeon 2019). WEGo is an illustration of a growing number of government officials and politicians who recognize the flaws of GDP and are willing to embark on the journey of putting other goals to the fore of policymaking.

For new goals to be taken up, new measures are required, as "indicators can be a useful tool for constructing new understandings, holding powerful actors to account and enabling engagement with policy end goals" (Jones et al. 2016). As already flagged, there is a rich terrain of beyond-GDP measures to explore and a suite of emerging projects.[2] They vary in terms of their focus, coverage, construction, and composition. Most of them are created by well-intentioned and very skilful practitioners. Most are valuable additions to a rich and still somewhat emergent terrain. Yet only some of these initiatives have the potential to be seen as putting communities or the general public in the driver's seat in terms of determining the purpose of the system. The merit of the remainder in terms of addressing political capture is thus dubious – despite their other credentials. The wide literature on alternative indicators and measures similarly pays relatively little attention to the patterns of power inherent in their construction (e.g., Jones et al. 2016; see White 2014 for a notable exception).

Policy and Participation

Accordingly, this section now turns to efforts that do make an attempt to encompass community participation to reflect on their potential to pioneer (or "prefigure") mechanisms by which the interests of those currently not well served by policymaking processes – and hence disadvantaged in the current economic system – can have their views elevated and their perspectives responded to in measures of progress. It examines the idea of prefiguration, the role of PMPs, then briefly sets out two examples, before finally (and by way of conclusion) reflecting on PMPs as possibly prefiguring a rebalancing of power.

Prefiguration came to prominence during the Occupy protests, but it has a longer history, with Carl Boggs as one of its original theorists. Boggs (1997) defines prefiguration as "the embodiment within the ongoing political practice of the movement, of those forms of social relations, decision making, culture, and human experience that are the ultimate goal." In other words, it entails constructing activities and interactions that exemplify – even in microcosm –

the sort of society, economy, or politics sought by the protagonists. As systems change expert Gopel (2014) explains, societal transformation can be built by smaller system transformations: small, alternative solutions which create "ripple effects" and irritate the status quo.

Many in the "new economy movement" celebrate prefigurative practice as "living" a new economy into existence, often citing Buckminster Fuller's advice that "you never change things by fighting the existing reality. To change something, build a new model that makes the existing model obsolete" (Fuller 1969). Embodying the desired future has demonstrative and symbolic merit, literally *showcasing* the merits of a changed way of doing things and thereby allowing the policy wheels to start turning in the right direction. For example, as Graeber (2013) observes, the prefigurative efforts of the Occupy movement reflect "the idea that the organisational form that an activist group takes should prefigure the kind of society we wish to create." The statement speaks to the integrity of an effort that practises what it preaches. As the organization Smart CSOs explains: "activists, organisations and campaigns can play a much more positive role in cultural change if they embody and communicate the values of the new system" (Narberhaus 2014).

Even to the extent that participatory measures of progress do feature in the beyond-GDP literature, attention is usually focused on their merit in terms of devising more appropriate, grounded, and accurate reflections of what progress or collective well-being entails (White 2014). For example, in 2009, when economists Joseph Stiglitz, Amartya Sen, and Jean-Paul Fitoussi delivered their final report for the *Commission on the Measurement of Economic Performance and Social Progress*, they called for a "global debate ... [and] discussion of societal values, for what we, as a society, care about, and whether we are really striving for what is important" (Stiglitz, Sen, and Fitoussi 2009). In the same vein, Canadian economist Mark Anielski (2007) declared that "future wellbeing indicator work should have a firm foundation in quality of life values expressed by citizens in the community." A recent report published by the Centre for Understanding Sustainable Prosperity (Jones et al. 2016) recommended that "the choice of indicators and their conceptualisation should be developed in a participatory way ... literature on participatory indicator development emphasises deliberative construction of visions in conjunction with a variety of stakeholders."

A more metaphorical way of making the point is Khalid Malik's observation that: "Only the wearer may know where the shoe pinches, but pinch-avoiding arrangements cannot be effectively undertaken without giving voice to the people and giving them extensive opportunities for public discussion. The importance of various elements in evaluating wellbeing and freedom of people can be adequately appreciated and assessed only through persistent dialogue among the population" (Malik 2013).

Those beyond-GDP initiatives that *do* have participation at their core thus have invariably been born of a desire to ensure the measures are an accurate reflection of what a constituency wants. They seem to call for participation in order to arrive at an appropriate suite of indicators and domains – which is, of course, important. Such rationales do not, however, engage with the power question, nor do they explore the potential of participation in the development of new measures of progress to help address political capture.

Walking the Talk

Despite these high-profile calls for conversations and dialogues and recognition of the importance of participation (for example, McGregor 2015), the recent spate of measurement initiatives remains dominated by indicator projects that lack public participation in their construction. They are often informed by sincerely held intentions to contribute to better outcomes for communities, but unless public engagement is part of their construction, they will not deliver the shift in power that is fundamental to a well-being economy. Measures devised by a small group of technical experts do not constitute the rebalancing of power that many people believe – and which political capture demonstrates – is required as part of a transition to a new economic model. Often the "experts" that determine the composition of these indices are the same intellectuals and technocrats that held influential roles as various ecological, financial, and human crises emerged. Indeed, to the extent that the emerging initiatives constitute something intuitively acceptable and plausible for the current policy regime, they are unlikely to usher in a meaningful shift in the locus of power. It is worth repeating here that the point of this discussion is not about criticizing the individuals involved (especially since they often share the goal of addressing many of the crises facing communities, they are making a vital contribution to moving beyond GDP and have greatly expanded the knowledge base and enhanced the rigour of measuring a wider set of objectives). Nor is it about condemning the initiatives – hence the lack of a list of examples. Instead, the point is about acknowledging the limitations of these projects in terms of helping to achieve a shift in power through prefiguration (Alperovitz 2013; Korten 1999).

Simply put, because injustice and poverty are about powerlessness, there is a need to place more power in the hands of those excluded from decisions that affect them (Polanyi Levitt 2013). Public participation in the construction of beyond-GDP measures can be a practical manifestation of this since it is a means for citizens to shape the very purpose of the economy in a way that shifts power and puts the interests of the general public, and especially the most disadvantaged, at the apex of policymaking.

Case Study 1: The Oxfam Scotland Humankind Index

In its work in Scotland, anti-poverty charity Oxfam deals with issues that can be considered an unfortunate consequence of excessive focus, over many decades, on GDP growth, i.e., wealth creation in a narrow sense. There is much financial wealth in Scotland, but there are also considerable levels of poverty, inequality, alienation, and social breakdown that are not reflected in GDP figures (Trebeck 2011; Collins and McCartney 2011). Pursuit of economic growth, and a belief (ostensibly held by many in economic development decision-making positions) that wealth would "trickle down," often from consumption-based activities, inadequately addresses these issues (Hastings 2009).

In 2010 Oxfam Scotland recognized a need for alternative measures of prosperity that would more accurately portray the needs of people living in deprived communities and those experiencing poverty, people in whose interests the prevailing policy regime was inadequately working. Oxfam wanted to elevate their needs on the radars of policymakers and undertook a project to devise a better measure of Scotland's collective prosperity than GDP. Rather than simply adopting the views of think tanks, academics, and other technical experts, and rather than using arbitrary weightings for respective components, the composition of the resulting Humankind Index was a direct reflection of the views and priorities of the people of Scotland. Using a diverse suite of participatory methods (focus groups, community meetings, street stalls, an online survey, and an opinion poll) – that all asked "What do you need to live well in your community?" – Oxfam engaged almost 3,000 people. In doing so it made particular efforts to reach out to seldom-heard communities and to create time and space for deliberation, discussion, and debate. Efforts generated a set of priorities which were weighted to reflect the relative importance of each factor of prosperity – the weightings directly flowed from the public consutlation. The priorities that emerged included: good physical and mental health; having decent, affordable, and secure housing; good relationships; satisfying work; and financial security (Dunlop and Trebeck 2012).

Liaison with subject-area experts (highlighting one of the key roles of technical expertise) enabled the priority areas to be matched to available data sets to ascertain Scotland's performance across these wider goals of progress. Often proxies were needed – some of which were rather inadequate, highlighting the data limitation challenge. Scotland's most deprived areas were compared to Scotland as a whole – revealing that they are falling behind on more than simply monetary aspects of life but also in terms of safety, health, and access to green space.

While the Humankind Index was an initial experimental effort with a very limited budget and much room for improvement should it be undertaken again, it sparked a wider conversation about the economy in Scotland and how it is measured that carries on today, some ten years later. In particular, the Humankind Index was debated in the Scottish Parliament with the then finance minister committing, at the end of the debate, to review Scotland's National Performance Framework (NPF). A series of roundtables and other inputs to this review resulted in the eventual revision of the NPF in 2018 with a broader definition of national success to include well being and the position ing of social and environmental progress on a par with economic progress. Its core values include kindness, compassion, and transparency. While of course not the singular initiative that led to the revision of the NFP, an independent evaluation of the policy impact of the Humankind Index reported that "a great amount of interest in the Index from politicians, policy makers and others, including audiences beyond … would not have occurred without the production of the HKI and the subsequent relationship-building across civil society and political networks" (Barlow et al. 2014).

Case Study 2: Australia's National Development Index

In a similar vein to the Humankind Index in Scotland, but with a substantially longer time frame, is Australia's National Development Index (ANDI). ANDI is in the midst of what might be described as development stages. In time, the goal is for ANDI to be able to generate annual "status" reports on Australia's progress in twelve priority areas (Salvaris, Lycett, and Stanley 2019).

It too utilizes the input of technical experts, but as with the Humankind Index they are "on tap rather than on top" in the formulation of the Index. ANDI is being constructed through a process of community consultation, with technical experts inputting rather than being at the centre of this process. ANDI is designed deliberately to reflect the "values and priorities of Australians" (Australian National Development Index 2019). As the team behind ANDI explain, experts inform the process, with the Index itself "defined by Australians." The aim is for up to half a million Australians to be involved in shaping the Index and specifically what should be measured in each domain. In constructing the Index, ANDI will ensure that weightings – within and between domains of the Index – are informed by community engagement. This takes place via events and other engagement mechanisms in partnership with a wide range of community organizations, umbrella bodies, businesses, local governments, faith-based organizations and media that will elicit the views of Australians on what they identify as mattering most for the well-being of Australia today and into the future and how to track steps toward these goals.

The team further explain that in this way "ANDI promotes democracy and citizen voice." This democratic aspect is core to ANDI's goals. Accordingly, the engagement of citizens is often highlighted by ANDI's project manager, Mike Salvaris (Trebeck, Salvaris, and Innes 2019). ANDI team members point to surveys showing that 76 per cent of Australians report being interested in participating in a national community program to express their views on national progress goals and measures (Salvaris, Lycett, and Stanley 2019).

ANDI's core democratic ethos is reflected in its principles that begin with inclusion, since, as they say: "everybody has a right to have a say about what wellbeing and progress towards it mean for them, their family, their community and their nation." Another ANDI principle is accessibility: "everybody should have access to easily understood information about different dimensions of wellbeing for our nation and our communities." The team have shared a hope that over time, with their extensive citizen engagement supported by rigorous research, ANDI "could help to build a shared vision and restore trust and democracy" (Salvaris, Lycett, and Stanley 2019).

Conclusion: Prefiguration and Power Shifts via Participatory Measures of Progress?

These two short vignettes illustrate mechanisms that attempt to bring the interests and priorities of communities and the public to the fore of new measures of progress. They are microcosms of the shift in power that a well-being economy demands: they *prefigure* how things might be done differently in a well-being economy. They thus constitute another crucial layer of the response to the multiple crises facing the world today.

This means many – though not all – existing beyond-GDP measures risk replacing or augmenting a problematic metric (GDP) with an (admittedly) better one, but one which nonetheless has a serious blind spot: insufficient attention to citizen participation. In this sense, initiatives such as the Humankind Index and ANDI, which seek to ensure marginalized communities and the general public are in the driving seat of the selection of alternative measures of progress, represent a very tentative and partial antidote to political capture (Fuentes-Nieva and Galasso 2014). The Humankind Index and ANDI add to a small but growing number of initiatives that showcase policymaking as a participatory process – that gathering people's views is part of building a mandate and legitimacy for a proposal (the Sustainable Development Goals are perhaps one of the largest examples of this, being informed by the *My World Survey* of over 2 million people). They, and other PMPs like them, in their different ways, seek to put people at the apex of policymaking, and some consciously reach out to seldom-heard communities and those in deprived communities to illuminate and elevate their voices. In a context where socio-economic inequalities are mirrored in inequalities of people's sense of political efficacy, taking the time to gather and elevate the voices and views of seldom heard communities is part of rebalancing power dynamics.

In their nascent way, PMPs arguably go to the heart of the structural problems driving today's multiple and interlocking crises. They embody – by their very construction – an example of the sort of power shifts that are necessary to address the crisis of democracy that sits alongside and exacerbates social and environmental crises.

NOTES

1   The authors acknowledge the input of Professor Allister McGregor on a much earlier iteration of some of the ideas contained in this chapter.
2   See http://wikiprogress.org/ for examples.

REFERENCES

Alperovitz, Gar. 2013. *What Then Must We Do? Straight Talk about the Next American Revolution*. White River Junction, VT: Green Press Initiative.

Anielski, Mark. 2007. *The Economics of Happiness: Building Genuine Wealth*. Gabriola, BC: New Society Publishers.

Australian National Development Index. 2019. "How ANDI Works." http://www .andi.org.au/how-andi-works.html.

Barber, Benjamin R. 1984. *Strong Democracy: Participatory Politics for a New Age*. Berkeley: University of California Press.

Barlow, Chris, Keith Burge, Tim Dixon, Kate Vittle, and Emma Ward. 2014. "Policy Influence in Scotland: Evaluation of Beyond the Horizon." Evaluation Report. Oxfam: Policy and Practice. https://policy-practice.oxfam.org.uk/publications /policy- influence-in-scotland-evaluation-of-beyond-the-horizon-336479.

Bivens, Josh, and Lawrence Mishel. 2015. "Understanding the Historic Divergence between Productivity and a Typical Worker's Pay: Why It Matters and Why It's Real." Economic Policy Institute, Washington, DC.

Boggs, Carl. 1997. "The Socialist Tradition: From Crisis to Decline." *Capital & Class* 21, no. 2: 201.

Callahan, David, and JM Mijin Cha. 2013. *Stacked Deck: How the Dominance of Politics by the Affluent and Business Undermines Economic Mobility in America*. New York: Demos.

Collins, Chik, and Gerry McCartney. 2011. "The Impact of Neoliberal 'Political Attack' on Health: The Case of the 'Scottish Effect.'" *International Journal of Health Services* 41, no. 3: 501–23.

Dunlop, Stewart, and Katherine Trebeck. 2012. *The Oxfam Humankind Index for Scotland: First Results*. Oxford: Oxfam GB.

Fioramonti, Lorenzo. 2013. *Gross Domestic Problem: The Politics behind the World's Most Powerful Number*. Economic Controversies. London: Zed Books.

Fuentes-Nieva, Ricardo, and V. Galasso. 2014. "Working for the Few: Political Capture and Economic Inequality." Briefing Paper, Oxfam: Policy and Practice. https://policy-practice.oxfam.org.uk/publications/working-for-the-few-political -capture- and-economic-inequality-311312.

Fuller, R. Buckminster. 1969. *Ideas and Integrities, a Spontaneous Autobiographical Disclosure*. Toronto: Collier-Macmillan.

Gopel, Maja. 2014. *Navigating a New Agenda: Questions and Answers on Paradigm Shifts and Transformational Change*. Berlin: Wuppertal Institute.

Graeber, David. 2013. *The Democracy Project*. London: Allen Lane.

Gramsci, Antonio. 1971. *Selections from the Prison Notebooks of Antonio Gramsci*. New York: International Publishers.

Hastings, Annette. 2009. "Poor Neighbourhoods and Poor Services: Evidence on the 'Rationing' of Environmental Service Provision to Deprived Neighbourhoods." *Urban Studies* 46, no. 13: 2907–27.

International Bank for Reconstruction & Development, and World Bank. 2012. *Inclusive Green Growth: The Pathway to Sustainable Development*. Washington, DC.

Jones, Aled, Simon Mair, Jonathan Ward, Angela Druckman, Fergus Lyon, Ian Christie, and Sarah Hafner. 2016. "Indicators for Sustainable Prosperity? Challenges and Potentials for Indicator Use in Political Processes." Centre for Understanding Sustainable Prosperity, Working Paper No. 03. Guildford: University of Surrey.

Korten, David C. 1999. *The Post-corporate World: Life after Capitalism*. 1st ed. San Francisco: Berrett-Koehler.

Kuznets, Simon (Acting Secretary of Commerce). 1934. "National income, 1929– 1932: Letter from the Acting Secretary for Commerce Transmitting in Response to Senate Resolution No. 220 (72nd Cong.)."

Lazonick, William, and Mariana Mazzucato. 2013. "The Risk-Reward Nexus in the Innovation-Inequality Relationship: Who Takes the Risks? Who Gets the Rewards?" *Industrial and Corporate Change* 22, no. 4: 1093–128.

McGregor, J. Allister. 2015. "Global Initiatives in Measuring Human Wellbeing: Convergence and Difference." CWiPP Working Paper Series 2, Centre for Wellbeing in Public Policy, University of Sheffield.

Meadows, Donella. 2010. "Leverage Points: Places to Intervene in a System." *Solutions Journal* 1, no. 1: 41–9.

Michaelson, Juliet, Saamah Abdallah, Nicola Steuer, Sam Thompson, Nic Marks, Jody Aked, Corrina Cordon, and Ruth Potts. 2009. *National Accounts of Wellbeing: Bringing Real Wealth onto the Balance Sheet*. New Economics Foundation.

Narberhaus, Micha. 2014. "Stirring Paper: Towards a New Activism to Effectively Support a Transition to a De-growth Economy." Degrowth Conference.

Nicholas, Chris. 2013. "Fairer Tax for a Better Economy." London: Institute for Public Policy Research.

O'Neill, Daniel, Andrew Fanning, William Lamb, and Julia Steinberger. 2018. "A Good Life for All within Planetary Boundaries." *Nature Sustainability* 1 (February): 88–95.

Otero, Iago, Katharine N. Farrell, Salvador Pueyo, Giorgos Kallis, Laura Kehoe, Helmut Haberl, Christoph Plutzar, et al. 2020. "Biodiversity Policy Beyond Economic Growth." Conversation Letters.

Polanyi Levitt, Kari. 2013. *From the Great Transformation to the Great Financialization: On Karl Polanyi and Other Essays*. Black Point, NS: Fernwood Pub.

Sachs, Jeffrey. 2019. "America's War on Chinese Technology." Project Syndicate. https://www.project-syndicate.org/commentary/cheney-doctrine-us-war-on -chinese-technology-by-jeffrey-d-sachs.

Salvaris, Mike, Kate Lycett, and Fiona Stanley. 2019. "Why We Won't Be Voting for the Australia We Want This Time," Australian National Development Index. http://www.andi.org.au/uploads/9/3/0/6/93064890/andi_conversation_april _2019.pdf.

Stiglitz, Joseph, Jean-Paul Fitoussi, and Martine Durand. 2018. *Beyond GDP: Measuring What Counts for Economic and Social Performance*. Paris: OECD Publishing.

Stiglitz, Joseph, Amartya Sen, and Jean-Paul Fitoussi. 2009. "Report by the Commission on the Measurement of Economic Performance and Social Progress." Paris: Commission on the Measurement of Economic Performance and Social Progress.

Stoddart, Hannah. 2014. *Food, Fossil Fuels and Filthy Finance*. Oxford: Oxfam International.

Sturgeon, Nicola. 2019. "Wellbeing Economy Governments (WEGo) Policy Labs: First Minister's Speech." Scottish Government. https://www.gov.scot/publications /wellbeing-economy-governments-wego-policy-labs/.

Trebeck, Katherine. 2011. *Whose Economy? The Winners and Losers in the New Scottish Economy*. Oxford: Oxfam.

Trebeck, Katherine, Mike Salvaris, and Carol Innes. 2019. "Extra – How to Make It Happen?" Luminary: The Regennarration. https://luminarypodcasts.com/listen /the-regennarration/rescope-radio/048-extra-how-to- make-it-happen-live-qanda -on-arriving-at-a-wellbeing-economy/653593a3-a87e-46f3- b21a-50bf30b31353.

Trebeck, Katherine, and Jeremy Williams. 2019. *The Economics of Arrival: Ideas for a Grown-Up Economy*. Bristol: Bristol University Press.

Watkins, Kevin. 2016. "Longer Lives and Unfinished Agendas on Child Survival." *The Lancet* 388, no. 10053: 1450–2.

WEAll. 2019. "Strategic Vision, 2019." Wellbeing Economy Alliance. https:// wellbeingeconomy.org/wp-content/uploads/2019/06/WEAll-brochure.pdf.

White, Sarah, and Asha Abeyasekera. 2014. *Wellbeing and Quality of Life Assessment: A Practical Guide*. Rugby, UK: Practical Action Publishing.

PART TWO

International Experiences and Perspectives

4 Beyond GDP, Beyond Numbers: Bhutan's Journey towards Gross National Happiness

JULIA C. KIM AND AMY MACKENZIE

Gross National Happiness – A New Narrative with Ancient Roots

Gross National Happiness (GNH) emerged in the early 1970s, as the Himalayan Kingdom of Bhutan was beginning to open to greater interaction and exchange with the modern world. It is widely held that the phrase was first expressed by Bhutan's fourth king, Jigme Singye Wangchuck, when, in response to a reporter's query about his country's Gross National Product (GNP), he replied that "Gross National Happiness is more important than Gross National Product" (Sachs 2012; Ura, Alkire, and Zangmo 2012). In so doing, the king succinctly expressed his vision that the country's happiness and well-being, rather than simply its economic output, should be the focus of development. In hindsight, it is striking to note that this critical assessment of GNP emanating from the East was being articulated at around the same time as the now historic critique of GNP voiced by senator Robert Kennedy: "it measures everything, in short, except that which makes life worthwhile" (Kennedy 1968).

While GNH carries multiple definitions and interpretations, the following has gained wide use: GNH "measures the quality of a country in a more holistic way [than GNP] and believes that the beneficial development of human society takes place when material and spiritual development occurs side by side to complement and reinforce each other" (Ura, Alkire, and Zangmo 2012, 111). The underlying roots of GNH can be traced to the Mahayana Buddhist views that historically informed Bhutan's society and governing structures (Brooks 2013; Givel 2015). Although not all Bhutanese are Buddhist, Buddhism's tenets have deeply influenced the country's development philosophy, legal system, and governance for centuries (Brooks 2013). Happiness as an early guiding principle in Bhutan is visible in the legal code of 1792, which states "if the Government cannot create happiness (*dekid*) for its people, there is no purpose for Government to exist" (Ura, Alkire, and Zangmo 2012).

Figure 4.1. GNH: Walking a balanced "middle path" of material and spiritual development

Photo: Julia C. Kim

Given this context, the term "happiness" in GNH carries a deeper meaning than the fleeting subjective feelings of joy often associated with the word in Western cultures (Ura, Alkire, and Zangmo 2012). In Bhutan, happiness is viewed as being relational and multidimensional – emphasizing responsibility, harmony with nature, and concern for the happiness of others (Ura, Alkire, and Zangmo 2012). It is therefore not focused on citizens attaining momentary positive feelings, but rather ensuring the conditions in which society can flourish in a holistic and sustainable way. As Bhutan's first prime minister stated in 2008: "We know that true abiding happiness cannot exist while others suffer, and comes only from serving others, living in harmony with nature, and realizing our innate wisdom and the true and brilliant nature of our own minds" (Khazan 2013). In contrast to a GDP-based paradigm, this concept of happiness suggests a higher purpose for development – one that encompasses the realization of our individual and collective human potential, in balance with the natural world. Thus, in Bhutan, the historical and cultural roots for an economy based on well-being run deep. In modern times, these have been codified in a constitution which proclaims the state's role as striving "to promote those conditions that will enable the pursuit of Gross National Happiness" (RGOB 2017, 18).

From Vision to Action: The Importance of New Goals and Measures

Bhutan's fourth king subsequently oversaw a peaceful transition to a constitutional monarchy, with the country's first democratic elections held in 2008. Previously, the understanding and application of GNH was largely intuitive. However, with democratization and increasing international engagement, the GNH vision needed to be further anchored in specific goals and frameworks for practical application (Choden 2015). Since then, key aspects for operationalizing GNH as a development framework have been articulated and formalized.

GNH: Four Pillars and Nine Domains

The core foundations of GNH are based on four pillars: sustainable and equitable socio-economic development, environmental conservation, preservation and promotion of culture, and good governance. These have subsequently been expanded and measured through the GNH Index, which is linked with a set of policy and program screening tools (Ura, Alkire, and Zangmo 2012). The index is informed by periodic, multidimensional national surveys which collect data across nine GNH domains that together create conditions for well-being: psychological well-being, time use, community vitality, cultural diversity and resilience, living standards, health, education, good governance, and ecological diversity and resilience (Figure 4.2). The 9 domains are measured by 33 clustered indicators that have a total of 124 variables, and all domains are weighted equally, as they are viewed as being equally important for achieving happiness (Ura, Alkire, and Zangmo 2012). A threshold level is used to assess sufficiency within the thirty-three indicators, and overall, an individual experiencing sufficiency in six or more of the nine domains is considered "happy" – that is, to have sufficient conditions for happiness. Disaggregating data from the survey allows for comparisons across different groups, e.g., by age, gender, educational level, occupation, or geographic district. For example, a recent GNH survey revealed that, in general, women reported lower happiness levels than men, and farmers lower levels than other occupations. Identifying such gaps should then guide policymakers to direct appropriate funding and interventions towards improving conditions for these groups (CBS 2016).

Figure 4.2. Bhutan's GNH Index

Linking Measurement to Policy and Action

Furthermore, to align government decision-making with GNH, the GNH Commission (a government planning body) uses a GNH policy-screening tool to provide a systematic appraisal of the potential effects of proposed projects on the nine domains. A policy that fails to receive a sufficiently high score is returned to the proponent agency, outlining why it fell short, along with ways to improve it. As noted above, the GNH Index can also be used to guide resource allocation and policy priorities, and since 2008 targets in the country's Five-Year Plans are based on components of the Index (CBS 2016).

Bhutan has conducted three rounds of GNH surveys, including a pilot survey in 2006 and nationwide surveys in 2010 and 2015. Guided by the GNH philosophy, the country has introduced a range of policies to achieve sustainable and equitable development while preserving its cultural traditions. Poverty reduction, universal primary school enrolment, free access to basic health services, distribution of land to landless farmers, expanded public services and infrastructure in rural areas, and increasing women's participation in elected office, have been recent priorities. There have been significant improvements in key social indicators, including a reduction in poverty and infant mortality, rising life expectancy, and substantial increases in primary school enrolment (World Bank 2014). Moreover, between 2005 and 2018, Bhutan's Human Development Index increased by 20.5 per cent, positioning the country in the Middle Human Development category (UNDP Bhutan 2019).

On the environmental front, Bhutan's constitution commits to maintaining a "minimum of 60% of the country's total land under forest cover for all time," and Bhutan has attracted attention as the world's first carbon-negative country – absorbing more greenhouse gases from the atmosphere than it emits (Climate Council 2017). Other notable initiatives include the striking absence of outdoor advertising due to a ban on billboards, as well as Bhutan's "high value, low impact" tourism policy, which seeks to balance the income derived from its considerable tourism appeal against potentially negative social and environmental impacts. Recognizing the importance of integrating GNH principles within the country's schools, the Ministry of Education has been implementing a nationwide Educating for GNH initiative since 2010 (Gyamsho, Sherab, and Maxwell 2017). In addition, a GNH survey tool was recently launched, with the aim of integrating GNH principles within the country's emerging private sector (CBS 2018). Finally, responding to the need for greater civil society engagement around GNH, the GNH Centre Bhutan (a national NGO), has been conducting youth leadership and advocacy programs, reaching thousands of youth in colleges and schools across Bhutan (Zangmo 2018). Table 4.1 summarizes some of Bhutan's key GNH institutions.

From Local to Global – Responding to Growing International Interest

In recent years Bhutan's efforts have converged with rising global concern regarding the profound financial, social, and environmental costs of inequitable and unsustainable economic growth. This concern, combined with several high-profile critiques of GDP from respected sources (e.g., Stiglitz, Sen, and Fitoussi 2010) has brought heightened international interest to Bhutan's experience of GNH. In response, Bhutan has contributed to a range of international initiatives that have brought growing attention to the importance of well-being and beyond-GDP measures. In 2011, under Bhutan's leadership, the

Table 4.1. Key GNH institutions in Bhutan

Centre for Bhutan & GNH Studies	The GNH Commission	The GNH Centre Bhutan
An autonomous social science research institute established by the government of Bhutan, which conducts and analyses the national GNH survey, alongside other interdisciplinary research https://www.bhutanstudies.org.bt/	The central government body responsible for ensuring all development policies and plans are formulated and implemented in line with the principles of GNH, including through the GNH Policy Screening Tool https://www.gnhc.gov.bt/en	A national NGO that aims to translate GNH into practical action at the grassroots level through collaboration with key stakeholders, and through leadership and action-learning programs in Bhutan and internationally https://www.gnhcentrebhutan.org

UN General Assembly adopted UN Resolution 65/309 "Happiness: Towards a holistic approach to development" (United Nations 2011). The following year, Bhutan convened a High-Level Meeting on Wellbeing and Happiness at UN headquarters in New York, bringing together over 800 delegates and launching a global movement. The vision for a New Development Paradigm was elaborated in a 2013 report, proposing holistic societal happiness as a core development objective in the lead up to the Sustainable Development Goals (NDP Steering Committee and Secretariat 2013).

Looking Ahead: New Challenges, New Opportunities

Ordinary Bhutanese citizens are often surprised and somewhat taken aback to find themselves the subject of such keen international interest. For visitors, the inclination to paint Bhutan with an exotic "Shangri La" brush is all too tempting and can sometimes project unrealistic expectations on this small Himalayan country. In many ways, GNH is a bold and vitally important work in progress. As acknowledged by the country's first prime minister: "Bhutan is not a country that has attained GNH ... Like most developing nations, we are struggling with the challenge of fulfilling the basic needs of our people. What separates us, however, from most others is that we have made happiness, the most fundamental of human needs as the goal of societal change" (Thinley 2012).

The road towards a well-being economy has not been without challenges and, as the country modernizes, new issues have emerged, including youth unemployment, rapid rural–urban migration, and an influx of global influences via the Internet and social media. As one Bhutanese minister put it, Bhutan "cannot be a GNH bubble in a GDP world" (K. Dorji 2012) – words which ring true whether considering the impacts of global warming on this carbon-negative country or the growing exposure of its youth to consumerist culture. However, these emerging challenges are simultaneously stimulating important debate and grassroots engagement about what GNH can and should look like moving forward. Some of these key challenges and emerging opportunities are highlighted below.

GNH and Economic Growth – Getting the Balance Right

A central challenge is striking a careful balance between equitable and sustainable socio-economic development on the one hand, and conventional, rapid GDP growth on the other. As some leaders have pointed out, GNH is not counter to economic growth, so long as such growth is viewed "not as an end in itself but rather as a means to achieve more important ends" (Planning Commission 1999a). Indeed, improving living standards (one of the GNH domains) and reducing poverty and income inequality are important enabling conditions for happiness and well-being. Another important end served by economic growth is greater self-reliance in financing state expenditure, which in turn would help enhance Bhutan's independence, sovereignty, and security (Planning Commission 1999b; Hayden 2015). GDP thus remains a visible and scrutinized reference point within Bhutan's political discourse.

Bhutan has now entered a preparatory period for graduating from least developed country (LDC) to lower middle-income country (LMIC) status by 2023 – signalling progress in its poverty reduction and self-reliance goals. In 2016, largely due to hydropower expansion, the country experienced an 8 per cent GDP growth rate, making it one of the world's fastest-growing economies (T. Palden 2019a). Such significant GDP growth has prompted some to question whether the country may begin to veer towards a more conventional productivist direction (Hayden 2015). In this context it is interesting to note that in 2018 Bhutan's new prime minister, Dr. Lotay Tshering and his DNT (Druk Nyamrup Tshogpa) party campaigned, and were elected to office, on the promise of "Narrowing the Gap" – creating a more inclusive society by reducing inequalities and focusing on social investments (T. Palden 2019b).

Since then, the government has introduced significant pay revisions that have made teachers and health care workers the highest-paid civil servants in Bhutan (Lamsang 2019). The prime minister has further asserted that GDP is not the best way to measure Bhutan's progress – particularly in narrowing the gap. Pointing out that longer-term social investments in education and health will not necessarily be reflected in GDP growth, he noted that a more modest growth rate would suffice, whereas one similar to the previous 8 per cent might widen inequality and cause more disharmony in society (Nima 2019).

GNH and a Young Democracy

Bhutan has benefitted from the influence of visionary leaders such as the fourth king, who have inspired and driven GNH efforts. As the country has transitioned to a democratic constitutional monarchy, there is growing awareness that with this comes an important shift in responsibility, and the need to exercise new democratic powers wisely. As one expert notes, GNH was quantified to help anchor politicians and bureaucrats to the long-term goals of GNH – in preparation for a time when democratically elected governments could potentially change every five years (S. Palden 2019). As another expert has queried: "After centuries of complete isolation, two and a half centuries of constructing a polity, and 100 years of Monarchy, the people are mandated to take on new responsibilities. Where will democracy take Bhutan and Bhutanese society?" As he and others are concluding, "it becomes the responsibility of the citizens who form political parties, elect governments, and function as civil society" to help achieve the vision of GNH (K. Dorji 2015).

An Expanding Role for Civil Society in Bhutan

To this end, Bhutan's expanding community of civil society organizations (CSOs) stands to play a vital role in ensuring that GNH values and principles are activated at a grassroots level. The concept of a formalized civil society only emerged in Bhutan in the late 1980s and, since 2009, civil society has secured the legal space and mandate to play a greater role in representing the voices and concerns of society (L. Dorji 2017). Many such organizations would not necessarily identify themselves as "GNH organizations," yet are actively engaged in creating the conditions for well-being across the nine GNH domains – addressing key issues, including health, rural economic development, gender equity, youth empowerment, promotion of traditional arts and artisans, media and communication, environmental conservation, and entrepreneurship. Recognizing the important role of such organizations, a former GNH commission secretary noted that "government can't create a GNH society alone. We need active citizen participation" (Colman 2017). While there have been considerable gains in promoting civil society's role within Bhutan, such organizations are still at a "fledgling stage," and more support is needed for them to realize their considerable potential (L. Dorji 2017).

GNH and the Growing Importance of the Private Sector

Similarly, Bhutan's private sector is growing and has the potential to play a more active role in shaping GNH, and Bhutan's development more broadly. However, as some have noted, it is currently dominated by a few business houses, and there is a need for a more balanced spectrum, where artists, intellectu-als, and diverse professionals can thrive and contribute to the country's growth (K. Dorji 2015). In addition, the GNH and business survey tool (CBS 2017) can encourage businesses to integrate GNH values – although additional techni-cal support will likely be needed. Incentives for adopting GNH certification could include improved access to business financing – for example, by linking such certification to business credit ratings or government procurement scores (Cheki 2017).

Until now, GNH in Bhutan has been primarily a top-down, government-led, policy-oriented approach. In contrast, encouraging a GNH orientation within the private sector requires a "bottom up, business led and practical approach" and, in this context, social entrepreneurship could play a vital role (Cheki 2017). As most registered businesses in the country are micro- or small enterprises, providing support to emerging entrepreneurs is a national priority (Cheki 2017). Against the backdrop of rising youth unemployment, Bhutan has invested in start-up centres, tech parks, and promoting an entrepreneur-ship culture (Kubota 2019). In addition, CSOs are providing youth entrepre-neurship training, interest-free loans, and professional mentorship for business development (Lhamo 2017). In alignment with GNH values and the broader aims of social enterprise, some seek to cultivate the ethos of a "bodhisattva entrepreneur" – evoking the image of a Buddhist hero who has the motiva-tion of serving society and starts a business as a means to that end (The Loden Foundation 2020).

Globalization, Rapid Change, and New Challenges for Bhutan's Youth

About 56 per cent of Bhutan's population is under the age of twenty-five, and youth make up about one-third of the electorate (UNDP Bhutan 2019). Glob-ally, this generation faces a complex array of new challenges, accelerated by the influence of the Internet and social media. Given Bhutan's relatively recent entry into this modern, globalized landscape, the impacts have been even more dramatic. As one Bhutanese historian has noted: "Being a young Bhutanese today, particularly in an urban settlement, is not easy. In about half a century, Bhutan has gone through changes that most other countries took many centu-ries to make" (Phuntsho 2016). The aspirations, values, and priorities of youth differ vastly from those of their parents and grandparents. Confronted by a barrage of new choices, practices, and products, it is no surprise that Bhuta-nese youth are experiencing a kind of cultural "identity crisis" (Phuntsho 2016; Choden 2015). They must constantly "balance their Bhutanese cultural roots and global citizenship, relate to the past and prepare for the future, make an honest living in a competitive world and uphold lofty ideals and values. Most of the challenges they face – unemployment, urbanism, social isolation and loneliness, the deluge of unverified information – are new problems" (Phunt-sho 2016).

Proposed responses to these challenges neither ignore the trends nor attempt a retreat towards a distant and romanticized past. Instead, recognizing the fluidity of culture, one author asserts that the emerging Bhutanese identity must be "a true blend of the past, present, and future. Even as we preserve our social, cultural, and spiritual memory, we must adapt to the reality of rapid change" (K. Dorji 2015). Others point to an opportunity at this cultural crossroads. Bhutanese youth are curious and ideologically open to new ways of thinking – and can therefore become a strong force for positive change. Amid growing disillusionment with modernity and its broken promises, some are witnessing a revival of youth interest in Bhutan's traditional practices, spirituality, and culture. Whereas many of their school-educated parents were enamoured of the new attractions of modernity and secular scientific education – and sometimes dismissive of Bhutan's spiritual and cultural heritage – this attitude may be changing. There is a renewed youth interest in Bhutan's Buddhist heritage, which may in part be due to the rising popularity of meditation in the West and the perception of Buddhism as a spiritual tradition that has withstood the test of time and can appeal to the modern rational mind (Phuntsho 2016). In this dynamic context, there is an important role for CSOs to play in meeting this generation's shifting needs – finding practical ways for them to shape their evolving identity and express GNH values for themselves through entrepreneurship, media literacy training, youth leadership, and related avenues (Zangmo 2018; Wangdi 2018).

As this section has shown, GNH reflects "the challenges and prospects of a nation and people grappling to find the middle ground between spiritualism and materialism, and between tradition and modernity" (Choden 2015). In some ways, the challenges young Bhutanese face in maintaining a connection to their cultural heritage and values amid an increasingly complex, globalized world are also experienced, to varying degrees, by their peers in other countries. Yet in Bhutan, the aspiration to find a balanced "middle ground" can uniquely draw on the foundation of GNH vision and values that are enshrined in the constitution and supported by a national measurement and policy framework. As many have highlighted, the path ahead cannot be tethered to a remote past but must remain fluid and forward looking. And as the country stretches its muscles as a young democracy, it will be vital that emerging generations redefine and enrich a "culture of GNH" while advancing towards a GNH society (Choden 2015).

Bhutan and Beyond: International Adaptations and Innovation

Growing global interest in GNH and other beyond-GDP approaches has led to a surge of international conferences and events, both in Bhutan and abroad

Figure 4.3.   Exploring modern GNH values – Youth Leadership Program, GNH Centre Bhutan

Photo: Julia C. Kim

(CBS 2018; Robert Wood Johnson Foundation 2018). In 2013 the GNH Centre Bhutan, together with the Global Leadership Academy (Germany) and the Presencing Institute (USA) launched "The Global Wellbeing Lab: Transforming Economy and Society." Designed as a multistakeholder action-learning platform, the lab aims to advance new ways of generating and measuring wellbeing at multiple levels of society (The Global Wellbeing Lab 2013). Activating participants from seventeen countries, the lab has inspired new projects and regional initiatives, including the Global Wellbeing in Business Lab, the WE-Africa Lab on Building Wellbeing Economies for Africa, and the Wellbeing Economies Alliance (Global Wellbeing Lab 2016).

In addition, the centre has collaborated with academic institutions, including Schumacher College (UK) to offer courses which seek to re-align the values of work and economy towards greater well-being and a more sustainable society (Kim and Richardson, forthcoming). These programs aim to convey a theoretical and technical understanding of GNH, as well as related disciplines, including new economics, sustainable development, and the growing science of well-being. Inner leadership and transformative education practices are emphasized to spark critical inquiry into the nature of the current economic system and how well-being is supported or undermined at both individual and systems levels. Moving from insight to action, participants are encouraged to innovate and apply what they have learned within their own personal and professional spheres (GNH Centre Bhutan 2017).

Over time, a range of GNH and well-being "prototypes" have emerged, applying well-being values, metrics, and interventions across various settings, including education, business and social enterprise, landscape architecture, urban spaces, and city planning, as well as public health (Kim and Richardson, forthcoming). By combining transformative leadership development (vision and values) with practical action, (well-being innovation and prototypes) these initiatives are generating insights into how well-being concepts can be applied and adapted across a range of contexts and scales. Beyond the projects and networks, participants have pointed to the value of the peer relationships formed through these experiences. Referring to the resistance they often face in introducing a well-being economy approach, many cite these deep, supportive relationships as a key condition for achieving impact despite such challenges (Global Wellbeing Lab 2016).

Beyond GDP, Beyond Numbers: Emerging Insights for a Global Economy of Well-Being

Drawing from Bhutan's unique heritage and still-evolving GNH experience, it is not feasible nor desirable to propose universal lessons to guide other contexts or countries. However, it is possible to reflect on Bhutan's rich experience and to draw out key insights that may hopefully inspire courageous experimentation and collaboration towards a global economy of well-being.

1. **The importance of acknowledging and balancing both the tangible and intangible aspects of happiness and well-being:** One early and enduring contribution of GNH to the beyond-GDP discourse has been the clear articulation by Bhutan's leaders of the importance of balancing "both material and spiritual development" or the "tangible and intangible" aspects of well-being (CBS 2016). That these are defined and measured through the GNH Index and its nine domains is one factor that distinguishes GNH so clearly from GDP. Although many national surveys routinely collect data on education, health, and living standards, the more intangible domains, such as time use, psychological well-being, community vitality, and cultural diversity and resilience, are equally

important in creating an enabling environment for well-being (Boniwell 2009; Layard, Clark, and Senik 2012). Beyond promoting such an environment, GNH posits that the inner transformation of mindsets and behaviour is as important for human flourishing as the transformation of outer living conditions (NDP Steering Committee and Secretariat 2013). In this respect, Bhutan's rich spiritual heritage draws on diverse traditions of teaching and meditative practices that emphasize the cultivation of wisdom and compassion as means towards genuine happiness (Phuntsho 2013). Globally, a growing body of interdisciplinary research (neuroscience, positive psychology, sociology, behavioural economics) highlights the role of well-being interventions (including mindfulness, compassion, altruism, volunteering, and other pro-social behaviours) in supporting the physical, psychological, and social aspects of well-being and happiness (Rinpoche 2007; Goleman and Davidson 2017; Greenfield and Marks 2004; Helliwell et al. 2018). Thus, addressing both the external and internal dimensions of well-being should be regarded as important and complementary approaches (Diener 2019).

2. **How much is enough? Notions of sufficiency, equity, and sustainability:** As described earlier, the GNH survey uses "sufficiency thresholds" to calculate whether individuals and groups have the requisite conditions to be happy. This has important practical and policy implications. Because the underlying principle behind sufficiency is that "more" does not necessarily translate into enhanced well-being, the analysis focuses on enabling as many people as possible to meet the threshold fixed for each of the thirty-three GNH indicators (Penjore 2017). Similarly, such data would help policymakers understand who is falling behind and, subsequently, what changes are needed to improve their well-being. At a macro-economic level, calls for sufficiency have drawn on research showing little, if any, connection between rising per-capita income and well-being once adequate material living standards have been achieved (Easterlin et al. 2019). Thus, the notion of sufficiency counters the productivist belief that ever-greater production and consumption is both desirable and feasible. From a sufficiency perspective, one must ask how much is enough and question infinite growth of production and consumption (Deitz and O'Neill 2013; Princen 2005). For some observers, sufficiency is essential to "justice in an age of limits" (Sachs and Santarius 2007). Thus, sufficiency is significant for GNH and for well-being economics more broadly, as it aims to promote equitable and sustainable socio-economic development, within the limits of planetary boundaries (NDP Steering Committee and Secretariat 2013; Raworth 2017).

3. **The importance of an "eco-centric" world view – Human beings embedded within an interdependent web of life:** Bhutan's approach

has been influenced by the Buddhist notion of a "middle path," based on avoiding extremes, living with moderation, and balancing the material and intangible conditions for well-being. The nine GNH domains are thus regarded as interdependent – a holistic view that does not privilege economic factors above others but places them alongside a range of social and environmental concerns. Moreover, human well-being is regarded as intimately interconnected with that of the natural world – an "eco-centric" rather than "ego-centric" view (Scharmer 2013), where balance among living systems is seen as integral, and the natural world itself has intrinsic value beyond its utility as a natural resource. In Bhutan, the natural world is still viewed by many as sacred. For example, in 1994, despite its attractive revenue potential, climbing mountains higher than 6,000 metres was prohibited. Local customs hold such peaks to be the rarefied domain of protective deities and spirits, and in 2003 mountaineering was banned entirely, leaving Bhutan with some of the world's highest untouched peaks (Verschuuren 2016). This sacred view of nature is shared by many indigenous cultures and has likely helped to protect Bhutan's environment well into the present time (Allison 2017). Similarly, in New Zealand, persistent advocacy and legal cases advanced by Māori people are showing how new policies that respect and protect forests and rivers are codifying such eco-centric cultural narratives. This profound shift in how nature is viewed could have important implications for other countries, where dominant narratives and policy currently place people at the "receiving end" of nature, rather than being part of a vibrant, interdependent whole (Acharya and Ng 2020).

4. **The power of a multilevel, multisector approach:** Bhutan has uniquely benefitted from leaders who have articulated a national development strategy based on happiness and well-being. As it continues to chart an alternative course against the tide of conventional GDP-based development, the journey ahead will undoubtedly be challenging. What is clear, however, is that the steps Bhutan has taken to integrate and operationalize a GNH approach (articulating the vision within key legal instruments, such as the constitution; developing and applying new survey and policymaking tools; and engaging influential sectors of society) are instrumental in taking a well-being approach beyond vision and into action. This multilevel, multisector approach can provide useful insights for other countries embarking on a similar course.

5. **Start where you are – Introducing well-being approaches across diverse scales and contexts:** While a national-level approach may not initially be feasible in many countries, it is possible to introduce well-being metrics and approaches at a smaller scale, where innovation and learning can progress in a supportive environment. Through its action-learning

Figure 4.4.   Nature is viewed as sacred – Taktsang monastery, Bhutan

Photo: Julia C. Kim

platforms, the GNH Centre Bhutan and its partners have supported stakeholders from a range of countries to introduce well-being values and metrics at different levels of scale (e.g., organization, community, municipality) and sectors of influence (e.g., education, social enterprise, business, city planning, health). As such initiatives grow over time, they can generate practical leverage points and popular support for subsequently mainstreaming new progress measures at a wider, systemic level. In the face of scepticism or resistance, it will be important to cultivate conscious leadership and build a community of practice and support for those individuals and institutions leading the change. In this way, a *culture of equity and well-being* can be grown from the grassroots level so that there is fertile soil for the seeds of new national-level well-being measures and policies to land (Robert Wood Johnson Foundation 2018).

6. **Going beyond numbers – The importance of transformative leadership for a unifying narrative of wellbeing:** New progress indicators and measures are critical in shifting national priorities and budgets towards

promoting greater well-being and equity. But numbers alone are not enough. Experience has shown that in the absence of deeply internalized values, reporting on measurements can remain an intellectual exercise, open to misinterpretation or manipulation in service of political agendas (Scharmer 2013). For this reason, *transformative leadership development* forms a central part of the GNH Centre's programs (Global Wellbeing Lab 2016). Demystifying economics and reconnecting it to ecology, well-being, and everyday lived experience is vital for understanding the deeper meaning behind the numbers. In this context, program participants have found it revealing to apply a "GNH lens" to their own personal lives. For those from high-GDP countries, such a lens can reveal, from the level of lived experience, how a country's pursuit of economic growth has often come at the cost of widening social disparities, loss of work-life balance, diminishing social connection, and worsening psychological well-being (Kim and Richardson, forthcoming). Participants can then begin to explore how a *unifying narrative of well-being* is supported, for example, by the growing research documenting how GDP growth and widening inequity negatively impacts the well-being not just of the poor but also the privileged within society (Wilkinson and Pickett 2010). This in turn can shift the level of inquiry from a position of trepidation to one of curiosity and hope – not simply asking *what do we stand to lose*, but what do we *hope to gain* by transitioning towards an economy of greater equity and well-being?

Concluding Reflections

From the inclusion of happiness within Bhutan's legal code of 1729 and the fourth king's articulation of GNH in the 1970s, to the modern-day integration of GNH within national surveys and policymaking tools, to the application of GNH-inspired values and metrics across new sectors in Bhutan and beyond, Bhutan's contribution to the collective learning and understanding of how to create a society based on happiness and well-being has steadily grown. In the face of high expectations and emerging modern challenges, there are those at home and abroad who question this small Himalayan country's ability to live up to the bold ideals and vision (Deidre 2017). Yet as some observers have noted, it may be "unrealistic to expect a small country such as Bhutan to have complete answers for how to move beyond a growth-based economy and avoid getting caught on the treadmill of production" (Hayden 2015). Indeed, whether Bhutan ultimately manages to blaze a trail towards a desirable post-growth future, it has already integrated environmental considerations and social equity into the development process to a much greater extent than in "business-as-usual" development strategies. Perhaps most valuable of all, it has elevated the importance, for the rest of the world, of asking critical questions about the ultimate purposes economic development should serve (Hayden 2015; J. Sachs 2012).

Given its deep historical roots, current cultural shifts, and long-term development aspirations, GNH should rightly be viewed as a *journey* rather than a final destination. As Bhutan's evolving story reveals, the journey towards GNH requires bold vision, committed leadership, and an actively engaged range of stakeholders, including government, the private sector, and civil society. Moreover, in an increasingly turbulent and interdependent world, it is a journey that cannot be undertaken alone. As this chapter has shown, Bhutan's experience is already revealing important challenges, opportunities and emerging lessons for creating an economy of well-being. Going forward, both in Bhutan and globally, it will be important to find innovative ways of combining vision with action, measurement with policymaking, and broad systems change with transformative leadership practice. All will be needed in order to cultivate the courage and the consciousness shift necessary to make the leap from propping up current, failing systems to embodying a new paradigm of planetary well-being – one that is still in emergence.

REFERENCES

Acharya, Karabi, and Tim Ng. 2020. "Meeting of the Minds, The Global Water Equity Article Series." *I Am The River, The River is Me: Prioritizing Well-being Through Water Policy.* https://meetingoftheminds.org/i-am-the-river-the-river-is -me-prioritizing-well-being-through-water-policy-33035.

Allison, Elizabeth. 2017. "Spirits and Nature: The Intertwining of Sacred Cosmologies and Environmental Conservation in Bhutan." *Journal for the Study of Religion, Nature and Culture* 11, no. 2.

Boniwell, I. 2009. *Time for Life: Satisfaction with Time Use and Its Relationship with Subjective Wellbeing.* Saarbrucken, Germany: VDM.

Brooks, Jeremy. 2013. "Avoiding Limits to Growth: Gross National Happiness in Bhutan as a Model for Sustainable Development." *Sustainability* 5, no. 9: 3640–64.

CBS. 2016. *A Compass towards a Just and Harmonious Society: 2015 GNH Survey Report.* Thimphu: The Centre for Bhutan Studies and GNH Research.

– 2017. *Proposed GNH of Business.* Centre for Bhutan Studies and GNH Research.

– 2018. "GNH of Business: Proceedings of the Seventh International Conference on Gross National Happiness." Edited by Karma Ura and Sangay Chophel. Centre for Bhutan Studies and GNH Research. 520.

Cheki, Karma. 2017. "92 Percent of Businesses in the Country are Micro or Small." *Kuensel*, 11 November 2017. https://kuenselonline.com/92-percent-of-businesses -in-the-country-are-micro-or-small/.

Choden, Tashi. 2015. "What Would a 21st Century Bhutanese Identity Be?" *The Druk Journal*, May 2015. http://drukjournal.bt/what-would-a-21st-century-bhutanese -identity-be/.

Climate Council. 2017. *Bhutan is the World's Only Carbon Negative Country – So How Did They Do It?* 2 April 2017. https://www.climatecouncil.org.au /bhutan-is-the-world-s-only-carbon-negative-country-so-how-did-they-do-it/.

Colman, Tashi Ronald. 2017. "Civil Society – Why it Matters." *The Druk Journal*. http://drukjournal.bt/civil-society-why-it-matters/.

Deidre, Rose. 2017. "A Modern History of Happiness as Economic Policy. History and Criticism of Gross National Happiness." *GRIN*. Munich. https://www.grin .com/document/366000.

Diener, Ed. 2019. "Well-Being Interventions to Improve Societies." In *Global Happiness and Wellbeing Policy Report*. Global Council for Happiness and Wellbeing.

Dietz, Rob, and Daniel O'Neill. 2013. *Enough is Enough: Building a Sustainable Economy in a World of Finite Resources*. San Francisco: Berrett-Koehler.

Dorji, Kinley. 2012. "Why Bhutan? A GNH Perspective." *Kuensel*, 29 December 2012. https://kuenselonline.com/why-bhutan-a-gnh-perspective/.

– 2015. "What Is the 'Bhutanese-ness' of the Bhutanese People?" *The Druk Journal*, Spring.

Dorji, Lam. 2017. "Emergence of Civil Society in Bhutan." *The Druk Journal*, Winter. http://drukjournal.bt/emergence-of-civil-society-in-bhutan/.

Easterlin, R.A., L.A. McVey, M. Switek, O. Sawangfa, and J.S. Zweig. 2019. "The Happiness-Income Paradox Revisited." *Proceedings of the National Academy of Sciences* 107, no. 52: 22463–8.

Givel, Michael S. 2015. "Gross National Happiness in Bhutan: Political Institutions and Implementation." *Asian Affairs* 46, no. 1: 102–17.

The Global Wellbeing Lab. 2013. *The Presencing Institute, The GNH Centre Bhutan, GIZ Global Leadership Academy*. https://vimeo.com/85855298.

– 2016. "The Global Wellbeing Lab 2.0 – Transforming Economy and Society, Summary Report." The Presencing Institute, The GNH Centre Bhutan, GIZ Global Leadership Academy. https://globalwellbeinglab.com/2016/10/14 /global-wellbeing-lab-2-0-2016-summary-report/.

GNH Centre Bhutan. 2017. *The Right Livelihood and GNH Program*. https://vimeo .com/384521262.

Goleman, Daniel, and Richard J. Davidson. 2017. *Altered Traits: Science Reveals How Meditation Changes Your Mind, Brain, and Body*. New York: Penguin Random House.

Greenfield, E.A., and N.F. Marks. 2004. "Formal Volunteering as a Protective Factor for Older Adults' Pscyhological Wellbeing." *The Journal of Gerontology Series B: Psychological Sciences and Social Sciences* 59, no. 5: s258–64.

Gyamsho, Deki C., Kezang Sherab, and T.W. Maxwell. 2017. "Teacher Learning in Changing Professional Contexts: Bhutanese Teacher Educators and the Educating for GNH Initiative." *Cogent Education*. https://www.cogentoa.com/article/10.1080 /2331186X.2017.1384637.pdf.

Hayden, Anders. 2015. "Bhutan: Blazing a Trail to a Postgrowth Future." *The Journal of Environment & Development* 24, no. 2: 161–86

Helliwell, J.F., L.B. Aknin, H. Shiplett, H. Huang, and S. Wang. 2018. "Social Capital and Pro-social Behavior as Sources of Wellbeing." In *Handbook of Wellbeing*, by E. Diener, S. Oishi, and L. Tay. Salt Lake City: DEF Publishers.

Kelly, Annie. 2012. "Gross National Happiness in Bhutan: The Big Idea from a Tiny State That Could Change the World." *The Guardian*, 1 December 2012.

Kennedy, Robert F. 1968. "John F. Kennedy Presidential Library and Museum." 18 March 1968. https://www.jfklibrary.org/learn/about-jfk/the-kennedy-family /robert-f-kennedy/robert-f-kennedy-speeches/remarks-at-the-university-of -kansas-march-18-1968.

Khazan, Olga. 2013. "Should Governments Try to Make Us Happy?" *The Atlantic*, 13 September 2013.

Kim, Julia, and Julie Richardson. Forthcoming. *Innovation toward a Wellbeing Economy: Lessons from the Right Livelihood and GNH Practitioner Programs.* The GNH Centre Bhutan.

Kubota, Azusa. 2019. "The Business Case for Innovation for Gross National Happiness in Bhutan." 3 December 2019. https://www.bt.undp.org/content /bhutan/en/home/presscenter/articles/the-business-case-for-innovation-for-gross -national-happiness-in-bhutan-by-azusa-kubota-resident-representative-undp -bhutan.html.

Lamsang, Tenzing. 2019. "Revolutionary Hike: Education and Health Wins as Teachers and Doctors Are Now the Highest Paid Civil Servants." *The Bhutanese*, 6 August 2019. https://thebhutanese.bt/revolutionary-hike-education-and-health -wins-as-teachers-and-doctors-are-now-the-highest-paid-civil-servants/.

Layard, Richard, Andrew Clark, and Claudia Senik. 2012. "The Causes of Happiness and Misery." In *World Happiness Report*, by John F. Helliwell, Richard Layard, and Jeffrey Sachs. New York: Sustainable Development Solutions Network.

Lhamo, Phurpa. 2017. "Helping the Young with Business and Education." *Kuensel*, 21 August 2017. http://www.kuenselonline.com/helping-the-young -with-business-and-education/.

The Loden Foundation. 2020. "The Loden Report." http://loden.org/wp-content /uploads/2020/02/Loden-Anual-Report-2019.pdf.

National Statistical Bureau. 2018. "Statistical Yearbook."

NDP Steering Committee and Secretariat. 2013. *Happiness: Towards a New Devlopment Paradigm. Report of the Kingdom of Bhutan*. Bhutan: Royal Government of Bhutan.

Nima. 2019. "We Will Not Measure Country's Progress Only by GDP: Prime
    Minister." *Kuensel*, 26 January 2019. https://www.dailybhutan.com/article
    /we-will-not-measure-bhutan-s-progress-only-by-gdp-prime-minister-dr-lotay
    -tshering.
Palden, Sonam. 2019. "GNH in Action." *Kuensel*, 12 January 2019. http://www
    .kuenselonline.com/gnh-in-action/.
Palden, Tshering. 2019a. "Bhutan Enters Period to Shed LDC Status." *Kuensel*,
    December 2019. http://www.kuenselonline.com/bhutan-enters-preparatory
    -period-to-shed-lcd-status/.
– 2019b. "Narrowing the Poverty Gap in the 12th Plan." *Kuensel*, 9 January 2019.
    https://kuenselonline.com/narrowing-the-poverty-gap-in-the-12th-plan/.
Penjore, Dorji. 2017. "Sustainable Development Goals and Gross National
    Happiness." *The Druk Journal*.
Phuntsho, Karma. 2016. "The Promise of Broken Youth: A Positive Perspective."
    The Druk Journal.
– 2013. *The History of Bhutan*. New Delhi: Random House India. Planning
    Commission. 1999a. "Bhutan 2020 (Part 1)." Thimphu, Bhutan, 20.
– 1999b. "Bhutan 2020 (Part II)." Thimphu, Bhutan, 7.
Princen, Thomas. 2005. *The Logic of Sufficiency*. Cambridge, MA: MIT Press.
Raworth, Kate. 2017. *Doughnut Economics: Seven Ways to Think Like a 21st-Century
    Economist*. London: Random House.
RGOB. 2017. *GNH*. The Permanent Mission of the Kingdom of Bhutan to the United
    Nations in New York. https://www.mfa.gov.bt/pmbny/?page_id=166.
Rinpoche, Yongey Mingyur. 2007. *The Joy of Living: Unlocking the Secret and Science
    of Happiness*. New York: Three Rivers Press.
Robert Wood Johnson Foundation. 2018. "Advancing Well-being in an Inequitable
    World: Moving from Measurement to Action. Summary of Insights from the
    Robert Wood Johnson Foundation;s Global Conference on Well-being." Bellagio:
    Robert Wood Johnson Foundation.
Sachs, Jeffrey. 2012. "Introduction." *World Happiness Report*. Edited by John
    Helliwell, Richard Layard, and Jeffrey Sachs. Columbia Earth Institute.
Sachs, Wolfgang, and Tilman Santarius. 2007. *Fair Future*. London: Zed Books.
Scharmer, C. Otto. 2013. *From Ego-system to Eco-system Economies*. 23 September 2013.
    https://www.opendemocracy.net/en/transformation/from-ego-system-to-eco
    -system-economies/.
Stiglitz, Joseph, Amartya Sen, and Jean-Paul Fitoussi. 2010. *Mismeasuring Our Lives:
    Why GDP Doesn't Measure Up*. New York: The New Press.
Thinley, Jigmi. 2012. "Address by the Honorable Prime Minister on Wellbeing and
    Happiness: Defining a New Economic Paradigm at the UN Headquarters New
    York." *Office of the Prime Minister and Cabinet*. 2 April 2012.
UNDP Bhutan. 2019. *Bhutan National Human Development Report: Ten Years
    of Democracy in Bhutan*. United Nations Development Programme Bhutan &
    Parliament of the Kingdom of Bhutan.

United Nations. 2011. *UN Resolution 65/309: Happiness: Towards a Holistic Approach to Development.* United Nations.

Ura, Karma, Sabina Alkire, and Tshoki Zangmo. 2012. "Case Study: Bhutan Gross National Happiness and the GNH Index." In *World Happiness Report*, edited by John Helliwell, Richard Layard, and Jeffrey Sachs. Columbia Earth Institute.

Verschuuren, Bas. 2016. "Nye within Protected Areas of Bhutan." In *Asian Sacred Natural Sites: Philosophy and Practice in Protected Areas and Conservation.* Milton Park, UK: Routledge.

Wangdi, Tempa. 2018. *News and Media Literacy for CSOs.* 17 July 2018. http://bcmd .bt/news-and-media-literacy-for-csos/.

Wilkinson, Richard G., and Kate Pickett. 2010. *The Spirit Level: Why Equality is Better for Everyone.* London: Penguin Books.

World Bank. 2014. "Bhutan Country Snapshot." Washington, DC.

Zangmo, Rinchen. 2018. "Promoting GNH Values among Bhutanese Youth." *Kuensel.* http://www.kuenselonline.com/promoting-gnh-values-among -young-bhutanese/.

5   Well-Being in British Politics and Policy[1]

IAN BACHE

Introduction

UK government activity in the second wave[2] of political interest in well-being can be traced back to the 1990s but took a leap forward with the election of David Cameron as prime minister (PM) of a Conservative-Liberal Coalition government in 2010. Cameron resigned as PM in 2016 in the wake of losing the referendum on Britain's membership of the European Union. From that point, momentum on well-being – as on many issues – slowed considerably, as Brexit came to dominate British politics. Yet some UK-level developments continued below the radar of political and public visibility, alongside some more visible developments in the devolved administrations of Scotland, Wales, and Northern Ireland. At UK level, the main focus has been on evidence accumulation on "what works" for well-being in policy, following the creation of the What Works Centre for Wellbeing (WWCW) in 2015. This is seen by many advocates as a crucial next step for bringing well-being into policy more fully. Moreover, developments following the 2019 general election suggested well-being might return more visibly to the UK agenda.

This chapter reviews key developments on well-being in British politics and policy. It considers how it rose on to the political agenda and the key policy initiatives that followed, before turning to the recent focus on accumulating evidence on how policies impact well-being. However, it argues that while evidence can play an important role, evidence alone is rarely decisive in policy change. The fact that new initiatives have advanced in the absence of robust evidence and in the context of ongoing disputes within epistemic communities on how well-being should be defined and measured demonstrates that the future prospects for well-being in British politics and policy – and indeed those elsewhere – will be shaped primarily by political will.

The Idea of Well-Being in Politics and Policy

As discussed in chapter one (Hayden and Wilson), there has been increasing interest in the idea of well-being as a goal of public policy. At the most ambitious level, well-being is seen as an idea that could reorient the overarching goals of public policy away from the dominant focus on economic goals, emblemized by the pursuit of GDP growth, which has long been taken as a proxy for social progress. For others, well-being can at least provide an important tool of analysis in policy appraisal and evaluation that might be used as an alternative (or complement to) more established techniques of neo-classical economics and thus reorient the focus of at least some policies.

As has often been observed, there are many ways of understanding well-being and, indeed, preferences for alternative, but closely related, concepts, such as happiness and quality of life. In this chapter, the focus on well-being reflects the dominant focus and terminology of UK policy debates. Specifically, well-being is used in terms defined by the Office for National Statistics (ONS) Measuring National Well-being program. This covers ten domains: personal well-being, our relationships, health, what we do (work and leisure), where we live, personal finance, economy, education and skills, governance, and environment (ONS 2019). However, in the UK context it is important to pay particular attention to the idea of subjective well-being (SWB), which relates to the personal well-being domain of the ONS framework and which is viewed as gaining currency in UK policy circles (Austin 2016). SWB has three aspects, which relate to pleasant or unpleasant affect, life satisfaction, and eudaimonia (experience of meaning) and is addressed by the ONS in four questions (the ONS4): Overall, how satisfied are you with your life nowadays? Overall, how happy did you feel yesterday? Overall, how anxious did you feel yesterday? Overall, to what extent do you feel the things you do in your life are worthwhile? Each question is measured on a scale from 0 to 10.[3]

There is not space here to detail the controversies around the use of SWB in policy. Briefly, though, it is viewed by advocates as anti-paternalistic and democratic (Diener et al. 2009) because SWB accounts for people's own evaluations of their lives. It also has the advantage of being relatively easily measured and requiring relatively few questions (and thus resources) in comparison to more complex multidimensional assessments of well-being. For critics, SWB is too a narrow measure of well-being that cannot adequately represent the complex idea of well-being. Moreover, it is criticized for focusing policy attention on individual responsibility rather than addressing the underlying structural conditions that shape the well-being prospects of many (Scott 2012; White 2017). While the preference for SWB for some is ideological, following Bentham (1996 [1823]), in others it can be more pragmatic because it is a relatively easy way to measure and present well-being: at its simplest, through a single number.

Multidimensional frameworks, by contrast, require a dashboard of indicators that is more difficult to communicate. While the ONS takes a multidimensional approach to measurement, it is the prioritization of the SWB component of this framework in policy discussions that has drawn attention and criticism in equal measure. We return to this issue below.

The Rise of Well-Being in UK Politics and Policy

Partly in response to developments internationally (see chapter one), in 2007 the ONS indicated its intention to elevate its analysis of societal well-being (Allin and Hand 2017, 6), and this is discussed below. However, interest in well-being in policy in the UK can be traced back significantly further. The Conservative government of John Major was one of the first to respond to the Earth Summit's recommendation that countries develop their own sustainable development strategies, with *Sustainable Development: The UK Strategy* published in 1994. The first indicators report, *Indicators of Sustainable Development for the United Kingdom*, was published in 1996 and placed a strong emphasis on environmental and economic factors but was criticized for its neglect of social issues (Scrivens and Iasiello 2010, 39). The Labour government that came to office in 1997 and set out a revised approach in the strategy report *A Better Quality of Life*, which was published in May 1999 and in the indicator set *Quality of Life Counts*, released seven months later. Beyond the sustainable development agenda, other notable developments in this period came in the departments of local government and health.

The Local Government Act 2000 gave local authorities the power to promote well-being in a "broader and more innovative" way than had been implied by previous legislation (Communities and Local Government 2008, 1). However, this power tended to be used symbolically or as reassurance in the use of other powers and therefore did not lead to significant policy changes (Communities and Local Government 2008, 4–5). In 2005, the Audit Commission published a list of forty-five local quality-of-life indicators for local authorities to use in order to help provide "a vision for the local area: to enhance local democracy; to provide information for effective policy formulation; to evaluate those policies; and to increase education and action around sustainability issues" (Scott 2012, 54). However, while the Audit Commission worked closely with local stakeholders to develop the indicators, they received limited support from local authorities and did not have much impact on policy (Scott 2012, 54).

The idea of QALYs (Quality Adjusted Life Years) was developed in the 1990s to provide a form of cost–benefit analysis in health care. QALYs are used by the National Institute for Health and Care Excellence (NICE) as a way of valuing the benefits gained from a variety of health interventions. The QALY has proved a popular tool for health policy decision-making because it takes into account both the quantity and quality of life generated by particular health care interventions in determining value. When the QALY figure is combined with the costs of providing the interventions, a cost–utility ratio results, which indicates "the additional costs required to generate a year of perfect health (one QALY)" (Phillips 2009, 1).[4]

In the mid-2000s, NICE published a raft of guidance on the effective treatment of mental health disorders, including depression, anxiety, and post-traumatic stress disorder, and made a strong case for more treatment through psychological therapies (for example, NICE 2004). At the same time, epistemic communities were making the economic case for psychological therapies. They argued that their use in the National Health Service would be cost effective by reducing other medical costs and the government's welfare bill. In addition, more-effective treatment would also increase tax revenue through people returning to work and would increase national productivity (Clark 2011, 319). At the vanguard of this activity was economist and Labour peer Richard Layard, who had played a leading role in the emerging "science of happiness." In the run up to the 2005 general election, Layard made the case to the Labour government for a radical expansion of mental health services, and Labour's election manifesto subsequently included a commitment to improving mental health services, referring to both behavioural and drug therapies. After the election, the returning Labour government established a program for Improving Access to Psychological Therapies (IAPTs), with £173 million to be spent by 2010/11 (Department of Health 2008, 4).[5]

The Coalition Government (2010–15)

The Coalition government that took office in 2010 consisted of two parties that had shown interest in well-being as a guide to public policy while in opposition. However, it was David Cameron's advocacy of well-being that was central to it rising up the British political agenda. In 2006, shortly after becoming leader of the Conservative Party, Cameron stated, "It's time we admitted there's more to life than money, and time we focused not just on GDP, but on GWB – General Well-Being" (Cameron 2006). He subsequently established the Quality of Life Policy Group as part of his party's internal policy review. This group concluded that "we are now confident enough of the dynamics of life satisfaction to start subjecting many areas of government policy to much more vigorous well-being tests" (Gummer and Goldsmith 2007, 57). Quality of life and well-being remained part of the Conservative Party's narrative in the run-up to the 2010 general election.

A pivotal moment came in November 2010 when Cameron, as the recently installed PM, publicly endorsed the Office for National Statistics (ONS) Measuring National Wellbeing (MNW) program. In launching the program

Cameron (2010) stated that "we will start measuring our progress as a country, not just by how our economy is growing, but by how our lives are improving; not just by our standard of living, but by our quality of life." He argued that the MNW program would "open up a debate about what really matters" and "would help the government work out, with evidence, the best ways of trying to help improve people's wellbeing" (Cameron 2010). The ONS subsequently conducted a "national debate" on what domains and measures of well-being should be used for the program. In response to this consultation, ten domains were decided upon in July 2012 (see above). Most of the data for these domains were already being collected by the ONS and were simply repackaged for the well-being framework. However, the four new SWB questions discussed above were added to national statistics to provide data for the personal well-being domain, and it was this move that attracted the most attention.

The ONS (2012, 36–7) highlighted three potential uses for its data: overall monitoring of national well-being; use in the policymaking process; and international comparisons.[6] It argued that the large sample size in the survey would allow comparison of different groups within the population and between different areas within the UK, which could allow policies to be targeted towards those whose well-being would benefit most. The first data from the program were presented to the government in 2012, and they have since been collected and reported on annually. In March 2014 the UK National Statistics Authority granted the ONS well-being statistics national statistics status, which means that they comply with a "wide-ranging" code of practice and are "readily accessible, produced according to sound methods and managed impartially and objectively in the public interest" (UK Statistical Authority 2014, 1).

The launch of the ONS program was accompanied by a flurry of activity within Whitehall. Responsibility for well-being was shifted from the Department for Food, Environment and Rural Affairs to the Cabinet Office, to provide a stronger cross-departmental focus. In addition, a Social Impacts Task Force was created, consisting of analysts from across Whitehall and the devolved administrations to help take the work forward within government departments. In 2011 the Treasury updated its Green Book policy guidance to government departments to include SWB analysis alongside the market-based approaches of Stated Preference and Revealed Preference for the valuation of non-market goods in policy appraisal (Fujiwara and Campbell 2011, 57–8).

However, the government was clear that the ONS SWB indicators were still in development and that "we should not expect at this stage to have examples of major decisions that have been heavily influenced by wellbeing research" (HM Government 2013, para. 4). Yet it also suggested that it had put in place some "new foundations" for instilling a well-being approach (HM Government

2013, para. 4). Among these new policy foundations were a number of new departmental surveys and narratives relating to well-being and examples of well-being emerging in policy appraisal and evaluations.

The increased interest in using well-being in policy appraisal has often been linked to the potential for SWB to be converted into a monetary valuation (see Helliwell et al., this volume). For example, in 2008 the Department for Culture, Media and Sport collaborated with other publicly funded organizations to invest in a *Culture and Sport Evidence Programme*, part of which sought to understand the short-term economic value of engagement with culture and sport using a SWB assessment (Marsh et al. 2010). The Department for Business, Innovation and Skills' attempt to understand the broader individual and community value of community learning led it to commission research that sought to monetize the value of adult learning using well-being and contingent valuation techniques (Dolan and Fujiwara 2012): social cost–benefit analysis techniques that are advocated in the Treasury's Green Book guidance to departments. The Cabinet Office, along with the Department for Work and Pensions, commissioned research to estimate the value of volunteering and other community-related variables using SWB data (Fujiwara, Oroyemi, and McKinnon 2012). In 2012 the government set up the Airports Commission to undertake an independent review of the UK's future airport capacity needs, which conducted a *Quality of Life Assessment* as part of its review – the first time such an analysis had been undertaken for an airport development (Airports Commission 2015, 213). The assessment drew partly on the ONS4 in order to assess the links between SWB and four aviation factors (proximity to airports, aviation noise, working in airports, and being at airports) (Airports Commission 2014, 29–44; see Bache and Reardon 2016, 110–12).

There are also examples of Whitehall departments using well-being measures as part of policy evaluation. The Department of Health's *Public Health Outcomes Framework* (introduced to guide national and local activity towards public health improvement), monitored "self-reported wellbeing" as an indicator of health improvement using the ONS4. The Department for Communities and Local Government suggested that well-being would play an "important part" in the evaluation of its *Troubled Families* program, with specific consideration given to assessing whether the program improved the well-being of participants. The Department for Work and Pensions included the ONS4 as part of its *Support for the Very Long Term Unemployed Trailblazer* study, which featured a randomized controlled trial of Job Seeker's Allowance claimants undergoing different elements of the *Work Programme*. Well-being also played an important role in the evaluation of one of the government's flagship civil society initiatives – the *National Citizen Service* (HM Government 2013, 32) (see Bache and Reardon 2016, 109–10).

Policy Developments

In addition to the use of well-being in surveys, appraisals, and evaluations, a limited number of policy initiatives were developed by the Coalition government informed by a well-being perspective. Prominent among these was the Care Act of 2014, which outlined the way local authorities should determine eligibility for care support and the obligations on local authorities to provide care services. The Care Act "puts wellbeing at the heart of care and support" and means that "local authorities must promote wellbeing when carrying out any of their care and support functions in respect of a person" (Department of Health 2014, 7). The *Children and Families Act* of 2014 reformed paternity, maternity, and adoption leave and introduced shared parental leave. A key component of the act was the extension of the right to request flexible working to all employees, whereas previously it had applied only to employees with child or caring responsibilities. In the Department for Business Innovation and Skills' assessment of the policy, improved well-being was mentioned as one of the "key non-monetised benefits" for the "main affected groups." Another example, the Social Value Act (2012), which applies to all public-sector bodies in England, requires them "to have regard to economic, social and environmental well-being in connection with public services contracts."

Well-being also became a more prominent goal within the health sector from 2010. In 2010 the government published the White Paper *Healthy Lives, Healthy People*, which outlined a "radical new approach" to public health in England, with well-being as a strong theme. Following the Health and Social Care Act in 2012, Public Health England was set up as an executive Agency of the Department of Health with the goal to "protect and improve the nation's health and wellbeing, and reduce health inequalities" (Public Health England 2015). The 2012 act also established Health and Wellbeing Boards as local fora for leaders from the health and care system to deliver on the same goals.

Evidence and the What Works Centre for Wellbeing

Despite these developments, the overall impact of well-being in policy has been relatively limited: established concerns relating to the economy in particular remain dominant. A perceived weakness of the idea of well-being in policy is the lack of robust evidence on what policies might enhance well-being, for whom, in what ways, and by how much: hence Cameron's reference to the need for evidence in launching the national wellbeing program in 2010 and his subsequent creation of the What Works Centre for Wellbeing (WWCW) in 2015 (below).

Scientific evidence is often seen to have an elevated status among forms of knowledge in the policy process, as the "dominant language of legitimation and persuasion in today's liberal societies" (Goodwin et al. 2001, 15). Scholars have long debated the influence of evidence in policy, with Carol Weiss (1979) shaping much of the scholarly debate (Dunlop 2014). In this literature it is commonplace to identify a continuum that places rationality at one end – where evidence is crucial in shaping policy – and politics at the other – where evidence is just one factor among a number, and generally not the most important (Marston and Watts 2003, 145; Cook 2011). The literature on *policy types* suggests that more complex policy areas tend to be more receptive to evidence than less complex areas (Boswell 2012). Yet while the degree of complexity may be important in shaping perceptions of the need for evidence, as Boswell (2012, 23) suggests, "it will reveal little about the function that research is playing in the policy process." This is because the use of evidence is often symbolic, and while policymakers may draw on knowledge and expertise, this does mean that it will necessarily shape policy. The extent to which this happens is an empirical question, although there is a clear demand for evidence in relation to well-being, which remains an idea characterized by complexity, uncertainty, and contestation.

For those who seek a more prominent role for well-being in public policy there are often different priorities: some are most concerned with promoting mental well-being (Layard 2005), others with greater equality (Wilkinson and Pickett 2009), others still with environmental sustainability (Jackson 2011), and so on. An evaluation of the use of well-being powers in UK local government found different interpretations and discourses of well-being across local authorities and "little consistency" in understanding of the new powers: "there was indeed no 'single' problem of wellbeing but rather a range of ongoing problematisations, which varied according to the interpretations of different stakeholders" (Griggs and Howarth 2011, 221). Such conclusions are reflected in the wider literature on well-being (e.g., Phillips 2006; Scott 2012; Tomlinson and Kelly 2013; McGregor 2015; Seaford 2018; Wallace 2018) and conflict over the nature of the problem and thus the potential solutions have led to it being described as a quintessential "wicked problem" (Bache, Reardon, and Anand 2016).

Thus, while well-being measurement has been described as "an idea whose time had come" (Bache and Reardon 2013), this is not the case in policy terms. Yet, despite slow progress, the idea of well-being as a prominent goal of public policy has survived. The director of the UK's Behavioural Insights Team,[7] David Halpern (2016), stated: "The real lacuna is around intervention studies … what can you do about it? There is a desperate need to collate and encourage intervention studies to see what could actually move the dial on." In short, a key challenge is to understand and act on "what works" for well-being in policy: the creation of the WWCW in 2015 was in response to this challenge.

The WWCW was established with seventeen founding partners, including various government departments, Public Health England, the ONS, the Big

Lottery Fund, and the Economic and Social Research Council (ESRC). The WWCW aims to develop a "strong and credible evidence base which will support these organisations to concentrate efforts on interventions that will have the biggest impact" on well-being (Cabinet Office 2015b). On behalf of the centre, the ESRC commissioned an initial research synthesis of "what works" and secondary data analysis in three policy areas: community well-being, culture and sport, and employment and learning (areas that Whitehall departments had already shown interest in). The initial work would also focus on "measuring, analysing data, definitions, and identifying areas for further research on wellbeing" (Cabinet Office 2015b).

However, the ESRC (2014, 4) provided a starting point for the WWCW on how well-being should be understood, drawing on the work of the ONS: "Well-being, put simply, is about 'how we are doing' as individuals, communities and as a nation and how sustainable this is for the future. We define wellbeing as having 10 broad dimensions [domains] which have been shown to matter most to people in the UK as identified through a national debate … [see above] … Personal wellbeing is a particularly important dimension." This definition set out common ground for the different programs in the WWCW but, as the ESRC acknowledged, would not resolve debate over definitional issues. The extent to which personal/subjective well-being should be emphasized remains a particularly contentious issue.

The newness of well-being to the policy agenda means that much extant research has not been conducted with this definition in mind and, often, relevant research has well-being as a secondary or even tertiary outcome (ESRC 2014, 5). As such, part of the WWCW's task is to address challenges such as "as the ability to establish cause and effect from such evidence" (ESRC 2014, 5). In short, the accumulation and transmission of evidence on how policies can enhance well-being is seen as a crucial next step in bringing well-being more fully into policy.

Well-Being and Policy: Moving Forward

In its advice to government departments and other agencies, the WWCW (2018) identified a number of ways in which well-being might change the approach to policy: at the strategic level (defining the overall objective of improving people's lives/improving well-being); at the policy or project level (designing options that improve well-being, based on evidence; using evidence to achieve better outcomes, as well-being in turn improves productivity, health, and pro-social behaviours); and in appraising options (considering the full potential of well-being impacts; quantifying well-being impacts and monetizing where possible; reflecting the well-being impacts on different groups). A well-being approach is said to understand policy impacts that may not have been previously considered by other approaches and also highlight the impact of policy on different groups. Evidence can help to estimate the potential scale of policy impacts and possibly quantify this impact by calculating the number of impacts x the length of time.

The WWCW (2018) provided a flavour of the types of evidence being collected and an indication of findings in relation to some of the drivers of well-being. The WWCW also summarized findings that quantify the effects of changes in key domains on life satisfaction, indicating the level of confidence in the effect and causality. These findings indicate that the levels of confidence across different findings vary significantly – although there is a consensus in some areas, not least those where a relationship with well-being would be widely expected (e.g., physical and mental health). In this sense, the evidence is likely to confirm what decision-makers already think they know. Where this kind of data might have more impact, however, is in identifying the challenges for particular groups (e.g., by age, gender, ethnicity, or location) and designing policies in relation to those whose well-being is relatively low.

Yet even where robust evidence is available, evidence alone is rarely decisive: there are significant challenges facing well-being as an idea moving further forward in politics and policy. These challenges relate to: the complexity of the idea of well-being, issues in the use of evidence, and a range of political factors (see Bache 2019).

Recent Developments

As noted above, there were some developments on well-being before the 2019 general election, despite the preoccupation with Brexit. In 2018, the Green Party proposed a *Free Time Index* to measure well-being, as an alternative to GDP, which would be based on the number of hours people spend outside of work and commuting (BBC News 2018). And in 2019 the Liberal Democrat Party's new elected leader, Jo Swinson, promised to introduce a well-being budget and put well-being "at the heart of government" and introduce a well-being budget if successful at the forthcoming general election. This commitment was included in her party's 2019 election manifesto, while the Labour Party manifesto pledged to introduce a Future Generations Well-being Act: although this did not refer to the ONS program or the wider well-being agenda but to "enshrining health aims in all policies and a new duty for NHS agencies to collaborate with directors of public health" (Labour Party 2019, 34). The heavy defeat suffered by the Liberal Democrats and Labour meant these commitments would not be carried forward into government.

Below the UK level, there were significant developments in the devolved administrations. In Scotland, a well-being approach informs the National Performance Framework,[8] whose stated purpose is "To focus on creating a more successful country, with opportunities for all of Scotland to flourish through increased wellbeing, and sustainable and inclusive economic growth" (Scottish Government 2018). In Wales, the Well-being of Future Generations Act (Wales) 2015 aims to improve the social, economic, environmental, and cultural well-being of Wales. It requires public bodies to set and publish well-being objectives and to "take all reasonable steps" to meet these objectives. Further, they are asked to take a more long-term perspective, work more effectively with people and communities, seek to prevent problems, and take a more joined-up approach to delivery (Welsh Government 2015). And, between 2015 and 2018, Northern Ireland produced a draft well-being framework and an outcomes delivery plan based on areas of economic and societal well-being that were decided following a period of consultation with the public. However, progress on this framework stalled due to political instability.[9]

In each case, policymakers have drawn eclectically on different philosophical traditions and combined objective and subjective measures, although objective measures are emphasized in each case. All three jurisdictions have taken a dashboard approach rather than a single indicator, and for the same reason: that "they believe that this is the best way to enable the use of wellbeing data in policy development" (Wallace 2018, 128). While aspects of the three approaches and the measures they employ overlap, they are driven by different purposes. In Scotland this is performance management, in Wales sustainable development and in Northern Ireland political "visioning." Moreover, while all three include measures of personal well-being within their frameworks, they are not the same one. Wallace (2018, 131) argues that: "those involved are seeking to balance political priorities, available data and stakeholder views. In no case did the civil servants involved run statistical regressions or modelling to identify the 'best fit' indicators either to a dominant indicator within the domain, or to personal wellbeing." The key difference between developments in the devolved administrations and those at the UK government level is that well-being measurement in the former is brought into a broader framework relating to the purpose of government and each has an emphasis on outcomes. As such, these are seen as significant political developments. However, while there have been "real social impacts" in Scotland, the overall policy effects in the three jurisdictions have been limited. Wallace (2018, 146) concluded that "While there is evidence of a shift towards a wellbeing approach, it is not overwhelming. The activities appear to remain on the margins of public services rather than being a 'golden thread.'" However, the first minister of Scotland, Nicola Sturgeon (2019), later gave a high-profile speech on "why governments should prioritize well-being." This speech highlighted cooperation between the network of Wellbeing Economy Governments (led by Scotland, Iceland, and New Zealand, later joined by Wales and Finland)[10], bringing further hope to well-being advocates.

To date, the different approaches taken in the component parts of the UK have not led to significant differences in average country-wide ratings on issues of life satisfaction, happiness, and worthwhileness in England, Scotland, and Wales; although Northern Ireland has shown consistently higher than average ratings on these indicators since the data were first collected in 2011. The reasons for this are not well understood. As the UK Government Statistical Service (2020) recently commented: "There does not appear to be research into whether this is due to questions being designed for Britain and not having the same meaning in Northern Ireland, or whether there truly are higher levels in Northern Ireland."

At UK government level, in 2018 the Treasury further revised its Green Book guidance to government departments, to strengthen the position of well-being in the evidence-based appraisal and evaluation of proposals to inform decision-making. Specifically, it stated that "Economic appraisal is based on the principles of welfare economics – that is, how the government can improve social welfare or wellbeing, referred to in the Green Book as social value" (HM Treasury 2018, 5). This change was described by the WWCW's Head of Evidence as a "subtle, yet important shift" that took well-being closer to the "heart of policy-making" (WWCW 2018). This shift appeared to underline the position of SWB within UK policy thinking: "Subjective wellbeing evidence aims to capture the direct impact of a policy on wellbeing. The evidence can challenge decision makers to think carefully about the full range of an intervention's impacts ... The evidence can also help challenge implicit values placed on impacts by providing a better idea of the relative value of non-market goods" (42).

The December 2019 general election returned a majority Conservative government and led to Britain's exit from the EU in January 2020. The increased Conservative majority had been secured largely by gains in the less prosperous regions of the UK normally held by the Labour Party. The returning government expressed its commitment to a "levelling up" agenda to address the relative disadvantage of these regions. Within two weeks of taking office, the government announced that it would "rip up public spending rules" (*The Times*, 27 December 2019) so that investment decisions would be less focused on economic growth, using the traditional metric of Gross Value Added (GVA)[11] and instead would be based partly on improving the well-being of citizens in the targeted regions.

At the time of writing (February 2020) it was not clear how well-being would be measured in this context, but the shift away from a focus on GVA – a metric seen to favour more economically vibrant regions – was welcomed in the targeted regions. Such an approach would be a significant culture shift in how the Treasury has traditionally taken major investment decisions. This announcement was potentially the most significant moment for well-being in British politics since the election of Cameron in 2010: although the devil might well be in the detail.

Taken together, these recent developments in the UK (and others beyond) indicate sustained interest in relation to well-being as a goal of public policy and momentum despite lack of consensus on definitional issues, measurement or the existence of incontrovertible evidence on "what works." Such cases highlight the importance of political will in moving forward: the measurement instruments and available evidence has been deemed "good enough" to get to the point of establishing well-being frameworks that frame an aspiration for government and for some concrete policy initiatives to advance.

Conclusion

Well-being is an idea that is relatively new to the policy arena and one that remains unsettled. It is a complex idea that faces particular challenges in an era of uncertainty and unpredictability in which simple solutions often appear increasingly attractive. There are disagreements within epistemic communities about how well-being should be defined and measured for public policy purposes and other challenges relating to securing wider support for the idea as a policy goal. Yet the idea is being taken seriously within the UK and beyond, although developments to date have not delivered the transformative change that many well-being advocates seek. The dominance of GDP as an indicator of progress has not been seriously threatened, and there is no suggestion that epistemic communities are close to a consensus on a persuasive alternative that is rooted in a clear theory of well-being. On this issue there often remains a significant gap between what scientists and statisticians would prefer and what politicians and the general public might find attractive.

However, the route to transformative change may not require a change in headline indicators. It is possible that this development may follow rather than lead change. Mulgan's (2005, 223) discussion of the spread of Keynesianism is interesting in this respect. He notes how the practice of Keynesian economics in different forms "was separately 'discovered' in New Zealand, Scandinavia and Roosevelt's US before, not after, the theory had been first formalised by Keynes himself. It was then popularised (some said bastardised) to become the conventional wisdom of the post-war era." It was in this context that GDP emerged and became dominant as the key indicator for this framework.

There are parallels with well-being. Various initiatives have emerged in quite different places, and this proliferation of initiatives may bring forward the possibility of further change through policy learning. Here, organizations such as the Wellbeing Economy Governments and the Wellbeing Economy Alliance, which brings together a broader range of organizations[12], could play a vital role. Well-being advocates generally view the prospect of transformative change as a long-term process in which, over time, evidence can foster learning, belief change, and policy change. Indeed, for many, this "bottom-up" approach is the likeliest strategy for success: a gradual accumulation of evidence and practice that in the longer term reduces resistance. As one prominent well-being advocate succinctly put it, "familiarity breeds consent" (Durant 2016).

Yet, whatever strategy is adopted to take well-being forward in policy, the way in which it is framed and communicated is crucial: politics is crucial to the destiny of this cause, and it will be interesting to see how this plays out in relation to recent developments in British politics. However, scientific evidence can make a significant contribution. It gives ideas substance and also offers legitimacy to well-being advocates. Thus, following Hunter's (2009, 596) comments on public health, it is important to recognize that while promoting the idea of wellbeing in policy is both an art and a science, it should not be an act of faith.

NOTES

1 Sections of this chapter draw on jointly produced work (Bache and Reardon 2016) and on Bache (2018) and Bache (2019). I am grateful to Louise Reardon for allowing me to draw on our jointly produced work here.
2 See chapter one for a discussion of the first and second waves of interest.
3 The ONS later added a "population mental well-being" measure to its personal well-being domain. This measure uses the Warwick-Edinburgh Mental Wellbeing Scale (WEMWBS) to assess mental well-being out of a total possible score of 35 (ONS 2018a).
4 To determine the health-related quality-of-life part of the QALY equation, scores are generated through the assessment of a patient's ability to function in five domains: mobility, pain/discomfort, self-care, anxiety/depression, and usual activities.
5 The funding was for the creation and implementation of a large training program to provide the specialist workforce of psychological therapists needed, and to fund the setting up of NICE-approved therapy centres across the country (Department of Health 2008, 4).
6 The ONS later added a fourth use: allowing individuals to make informed decisions about their lives (ONS 2018b).
7 The Behavioural Insights Team is a social purpose company jointly owned by the UK government. It seeks to shape public policy through drawing on the ideas from the behavioural science literature. It is often colloquially known as the "nudge unit."
8 The National Performance Framework was created in 2007 and later became more closely associated with well-being (see Wallace 2018).
9 The Northern Ireland assembly was suspended for three years, from January 2017 to January 2020, following disputes between the major parties.
10 https://www.gov.scot/groups/wellbeing-economy-governments-wego/.

11 Gross Value Added is the value generated by any unit engaged in the production of goods and services (ONS 2020).

12 See https://wellbeingeconomy.org/weall-members.

REFERENCES

Airports Commission. 2014. *Quality of Life Assessment: Airports Commission*. London: Price Waterhouse Coopers.

– 2015. *Airports Commission: Final Report*. London: Airports Commission.

Allin, Paul. 2017. "The Well-Being of Nations." *Wiley StatsRef: Statistics Reference Online*. https://doi.org/10.1002/9781118445112.stat07926.

Allin, Paul, and David J. Hand. 2014. *The Wellbeing of Nations: Meaning, Motive and Measurement*. London: Wiley.

– 2017. "New Statistics for Old – Measuring the Wellbeing of the UK." *Journal of the Royal Statistical Society* 180, part 1: 1–22.

Austin, Annie. 2016. "On Well-Being and Public Policy: Are We Capable of Questioning the Hegemony of Happiness?" *Social Indicator Research* 127, no. 1: 123–38.

Bache, Ian. 2019. *Evidence, Policy and Wellbeing*. Cham, Switzerland: Palgrave Macmillan.

Bache, Ian, and Louise Reardon. 2013. "An Idea Whose Time Has Come? Explaining the Rise of Well-Being in British Politics." *Political Studies* 61, no. 4: 898–914.

– 2016. *The Politics and Policy of Wellbeing: Understanding the Rise and Significance of a New Agenda*. Cheltenham: Edward Elgar.

Bache, Ian, Louise Reardon, and Paul Anand. 2016. "Wellbeing as a Wicked Problem: Navigating the Arguments for the Role of Government." *Journal of Happiness Studies* 17, no. 3: 893–912.

BBC News. 2018. "Free Time Should Be Measure of UK's Well-Being, Say Greens." https://www.bbc.co.uk/news/uk-politics-45750920.

Bentham, Jeremy. 1996. *An Introduction to the Principles of Morals and Legislation*. Edited by James Henderson Burns and Herbert Lionel Adolphus Hart. Oxford: Clarendon.

Boswell, Christina. 2012. *The Political Uses of Expert Knowledge: Immigration Policy and Social Research*. Cambridge: Cambridge University Press.

Cabinet Office. 2015a. *Social Value Act Review*. London: Cabinet Office.

– 2015b. "Government Guidance – What Works Network." https://www.gov.uk /guidance/what-works-network.

Cameron, David. 2006. "David Cameron's Speech to Google Zeitgeist Europe 2006." *The Guardian*, 22 May 2006. https://www.theguardian.com/politics/2006/may/22 /conservatives.davidcameron.

– 2010. "PM Speech on Well-Being." https://www.gov.uk/government/speeches/pm-speech-on-wellbeing.

Clark, David M. 2011. "Implementing NICE Guidelines for the Psychological Treatment of Depression and Anxiety Disorders: The IAPT Experience." *International Review of Psychiatry: International Guidelines in Mental Health* 23, no. 4: 318–27.

Cook, F. 2011. "Evidence-Based Policy-Making in a Democracy: Exploring the Role of Policy Research in Conjunction with Politics and Public Opinion." Paper presented for delivery at the 2001 annual meeting of the American Political Science Association, San Francisco, 30 August–2 September 2011.

Communities and Local Government. 2008. *Practical Use of the Well-Being Power.* London: Communities and Local Government.

Department of Health. 2008. *Improving Access to Psychological Therapies Implementation Plan: National Guidelines for Regional Delivery.* London: Department of Health.

– 2014. *Improving Outcomes and Supporting Transparency, Part 2: Summary Technical Specifications of Public Health Indicators.* London: Department of Health.

Diener, Ed, and Richard E. Lucas. 1999. "Personality and Subjective Well-being." In *Well-Being: The Foundations of Hedonic Psychology,* edited by Daniel Kahneman, Edward Diener, and Norbert Schwarz, 213–29. New York: Russell Sage Foundation.

Diener, Ed, Richard Lucas, Ulrich Schimmack, and John Helliwell. 2009. *Well-Being for Public Policy.* Oxford: Oxford University Press.

Dolan, Paul, and Daniel Fujiwara. 2012. *BIS Research Paper Number 85: Valuing Adult Learning: Comparing Wellbeing Valuation to Contingent Valuation.* London: Department for Business Innovation and Skills.

Dunlop, Claire. 2014. "The Possible Experts: How Epistemic Communities Negotiate Barriers to Knowledge Use in Ecosystems Services Policy." *Environment and Planning C: Government and Policy* 32, no. 2: 208–28.

ESRC. 2014. "What Works Centre for Wellbeing 2014/15: Common Specification." Swindon: Economic and Social Research Council. www.esrc.ac.uk/_ ... /what-works-wellbeing-common-specification_tcm8.

Fujiwara, Daniel, and Ross Campbell. 2011. *Valuation Techniques for Social Cost-Benefit Analysis: Stated Preference, Revealed Preference and Subjective Well-Being Approaches. A Discussion of the Current Issues.* London: HM Treasury, DWP.

Fujiwara, Daniel, Paul Oroyemi, and Ewen Mckinnon. 2012. *Working Paper No 112: Wellbeing and Civil Society: Estimating the Value of Volunteering Using Subjective Wellbeing Data.* London: Department for Work and Pensions.

Griggs, Steven, and David Howarth. 2011. "Discourse and Practice: Using the Power of Well Being." *Evidence and Policy* 7, no. 2: 213–26.

Gummer, John, and Zac Goldsmith. 2007. *Blueprint for a Green Economy: Submission to the Shadow Cabinet.* London: Conservative Party. http://conservativehome.blogs.com/torydiary/files/blueprint_for_a_green_economy110907b.pdf.

Halpern, David. 2016. "Subjective Well-Being over the Life Course: Evidence and Policy Implications." Comments to the Conference at the London School of Economics and Political Science, 12–13 December 2016.

HM Government. 2013. *Well-Being Evidence Submitted by the Government to the Environmental Audit Committee Well-Being Inquiry.* http://data.parliament.uk /writtenevidence/committeeevidence.svc/evidencedocument/environmental -audit-committee/wellbeing/written/1069.pdf.

HM Treasury. 2018. *The Green Book: Central Government Guidance on Appraisal and Evaluation.* https://assets.publishing.service.gov.uk/government/uploads/system /uploads/attachment_data/file/685903/The_Green_Book.pdf.

Hunter, D.J. 2009. "Relationship between Evidence and Policy: A Case of Evidence-Based Policy or Policy-Based Evidence?" *Public Health* 123, no. 9: 583–6.

Jackson, Tim. 2011. *Prosperity without Growth.* Oxford: Earthscan.

Labour Party. 2019. *It's Time for Real Change: Labour Party Manifesto 2019.* United Kingdom: Labour Party. file:///C:/Users/ian/Documents/PolQual%20research /Real-Change-Labour-Manifesto-2019.pdf.

Layard, Richard. 2005. *Happiness: Lessons from a New Science.* New York: Penguin Press.

Marsh, Kevin, Sam MacKay, David Morton, Will Parry, Evelina Bertranou, Jennie Lewsie, Rashmi Sarmah, and Paul Dolan. 2010. *Understanding the Value of Engagement in Culture and Sport: Summary Report.* London: Department for Culture, Media and Sport (DCMS).

Marston, Greg, and Rob Watts. 2003. "Tampering with Evidence: A Critical Appraisal of Evidence-Based Policy-Making." *The Drawing Board: an Australian Review of Public Affairs* 3, no. 3: 143–63.

McGregor, J. Allister. 2015. *Global Initiatives in Measuring Human Wellbeing: Convergence and Difference.* CWiPP Working Paper No. 2. Centre for Wellbeing in Public Policy, University of Sheffield.

Mulgan, Geoff. 2005. "Government, Knowledge and the Business of Policy Making: The Potential and Limits of Evidence-Based Policy." *Evidence and Policy* 1, no. 2: 215–26.

NICE. 2004. *Depression: Management of Depression in Primary and Secondary Care.* London: National Institute for Health and Care Excellence.

Nickson, Sofi. 2020. "Personal Wellbeing Harmonised Standard." Government Statistical Service, 19 May 2020. https://gss.civilservice.gov.uk/policy-store /personal-well-being/.

ONS. 2012a. *First ONS Annual Experimental Subjective Well-being Results.* London: Office for National Statistics.

– 2012b. "Gross Value Added (GVA)." https://www.ons.gov.uk/economy /grossvalueaddedgva.

– 2018a. "Personal Well-Being: Frequently Asked Questions." https://www.ons.gov .uk/peoplepopulationandcommunity/wellbeing/.

– 2018b. "Personal Well-Being in the UK QMI." https://www.ons.gov.uk/ … /wellbeing/methodologies/personalwellbeingintheukqmi/pdf.

– 2019. "Measures of National Well-Being Dashboard." https://www.ons.gov.uk
/peoplepopulationandcommunity/wellbeing/articles/measuresofnationalwellbeing
dashboard/2018-09-26.

Phillips, David. 2006. *Quality of Life Concept, Policy and Practice*. London: Routledge.

Public Health England. 2015. "What We Do." https://www.gov.uk/government
/organisations/public-health-england/about.

Scott, Karen. 2012. *Measuring Wellbeing: Towards Sustainability?* Abingdon:
Earthscan.

Scottish Government. 2018. *Developing an Environment Strategy for Scotland:
Discussion Paper*. https://www.gov.scot/publications/developing-environment
-strategy-scotland-discussion-paper/pages/13/.

Scrivens, Katherine, and Barbara Iasiello. 2010. *Indicators of "Societal Progress":
Lessons from International Experiences*. Paris: OECD. DOI: 10.1787/18152031.

Seaford, Charles. 2018. "Is Wellbeing a Useful Concept for Progressives?" In *The
Politics of Wellbeing: Theory, Policy and Practice*, edited by Ian Bache and Karen
Scott, 97–120. Cham, Switzerland: Palgrave Macmillan.

Sturgeon, Nicola. 2019. "Why Governments Should Prioritize Well-being." Filmed
July 2019 at TEDSummit 2019, Edinburgh. https://www.ted.com/talks
/nicola_sturgeon_why_governments_should_prioritize_well_being?language=en.

Tomlinson, Mike, and Grace Kelly. 2013. "Is Everybody Happy? The Politics and
Measurement of National Wellbeing." *Policy & Politics* 41, no. 2: 139–57.

UK Statistical Authority. 2014. *Assessment of Compliance with the Code of Practice
for Official Statistics: Statistics on Personal Well-Being*. London: UK Statistics
Authority.

Wallace, Jennifer. 2018. *Wellbeing in Scotland: Reframing the Role of Government in
Scotland, Wales and Northern Ireland*. Cham, Switzerland: Palgrave Macmillan.

Weiss, Carol H. 1979. "The Many Meanings of Research Utilization." *Public
Administration Review* September/October: 426–31.

Welsh Government. 2015. *Well-Being of Future Generations (Wales) Act 2015*. https://
futuregenerations.wales/wp-content/uploads/2017/02/150623-guide-to-the-fg
-act-en.pdf.

White, Sarah C. 2017. "Relational Wellbeing: Re-centring the Politics of Happiness,
Policy and the Self." *Policy & Politics* 45, no. 2: 121–36.

Wilkinson, Richard G., and Kate Pickett. 2009. *The Spirit Level: Why Equality is
Better for Everyone*. London: Penguin.

WWCW. 2018. *Wellbeing in Policy Analysis*. https://www.whatworkswellbeing
.org/wp-content/uploads/2018/03/Overview-incorporating-wellbeing-in-policy
-analysis-vMarch2018.pdf.

6 Integrating Well-Being Indicators in Budgetary Procedures: Four Shades of Sincerity

ÉLOI LAURENT

Introduction: The Performative Age of Well-Being Indicators

It can be said that the criticism of economic growth is now in its third age. The first age, the age of philosophical criticism, is as old as the Industrial Revolution itself. It was born with the questioning by John Stuart Mill of the purpose of the economy. The question asked by Mill in Chapter VI of Book IV ("Of the Stationary State") of his *Principles of Political Economy* (1848) is that of the fundamental purpose of economic activity: "To what goal? Towards what ultimate point is society tending by its industrial progress?"[1]

In a series of papers published between 1972 and 1973, economists William Nordhaus and James Tobin contributed to the advent of the second age of growth criticism, the empirical age, picking up on the acknowledgment of Simon Kuznets himself, the inventor of GDP, that it was not a measure of human welfare. They suggested that "growth" (understood as the increase of real gross domestic product, or GDP, in real terms) had become "obsolete" and attempted for the first time to offer not just an ethical or theoretical criticism of economic growth but a statistical alternative to GDP in the form of a Measure of Economic Welfare (MEW) (Nordhaus and Tobin 1973).[2]

This research and policymaking agenda have greatly expanded since then. In the last decade alone since the beginning of the "great recession," dozens of commissions have produced as many reports, and hundreds of welfare and sustainability indicator proposals have emerged, some ready for use (see Laurent [2018] for an overview). Building upon this unprecedented effort, the United Nations adopted in September 2015 a scoreboard of seventeen Sustainable Development Goals, or SDGs, designed to guide development policies in the coming years, where GDP plays only a minor role (as part of goal 8).

With the adoption of the SDGs has come the third age of alternative indicators: the age of institutionalization. The purpose of the dynamic under way in many parts of the planet at different levels of governance – that can be labelled the "well-being transition" – is clear: instead of growth, policymakers should be concerned with the advancement of well-being (human flourishing), resilience (resisting shocks, especially environmental ones) and sustainability (caring about future well-being by preserving the biosphere). For this well-being transition to become a reality, alternative indicators prioritizing human well-being over growth need to be integrated into public policies.

Measuring well-being profoundly changes the way we see the world, like when one looks at the US economy at the beginning of 2019 through the lens of life expectancy (structurally declining) instead of GDP growth (increasing in the short term). But indicators of well-being should now become performative: they should inform *and* reform policy. Measuring, indeed, is governing and well-being indicators have already started to deliver progress. But more is needed.

From this perspective, this chapter considers four strategies that have been implemented in recent years in Europe to integrate alternative indicators into budgetary procedures. It concentrates on European countries because the European Union has been one of the first world powers to recognize the need to go "beyond GDP." It focuses on budgetary procedures because voting on the budget has been the core historical task of parliamentary democracy since the seventeenth century.[3]

The following sections present four integration strategies, from the least to the most ambitious. This gradation attempts to show how much has been achieved on the path of the well-being transition and, more importantly, how much remains to be done.

Strategy 1: Manipulation (France)

France suffers from a severe form of statistical distrust. Chiche and Chanvril (2016), using the data of the seventh wave of Cevipof's[4] confidence barometer, report that only 38 per cent of French respondents say they trust official inflation data, 36 per cent economic growth data, and 28 per cent unemployment data. According to the authors, France stands among the most distrustful countries in Europe towards official statistics, ranking twenty-sixth in 2009 and twenty-seventh in 2015 among the twenty-eight European countries surveyed.

The law of 13 April 2015, known in France as the "Sas law" (named after the ecologist MP Eva Sas, who drafted it and tabled it in Parliament), was unanimously adopted by the National Assembly on 29 January 2015. What the law proposed was essentially a cure to statistical distrust, aiming "at considering new indicators of wealth in the definition of public policies" (see Box 6.1).

BOX 6.1. THE FRENCH LAW NO. 2015–411 OF 13 APRIL 2015

The Government shall submit annually to Parliament, on the first Tuesday of October, a report presenting the evolution, over the past years, of new wealth indicators, such as indicators of inequality, quality of life and sustainable development, as well as a qualitative or quantitative assessment of the impact of the main reforms initiated the previous year and the current year and those envisaged for the following year, notably in the context of the finance laws, with regard to these indicators and that of the evolution of the gross domestic product. This report can be debated in Parliament.

Source: Journal Officiel.

The French government has implemented this innovative law in two ways: on the one hand by organizing a process of selection of the indicators to appear in the report to Parliament each year; on the other hand, by publishing the report in question in 2015, 2016, and 2017 for consideration by Parliament and the general public. Alas, in both cases, public action did not live up to the challenge of truly informing and reforming public policy using alternative indicators.

The general orientation of the indicator selection process posed a problem right away: the first official documents referred to the search for relevant indicators of "quality of growth," not post-growth or alternative indicators to GDP. Then, the "consultation" process, supposedly open to independent expertise and citizens input, was emptied of its meaning and reduced to a mere validation of discretionary and eminently questionable choices made by the executive before and after the process. The framing a priori by France Strategy (a government agency) and the reframing *a posteriori* directly by the prime minister's office, without consultation in both cases, have resulted in the executive choosing seven of the ten final indicators (labelled "new wealth indicators") (see Table 6.1).

Given the lack of sincerity displayed by the French government in this "consultation process," it is hardly surprising that the final reports were deeply flawed. The first two annual reports, issued by the executive and published in 2015 and 2016, are peppered with passages that can be read as manipulation of the "new indicators of wealth" it puts forward for purposes of enhancing government action.

Table 6.1. "New wealth indicators" selection process, 2014–15

Initial selection by France Stratégie (September 2014)	Selection at the end of the "consultation" process (June 2015)	Final selection by the government (October 2015)
Net public debt as a ratio of GDP	Debt of different non-financial economic agents (general government, enterprises, households) as percentage of GDP	Debt (public debt, household debt, corporate debt) as percentage of GDP
Net foreign debt as a ratio of GDP		
Ratio between the incomes of the richest 20 per cent of the population and poorest 20 per cent	Ratio of the income pool held by the richest 10 per cent and the poorest 10 per cent	Inequalities of income between the richest 20 per cent and the poorest 20 per cent
	Subjective index of life satisfaction	Subjective index of life satisfaction
Annual French carbon footprint, including imports	Carbon footprint including imports	Carbon footprint including imports
Evolution of stocks of productive, physical, and intangible assets, as a percentage of GDP	Physical and intangible productive assets in percentage of Net Domestic Product	
	Waste recycling rate	
	Life expectancy in good health at birth	Life expectancy in good health at birth
"Soil artificialisation" (a measure of excessive urbanization)	Bird abundance index	"Soil artificialisation" (a measure of excessive urbanization)
Proportion of people between twenty-five and sixty-four years of age with a college diploma	Higher education graduation rate among twenty-five to thirty-four-year-olds	Early exit from the school system
	Employment rate	Employment rate
		Research effort (in percentage of GDP)
		Poverty in living conditions

Source: France Stratégie and French government.

The first report (Gouvernement Français 2015) comments on an indicator that was not retained at the end of the consultation process and that the government itself selected: "The rate of early leavers [from the education system] in France is significantly lower than the one observed on average in the European Union (8.5% for France compared to 11.1% Europe in 2014)." It then adds "relatively stable in the past, the rate experienced a significant decrease between 2012 and 2014 (-3 points)" (the new government was elected in 2012). It concludes: "Partly related to an improvement in the statistical measurement of this indicator, this decrease is also due to a real drop in the number of dropouts, linked to a very proactive and more and more systemic policy in this area."

The second report, in October 2016 (Gouvernement Français 2016), with a foreword from the prime minister himself, is marked by the same partisan tone. It notes, in light of some of the indicators selected by the executive, that "the effects of the crisis of 2008, the hardest in our recent history, have been erased, while preparing the future. The energy transition is under way, business and state investment in R & D is still at a high level, the fight against school failure has been revived." The "new wealth indicators" are directly used for political comparisons: "Since 2012, the Government has been trying to stabilize public debt – which had increased by 25 percentage points of GDP between 2007 and 2012 – by reducing the deficit while preserving the conditions to accelerate the economic recovery." Evaluations of selected government reforms presented at the end of the two reports, which are almost exclusively positive, further accentuate the feeling of bias.

Ultimately, not only has the potential performative power of the selected indicators been neutralized because of a biased selection process, but their manipulation for short-sighted political gain by the government contravenes the very purpose of human well-being indicators, which is to shed light on poorly understood albeit important realities for the benefit of citizens (like growing domestic inequality in a context of strong GDP growth). The publication of the 2017 report, long delayed, took place in February 2018 in the greatest indifference of public opinion (with hardly any media coverage). It is very likely that the misuse of well-being indicators by the French government on the basis of a useful but hijacked law has further increased statistical distrust in France instead of helping mitigate it.

A first simple step to redress the situation and restore confidence would be to take the indicators selection and report drafting out of the hands of the executive to entrust it to a tripartite collegiate body (MPs, experts, and citizens). A genuine parliamentary and public debate could then be organized on the data contained in this report prior to voting on the budget. It should be made clear that the government chooses to delegate its responsibility to better ensure the impartiality, legitimacy, and in the end efficiency of the whole process (the "Sas law" specifies that the report is to be tabled by the government but does not prevent it from entrusting it to an *ad hoc* body).

The question would then arise to determine the type of well-being metrics, currently absent from official documents, that could better inform Parliament in its principal act: the vote of the budget. It would be up to the collegiate body to determine it, but some well-being dimensions appear especially useful to grasp: the evolution of inequalities, the state of national wealth understood in its widest sense (including ecosystems and biodiversity) and the impact of France in the world (including environmental footprint). These three dimensions are in line with international norms adopted by the Conference of European Statisticians (CES) in 2013, which highlighted the need for indicators measuring well-being "here and now," "later," and "elsewhere."[5]

This is not out of reach: these proposals, originally formulated in 2017 (Laurent 2017), were picked up in a recent Senate bill aimed at establishing a Parliamentary Council for the Evaluation of Public Policy and Well-being.[6] This proposal should now be carried out by the executive and adopted by Parliament.

Strategy 2: Window-Dressing (Slovenia)

To date, twenty-three countries have taken steps to integrate the United Nations Sustainable Development Indicators (SDIs) into their budgetary process. But the vast majority are procedures of budgetary framing rather than budgetary allocation (of public resources). Thirteen of the G20 countries surveyed answered "no" in 2018 to the question "Does the latest central/federal budget reflect incremental SDG investment needs?" (Sachs et al. 2018).

Slovenia is a good case in point of this window-dressing strategy. The Eastern European country has recently made significant progress on the path of the well-being transition: in the Slovenian Development Strategy for 2030 adopted by the Government of the Republic of Slovenia on 7 December 2017,[7] five new strategic orientations have been adopted that seem to redefine development priorities under the banner of "a high quality of life" (these orientations are "an inclusive, healthy, safe and responsible society," "learning for and through life," "a highly productive economy that creates added value for all," "well-preserved natural environment," and a "high level of cooperation, competence and governance efficiency"). Twelve sub-objectives have been defined accordingly (see Box 6.2).

BOX 6.2. THE TWELVE OBJECTIVES TO ACHIEVE A "HIGH QUALITY OF LIFE" IN SLOVENIA

1. Healthy and active life
2. Knowledge and skills for a high quality of life and work
3. Decent life for all
4. Culture and language as main factors of national identity
5. Economic stability
6. Competitive and socially responsible entrepreneurial and research sector
7. Inclusive labour market and high-quality jobs
8. Low-carbon circular economy
9. Sustainable natural resource management
10. Trustworthy legal system
11. Safe and globally responsible Slovenia
12. Effective governance and high-quality public service

Source: Slovenian Development Strategy for 2030.

But the means to implement this strategy appear to be lacking. First, only six "key performance indicators" have been defined, which don't cover the objectives and orientations announced (they are Healthy Life Years; PISA, Mean Score in Mathematics, Reading and Science; GDP per Capita in Purchasing Power Parities; Employment Rate, age twenty to sixty-four; and Share of Renewable Energy in Gross Final Energy Consumption). These indicators fall into three categories: conventional macroeconomic indicators that are already widely used in Slovenia and the rest of the world (GDP and employment), EU strategy indicators (the share of renewable energy is part of the European 20–20–20 climate strategy), and basic public policy indicators also already in use (health and education).

The method of implementation is even less convincing: the "Slovenian Development Strategy for 2030" aims at respecting EU fiscal criteria (putting forward a "medium-term fiscal framework for implementing the principle of medium-term balance of state budget revenues and expenditure without borrowing"), which is already an obligation for Slovenia since joining the Eurozone in January 2007. It further proposes that "the Institute of Macroeconomic Analysis and Development monitors the achievement of the goals set out in the Slovenian Development Strategy" without mentioning any instrument of integration of these goals into policymaking or budgetary procedure. In fact, little if anything has really changed since 2017 in terms of policy, as noted recently by the OECD (2018).

Strategy 3: Juxtaposition (European Union)

The proposals recently put forward by the European Commission (2019b) to achieve a 2030 agenda clearly shows the confusion resulting from juxtaposing indicators of fiscal discipline as a percentage of GDP and alternative indicators to GDP and growth. In its "reflection paper" (the least binding document in the EU legal hierarchy), the European Commission favours a strategy in which alternative indicators (in this case UN SDGs) serve as a source of "inspiration" (Box 6.3), while EU member states continue to be governed by the so-called Maastricht criteria.

BOX 6.3. CONTINUED MAINSTREAMING OF THE SDGS IN ALL RELEVANT EU POLICIES BY THE COMMISSION, BUT NOT ENFORCING MEMBER STATES' ACTION

The SDGs will continue to inspire the Commission's political decision-making and guide the development of the post-EU2020 growth strategy, while not excluding other political priorities, and not forcing the work of Member States to reach the SDGs collectively and EU-wide. This approach would leave more freedom to Member States, including regional and local authorities, to decide whether and how they adjust their work to deliver on the SDGs.

Source: European Commission (2019b).

The Maastricht Treaty, which created the European Union (1992), is the economic constitution of contemporary Europe.[8] In it, the political power of conventional macroeconomic indicators is very tangible: fiscal discipline ratios govern the admission of countries into the EU and the euro area and are supposed to guarantee the continent's stability, unity, and prosperity. Countries wanting to join the euro area when it was devised in the early 1990s had to conform to five criteria of convergence, three of which still govern the region's cohesion: inflation of no more than 1.5 percentage points above the average rate of the three EU member states with the lowest inflation over the previous year, a national budget deficit at or below 3 per cent of gross domestic product, and national public debt not exceeding 60 per cent of GDP.

These rules have been only marginally modified in the past two decades. The European Central Bank (ECB) was assigned an inflation target of below but close to 2 per cent when it was created in 1998 and the Stability Pact governing fiscal policy includes a sanction procedure for "excessive" deficits and debt – over 3 per cent and 60 per cent of GDP, respectively – and now forces governments to commit themselves to reaching "the medium-term objective of a budgetary position close to balance or in surplus."[9]

Countries belonging to the euro area, the most integrated part of the European project, have relied on these economic rules to govern their common policies. This project is officially motivated by the goal of paving the way for a better common future for European peoples, but the Stability Pact and the ECB statutes give priority in reality to "price stability" and "fiscal sustainability," even if this means reducing governments' ability to deliver employment and well-being expansion. If they have brought about an apparent culture of discipline, these indicators were not able to create a lasting culture of cooperation: the "great recession" of 2008–9 triggered a confidence crisis among member states that has, in recent years, turned into a crisis of political trust among European citizens. While economic discipline through numbers was supposed to ease peacetime relations, it has instead created divergence among nations and conflicts within their borders, as the rise of populist parties all over the continent makes clear.

It is in fact more and more apparent that the intermediate objectives that prevail in the governance of the EU (fiscal balance, currency strength, price stability) are at odds in practice with the attainment of the ultimate social objectives (such as health and employment) that matter the most to populations.

There has actually been a real European paradox regarding well-being indicators in the last decade: on the one hand, the EU has tried to capitalize on the discontent with standard economics by embracing the beyond-GDP agenda; on the other, it has become even more rigid in applying its ill-advised targets. The communication "GDP and Beyond: Measuring Progress in a Changing World," released in 2009 by the European Commission, described ways to improve policy indicators to better reflect societal concerns. The commission's intent was to adjust and complement GDP with indicators that monitored social and environmental progress.[10] But soon after, the EU institutions embarked on coercing the Greek government, from 2010 onward, into reaching European ratios in a time of recession, delaying the country's economic recovery by several years, imposing extremely difficult social conditions on the Greek population[11] and creating perilous political tensions among member states.[12] By the same token, the EU is supposed to abide by a broad "2020 strategy"[13] but in practice only governs itself through narrow macroeconomic indicators.

Instead of this contradiction that borders on policy schizophrenia, indicators of well-being and sustainability that are already largely monitored by the statistical agency Eurostat should be built into European public decisions.

In fact, everything remains to be done at the European level to integrate well-being indicators into budgetary procedures, but new and practical ideas are already on the table. The EU could for instance conceive and organize, during the "European Semester,"[14] a debate in the European Parliament and in all the parliaments of the Member States informed by indicators of well-being and sustainability, guided by European values and national priorities aimed at determining budgetary choices (European and national) beyond the sole criteria of fiscal discipline. The recent proposals by the Independent Commission on Sustainable Equality (ICSE 2018) offer precise and practical ways to achieve this objective (Box 6.4).

BOX 6.4. THE ICSE PROPOSALS FOR "SUSTAINABLE EUROPEAN GOVERNANCE"

Horizon and scope

Sustainable development implies a different timeframe for policymaking, from short-termism to a long-term perspective. Therefore, it is necessary to replace the current annual fiscal and macroeconomic surveillance exercise with a multi-annual sustainable development pact. In order to set a policy direction and to ensure coherence with other EU policies, the new Semester needs to be part of an overarching sustainable development strategy based on the SDGs as policy goals.

Indicators and targets

What we measure affects what we do in terms of policy outcome. Referring solely to GDP will lead to policies that take into account only their economic impact. Therefore, it is necessary to enlarge the reference indicators by including social and environmental indicators in order to design truly sustainable reforms, not just structural reforms for public finance sustainability. It is essential that these indicators are also compatible with the UNSDGs (but could go beyond them).

Governance

Silo-based governance gives birth to silo-based policies. Therefore, it is required to open up the current decision-making process both internally (enlarging the ownership of the semester to other Commission services beyond the Directorate-General for Economic and Financial Affairs such as the Directorate-General for Environment) and externally (promoting structural dialogues with stakeholders). The European Parliament needs to be given a key role to ensure proper democratic control, and social partners and NGOs should be well involved, including the Multi-Stakeholder Platform on sustainable development. The

Semester must also be community-oriented to adapt to the different national and territorial needs and particularities.

The **new Sustainable Development Cycle** will be a multi-annual exercise aiming at implementing sound fiscal policy on an equal footing with sustainable development policies. The Sustainable Development Cycle will be founded on a new and legally enshrined Sustainable Development Pact which would encompass the existing Stability and Growth Pact in an alternate form, excluding public investment such as the investment needed to achieve the low carbon transition of European economies from the deficit so that these investments are not reined in.

Source: ICSE (2018).

Furthermore, the adoption of the European Green Deal in December 2019 offers a clear window of opportunity. In the main document outlining the project, the European Commission writes that "The Green Deal is an integral part of this Commission's strategy to implement the United Nation's 2030 Agenda and the sustainable development goals" and that it "will refocus the European Semester process of macroeconomic coordination to integrate the United Nations' sustainable development goals, to put sustainability and the well-being of citizens at the centre of economic policy, and the sustainable development goals at the heart of the EU's policymaking and action" (European Commission 2019a).

These are laudable intentions, but there is still considerable uncertainty as to the method chosen to arbitrate between indicators which, as they stand, are not compatible. In addition, the European Commission does not have the political legitimacy to arbitrate between the various indicators which must guide the European project over the next decade. Yet conflicts and trade offs exist and must be sorted out. Therefore, the Green Deal could be an opportunity to define as a reference a set of indicators of human well-being rather than GDP alone and entrust the European Parliament with the responsibility of rethinking the European semester by defining the dimensions of European well-being that should be given priority, the corresponding indicators and their articulation with the United Nations Sustainable Development Goals and the Stability and Growth Pact.

Strategy 4: Integration (Finland)

Finland is a poster child for well-being and sustainability: the country was ranked third best in the assessment of sustainability in all UN Member States published in 2018,[15] first in the 2019 World Happiness Report and tenth in the 2018 Environmental Performance Index. On the policy front, its "Finnish National Commission on Sustainable Development"[16] has informed policy since 1993.

Finland adopted in 2017 an original new sustainable development implementation strategy relying on just two objectives: a well-being goal (a nondiscriminatory, equal, and competent Finland) and a sustainability goal (a carbon-neutral and resource-wise Finland) (Prime Minister's Office 2017).

But what is more important is that Finland has devised practical ways to implement this strategy using public resource allocation. The budget review of 2018, for instance, examined whether current taxes and spending promoted or hindered the sustainability goal as a first step (Ministry of Finance 2018).

This is a crucial point because a number of forms of environmental pollution or degradation do not result from free and undistorted competition (which exists only in the minds of orthodox economists), but from incentives or public disincentives, including taxes and subsidies. It is estimated, for instance, that from 2014 to 2016, 997 different fossil fuel subsidies were provided by EU member states and EU institutions representing €112 billion per year (or as much as 80 per cent of the whole EU budget) (Gençsü et al. 2017).

The government proposed to go further so that the 2019 budget integrated these objectives in the allocation of public resources by obliging the Finnish ministries to justify their expenditures in terms of the "carbon-neutral and resource-wise Finland criterion" (Ministry of Finance 2019). In September 2019 it was announced that additional funding would be allocated to conservation and low-carbon transition policies.

The "PATH2030" Report that was drafted by independent scholars commissioned by the Finnish government to evaluate Finland's Sustainable Development Policy and published in May 2019[17] recommends that "the governmental budgeting process of taking into account sustainable development is to be continued and widened."

More precisely, the authors argue that there should be targets set for the budget, such as phasing out support for environmentally harmful activities and increasing investments that support sustainable development in both the public and private sectors. "Ideally," they write, "the budget should be designed so that funds are allocated in such a way that makes it possible to monitor governmental support as a whole for phenomena that are central to sustainable development."

The 2021 budget, agreed upon in September 2020, reaffirms the executive's commitment to well-being and sustainability goals, notably by "pursuing measures that will make Finland carbon neutral by 2035 and carbon negative soon after that," especially by increasing taxation on heating fuels, such as coal, natural gas, and fuel oil (Prime Minister's Office of Finland 2020).

The strategy of integration of well-being indicators pursued by Finland has not been limited to including them in public finance, but also in the country's response to the COVID-19 crisis. Finland has been one of the least affected countries in the world in terms of mortality and morbidity and the least affected EU country because it has strongly prioritized health instead of economic growth (the opposite choice was made in France, with dire health and economic consequences).

The irony of the situation is that because of this choice, Finland has also fared much better in economic terms, enjoying a double dividend while neighbouring Sweden has suffered from a double health and economic penalty (with mortality per capita almost ten times higher and a twice as severe economic contraction in 2020).

Conclusion: The Sustainability–Justice Nexus, Embedding Alternative Indicators in a New Narrative

Going beyond growth as a social goal means complementing and eventually replacing GDP with indicators of well-being, resilience, and sustainability that better reflect the social and ecological realities and challenges of our world. It also means integrating them into policymaking, starting with the budgetary process, as this chapter has argued. But this is still not enough: it also implies linking those objectives in a common positive narrative that can give them meaning.

Indicators of well-being indeed need to be embedded in a new narrative that can convince individuals to change not only their behaviours but also their attitudes. William Cronon (1992) has argued that "what we most care about in nature is its meaning for human beings." In fact, one can think that current ecological crises, however severe they become, won't be fully addressed until they make ethical and social sense to humans.

Any meaningful conversation among humans about change and progress starts with debating justice principles and imagining institutions able to embody these principles. This is especially true of the titanic shift in attitudes and behaviours required by the ecological transition, whose goal is nothing short of saving the habitability of the planet for humans. In this respect, the notion of "ecological transition" can be misleading: it is really a social-ecological transition that must be built in coming years, combining social issues with ecological challenges.

This new narrative is actually emerging: by linking justice and sustainability in a sustainability–justice nexus,[18] a number of scholars argue that our societies will be more just if they are more sustainable and more sustainable if they are more just.[19] In other words, in the twenty-first century, it makes environmental sense to mitigate our social crisis and social sense to mitigate our environmental crises (Laurent 2019).

This new vision of the world needs to rely on new institutions, such as reformed budgetary procedures gradually leading to a true "social-ecological State" (Laurent 2019), as much as these new institutions need to be embedded on a new vision of the world. From this perspective, the emerging narrative of the "Green New Deal" in the United States, the EU, and elsewhere should be welcome, provided it stays clear of the pursuit of economic growth.[20]

In other words, in the decisive decade of the 2020s, the beyond-GDP agenda faces two intertwined imperatives: building a consistent framework linking well-being and sustainability; and operationalizing indicators, i.e., changing not only indicators but policies (Laurent 2021). In this respect, the immense suffering endured through the COVID-19 crisis should not be in vain: if we continue to destroy our habitat by squandering biodiversity and ecosystems, we will end up destroying our humanity, whose core is our social links.

The first objective requires that human health is used as a mediator between well-being and sustainability, especially the health of children, a task already underway (Clark et al. 2020). The second objective requires that the most efficient and sincere well-being-driven reforms of budgetary decisions are adopted. This means, in the light of this chapter, that strategies of integration should be favoured over strategies of manipulation, window-dressing, and juxtaposition.

NOTES

1 Mill goes on to note: "If the earth must lose that great portion of its pleasantness which it owes to things that the unlimited increase of wealth and population would extirpate from it, for the mere purpose of enabling it to support a larger, but not a better or a happier population, I sincerely hope, for the sake of posterity, that they will be content to be stationary, long before necessity compel them to it."
2 Interestingly, Nordhaus later stuck to conventional economic indicators and GDP when attempting to model economic impacts of climate change.
3 The principle of budgetary sincerity implies the completeness, coherence, and accuracy of the information provided in a given budget.
4 Cevipof, the Centre for Political Research at Sciences Po, produces influential surveys on political behaviours and attitudes in France.
5 Framework and suggested indicators to measure sustainable development, Joint UNECE/Eurostat/OECD Task, 2013. http://www.unece.org/fileadmin/DAM/stats/documents/ece/ces/2013/SD_framework_and_indicators_final.pdf.
6 Proposition de loi by Franck Montaugé (Senator of Gers), 5 July 2017.
7 An outline and empirical evaluation of which is presented in IMAD (2019) and Government Office for Development and European Cohesion Policy of the Republic of Slovenia (2018).
8 This conception was formally advanced by Finn Kydland and Edward Prescott (1977), who intended to develop and legitimize, on behalf of individual

freedoms and the effectiveness of public policy, an economic constitutional order constraining the state's power. According to this perspective, public policies ought to be governed by principles with which the state cannot interfere.

9 The EU's fiscal rules have been amended in recent years, but the philosophy of the Stability Pact remains. Recent reforms include the European Union Fiscal Treaty (in full, the "Treaty on Stability, Coordination and Governance"), which was signed by only twenty-five EU member states on 2 March 2012 and ratified by the national parliaments, which set an agenda for fiscal consolidation that might prove too drastic for many member states in the current economic conditions and eventually prevent the reduction of public deficit and debt.

10 The communication identified five key actions for the short to medium term: complement GDP with environmental and social indicators (environmental index and quality of life and well-being); provide near real-time information for decision-making; report more accurately on distribution and inequalities; develop a European sustainable development scoreboard (including thresholds for environmental sustainability); and extend national accounts to environmental and social issues.

11 The *Lancet* reported that the health of the Greek population had suffered tremendously during the worst of the austerity policy and even talked about a "Greek public health tragedy." HIV incidence in injectable-drug users rose more than tenfold from 2009 to 2012 and tuberculosis incidence in this population more than doubled in 2013; state funding for mental health decreased by 55 per cent between 2011 and 2012; major depression grew to two and a half times its 2008 rate by 2011; suicides increased by 45 per cent between 2007 and 2011; and infant mortality jumped by 43 per cent between 2008 and 2010 (Kentikelenis et al. 2014).

12 By the same token, in July 2016 the EU triggered the sanction mechanisms of the Stability Pact against Portugal and Spain for failing to respect deficit-reduction targets, while the two countries were still economically and politically very weak.

13 The Europe 2020 strategy "emphasises smart, sustainable and inclusive growth in order to improve Europe's competitiveness and productivity and underpin a sustainable social market economy."

14 Introduced in 2010, the European Semester enables the EU member countries to coordinate their economic policies throughout the year and address the economic challenges facing the EU. But its goals rely on conventional macroeconomic thinking and policymaking, such as "ensuring sound public finances (avoiding excessive government debt)" and "preventing excessive macroeconomic imbalances in the EU supporting structural reforms."

15 According to the 2018 report (Sachs et al. 2018), Finland has been particularly successful in achieving the SDG #1 (No Poverty) and SDG #7 (Affordable and Clean Energy) targets. Like wealthy countries in general, the biggest challenges facing Finland are the achievement of SDG #12 (Responsible Consumption and Production), #13 (Climate Action) and #14 (Life Below Water).

16 Chaired by the prime minister or a minister, its members have represented a broad range of sectors of society from political decision-making to ministries, research institutes, interest groups, and NGOs.

17 PATH2030, May 2019. https://julkaisut.valtioneuvosto.fi/bitstream/handle/10024/161601 /VN_TEAS_23_Path%202030.pdf?sequence=1&isAllowed=y.

18 Agyeman, Bullard, and Evans (2002) first mentioned the idea of a nexus between "sustainability, environmental justice and equity."

19 See, for instance, Laurent (2011 and 2018), Dasgupta and Ramanathan (2014), Motesharrei et al. (2014), and Gough (2017).

20 The original new deal, in the 1930s, did raise GDP growth, but that was never its intention (gross domestic product was in fact invented in 1934 by Simon Kuznets to measure the magnitude of the Great Depression). "In 1932 the issue was the restoration of American democracy," said Franklin Delano Roosevelt in 1936. In the same speech, he defines peace as the ultimate goal of the New Deal. See "Transcript of President Franklin Roosevelt's 1936 Radio Address Unveiling the Second Half of the New Deal: https://www.ourdocuments.gov/doc.php?flash=false &doc=69&page=transcript.

REFERENCES

Agyeman, Julian, Robert Bullard, and Bob Evans. 2002. "Exploring the Nexus: Bringing Together Sustainability, Environmental Justice and Equity." *Space and Polity* 6, no. 1: 70–90.

Boyce, James K. 1994. "Inequality as a Cause of Environmental Degradation." *Ecological Economics* 11, no. 3: 169–78.

Chiche, Jean, and Flora Chanvril. 2016. "Confiance dans les statistiques publiques: une relation contrariée." *Statistique et société* 4, no. 3: 55–63.

Clark, Helen, Awa Marie Coll-Seck, Stefan Peterson, Sarah L. Dalglish, Shanti Ameratunga, Dina Balabanova, Maharaj Kishan Bhan et al. 2020. "A Future for the World's Children? A WHO–UNICEF–Lancet Commission." *The Lancet* 395, no. 10224: 605–58.

Dasgupta, Partha, and Veerabhadran Ramanathan. 2014. "Pursuit of the Common Good." *Science* 345, no. 6203: 1457–8.

European Commission. 2019a. "The European Green Deal." COM(2019) 640 final. Brussels: European Commission.

– 2019b. "Reflection Paper: Towards a Sustainable Europe by 2030." Brussels: European Commission. https://ec.europa.eu/commission/publications/reflection -paper-towards-sustainable-europe-2030_en.

Gençsü, Ipek, et al. 2017. "Phase-Out 2020: Monitoring Europe's Fossil Fuel Subsidies." London/Brussels: Overseas Development Institute and Climate

Action Network Europe. https://www.odi.org/sites/odi.org.uk/files/resource
-documents/11762.pdf.

Gough, Ian. 2017. *Heat, Greed and Human Need: Climate Change, Capitalism and Sustainable Wellbeing*. London: Edward Elgar.

Gouvernement Français. 2015. "Les nouveaux indicateurs de richesse." Paris: Service d'information du Gouvernement. https://www.strategie.gouv.fr/sites/strategie .gouv.fr/files/atoms/files/a9rb245.pdf.

– 2016. "Les nouveaux indicateurs de richesse." Paris: Service d'information du Gouvernement. https://www.gouvernement.fr/sites/default/files/document /document/2016/10/indicateur_de_richesses_2016.pdf.

Government Office for Development and European Cohesion Policy of the Republic of Slovenia. 2018. "Slovenia: Implementing the 2030 Agenda for Sustainable Development, 2018 Update." https://www.gov.si/assets/vladne-sluzbe/SVRK /Agenda-2030/Implementing_the_Agenda2030_update_2018.pdf.

Helliwell, John, Richard Layard, and Jeffrey D. Sachs. 2017. *World Happiness Report*. New York: Sustainable Development Solutions Network.

ICSE. 2018. *Sustainable Equality*. Independent Commission for Sustainable Equality. https://www.progressivesociety.eu/publication/report-independent-commission -sustainable-equality-2019-2024.

IMAD. 2019. "Development Report." Ljubljana: Institute of Macroeconomic Analysis and Development. http://www.umar.gov.si/fileadmin/user_upload/razvoj _slovenije/2019/angleski/POR 2019_ANG_splet.pdf.

Kentikelenis, Alexander, Marina Karanikolos, Aaron Reeves, Marin McKee, and David Stuckler. 2014. "Greece's Health Crisis: From Austerity to Denialism." *The Lancet* 383, no. 9918: 748–53.

Kydland, Finn E., and Edward C. Prescott. 1977. "Rules Rather Than Discretion: The Inconsistency of Optimal Plans." *Journal of Political Economy* 85, no. 3: 473–91.

Laurent, Éloi. 2011. *Social-écologie*. Paris: Flammarion.

– 2017. "Inscrire les indicateurs de bien-être et de soutenabilité au cœur du débat budgétaire." OFCE Policy Brief 14 (March): 1–8.

– 2018a. *Measuring Tomorrow: Accounting for Well-being, Resilience and Sustainability in the 21st Century*. Princeton, NJ: Princeton University Press.

– 2018b. "Toward a Well-being Europe." In *The Euro at 20 and the Futures of Europe*, edited by Jerome Creel, Éloi Laurent, and Jacques Le Cacheux. Palgrave Macmillan.

– 2019. *The New Environmental Economics: Sustainability and Justice*. Cambridge: Polity.

–, ed. 2021. *The Well-being Transition: Analysis and Policy*. Palgrave MacMillan.

Ministry of Finance. 2018. Budget Review 2018, Ministry of Finance Publications, September 2018.

– 2019. Budget Review 2019, Ministry of Finance Publications, January 2019.

Motesharrei, Safi, Jorge Rivas, and Eugenia Kalnay. 2014. "Human and Nature Dynamics (HANDY): Modeling Inequality and Use of Resources in the Collapse or Sustainability of Societies." *Ecological Economics* 101: 90–102.

Nordhaus, William D., and James Tobin. 1973. "Is Growth Obsolete?" In *The Measurement of Economic and Social Performance*, edited by Milton Moss, 519–64. New York: National Bureau of Economic Research.

OECD. 2018. "Country Profiles: Institutional Mechanisms for Policy Coherence." In *Policy Coherence for Sustainable Development 2018: Towards Sustainable and Resilient Societies.* Paris: OECD Publishing.

Prime Minister's Office of Finland. 2017. "Government Report on the Implementation of the 2030 Agenda for Sustainable Development. Sustainable Development in Finland – Long-term, Coherent and Inclusive Action." VNS 1/2017.

– 2020. "Budget Proposal for 2021 Provides a Route for Exiting the COVID-19 Crisis." Government Communications Office, Ministry of Finance. https://vnk.fi /en/-/budget-proposal-for-2021-provides-a-route-for-exiting-the-covid-19-crisis.

Sachs, Jeffrey, Guido Schmidt-Traub, Christian Kroll, Guillaume Lafortune, and Grayson Fuller. 2018. *SDG Index and Dashboards Report 2018.* New York: Bertelsmann Stiftung and Sustainable Development Solutions Network (SDSN).

7 Beyond "Beyond GDP" in the EU: What's Next?

BRENT BLEYS AND GÉRALDINE THIRY

Introduction

In November 2007, the European Commission, the European Parliament, the Club of Rome, the OECD, and WWF hosted the *Beyond GDP* conference in Brussels, a high-level event that brought together academics, policymakers, and politicians to discuss alternative measures of societal progress and their potential for influencing decision-making processes and informing the public debate. The conference attracted over 600 attendees and also featured an indicator exhibition in which different research institutes presented the many alternative indicators to GDP developed over the previous years. At the conference José Manuel Barroso, then president of the European Commission, called for the development of new tools and indicators to face the problems of the twenty-first century and stated that we should aim for a breakthrough that adapts or complements GDP with indicators better suited to our needs today, in a similar fashion to the breakthrough in the 1930s when the System of National Accounts (SNA) was developed. Partially inspired by this event, former French president Nicolas Sarkozy installed the Commission on the Measurement of Economic Performance and Social Progress in February 2008. This commission was headed by leading economists such as Joseph Stiglitz, Amartya Sen, and Jean-Paul Fitoussi. Its final report (Stiglitz, Sen, and Fitoussi 2009) provided a documented, yet largely economics-oriented, synthesis of the existing academic literature on measuring societal progress and sustainability.

The debate on the problems with GDP, both as a measure of progress and as a goal for economic policy, has a long tradition (Kuznets 1934; Meadows et al. 1972; Hirsch 1995 [1972]; Cobb, Halstead, and Rowe 1995; Méda 2008 [1999]; Viveret 2004; Goossens et al. 2007), yet the Beyond GDP conference and the Stiglitz-Sen-Fitoussi report reignited the discussions. The conference and the report respectively provided political and academic recognition of

GDP's problems and, fuelled by the financial and economic crisis of 2008–9, beyond-GDP proponents had high hopes for breaking down GDP's dominance in economic decision-making. However, thirteen years after the Beyond GDP conference, it feels like the momentum for Beyond GDP has passed.

In this chapter, we will focus on the rise and fall of Beyond GDP in the EU and analyse in what ways a more traditional economic agenda was restored in the 2010s, moving beyond-GDP initiatives away from their initial transformative ambitions. We will do so by looking at Beyond GDP as a multifaceted combination of processes encompassing:

- An *intellectual process* led by several scholars who think about redefining prosperity, clarifying ends and means for a flourishing collective and individual life (Cassiers 2014; Cassiers, Maréchal, and Méda 2019; Jackson 2017), and seek to provide a new theoretical framework able to provide an ecological macroeconomics (Jackson et al. 2014).
- A *statistical endeavour* that results in the development of a plethora of new indicators of prosperity – see Gadrey and Jany-Catrice (2006) and Bleys (2012) for reviews of indicators and classification schemes.
- An *institutional process*, embarking local, regional, national, and supranational institutions on a journey to renew the criteria on the basis of which political and economic decisions are taken and socio-economic policies are assessed.

Before analysing the reasons why Beyond GDP in the EU has had limited success, we will give an overview of the most important beyond-GDP milestones in different policy processes at the EU institutions. We will conclude the chapter with an outlook into the future, focusing on the emergence of a post-growth movement, insights from the OECD's New Approaches to Economic Challenges initiative, and ideas to merge the beyond-GDP agenda with the Sustainable Development Goals (SDGs) by 2030.

Beyond GDP in the EU

The financial and economic crisis of 2008–9 was initially regarded as an ally to the beyond-GDP cause as the traditional models focusing on economic growth and GDP failed to signal the problems in the financial sector. Yet, the impact of the crisis was so severe that soon after its onset, policymakers around the world turned to the long-established recipes of fiscal and monetary expansion to combat the economic recession. As a result of the financial and economic crisis, the EU delayed further communication on Beyond GDP until summer 2009.

In August 2009 the European Commission released a policy paper entitled "GDP and Beyond: Measuring Progress in a Changing World" in which it outlined a road map for action following the commitments made at the Beyond GDP conference in 2007. In the paper, the following five actions were outlined:

- complementing GDP with environmental and social indicators
- moving towards near real-time information for decision-making
- more accurate reporting on distribution and inequalities
- developing a European Sustainable Development Scoreboard
- extending national accounts to environmental and social issues

By and large, the road map focused on the development of new indicators relevant to the challenges of that time that provide a richness in data for improved policymaking and public debate.

Two years later, in June 2011, the European Parliament adopted a Resolution on "GDP and Beyond: Measuring Progress in a Changing World" to support the actions proposed by the European Commission and stressed the need to develop clear and measurable indicators of economic and social progress. However, the initial motion by MEP Anna Rosbach also called on the commission "to submit a tiered strategy for the Beyond GDP approach that should show how the new approach can be used pragmatically in day-to-day political work. Unless there is clarity on this issue, I consider that there can be little progress in this debate" (EU Parliament 2011, 8).

At the same time, the final report of the "Sponsorship Group on Measuring Progress, Well-Being and Sustainable Development" was adopted by the European Statistical System Committee (ESSC) in November 2011. The report summarized the main actions taken by the European Statistical System to implement the recommendations from the 2009 "GDP and beyond" communication from the EC and the Stiglitz-Sen-Fitoussi report (Stigltz, Sen, and Fitoussi 2009). The report lists about fifty concrete actions to respond to the changing needs for new information. The actions focused on three main areas: 1) multidimensional measurement of quality of life, 2) the household perspective and distributional aspects, and 3) environmental sustainability – see Figure 7.1 for examples of concrete actions. Since the report's release, these suggested actions have been integrated in the European Statistical Programme and are gradually being implemented by Eurostat.

In August 2013 the European Commission published its last official communication on GDP and Beyond – the Staff Working Document on "Progress on 'GDP and Beyond' Actions" (European Commission 2013). The document reported on progress made in different areas since publication of the road map in 2009. In terms of environmental indicators, two summary indices have been

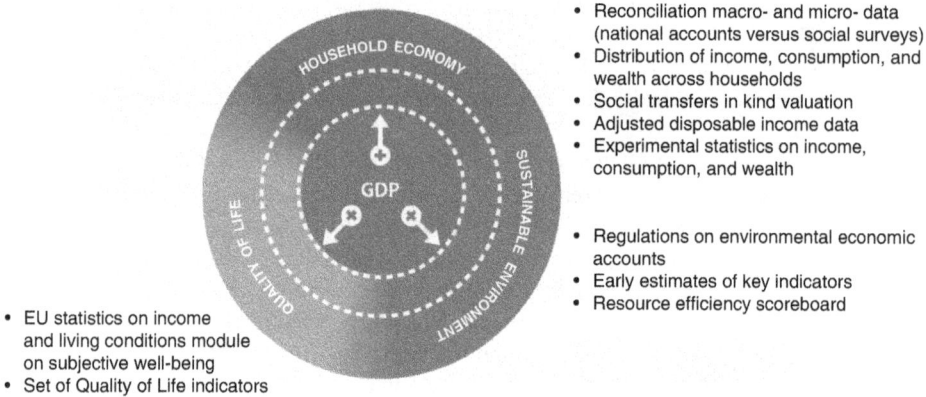

Figure 7.1. The three main "GDP and beyond" priority areas identified by the European Statistical System Committee

developed on environmental pressures at the EU level and the global environmental impacts of EU consumption. With regard to the quality-of-life indicators, headline indicators were made available to provide objective information on quality of life. In this domain, an aggregate indicator measuring "people at risk of poverty or social exclusion" was developed, and a wide range of statistics on income and living conditions was established. Finally, progress has been made by Eurostat and the European Environmental Agency on the timeliness of data as "early estimates" of key environmental indicators are now being produced to inform policy decisions. At the same time, the SNA has been extended to include environmental and social data.

Since 2013 "GDP and beyond" at the EU level has entered a long period of radio silence. The website on "Beyond GDP: Measuring Progress, True Wealth, and Well-Being"[1] of the Directorate-General for Environment of the European Commission is still up and now lists a broad range of recent developments and ongoing work in different member states, illustrating the many different initiatives being undertaken. Eurostat's "GDP and Beyond" web page[2] indicates that all measures regarding the topic have been integrated in the yearly Commission Statistical Work Programmes, but no specific updates are listed.

While many people working on going Beyond GDP had high hopes for dethroning GDP as the main economic policy indicator and for reorienting policies away from focusing first and foremost on economic growth, the momentum now seems lost. The past thirteen years have shown that Beyond GDP in the EU has mostly focused on producing new statistics, rather than changing the policy course. This became especially clear after the financial and economic crisis hit the EU in 2008/9.

Going beyond GDP: An Unsurpassable Complexity?

Why have beyond-GDP initiatives only had partial and limited success to date? Why does GDP remain predominant – as a reference in economic theory, as a target in policymaking and as the single most important indicator in the national accounts – despite a long tradition of criticism and challengers? We suggest that the lack of a unified beyond-GDP movement that is able to carry a coherent political vision, and supported by robust intellectual contributions and an accurate statistical apparatus, is anchored in the deep *complexity* of the issues addressed.

By broadening the scope of quantification from the monetary values of goods and services produced on a territory during a given period of time to issues such as well-being and sustainability, going beyond GDP involves confronting *complexity*. We understand complexity in the double sense that 1) the issues at stake are hard to understand and 2) they imply value conflicts. Sustainability and well-being can hardly be reduced to monistic definitions and measures, as both concepts encompass radical uncertainty due to social indeterminacy and limited computing skills, value conflicts – i.e., which kind(s) of sustainability, sustainability for whom, and to what purpose? – and diverging beliefs about what dimensions to include and prioritize. "These beliefs depend upon our perceptions about what the issues are and how the physical and social worlds 'work'. Due to great complexity and the subsequent high levels of ignorance and uncertainty, 'fixing beliefs' is not in any way straightforward" (Vatn 2017, 33), and quantifying them seems even harder. So, be it as an intellectual process, as a political (re)orientation, or as a statistical innovation, any endeavour to go beyond GDP is confronted with issues of uncertainty, value conflicts, and a plurality of legitimate perspectives (Funtowicz and Ravetz 1994).

Analysing beyond-GDP initiatives – understood here as the multifaceted combination of intellectual, statistical, and institutional processes – through the lens of complexity provides an interesting framework to understand the decline of the movement.

At the Intellectual Level: Beyond GDP, a Complex Object

At the intellectual level, several aspects of Beyond GDP can be identified that prevent the emergence of a coherent systemic vision or theoretical framework.

First, the *scope* of what should be covered by the beyond-GDP movement is multidimensional (Abdallah and Seaford 2013). In essence, going beyond GDP implies considering several dimensions such as inequality and (multidimensional) poverty, the definition of prosperity, sustainability, and well-being to name just a few of the most important ones. All these concepts are themselves subject to different – often contradictory – interpretations and do not properly exist independently of their definition. Moreover, these dimensions are hard to grasp within a single indicator, or even in a set of indicators. For most of them, it is even impossible to robustly measure them because of radical uncertainty and social indeterminacy. Desrosières (2013) defines quantification as the combination of *convention*, that is, agreeing on a common definition, and *measurement*, that is, attributing a quantitative value to the conventionally defined phenomenon. In the case of beyond GDP, the multidimensionality of the scope implies both that it is hard to agree on common definitions of these dimensions and that some of these dimensions are fundamentally impossible to measure. So, while the scope of GDP is very clearly delineated and historically results from a convention that today is broadly accepted and institutionalized, the scope of beyond-GDP initiatives is extremely – infinitely? – broad and subject to debate, which gives rise to deep debates among scholars.

Second, *scholars' normative positions* diverge vis-à-vis GDP and the economic model it underpins. Intellectual contributions to Beyond GDP are fragmented, and criticism of GDP has been around for a long time. Yet, there exist different, and often conflicting, traditions. While some scholars working on Beyond GDP formulate strong criticisms of the current economic system based on the perpetual pursuit of economic growth (O'Neill 2012; Buch-Hansen 2018; D'Alisa, Demaria, and Kallis 2014) and therefore expect from new indicators that they carry a radically new organization of the economy, others conceive new indicators as an opportunity for refining our quantitative knowledge of society and therefore expect from new measures to enrich decision-making without necessarily questioning the economic system as such (Stiglitz, Fitoussi, and Durand 2018; Fleurbaey 2013). These different views can be related to different disciplines and discourses: criticism of GDP and economic growth is much stronger in ecological economics and degrowth, while within sustainable development and circular economy, continued economic growth is questioned less (and sometimes even regarded as desirable). Some authors (e.g., van den Bergh 2011) even argue in favour of "agrowth" – being agnostic and indifferent about GDP growth. As a result, Beyond GDP has no unified voice, and its main "champions" in the movement promote different, yet closely related, ideas.

Last but not least, while GDP benefits from a *strong macro-micro coherence*, it is not the case for the myriad of indicators produced in a beyond-GDP perspective. There is a coherent link between the three approaches to GDP in the SNA and accounting at the micro (firm) level: in the production perspective, GDP is the sum of the value-added by each firm; in the spending perspective, GDP is the sum of all expenditures on final goods and services in the economy; and in the income perspective, GDP is the sum of all incomes generated in the production processes. To date, no effort has been successfully made to foster the micro-macro coherence between alternative macro-level indicators and changes in economic behaviours at the micro level. Such a coherent accounting framework is lacking in the beyond-GDP literature, making it very difficult to challenge GDP. Furthermore, GDP is strongly embedded in current macroeconomic thinking: at the time GDP was institutionalized, Keynes's General Theory constituted a crucial intellectual foundation providing a systemic understanding of the economic system, theorizing the functioning of the economic system, and the role of the state in the economy. Traditional macroeconomic models focus on different types of policies to foster economic growth: monetary and fiscal policy, labour market policy, policies promoting competitiveness in product markets and policies oriented towards achieving technological progress. Although some efforts have been made, Beyond GDP has to date not managed to develop a theoretical framework that fully grasps the interactions between economic, social, and biophysical systems and makes possible *ex ante* analysis of the impact of different macroeconomic policy options.

At the Political Level: No Political Identity, Focus on Statistics

The complexity of the stakes addressed by the beyond-GDP movement also impacts the institutional and political processes that claim it. The most striking observation is related to the fact that the beyond-GDP issue has been appropriated across the whole political spectrum. Such wide appropriation is directly related to the intellectual fuzziness around the notion of Beyond GDP and to the lack of overall coherence of the initiatives. Each political or institutional actor can pragmatically seize one aspect of the movement that is convenient to its objectives or constraints and claim to take part in the beyond-GDP movement – in a similar fashion that all actors are in favour of promoting sustainable development, a related umbrella concept. The diversity of theoretical approaches and normative positions regarding the different routes to Beyond GDP makes it difficult to clearly identify the normative position of the actors and the power balances ruling the debates (Thiry et al. 2016). While some actors mobilize Beyond GDP as a new rhetoric to avoid confronting the structural economic problems resulting from the financial crisis, others see beyond-GDP initiatives as a window of opportunity for a more radical debate on the organization of society. Yet, at the institutional level, we have observed that dominant interests are focused on short-term objectives and constraints where GDP growth remains pivotal (Thiry et al. 2016). The interest of institutional actors in going beyond GDP often reflects the need to adapt public management and policies to new constraints rather than a critical stance towards the economic growth model.

While politicians and policymakers questioned to some extent economic growth as the main goal for the EU at the Beyond GDP conference in 2007, it became clear by the time of the European Commission's next communication on Beyond GDP in 2009 that tackling the recession was the number one priority. The fact that the policy paper was titled "GDP and Beyond" instead of "Beyond GDP" is telling for how a stronger implementation of Beyond GDP was toned down, as it was considered to be incompatible with the pressing policy agendas of stabilizing the economy. This became very clear when the EU launched the Europe 2020 Strategy in 2010 that put forward an agenda for growth and jobs for the decade to come. The strategy emphasized smart, sustainable, and inclusive growth that would improve the EU's competitiveness and productivity while also contributing to a sustainable social market economy. The EU adopted targets to be reached by 2020 in five main areas: employment, R&D, climate change and energy, education, and poverty and social exclusion – and economic growth was deemed central to reaching these goals. Parallel to the Europe 2020 Strategy, the EU introduced the "European Semester" to guide its member countries in coordinating their economic policies and addressing the EU's shared economic challenges. The goals of the European Semester are strongly focused on the economy and include, among others, structural reforms required to create more jobs and economic growth (see also Laurent, this volume).

Along the way, the institutional focus of Beyond GDP has shifted almost completely towards the direction of statistical production, as revealed by the actions outlined in the European Commission's 2009 "GDP and Beyond" policy paper. The paper included a plethora of statistical initiatives that largely lacked an overarching vision of how the new indicators could facilitate a change in policymaking. This was also highlighted in the European Parliament's resolution on "GDP and Beyond" in 2011, as in the work of several scholars in the field. In that respect, Bauler (2012) refers to a lack of "institutional embeddedness," while Hege and Brimont (2018) are critical of the EU's narrow focus on producing indicators without a strong and coherent policy basis. Looking today at the output of the EU's work on Beyond GDP/GDP and beyond, new indicators are central. An overarching policy strategy for the use of such indicators has never materialized, and over the last ten years, the Europe 2020 Strategy and the European Semester have dominated EU economic policy.

At the Statistical Level: Disparate Initiatives Rather than a Comprehensive Endeavour

Development of beyond-GDP indicators has been troubled by the conceptual complexity outlined above in at least two ways. First, as Beyond GDP was regarded as an umbrella concept, a wide range of alternative indicators were labelled as "beyond-GDP indicators." Most of these indicators focus on specific beyond-GDP dimensions – e.g., the ecological footprint that looks at the ecological dimension, or measures of (multidimensional) poverty focusing more on the social dimension. It is clear that if GDP is to be challenged using such indicators, a set of indicators is needed – and agreeing on such a set is a daunting, if not impossible, task. At the Indicator Expo of the Beyond GDP conference in 2007, different research institutes and NGOs were promoting their indicators as beyond-GDP indicators, and it had a certain dog-eat-dog feel to it, as each group was trying to attract as much interest as possible for their work. Second, we observe different views on the position of beyond GDP indicators vis-à-vis GDP. Should the indicators be regarded as complements to GDP or as substitutes? Or should we try to adjust GDP to turn it into a better measure of economic welfare? These debates on indicators date back to the 1990s, when sets of indicators for sustainable development were being discussed. In a way, Beyond GDP can be regarded as a "rebranding" of this debate.

Eurostat's development of a number of new indicators is probably the most visible outcome of the beyond-GDP movement at the EU level to date. These indicators are labelled "GDP and beyond" indicators and focus on different subdimensions of Beyond GDP. They can thus be regarded as supplementary indicators that do not really challenge GDP's dominant position in policymaking. Furthermore, the indicators are hard to find on the website of Eurostat – indicating a sharp decline in interest in the topic. It is clear that Eurostat is promoting some indicator sets more prominently than others. The most important sets of indicators are currently the ones focusing on the EU 2020 Strategy and, since 2015, the Sustainable Development Goals (SDGs). In many European countries the SDGs have hijacked at least part of the beyond-GDP work on indicators, and yet, although they are nowadays increasingly being used in policy evaluations, the SDGs largely fail to promote alternative policies.

GDP Remains Central for Now, but What's Next?

As argued in the previous section, Beyond GDP's impact at the EU level has been rather limited – at first sight, at least. Yet, it might take some time to shift minds in the direction of other indicators and a policy focus in which economic growth is no longer central. In this section, we will focus on the most recent developments related to the different beyond-GDP processes. At the intellectual level, the emergence of ecological macroeconomics is providing a theoretical foundation for more heterodox policies, while we also observe, to some extent, a tendency to unify voices in the debate. At the policy level, green growth is starting to be questioned, and at least one initiative within the OECD is arguing that a paradigm shift is needed to be able to outline policy recommendations for the problems and challenges we face today. Finally, the development of ecological macroeconomics also offers new opportunities for a wider use of beyond-GDP indicators (*ex ante* policy evaluation), while beyond-GDP initiatives also need to bridge the gap with the UN SDGs. In this regard, 2030 will be an important focal point as both the EU 2030 agenda and the SDG agenda will be rediscussed and renegotiated. These developments are at least partially inspired by the work on beyond-GDP initiatives and that of others with a similar agenda before 2007.

At the Intellectual Level: Post-growth and Ecological Macroeconomics

At the intellectual level, we see signs of scholars linking up to raise common concerns and to have greater influence on the public debate. For instance, in September 2018, 238 academics signed an open letter[3] published in more than 15 countries calling on the EU, its institutions, and member states to explore possibilities for a post-growth future. More specifically, the scientists demanded 1) the establishment of a special Commission on Post-Growth Futures in the European Parliament, 2) the use of alternative indicators in the policy framework of the EU and its member states, 3) the reconversion of the Stability and Growth Pact into a Stability and Well-Being Pact, and 4) the establishment of a Ministry for Economic Transition in each member state. The open letter was signed, among others, by Giorgos Kallis and other degrowth thinkers, Tim Jackson, Kate Raworth, and many leading scholars in ecological economics. Another example of this unification process is the Well-Being Economy Alliance (WE-All), a global initiative that is making connections between different movements that want to challenge GDP and the strong policy focus on economic growth by promoting a well-being economy that serves people and communities first and foremost (see Rodgers and Trebeck, this volume).

A second important development at the intellectual level is the emergence in the 2010s of the field of ecological macroeconomics, which can be used to evaluate policy proposals related to post-growth (e.g., limits on resource use, progressive taxation to stem the tide of rising inequality, and a gradual reduction in working time). The literature on ecological macroeconomics is growing rapidly and includes several new modelling approaches. The common denominator of these new models is that the assumption of optimization – either for the model as a whole or for the description of the behaviour of agents in the model – is abandoned (Scrieciu et al. 2013). In a recent review of the ecological macroeconomics literature, Hardt and O'Neill (2017) classify twenty-two different models according to two important aspects, namely, the modelling techniques (analytical versus numerical models) that they use. The authors argue that, although current models are still at an early stage of development, "the combination of environmentally extended input-output analysis and [system dynamic] stock-flow consistent modelling stands out as a promising avenue for integrating concerns about ecological impacts and financial stability" (Hardt and O'Neill 2017, 208). Ecological macroeconomics provides important new tools for moving towards a sustainable post-growth economy.

Launched in October 2018, the EUROGREEN model (D'Alessandro et al. 2018) allows the exploration of the impact of a wide range of public policies related to post-growth, ranging from basic income programs to radical decarbonization plans. EUROGREEN is a system dynamic ecological macroeconomic model based on initial values and parameters from the French economy (2014–50) due to data availability – most importantly the distribution of wealth – but which allows for policy analysis for the wider euro area. The model explores the viability, effectiveness, and possible synergies between alternative policy options to low-carbon transition and social justice. The authors conclude that, according to their model, the only scenario that achieves the GHG reduction goal set for 2050 and improvements in social equity is one in which radical public policies (working time reduction, job guarantee, changes in the energy mix, introduction of a carbon tax with border adjustment) are combined with a voluntary choice to reduce consumption.

At the Policy Level: The End of Green Growth?

The idea of green growth is increasingly being challenged by NGOs and academics. The European Environment Bureau, the umbrella organization for environmental NGOs in Europe, recently published a report entitled "Decoupling Debunked: Why Green Growth is Not Enough" in which the validity of the decoupling hypothesis is assessed (Parrique et al. 2019). The report finds that there is "no empirical evidence supporting the existence of an absolute, permanent, global, substantial and sufficiently rapid decoupling of economic growth from environmental pressures." It also lists seven reasons to be sceptical about sufficient decoupling in the future, including rebound effects and insufficient and inappropriate technological change. At the same time, we see these concerns to some extent translated into policy reports both at the EU level (e.g., EEA 2019) and at the OECD (e.g., OECD 2019). To us, this indicates that the importance of achieving economic growth in policymaking is dwindling somewhat. However, two important issues remain. First, we observe a lack of internal coherence both within the EU and the OECD, as we find a strong parallel policy discourse on promoting (green) growth – e.g., the OECD published the "Going for Growth" report in 2019, in which green growth still plays a central role. Second, the question remains as to what extent this shift in policy focus is taking place quickly enough to avoid large-scale environmental degradation and an unequal distribution of the costs and benefits involved in this process.

In July 2019 the European Parliament elected Ursula von der Leyen as president of the European Commission. Von der Leyen announced that she would focus on an ambitious climate agenda that will make Europe the first climate-neutral continent by 2050. At the same time, she also set out to engage with the European Parliament to strengthen democracy and the fair and social market economy in Europe. In her political guidelines, von der Leyen also put forward the idea to expand the scope of the European Semester system to look beyond economic indicators and also focus on the UN Sustainable Development Goals, while also proposing to make use of the full flexibility allowed within the Stability and Growth Pact to increase investments in countries with large public debt. When the commission presented its Green Deal (European Commission 2019) in December 2019, Von der Leyen referred to it as "Europe's new growth strategy," indicating the difficulty of giving up on economic growth. The focus on growth is, however, less strong than in the Europe 2020 Strategy, as the Green Deal put forward other goals for the EU: cutting down greenhouse gas emissions, creating jobs, and improving quality of life. It remains to be seen how the guidelines will be translated into actual policies by the European institutions in the coming years.

In September 2019 the OECD's New Approaches to Economic Challenges (NAEC) initiative published a report (OECD 2019) in which its Advisory Group[4] synthesized a wide reflection on new ways of thinking about economic policymaking. The report encompasses a new set of goals and measures of economic progress, new frameworks of economic analysis and new approaches to policymaking. The authors argue that politicians and policymakers need to move "beyond growth" and that there is a "need to ensure that, alongside rising GDP – and as a result of it – economic policy is achieving a wider set of objectives and measures of economic and social progress" (OECD 2019, 6). In their view, four objectives for economic policymaking should be paramount today: environmental sustainability, rising well-being, falling inequality, and system resilience. The NAEC Advisory Group argues that a new paradigm shift is needed, as "the frameworks and prescriptions which have dominated policymaking in recent decades are no longer able to generate the solutions to the problems and challenges we face today" (ibid., 21). It is time for more profound change, moving away from taking only incremental steps.

At the Statistical Level: Moving beyond "Beyond GDP"

One main barrier in the uptake of beyond-GDP indicators is their inability to inform policymakers *ex ante* (Bleys and Whitby 2015). The timeliness of production of most beyond-GDP measures is problematic, as some of these indicators are published with a delay of one or two years – compared to having flash GDP estimates for each quarter at t+30 days. This makes a holistic evaluation of post-growth policy measures, such as green taxation or climate policy, using beyond-GDP indicators very difficult. A potentially significant way to work around this is to expand the ecological macroeconomic models introduced in earlier in such ways that allow for *ex ante* welfare assessments in terms of beyond-GDP indicators. As a result, policy scenarios could be evaluated in a more heterodox way – i.e., by not only relying on GDP impacts. At the moment, important data gaps to make post-growth welfare assessments – using, for instance, the Index of Sustainable Economic Welfare (ISEW) – include data on time use and data on the international social and environmental impacts related to national consumption. The post-growth economics network[5] is currently applying for EU research funding to expand ecological macroeconomic models in this way, while in Germany, Diefenbacher et al. (2019) have explored how ecological and social indicators can be better integrated into macroeconomic models. Building on this work, Gran et al. (2019) look at new ways to integrate ecological and social indicators into QUEST, the global macroeconomic policy simulation model of the EC's Directorate-General for Economic Affairs and Finance (DG ECFIN).

In anticipation of the EU 2030 Agenda and its indicators, Hoekstra (2019) has identified 2030 as a pivotal year for beyond-GDP indicators. The Sustainable Development Goals (SDGs) of the United Nations have a time frame of 2015–30, so they will require replacement in 2030. This coincides with the launch of the next ten-year agenda for the EU (2030–40), so it will be an opportunity to establish a different view on how to measure societal progress towards well-being and sustainability. In his book *Replacing GDP by 2030*, Hoekstra (2019) describes a strategic pathway to arrive at such a view. First, a statistical community should be established that outlines a coherent scientific and multidisciplinary foundation to underpin coherent policies. We think that post-growth economics can play an important role here, although Hoekstra stresses that the statistical community he envisions should not be led by economists, however heterodox the group might be. Next, this community should set a clear goal, develop a coherent structure and a common language, and it should aim to get institutionalized. Hoekstra (2019) describes in detail one way in which this could be operationalized, focusing on a system of global and national accounts that would deliver key well-being and sustainability indicators using four system accounts – for the environment, society, the economy, and distribution. These system accounts should be based on a number of statistical blocks – stock-flow accounting, networks, and the concept of limits – and capitalize, where possible, on new developments in big data. The biggest challenge will probably lie in the institutionalization: the UN has had a mandate to work on this topic since 1992, yet so far the institutes have failed to develop a comprehensive process (Hoekstra 2019). However, the author also refers to more successful community-building processes, such as the SNA, the IPCC, and the SDGs, and his book certainly helps building its case.

Conclusion

European beyond-GDP initiatives made a promising start during the end of the 2000s with the Beyond GDP conference in the European Parliament and the Stiglitz-Sen-Fitoussi Commission in France. At first sight, the impact of these initiatives thirteen years later appears to be limited. The financial and economic crisis of 2008–9 caused the EU and many of its member states to largely abandon the beyond-GDP agenda and turn instead to the more traditional economic policy recipes of providing jobs through economic growth. In the 2010s the EU strived for smart, sustainable, and inclusive growth, yet the emphasis was put on "growth," as became clear from both the EU 2020 Strategy and the European Semester. Beyond-GDP initiatives were fragmented and partially competing with each other so that a coherent beyond-GDP strategy never materialized, and "Beyond GDP" was downgraded to "GDP and beyond." The most visible impact of the beyond-GDP initiatives today is the development of a number of new indicators by Eurostat, the EU's statistical office. In the EU, Beyond GDP nowadays largely refers to the statistical endeavour and less to the intellectual and institutional processes that were initially also associated to it.

In recent years, however, we have also observed a shift from Beyond GDP to "post-growth" or "beyond growth." In both fields, attention has shifted from the indicator (GDP) to the policy agenda that it promotes (economic growth), and efforts are made to develop a different narrative and an accompanying set of policy recommendations to support this. The paradigm shift promoted by the advisory group of the OECD's New Approaches to Economic Challenges (NAEC) initiative and the academic work in ecological macroeconomics are probably the best examples here. These developments could signal the arrival of the much-needed policy strategy in which economic growth is no longer central. In this way, we could think of Beyond GDP as a placeholder for a set of ideas that have been around for many decades, with Beyond GDP bridging the gap between sustainable development in the 1990s and early 2000s and post-growth/beyond growth today. In that sense, the beyond-GDP initiatives might have had a bigger impact than what the "GDP and beyond" website is showing.

Finally, we have to be clear that economic growth is still very much central in policymaking in the EU and its member states. The observations we make in this article are not at all mainstream, neither in academic research nor in policy recommendations. The field of ecological macroeconomics, though expanding rapidly, is still at the very margin of macroeconomic literature, and many of the policy recommendations that are derived from its models are fiercely opposed by the more dominant neoclassical field. At the same time, the new approaches to economic policy outlined by the OECD's NAEC initiative contradict most of the OECD's policy advice in other documents, indicating that the "beyond growth" agenda is also very peripheral in policy terms. Similarly, it remains to be seen to what extent the political guidelines of the new president of the European Commission will be translated into actual EU policies.

NOTES

1   https://ec.europa.eu/environment/beyond_gdp/index_en.html
2   https://ec.europa.eu/eurostat/web/gdp-and-beyond. Accessed 11 March 2020.
3   https://degrowth.org/2018/09/06/post-growth-open-letter/.
4   Acting in a personal capacity, the Advisory Group comprised Andy Haldane, Michael Jacobs, Nora Lustig, Mariana Mazzucato, Robert Skidelsky, Dennis Snower, and Roberto Unger.
5   http://www.postgrowtheconomics.org

REFERENCES

Abdallah, Saamah, and Charles Seaford. 2013. "Case Study: Opportunities for Use of Alternative Indicators in the OECD." BRAINPOoL Report.

Bleys, Brent. 2012. "Beyond GDP: Classifying Alternative Measures for Progress." *Social Indicators Research* 109, no. 3: 355–76.

Bleys, Brent, and Alistair Whitby. 2015. "Barriers and Opportunities for Alternative Measures of Economic Welfare." *Ecological Economics* 117: 162–72.

Buch-Hansen, Hubert. 2018. "The Prerequisites for a Degrowth Paradigm Shift: Insights from Critical Political Economy." *Ecological Economics* 146: 157–63.

Cassiers, Isabelle, ed. 2014. *Redefining Prosperity*. New York: Routledge.

Cassiers, Isabelle, Kevin Maréchal, and Dominique Méda. 2019. *Post-Growth Economics and Society: Exploring the Paths of a Social and Ecological Transition*. London: Routledge.

Cobb, Clifford, Ted Halstead, and Jonathan Rowe. 1995. "If the GDP Is up, Why Is America Down?" *The Atlantic Monthly* 276, no. 4: 59–78.

D'Alessandro, Simone, Kristofer Dittmer, Tiziano Distefano, and André Cieplinski. 2018. "EUROGREEN Model of Job Creation in a Post-Growth Economy." The Greens and EFA in the European Parliament.

D'Alisa, Giacomo, Federico Demaria, and Giorgios Kallis, eds. 2015. *Degrowth: A Vocabulary for a New Era*. New York: Routledge.

Desrosières, Alain. 2013. *Gouverner par les nombres: L'argument statistique II*. Paris: Presses des Mines via OpenEdition.

Diefenbacher, Hans, Sebastian Gechert, Christoph Gran, Kai Neumann, Linsenmeier Manuel, Malte Oehlmann, et al. 2019. "Environmental Costs and Alternative Welfare Measures." Analysis of the Integration of Environmental Costs and Alternative Welfare Measures into Economic Models. Edited by Umweltbundesamt.

EEA. 2019. "The European Environment – State and Outlook 2020: Knowledge for Transition to a Sustainable Europe." Copenhagen: European Environment Agency.

EESC. 2008. "Opinion of the EESC on Beyond GDP—Measurements for Sustainable Development." Brussels: European Economic and Social Committee.

EU Parliament. 2011. "Report on GDP and Beyond – Measuring Progress in a Changing World." Brussels: European Parliament.

European Commission. 2013. "Commission Staff Working Document – Progress on 'GDP and Beyond' Actions." SWD (2013) 303 final, Volume 1 of 2. Brussels: European Commission.

– 2019. "Communication from the Commission to the European Parliament, the European Council, the Council, the European and Social Committee and the Committee of Regions. The European Green Deal." COM (2019) 640 Final. Brussels: European Commission.

Fleurbaey, Marc, and Didier Blanchet. 2013. *Beyond GDP: Measuring Welfare and Assessing Sustainability*. Oxford: Oxford University Press.

Funtowicz, Silvio O., and Jerome R. Ravetz. 1994. "The Worth of a Songbird: Ecological Economics as a Post-Normal Science." *Ecological Economics* 10, no. 3: 197–207.

Gadrey, Jean, and Florence Jany-Catrice. 2006. *The New Indicators of Well-Being and Development*. Basingstoke: Palgrave Macmillan.

Goossens, Yanne, Arttu Mäkipää, Philipp Schepelmann, Isabel van de Sand, Michael Kuhndt, and Martin Herrndorf. 2007. "Alternative Progress Indicators to Gross Domestic Product (GDP) as a Means Towards Sustainable Development." European Parliament.

Gran, Christoph, Sebastian Gechert, and Jonathan Barth. 2019. "Growth, Prosperity and the Environment: Integrating Environmental and Social Indicators into QUEST." Bonn: ZOE Institut für zukunftsfähige Ökonomien.

Hardt, Lukas, and Daniel W. O'Neill. 2017. "Ecological Macroeconomic Models: Assessing Current Developments." *Ecological Economics* 134, no. C: 198–211.

Hege, Elisabeth, and Laura Brimont. 2018. "Integrating SDGs into National Budgetary Processes." Paris: IDDRI.

Hirsch, Fred. 1995 [1972]. *Social Limits to Growth*. London: Routledge.

Hoekstra, Rutger. 2019. "Replacing GDP by 2030: Towards a Common Language for the Well-Being and Sustainability Community." Cambridge: Cambridge University Press.

Jackson, Tim. 2017. *Prosperity without Growth: Foundations for the Economy of Tomorrow*. 2nd ed. London: Routledge.

Jackson, Tim, Ben Drake, Peter Victor, Kurt Kratena, and Mark Sommer. 2014. "Foundations for an Ecological Macroeconomics: Literature Review and Model Development." WWW for Europe Working Paper No. 65.

Kuznets, Simon. 1934. "National Income 1929–1932. A report to the U.S. Senate, 73rd Congress, 2nd Session." Washington, DC: US Government Printing Office.

Meadows, Donella H., Dennis L. Meadows, Jørgen Randers, and William W. Behrens III. 1972. "The Limits to Growth. A Report to the Club of Rome." New York: Universe Books.

Méda, Dominique. 2008. *Au-delà du PIB: Pour une autre mesure de la richesse*. Paris: Flammarion.

OECD. 2019. "Beyond Growth: Toward a New Economic Approach. Report of the Secretary General's Advisory Group on a New Growth Narrative." Paris: OECD.

O'Neill, Daniel W. 2012. "Measuring Progress in the Degrowth Transition to a Steady State Economy." *Ecological Economics* 84: 221–31.

Parrique, Timothée, Jonathan Barth, François Briens, Christian Kerschner, Alejo Kraus-Polk, Anna Kuokkanen, and Joachim H. Spangenberg. 2019. "Decoupling Debunked: Evidence and Arguments against Green Growth as a Sole Strategy for Sustainability." Brussels: European Environmental Bureau.

Stiglitz, Joseph, Jean-Paul Fitoussi, and Martine Durand. 2018. "Beyond GDP: Measuring What Counts for Economic and Social Performance." Paris: OECD.

Stiglitz, Joseph E., Amartya Sen, and Jean-Paul Fitoussi. 2009. "Report by the Commission on the Measurement of Economic Performance and Social Progress." Paris. http://www.stiglitzsen-fitoussi.fr/en/index.htm.

Thiry, Géraldine, Léa Sébastien, and Tom Bauler. 2016. "Ce que révèlent les discours des acteurs institutionnels sur un 'au-delà du PIB.'" *Natures Sciences Sociétés* 24, no. 1: 3–14.

van den Bergh, Jeroen C.J.M. 2011. "Environment versus Growth – A Criticism of 'Degrowth' and a Plea for 'A-growth.'" *Ecological Economics* 70, no. 5: 881–90.

Vatn, Arild. 2017. "Critical Institutional Economics." In *Routledge Handbook of Ecological Economics: Nature and Society*, edited by Clive L. Spash, 29–38. New York: Routledge.

Viveret, Patrick. 2004. *Reconsidérer la richesse*. Paris: Editions de l'aube.

8 Contributions of the Genuine Progress Indicator to Measuring and Promoting Welfare

GÜNSELI BERIK

Introduction

The early twenty-first century has witnessed a proliferation of aggregate welfare measures that seek to either complement or replace per capita gross domestic product (GDP) as a measure of well-being. Among the most prominent "beyond-GDP" alternatives at the international level are the Human Development Index, the Happy Planet Index, happiness (i.e., life satisfaction), the Better Life Initiative, and the Genuine Progress Indicator. These measures implement different well-being concepts and pursue different approaches to aggregation. In addition, there are home-grown national indicators, such as the Gross National Happiness Index, the Canadian Index of Wellbeing, the UK's national well-being dashboard, and New Zealand's Living Standards Framework. While the point of departure of each of these measures was GDP's shortcomings as a well-being indicator, many do not respond to the criticisms of GDP, nor are they equipped to address modern-day challenges that can adversely affect well-being (such as climate change, ecological degradation, and changing labour dynamics). Moreover, each has theoretical or practical shortcomings as a welfare indicator.

This chapter examines the case for using the Genuine Progress Indicator (GPI), also known as the Index of Sustainable Welfare (ISEW) in European research communities, to measure aggregate well-being and guide policymaking. The GPI is a comprehensive welfare indicator that incorporates economic, environmental, and social components. In recent years it has attracted attention for its potential to assess sustainability, shared prosperity, and quality of life (Brown 2017) and to undermine the dominant GDP-growth-centric thinking (Held et al. 2018). It is the subject of a growing number of studies and of methodological innovation.

The chapter shows that among prominent international beyond-GDP indicators, GPI stands out as the most responsive to GDP's shortcomings and in incorporating concerns about income inequality, the environment, unpaid care work, underwork, and overwork. As a monetary indicator, it is also a potentially powerful policy tool, a feature which is underutilized by GPI researchers so far, even as the contending indicators often resort to monetization to make policy recommendations. While GPI does not yet have a standard methodology that enables cross-country comparability, the chapter argues that policy use of GPI could start at the subnational (state/province) level with a customized GPI, that could be used for conversations on sustainable well-being and showing the relevance of GPI in moving towards sustainability. Grassroots support for GPI can, in turn, translate into institutional support and pave the way for standardization as well as local adaptations of GPI.

GPI: History and Features

GPI's origins go back to the debates around the creation of the System of National Accounts (SNA) and choice of an indicator to assess impacts of macroeconomic policy on the nation's welfare during the Great Depression. One of the architects of these accounts, Simon Kuznets, favoured an indicator that went beyond a gauge of market activity, to include non-market activities that enhance welfare and leave out market activities that do not directly add to people's welfare. Ultimately, however, under the ascendant Keynesian approach, national income was defined as the sum of market exchanges, specifically the sum of value added by production, and became a measure of value creation in the economy. Over time, GDP has become a powerful measure of economic and even national performance. It is routinely used to assess a country's welfare, despite warnings from the outset against such interpretations and those found in United Nations System of National Accounts (SNA) documents (European Commission et al. 2009).

Kuznets's call for an aggregate national welfare indicator was not heeded until Nordhaus and Tobin (1972) proposed the Measure of Economic Welfare (MEW), the precursor of the ISEW and GPI. MEW built on the GDP framework and expressed welfare in monetary terms. Nordhaus and Tobin took personal consumption expenditure in the national accounts as the starting point, added the imputed value of leisure and household services, and deducted "disamenities" associated with urbanization (e.g., commuting costs). They estimated per-capita MEW between 1929 and 1965 in the United States and found that it was higher than GDP.

The MEW was followed by the ISEW (Daly and Cobb 1989), later renamed the GPI (Cobb, Halstead, and Rowe 1995; Anielski and Rowe 1999).[1] The GPI has more components than the MEW, representing the three "pillars" of sustainability (economic, environmental, and social) widely embraced since the Brundtland Report (World Commission on Environment and Development 1987). Underlying the single-value GPI is a set of accounts that weights personal consumption expenditures (GDP's largest component) by income inequality and incorporates both the value of non-market services and activities, such as household production and leisure, and the social and environmental costs associated with market activity.

The GPI incorporates about two dozen adjustments to personal consumption, making it mostly an externality-corrected GDP. Figure 8.1 illustrates the components of the GPI study conducted in the US state of Utah, and the Appendix summarizes the methodology. The GPI can be viewed as a set of satellite accounts that are then merged with the primary accounts to come up with an adjusted bottom-line number on total consumption.[2] Each adjustment, consistent with microeconomic theory, reflects an external effect weighted by its marginal value. These values include damage costs, option values, willingness-to-pay estimates from contingent valuation surveys, and market costs.

GPI has faced criticisms for having a weak theoretical foundation and an arbitrary list of components. In response, GPI researchers have affirmed the theoretical foundations of GPI in utilitarian theory (welfare economics) as a measure of current welfare. However, in the most recent articulation of the theory underlying GPI, Talberth and Weisdorf (2017) observe that many GPI studies have been less rigorous in applying the theory, which may have contributed to the perception of a weak theoretical foundation. In addition, Fox and Erickson (2018) note that GPI's initial design (as ISEW) did not provide clear criteria for which components to include or exclude, giving rise to the perception of arbitrariness.

The choice-of-components criticism is not unique to the GPI but applies to all approaches that generate an aggregate indicator top-down, whether on an ad-hoc basis or from theoretical frameworks. The GPI faces a larger dose of criticism possibly because it has a large number of non-market components. Some critics do not consider extreme inequality as a problem and may have low levels of environmental literacy.[3] At best, each aggregate indicator strives to reflect a consensus on what is important to measure. Moreover, it is important to remember that GDP itself – the SNA production boundary – incorporates many arbitrary decisions. Striking examples in SNA accounting include the imputation of rent to services of owner-occupied houses while imputing value to unpaid household services is rejected (Folbre 2002), and the movement of the (unproductive) financial sector into the production boundary over time (Mazzucato 2018).

There have also been debates about the valuation (imputation) methods used for some individual components of GPI, but these are consonant with current debates in microeconomic theory (e.g., how to value resource depletion).

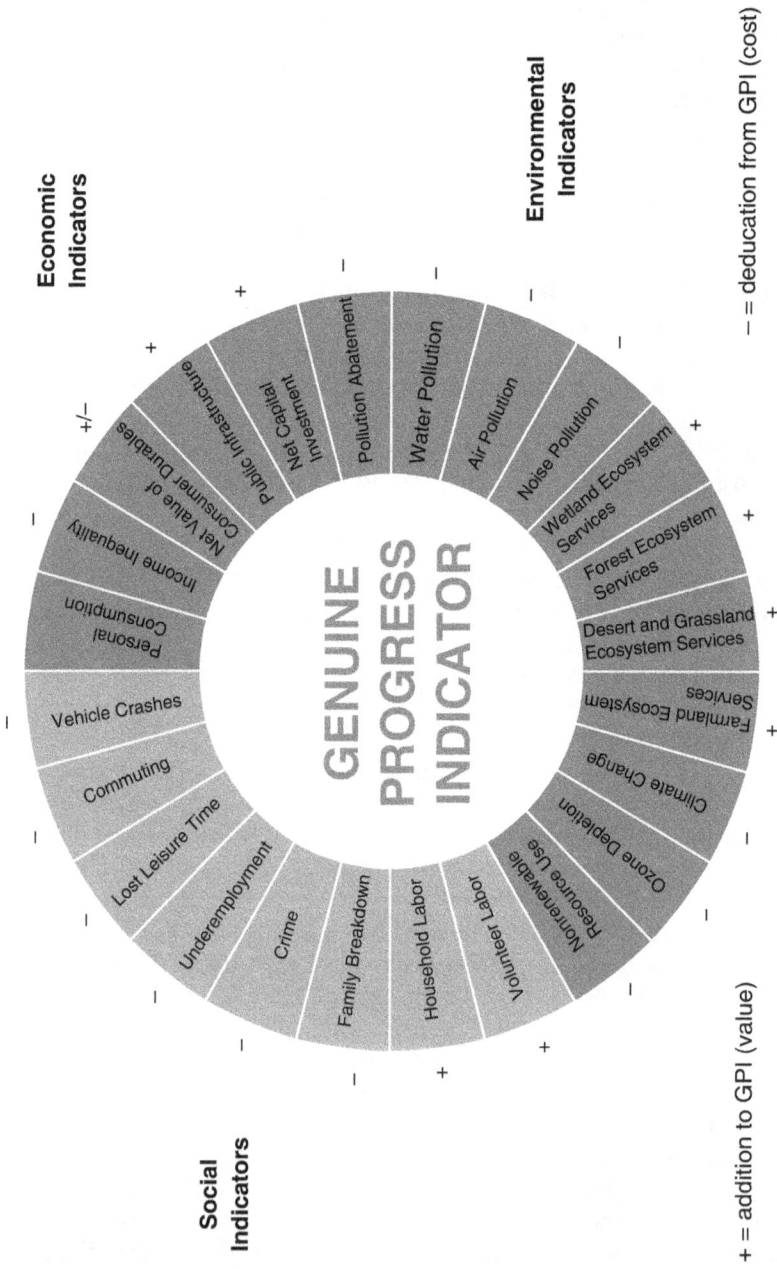

Figure 8.1. GPI components, state of Utah, United States

Note: See Appendix for details on the calculation of the components.
Source: Author's formulation based on Berik and Gaddis (2011).

+ = addition to GPI (value)   − = deducation from GPI (cost)

Economic Indicators

- Pollution Abatement +
- Net Capital Investment +
- Public Infrastructure +
- Net Value of Consumer Durables +/−
- Income Inequality −
- Personal Consumption

Environmental Indicators

- Water Pollution −
- Air Pollution −
- Noise Pollution −
- Wetland Ecosystem Services +
- Forest Ecosystem Services +
- Desert and Grassland Ecosystem Services +
- Farmland Ecosystem Services
- Climate Change −
- Ozone Depletion −
- Nonrenewable Resource Use −

Social Indicators

- Vehicle Crashes −
- Commuting −
- Lost Leisure Time −
- Underemployment −
- Crime −
- Family Breakdown −
- Household Labor +
- Volunteer Labor +

GENUINE PROGRESS INDICATOR

Finally, while the main contributors to the GPI's development are critics of growth-centric thinking, others are sceptical of GPI's potential to transform contemporary growth-oriented economies. As a monetary metric, it is perceived as reinforcing reliance on market values, and its value is dominated by the very large market-sourced consumption component (Bleys and Whitby 2015).

Measuring What Matters: Responding to GDP's Shortcomings and the Challenges of Our Times

A close-up on GPI shows that, despite its dated design, it is still well equipped to reflect major contemporary well-being concerns and, this chapter argues, performs better in comparison to other prominent international beyond-GDP indicators in this regard. By way of background, the Human Development Index (HDI) of the United Nations Development Programme (UNDP) is one of the earliest aggregate measures. It conceptualizes well-being in terms of the capability approach (Sen 1999) and incorporates the capabilities to live a long, healthy life, to be educated, and enjoy a decent standard of living (UNDP 2020). Another composite index is the Happy Planet Index (HPI), which measures welfare in terms of life expectancy and subjective well-being but also takes into account the effect of inequality and the ecological footprint (New Economics Foundation 2016). The subjective evaluation approach measures well-being on the basis of people's evaluation of their own lives, usually in terms of Cantril Ladder scores that range from 0 to 10 (Helliwell, Layard, and Sachs 2019). The Organisation for Economic Co-operation and Development's (OECD) Better Life Initiative exemplifies the dashboard approach that does not aggregate the selected well-being dimensions (Durand 2015; OECD 2020). The dashboard features three material dimensions (income and wealth, jobs and earnings, housing) and eight quality-of-life dimensions (health status, work-life balance, education and skills, social connections, civic engagement and governance, environmental quality, personal security, subjective well-being).

Table 8.1 summarizes GPI's relative strengths and weaknesses compared to these indicators, focusing on the extent to which each seeks to remedy GDP's shortcomings, addresses the pressing well-being concerns (income inequality, environmental sustainability, unpaid work, underwork, and overwork), and serves as a guide for policy.

Inequality

The GPI was the first aggregate welfare indicator to incorporate an inequality adjustment that deducts the cost of inequality from personal consumption expenditures. Underlying the inequality adjustment is the notion that inequality

Table 8.1. Strengths and shortcomings of the main beyond-GDP indicators

	GPI (1989) 2006 version	HDI (1990) 2010 version	HPI (2006) 2016 version	Cantril Ladder (2012) 2019 version	OECD Better Life Index (2011)
Approach	Monetary	Composite index	Composite index	Subjective evaluation	Dashboard
Relation to GDP	Adjusts	Includes	No	No	No
Incorporates:					
Inequality	Yes	No	Yes	No	No
Environment	Yes	No	Yes	No	Yes
Non-market activities	Yes	No	No	No	Yes
Dynamics of paid work	Yes	No	No	No	Yes
Enables:					
Cross-country comparability	No	Yes (189 in 2019)	Yes (140 in 2016)	Yes (156 in 2019)	Yes (35 in 2017)
Assessment of change over time for each country (%)	Yes	No	No	No	No

Notes: The year indicated in parentheses in the column headings denotes the year in which the indicator/dashboard was launched and is followed by the year of the version for which characteristics are indicated in the table. The OECD dashboard tracks water and air quality, leisure and personal care time, and excessive paid work hours. "Cross-country comparability" refers to the use of standard data and methodology across countries. The number of countries considered in the latest report and the report year are in parentheses. "Assessment of change over time for each country (%)" refers to use of the indicator to measure a percentage increase or decrease in outcome between two periods for a specific country.

results in lower total welfare because one unit of consumption has greater value (utility) for a poor person than a rich one. The adjustment involves calculating the cost of inequality relative to the lowest recorded inequality level, measured in terms of the Gini coefficient. The intuition is to track the inequality associated with economic process (growth), or in effect to treat inequality as an externality (positive or negative).

Among the prominent indicators covered in this chapter, only the GPI and HPI include inequality adjustments (Table 8.1). Inequality adjustment is not part of the HDI, although an inequality-adjusted version has been reported since 2010. The OECD's Better Life dashboard does not track inequality, although it reports income- or education-inequality adjusted values for some indicators on the dashboard (OECD 2020).

Environmental Sustainability

A unique GPI feature is that it provides an approximation of a nation's sustainable economic welfare by distinguishing between activities that enhance welfare and those that reduce it. In environmental terms, the GPI tracks changes in both the quantity of various types of natural capital (e.g., wetlands, farmland, and forests) and the quality of others (e.g., water pollution, air pollution, and noise pollution), each in both physical and monetary terms.[4] It also measures the costs of energy-resource depletion, ozone depletion, and carbon emissions. These environmental components are relevant for both current welfare and the sustainability of that welfare. However, relatively early in the GPI's development, critics established that GPI does not measure sustainability (Neumayer 1999). The problem is that as a monetary measure GPI allows substitution of different flows of income to increase the GPI (Neumayer 2010). For example, increases in personal consumption expenditures could offset rising costs of air or water pollution. Indeed, in many studies, the GPI is dominated by consumption expenditures. In addition, the GPI underestimates environmental costs, such as the transboundary impact of economic growth (i.e., exporting costs of growth to other locations).

To operationalize "strong sustainability," the GPI income statement has to be supplemented with a balance sheet of assets to determine whether a nation's stock of natural resources has declined to a degree that makes welfare ecologically unsustainable. To assess how close we are to ecological boundaries, a "red flag" needs to be added to all simulations and evaluations of sustainability, to indicate when a natural resource is close to breaking point and must be protected at all costs. The United Nations System of Environmental-Economic Accounting provides such balance sheet accounts.

Among the beyond-GDP alternatives considered in this chapter, ecology figures in the HPI, which divides inequality-adjusted "Happy Life Years" by the ecological footprint, and the OECD Better-Life dashboard tracks two environmental-quality indicators – water pollution (in terms of subjective assessments of water quality) and air pollution (Table 8.1). The HDI does not address environmental sustainability, and cross-country analysis shows that very high and high HDI levels are associated with greater environmental degradation (Neumayer 2012). And, given subjective well-being's close association with GDP, high levels of subjective well-being can be associated with high levels of ecological degradation.[5]

Unpaid Work, Underwork, and Overwork

Another unique feature of the GPI compared to other international beyond-GDP indicators is that it incorporates unpaid household and volunteer work as contributors to current welfare. These activities reproduce the labour force and provide care that enhances quality of life and builds social relationships. Time-use surveys, used in a growing number of countries, indicate that, globally, women do most of the unpaid household and volunteer work (Charmes 2019), yet these services are not counted in the SNA. In addition, the GPI gauges the current bifurcation of paid working hours: overwork (loss of leisure time of full-time employed workers) for some and underwork (underemployment) for others. Each of these components is measured in terms of time use, which is typically valued at market wage rates. These components, along with rising inequality, are central to discussions about the future of work and the dimensions of work that belong in a more comprehensive measure of well-being (Ryder 2019).

GPI's inclusion of unpaid work responds to long-standing calls by feminist economists to make the contribution of non-market work to well-being statistically visible (Benería et al. 2016). It is important to track changes in time spent on non-market activities, as they reflect both the commodification of goods and services and changes in technology. Unpaid household work and volunteer work complement, and at times replace, market work. In the Global North, the time devoted to household work is shrinking owing to increasing reliance on market substitutes, although economic or health crises could disrupt this trend and increase unpaid work as families reduce outsourcing, as illustrated by the COVID-19 crisis. The spread of market-provisioned services would be reflected in a decline in the value of unpaid household work accompanied by a rise in personal consumption expenditures, which could leave the GPI potentially unchanged. But the GPI dashboard can track the underlying shifts in time use: a decline in unpaid care hours can be associated with a rise in paid labour (that enables the purchase of consumer goods), increased leisure time, or increased volunteer work. Similarly, the GPI can track greater reliance on new technologies, such as self-driving personal cars, which could reduce commute times (and costs) while increasing the leisure time of full-time workers, resulting in both a compositional change and a net increase in GPI.

In the Global South, commodification is taking place more slowly and unevenly (differentiated by class, region, and rural versus urban areas), and routine household tasks are still time-consuming, owing to shortfalls in household and public infrastructure. These hours have to be tracked to make the case for public funding to reduce the drudgery involved. Within the GPI framework, such investments would be reflected in fewer unpaid household work hours that may enable more paid work hours, hence an increase in expenditures on consumer goods and services.

GPI's underemployment component allows tracking the cost of unprovided hours (indicated in labour force surveys by workers wishing to work longer hours but unable to do so) to economic performance. The cost of underemployment – unprovided hours multiplied by the market wage rate – is deducted from the GPI. Underemployment is broader than unemployment and seeks to measure the social cost of underutilization of labour resources. For example, the growing prevalence of just-in-time scheduling practices that place workers on call and force them to work part time contributes to underemployment.

At the other extreme is overwork, when an increase in total (paid and unpaid household) work hours by full-time, year-round employed workers erodes leisure hours, raising the cost of lost leisure. In addition, GPI components could track the impact of spatial reorganizations of work leading to shorter commutes and less air pollution. Overall, even if these adjustments may not change the GPI's value, the GPI framework is equipped to track changes in the dynamics of work.

None of the major international beyond-GDP indicators incorporates the value of household and volunteer work. Only the OECD Better Life dashboard includes indicators that track excessive hours of paid work (more than fifty hours per week) and leisure time.

Other Conceptual and Measurement Issues

Each contending approach to aggregate well-being measurement has theoretical or practical shortcomings (Fleurbaey and Blanchet 2013; Brown 2017). In a nutshell, monetary indicators, like GPI, and composite indices, like HDI and HPI, raise questions about aggregation methods – the components and how they are weighted. Monetary indicators tend to rely on imputed prices for valuation of non-market components, which can be difficult to calculate and may be considered arbitrary. Seemingly neutral composite indices, on the other hand, tend to have implicit biases hidden in the aggregation process. Monetary or not, aggregation implies that the components are substitutable (Fleurbaey and Blanchet 2013).

The subjective approach, implemented in happiness measurement, has been criticized on conceptual and methodological grounds (Sen 1999; Stewart 2014). The approach embodies an adaptation problem: individuals adapt to their living conditions, no matter how poor or lavish, and may express the same happiness level across disparate material conditions. Similarly, cultural norms of life satisfaction are dynamic. These issues undermine the indicator's cross-country and intertemporal comparability.

The dashboard approach, which is gaining traction, tends to suffer from the "too-much-information" problem. A major drawback of using an array of indicators instead of a single-value indicator is that it is not possible to assess changes in overall well-being over time. As many authors have pointed out (e.g., Fleurbaey and Blanchet 2013), the dashboard approach is no match for the simplicity of one aggregate, headline indicator. In fact, as insightful as they are, dashboards tend to be sidelined and signal lesser importance, and "naming and shaming is much harder based on a dashboard" (Klasen 2018, 22). Moreover, as discussed below, dashboards are of limited use in guiding policy, other than spotlighting issues for policy attention (Berik 2020). Some authors (e.g., Felice 2016) argue that an indicator dashboard can be used as a transitional step until strong interest in an alternative composite single-valued indicator emerges.

Thus, each prominent beyond-GDP alternative is less than perfect for measuring aggregate well-being. Some recent evaluations suggest that policy discussions should be based on either a multiplicity of indicators (since each highlights a different dimension of welfare) or on indicators selected as being best suited to the country's income level, e.g., use GPI for affluent economies and HDI for low-income countries (Brown 2017). This chapter argues that usefulness in policymaking should also be a major consideration in indicator selection.

Guiding Policy

While the primary purpose of measuring welfare is to inform policy, measurement does not guarantee policy use. Accordingly, the key questions are, first, whether each beyond-GDP indicator is designed to be useful in guiding policy and, second, whether it is being used to that end. Usefulness for policy may be viewed in various terms, ranging from highlighting problem areas to assisting policy choice.

A common use of aggregate indicators is to highlight the relative standing of countries and thereby to indicate potential policy initiatives. In this sense, arguably only the HDI has effectively been used to shape policy. Developed in the political-economic context of structural adjustment programs that mandated cuts in social spending, the HDI has been useful in indicating short-falls in health and education outcomes. If a country's HDI rank is considerably below its Gross National Income (GNI) rank, this calls for greater allocation of budgets to education and health.

Comparison of alternative indicators to the GDP has also served an important policy role. For example, divergence of happiness from GDP (Easterlin 1995) shows that measured welfare is not growing as fast as GDP. In the case of GPI, typically, per capita GPI values fall below per capita GDP, and often the GPI stagnates above a certain GDP level. The meta-analysis of GPI studies by Kubiszewski et al. (2013) illustrates this relationship over the period 1950–2005 for seventeen countries that generated 59 per cent of world GDP in 2005. The divergence of GPI from GDP is largely the result of the rising costs of growth, which drags GPI values down. However, the divergence of the GPI and GDP beyond a threshold-income level may not necessarily hold to the extent that policies address GPI's cost components by, for example, shifting to renewable energy, reducing underemployment, or increasing leisure time of full-time workers. Thus, the GPI–GDP comparison itself is a useful tool to design a policy agenda to raise the GPI.

Policymakers value GDP because they can use it in simulations and to assess policy trade-offs. Among the prominent international aggregate indicators considered in this chapter only the GPI is suitable for these policymaking tasks (Table 8.1): as a monetary indicator it can show the percentage change in the indicator value over time for a given country/region and can be used to assess potential impacts of prospective policies. By contrast, composite non-monetary indices, such as the HDI or HPI, are of limited use for this task. Changes in a country's HDI can indicate whether the situation is improving or worsening, but the percentage change over time in an index is of limited usefulness in policy.

Stiglitz, Fitoussi, and Durand (2018) favour supplementing GDP with an indicator dashboard, but a dashboard cannot give a sense of overall change in well-being and cannot readily serve key tasks that enable policymaking. To be sure, dashboards are useful for highlighting and tracking specific problems, for example, quality-of-life assessments or detailed assessments of labour market performance, biodiversity, and ecosystem boundaries. Thereby they can provide rough or imprecise guidance for budget decisions. But they do not provide a decision rule on how policymakers will use them in making decisions involving trade-offs: to distinguish policy priorities, assess benefits and costs of options, and guide budget and financing decisions. Decision-making rules have to be developed, and dashboard indicators often have to be translated into monetary equivalents to apply cost–benefit analysis (Ng, this volume; New Zealand Treasury 2019).

As regards the actual use of alternative indicators in guiding policy, this is a recent, emerging development. The latest beyond-GDP assessment by Stiglitz, Fitoussi, and Durand (2018) reports that some OECD countries have begun using well-being metrics in their policy processes. Among the national efforts, the UK and New Zealand have launched well-being frameworks for policy evaluation (Bache; Ng, this volume). New Zealand has used its Living Standards Framework to inform its 2019 well-being budget. A prominent and controversial metric in the UK's framework is subjective well-being, considered attractive by its proponents for its potential to be converted into monetary terms, which enables application of social cost–benefit analysis. Bhutan's Gross National Happiness (GNH) Index can be used to determine areas where policy intervention is needed, while the related GNH Policy Screening Tool has been used to evaluate policy initiatives by scoring how they would affect various dimensions of GNH (Hayden 2015).

The GPI's direct policy impact has been limited thus far, despite its policy advantage as a monetary indicator. A few US studies, for example Bagstad and Shammin (2012), have used GPI in policy analysis. In the context of Belgium and Germany, Bleys and Whitby (2015) identify three main obstacles to the GPI's adoption and policy use: the attractiveness of GDP growth in the aftermath of the Great Recession; infrequent releases of new GPI figures to meet needs of potential users; and scepticism about GPI's usefulness in moving towards sustainability.

Similar obstacles, as well as bureaucratic hurdles, are highlighted by Hayden and Wilson (2018) in their study of the adoption of GPI in the US state of Maryland.

A drawback of GPI for potential users is that it is not yet ready for use in cross-country analyses (Table 8.1). Given its high data demands, as of 2021, GPI has been estimated for only about forty, mostly affluent, countries and for subnational entities in ten of them.[6] While most GPI studies estimate a standard set of components, such as those shown in Figure 8.1, divergent methods have been used for some components. The only study that has applied a consistent methodology to calculate comparable GPIs for a large number of states is the fifty-state US study by Fox and Erickson (2018).

The GPI at the Crossroads

In recent years methodological divergence has increased as GPI gained attention. The main source of increasing divergence is researchers' use of latest data sources and cutting-edge scholarship in calculating the GPI for high- and middle-income countries (Bagstad, Berik, and Gaddis 2014; Talberth and Weisdorf 2017; Brown and Lazarus 2018; O'Mahony, Escardó-Serra, and Dufour 2018). As these innovations put the GPI on the path to becoming a more robust indicator, the GPI research community has also emphasized the desirability of a standard methodology. Such method resets are common for both GDP and the other beyond-GDP indicators, as attested by the major overhauls of the HDI in 2010 and US GDP in 2013. To generate a standard GPI, methodology discussions have focused on how to improve measurement of the welfare gains and losses associated with various components, while avoiding double counting. Proposals include improving measurement of existing components: for example, moving away from calculating accumulated costs relative to a benchmark year in the ecosystem, leisure time, and inequality calculations (Bagstad, Berik, and Gaddis 2014); incorporating the value of government spending on health and education (Brown and Lazarus 2018); and using an alternative inequality adjustment (Howarth and Kennedy 2016; Talberth and Weisdorf 2017). In addition, recent GPI studies have favoured dropping GPI components that are no longer pressing issues (e.g., cost of ozone depletion) or on which there is less consensus (e.g., cost of family breakdown). A related proposal is to consider a smaller component list so as to economize on data demands and allow a standard methodology that would enhance cross-country comparability (Fox and Erickson 2018; Kenny et al. 2019). Transparent and inclusive GPI research practices – in data reporting, routine use of sensitivity tests to provide conditional input for policy, and supporting the voice of local groups through GPI research – are also emphasized (Berik 2018). These practices can increase confidence in GPI as a planning tool.

However, there is no guarantee that these proposals will be widely adopted, since GPI studies are largely driven by academic researchers (through peer-reviewed scholarly publications) or non-profit organizations. Thus, a standard

GPI methodology may be difficult to attain without institutional sponsorship of the sort received by other prominent indicators, supported by foundations and international organizations that periodically convene expert groups and maintain and update the indicator.

The alternative to standardization is localization. National or subnational adaptations of methodology and use of superior data sources, which may not be available across provinces/states/countries, make GPI more relevant to policy-making. These adaptations have entailed incorporating locally relevant variants of components (e.g., desert ecosystems for Utah and coastal watershed ecosystems for Hawaii) (Berik and Gaddis 2011; Ostergaard-Klem and Oleson 2014) and country-/province-specific public concerns, such as the cost of nuclear energy (Held et al. 2018). Localization opens up the possibility of strengthening local ownership of GPI. Brown and Lazarus (2018) argue that standardization could proceed along with localization, calculating both a customized GPI, for use by policymakers, and a GPI based on the standard methodology (subject to any reset) that would enable comparability across states/countries.

Concluding Thoughts

This chapter has argued that in the contemporary landscape of competing aggregate measures GPI is superior in measuring what matters and guiding policy. GPI provides an alternative monetary indicator that tells how well the macroeconomy is performing in generating well-being. In doing so, GPI responds to GDP's shortcomings as an economic welfare indicator and tracks major contemporary challenges to well-being in a single framework: it makes visible non-market contributors to and detractors from well-being, such as unpaid labour, overwork, underemployment, ecological challenges, and inequality. Each of these components can be tracked in non-monetary and monetary terms. Thus, GPI is not solely a single-value indicator but also a dashboard/set of satellite accounts that is suitable for demonstrating the effect of policies on its various components. Importantly, as a monetary indicator, it is well suited to evaluate the welfare impact of policy proposals – it enables policy simulations and allows assessment of trade-offs – which is a feature that tends to be overlooked in discussions of beyond-GDP indicators. Neither the dashboard approach nor a composite non-monetary index is readily available for these policy purposes, which require monetary units (or specialized tools to translate changes in indicators into monetary units).

Despite these valuable features, GPI has faced opposition from some critics. As discussed in this chapter, this may be partly due to GPI's perceived theoretical weakness. But the other beyond-GDP approaches also have theoretical and practical limitations. As summarized in Table 8.1, the GPI at least minimizes the problems and strikes a better balance between its weaknesses and strengths. Another drawback is that GPI is not yet available for cross-country analyses because of its evolving methodology, high data demands and independent researcher–driven studies. Even without a standard methodology, however, growing interest in using the GPI to inform policy has helped generate new studies and updated GPI estimates. Increasing availability of internationally comparable data and research developments will be valuable for the methodological update of GPI: time-use data infrastructure and availability are likely to improve further with the pursuit of Sustainable Development Goal 5 (Gender Equality and Women's Empowerment), the growing reliance on gender-budget analysis in evaluating fiscal policy (Chakraborty 2013), and the International Labour Organization's recognition of unpaid care services as a productive activity (ILO 2013). In turn, gender-/race-/class-differentiated time-use data may enable development of GPI methodology to incorporate broader inequality concerns. Similarly, recent ecosystems research and growing availability of environmental and natural resource data provide invaluable input for estimating the GPI regularly and addressing GPI's shortcomings, such as transboundary impact problems (Schröter et al. 2018).

A more subtle and formidable obstacle to the adoption and use of GPI to inform policy may be resistance to full accounting of the costs of the economic process. The GPI is the only prominent beyond-GDP indicator that assesses overall economic performance by adjusting for the negative externalities of the economic process. Arguably, the ascendant dashboard approach to measuring well-being receives a lot of support because it avoids controversy by leaving off the dashboard the costs of economic growth to the environment.

To overcome the obstacle mounted by the growth mindset, GPI research needs institutional support – sponsorship by a central entity that would convene a high-level group to review and periodically reset GPI methodology and provide blueprints for policy simulations. However, institutional support is unlikely without grassroots support. GPI researchers have to generate conversations on local social and ecological sustainability concerns among activists and policymakers, such as air or water pollution, and showcase GPI's policy relevance in moving towards a sustainable future. It also means positioning GPI in both activist and academic circles as one tool in a plural and conditional decision-making process (Berik 2018). If the GPI were to receive institutional support it would be ready for adoption, local adaptation, frequent releases, and tracking by governments or independent research organizations.

NOTES

1   Another variant of MEW is a consumption-equivalent measure of welfare (utility) implemented by Jones and Klenow (2016). This measure does not incorporate negative externalities and is highly correlated with per capita GDP.
2   Satellite accounts are a response to GDP's neglect of non-market services, such as unpaid household work, services of consumer durables, and childcare (Kanal and

Kornegay 2019; Suh and Folbre 2016), or of environmental assets and service flows in the case of the United Nations System of Environmental-Economic Accounting (see https://seea.un.org/). But these two satellite accounts are not combined.

3   In a typical objection, Worstall (2014) charges that the GPI's proponents are attempting to "codify ... highly contentious ideas" into a single-value indicator when the welfare implications of increase in income inequality and decline in wetlands or farmlands are not "universally agreed upon."

4   The GPI also incorporates social sustainability in terms of erosion of the social fabric (e.g., costs of family breakdown and underemployment) and the costs of urbanization (e.g., commuting and car crashes).

5   While this chapter focuses on prominent international indicators, one prominent Canadian indicator, the Canadian Index of Wellbeing (CIW), does take into account environmental conditions, as well as unpaid and volunteer labour, and the value of leisure time discussed in the next section (see Dasilva and Hayden, this volume).

6   GPIs for low-income countries have fewer components. GPI researchers nevertheless argue that starting with a more limited GPI is a useful first step towards full-cost accounting of welfare (Bleys 2007; Lawn and Clarke 2008; Menegaki 2018).

REFERENCES

Anielski, Mark, and Jonathan Rowe. 1999. "The Genuine Progress Indicator – 1998 Update." San Francisco: Redefining Progress.

Bagstad, Kenneth J., Günseli Berik, and Erica J. Brown Gaddis. 2014. "Methodological Developments in US State-level Genuine Progress Indicators: Toward GPI 2.0." *Ecological Indicators* 45 (October): 474–85.

Bagstad, Kenneth J., and Md Rumi Shammin. 2012. "Can the Genuine Progress Indicator Better Inform Sustainable Regional Progress?—A Case Study for Northeast Ohio." *Ecological Indicators* 18 (July): 330–41.

Benería, Lourdes, Günseli Berik, and Maria Floro. 2016. *Gender, Development and Globalization: Economics as if All People Mattered*. 2nd ed. New York: Routledge.

Berik, Günseli. 2020. "Measuring What Matters and Guiding Policy: An Evaluation of the Genuine Progress Indicator." *International Labour Review* 159, no. 1 (March): 71–94.

– 2018. "To Measure and to Narrate: Paths toward a Sustainable Future." *Feminist Economics* 24, no. 3 (April): 136–59.

Berik, Günseli, and Erica J.B. Gaddis. 2011. "The Utah Genuine Progress Indicator (GPI), 1990 to 2007: A Report to the People of Utah." https://utahpopulation.org/our-projects/genuine-progress-indicator.

Bleys, Brent. 2007. "Simplifying the Index of Sustainable Economic Welfare: Methodology, Data Sources and a Case Study for the Netherlands." *International Journal of Environment, Workplace and Employment* 3, no. 2: 103–18.

Bleys, Brent, and Alistair Whitby. 2015. "Barriers and Opportunities for Alternative Measures of Economic Welfare." *Ecological Economics* 117 (September): 162–72.

Brown, Clair. 2017. *Buddhist Economics: An Enlightened Approach to the Dismal Science*. New York: Bloomsbury.

Brown, Clair, and Eli Lazarus. 2018. "Genuine Progress Indicator for California: 2010–2014." *Ecological Indicators* 93 (October): 1143–51.

Chakraborty, Lekha. 2013. *Integrating Time in Public Policy: Any Evidence from Gender Diagnosis and Budgeting*. NIPFP Working Paper No. 127. New Delhi, National Institute of Public Finance and Policy. http://www.nipfp.org.in/media /medialibrary/2013/10/WP_2013_127.pdf.

Charmes, Jacques. 2019. "The Unpaid Care Work and the Labour Market. An Analysis of Time Use Data Based on the Latest World Compilation of Time-Use Surveys." International Labour Office, Geneva: ILO.

Cobb, Clifford, Ted Halstead, and Jonathan Rowe. 1995. "If the GDP Is up, Why Is America Down?" *The Atlantic* (October): 59–79.

Daly, Herman E., and John B. Cobb Jr. 1989. *For the Common Good: Redirecting the Economy toward Community, the Environment, and a Sustainable Future*. Boston: Beacon Press.

Durand, Martine. 2015. "The OECD Better Life Initiative: How's Life? And the Measurement of Well-Being." *Review of Income and Wealth* 61, no. 1 (March): 4–17.

Easterlin, Richard A. 1995. "Will Raising the Incomes of All Increase the Happiness of All?" *Journal of Economic Behavior & Organization* 27, no. 1 (June): 35–47.

European Commission, International Monetary Fund, OECD, United Nations, and World Bank. 2009. *System of National Accounts 2008*. New York: EC, IMF, OECD, UN, and World Bank.

Felice, Emanuele. 2016. "The Misty Grail: The Search for a Comprehensive Measure of Development and the Reasons for GDP Primacy." *Development and Change* 47, no. 5 (September): 967–94.

Fleurbaey, Marc, and Didier Blanchet. 2013. *Beyond GDP: Measuring Welfare and Assessing Sustainability*. New York: Oxford University Press.

Folbre, Nancy. 2002. "Measuring Success." In *The Invisible Heart: Economics and Family Values*, 53–80. New York: The New Press.

Fox, Mairi-Jane V., and Jon D. Erickson. 2018. "Genuine Economic Progress in the United States: A Fifty State Study and Comparative Assessment." *Ecological Economics* 147 (May): 29–35.

Hayden, Anders. 2015. "Bhutan: Blazing a Trail to a Postgrowth Future? Or Stepping on the Treadmill of Production?" *The Journal of Environment & Development* 24, no. 2 (April): 161–86.

Hayden, Anders, and Jeffrey Wilson. 2018. "Taking the First Steps beyond GDP: Maryland's Experience in Measuring 'Genuine Progress.'" *Sustainability* 10, no. 2 (February): 462.

Held, Benjamin, Dorothee Rodenhäuser, Hans Diefenbacher, and Roland Zieschank. 2018. "The National and Regional Welfare Index (NWI/RWI): Redefining Progress in Germany." *Ecological Economics* 145 (March): 391–400.

Helliwell, John F., Richard Layard, and Jeffrey D. Sachs, eds. 2019. *World Happiness Report 2019*. New York: Sustainable Development Solutions Network.

Howarth, Richard B., and Kevin Kennedy. 2016. "Economic Growth, Inequality, and Well-Being." *Ecological Economics* 121 (January): 231–6.

ILO (International Labour Organization). 2013. *Resolution Concerning Statistics of Work, Employment and Labour Underutilization*. Resolution adopted by the 19th Conference of Labour Statisticians, Geneva, 2–11 October 2013.

Jones, Charles I., and Peter J. Klenow. 2016. "Beyond GDP? Welfare across Countries and Time." *The American Economic Review* 106, no. 9 (September): 2426–57.

Kanal, Danit, and Joseph Ted Kornegay. 2019. "Accounting for Household Production in the National Accounts." *Survey of Current Business* 99, no. 6 (June): 1–9.

Kenny, Daniel C., Robert Costanza, Tom Dowsley, Nichelle Jackson, Jairus Josol, Ida Kubiszewski, Harkiran Narulla, Saioa Sese, Anna Sutanto, and Jonathan Thompson. 2019. "Australia's Genuine Progress Indicator Revisited (1962–2013)." *Ecological Economics* 158 (April): 1–10.

Klasen, Stephan. 2018. "Human Development Indices and Indicators: A Critical Evaluation." *Human Development Report Office Background Paper* 1, 5 October 2018. http://hdr.undp.org/en/content/human-development-indices-and -indicators-critical-evaluation.

Kubiszewski, Ida, Robert Costanza, Carol Franco, Philip Lawn, John Talberth, Tim Jackson, and Camille Aylmer. 2013. "Beyond GDP: Measuring and Achieving Global Genuine Progress." *Ecological Economics* 93 (September): 57–68.

Lawn, Philip A., and Matthew Clarke, eds. 2008. *Sustainable Welfare in the Asia-Pacific: Studies Using the Genuine Progress Indicator*. Cheltenham: Edward Elgar.

Mazzucato, Mariana. 2018. *The Value of Everything: Making and Taking in the Global Economy*. New York: Public Affairs.

Menegaki, Angeliki. 2018. "The Basic, the Solid, the Site-Specific and the Full or Total Index of Sustainable Economic Welfare (ISEW) for Turkey." *Economies* 6, no. 2 (April): 24.

Neumayer, Eric. 1999. "The ISEW: Not an Index of Sustainable Economic Welfare." *Social Indicators Research* 48, no. 1 (September): 77–101.

– 2010. *Weak versus Strong Sustainability: Exploring the Limits of Two Opposing Paradigms*. 3rd ed. Cheltenham: Edward Elgar.

– 2012. "Human Development and Sustainability." *Journal of Human Development and Capabilities* 13, no. 4 (July): 561–79.

New Economics Foundation. 2016. "Happy Planet Index 2016: Methods Paper." London: New Economics Foundation.

New Zealand Treasury. 2019. "CBAx Tool User Guidance: Guide for Departments and Agencies Using Treasury's CBAx Tool for Cost Benefit Analysis." https:// treasury.govt.nz/sites/default/files/2019-09/cbax-guide-sep19.pdf.

Nordhaus, William D., and James Tobin. 1972. "Is Growth Obsolete?" In *Economic Research: Retrospect and Prospect*, vol. 5: *Economic Growth*, edited by William D. Nordhaus and James Tobin, Chapter 1, 1–80. Cambridge: National Bureau of Economic Research.

OECD. 2020. *How's Life?* Paris: OECD. https://stats.oecd.org/Index .aspx?datasetcode=HSL.

O'Mahony, Tadhg, Paula Escardó-Serra, and Javier Dufour. 2018. "Revisiting ISEW Valuation Approaches: The Case of Spain Including the Costs of Energy Depletion and of Climate Change." *Ecological Economics* 144 (February): 292–303.

Ostergaard-Klem, Regina, and Kirsten L.L. Oleson. 2014. "GPI Island Style: Localizing the Genuine Progress Indicator to Hawaii." *Environmental Practice* 16, no. 3: 182–93.

Ryder, Guy. 2018. "Correctly Valuing the Work of the Future." *Journal of International Affairs* 72, no. 1 (Fall/Winter): 23–36.

Schröter, Matthias, Thomas Koellner, Rob Alkemade, Sebastian Arnhold, Kenneth J. Bagstad, Karl-Heinz Erb, Karin Frank, et al. 2018. "Interregional Flows of Ecosystem Services: Concepts, Typology and Four Cases." *Ecosystem Services* 31 (June): 231–41.

Sen, Amartya. 1999. *Development as Freedom*. New York: Oxford University Press.

Stewart, Frances. 2014. "Against Happiness: A Critical Appraisal of the Use of Measures of Happiness for Evaluating Progress in Development." *Journal of Human Development and Capabilities* 15, no. 4 (May): 293–307.

Stiglitz, Joseph E., Jean-Paul Fitoussi, and Martine Durand. 2018. *Beyond GDP: Measuring What Counts for Economic and Social Performance*. Paris: OECD.

Stiglitz, Joseph E., Amartya Sen, and Jean-Paul Fitoussi. 2010. *Mismeasuring Our Lives: Why GDP Doesn't Add Up*. New York: The New Press.

Suh, Jooyeoun, and Nancy Folbre. 2016. "Valuing Unpaid Child Care in the US: A Prototype Satellite Account Using the American Time Use Survey." *Review of Income and Wealth* 62, no. 4 (December): 668–84.

Talberth, John, Clifford Cobb, and Noah Slattery. 2007. "The Genuine Progress Indicator 2006: A Tool for Sustainable Development." Oakland: Redefining Progress.

Talberth, John, and Michael Weisdorf. 2017. "Genuine Progress Indicator 2.0: Pilot Accounts for the US, Maryland, and City of Baltimore 2012–2014." *Ecological Economics* 142 (December): 1–11.

UNDP. 2020. *Human Development Report 2020*. New York: United Nations Development Program.

World Commission on Environment and Development. 1987. *Our Common Future*. Oxford: Oxford University Press.

Worstall, Tim. 2014. "The Problems with Using GPI Rather than GDP." *Forbes*, 5 June 2014. https://www.forbes.com/sites/timworstall/2014/06/05 /the-problems-with-using-gpi-rather-than-gdp/#1a4694a752a5.

Appendix 8.1: Methods Used in the Utah Genuine Progress Indicator Study

The Utah GPI study for the 1990–2007 period retains the methodology used in studies conducted in the United States by Anielski and Rowe (1999) and Talberth, Cobb, and Slattery (2007), while updating some methods based on the availability of new data (e.g., time-use and ecosystem value data), introducing new methods (such as estimating the value of available ecosystem functions, as opposed to their loss from a distant benchmark year), and adding the value of locally relevant ecosystems (such as desert grasslands and scrublands). See Berik and Gaddis (2011) for a detailed description of the rationale, data, and methodology of the Utah GPI study. The report and data spreadsheet are available at http://www.utahpopulation.org/our-projects /genuine-progress-indicator/.

Components	Contributor or detractor from economic welfare	Brief description of methodology
Personal consumption expenditure (PCE)		Start with US consumption data; use the Utah–US consumption ratio from Environmental Systems Research Institute (ESRI) data to obtain an estimate of consumption for Utah; deduct the percentage of tobacco, alcohol, and food as harmful to health per Lawn (2003) (deduction amounts to 3 per cent lower PCE in 2007)
Income inequality	Negative	PCE (1/income distribution index-1) where the income distribution index = Gini coefficient in current year/Gini coefficient for reference year (1970, the lowest Gini on record in the US Population Census)
Income inequality-adjusted personal consumption		PCE/income distribution index

(*Continued*)

Components	Contributor or detractor from economic welfare	Brief description of methodology
Net value of consumer durables	Positive/negative	Use ESRI consumption data for Utah. Calculate the annual service value of durables purchased in a given year and deduct spending on consumer durables (negative values observed, suggesting acceleration of built-in obsolescence)
Public infrastructure services (streets and highways)	Positive	Annual service value of Utah roads = Utah–US mileage ratio x US stock value of roads x 75 per cent of vehicle miles for non-commuting x 10 per cent (= 2.5 per cent depreciation + 7.5 per cent interest rate)
Net capital investment	Positive	Scaled down from US data; change in the value of built capital stock over and above that needed to maintain a constant capital–labour ratio
Household work	Positive	Based on American Time Use Survey (ATUS), identify the number of housework and care labour hours of employed, unemployed, and out-of-the-labour-force women and men x the hourly wage rate of housekeepers and maids and housekeeping cleaners in the state
Volunteer work	Positive	Weight population by education level (assumption: more educated provide more volunteer labour) x the hourly wage for volunteer labour reported for the state

Components	Contributor or detractor from economic welfare	Brief description of methodology
Underemployment	Negative	Measures social cohesion erosion, in some cases captured by crime or divorce. Measured by earnings forgone by the underemployed = numbers who worked involuntarily fewer hours in the March CPS x hours they could not provide (i.e., hours of full-time, year-round [FTYR] worker – underemployed hours) x hourly wage for Utah
Lost leisure time	Negative	Measures overwork experienced by those employed FTYR. Based on ATUS, calculate value of lost leisure time = number of FTYR workers x lost leisure hours x hourly wage. (Lost leisure = Benchmark 2,800 leisure hours in US in 1969 – [total disposable hours per year (5475)] – paid work hours of FTYR – unpaid care work hours of employed workers). Hourly wage is weighted by 1.28 based on the assumption that fully employed workers value one leisure hour more than a paid-work hour)
Commuting	Negative	Sum of cost of driving one's own vehicle (= miles driven to job x mileage reimbursement rate) + cost of commuting time (Utah hours from ATUS x Utah hourly wage) + public transit fares

(Continued)

Components	Contributor or detractor from economic welfare	Brief description of methodology
Crime	Negative	Direct costs of crime + indirect costs (crime prevention) based on Utah data on number of violent and property crimes; US cost per crime data based on victim cost estimates in crime studies
Motor vehicle accidents	Negative	Direct costs (property damage and health care expenses) + indirect costs (value of lost life and lost wage associated with injury and death) based on data on total fatalities, injuries, and crashes involving property damage
Family breakdown	Negative	Cost of setting up new households after divorce + cost of excessive television viewing in families with children (more than two hours per day)
Pollution abatement	Negative	Household spending to reduce or dispose of pollution from automobile emissions, wastewater treatment, solid waste disposal (using ESRI data for Utah)
Water pollution	Negative	Water impairment data for four primary designated water uses in Utah x per-capita value of beneficial uses (based on US estimates)
Air pollution	Negative	Emissions data on six major pollutants for Utah x damage cost estimates per unit ton of each type of pollutant produced, estimated for each county in the United States

Components	Contributor or detractor from economic welfare	Brief description of methodology
Noise pollution	Negative	Average damage cost per person scaled down from US estimates for urban areas x urban population in Utah
Wetland services	Positive	Wetland acreage in Utah x wetland value per acre for the western United States (value based on various types and functions of wetlands)
Farmland services	Positive	Farmland acreage in Utah x the option value of preserving agricultural land for the future (option value = market value of conservation easements in Utah)
Forest services	Positive	Forest acreage in Utah x forest value per acre for the western United States (value based on various forest types and functions)
Desert grassland and scrubland services	Positive	Grassland and scrubland acreage in Utah x value per acre for the western United States (value based on various grassland types and functions)
Non-renewable energy resource depletion	Negative	Total consumption of each energy source (coal, natural gas, petroleum, electricity) x the cost per unit of energy consumed (based on the replacement cost approach, namely, the assumption that the cost of replacing the particular resource with renewable energy is established at the point of consumption)

(*Continued*)

Components	Contributor or detractor from economic welfare	Brief description of methodology
Ozone depletion	Negative	US cost per ton ozone-depleting chemicals emitted x per-capita emissions in Utah
Climate change (carbon emissions)	Negative	Carbon emissions from consumption in Utah (metric tons of carbon emitted per dollar of each category of consumption from ESRI) x global cost of carbon estimates (a median value per ton from a meta study of the cost of carbon)

Note: The signs reflect the estimated values in the Utah study.

9 Measuring What Matters: Policy Applications in New Zealand

TIM NG[1]

Introduction

This chapter describes New Zealand's experience thus far in developing and using well-being measures to strengthen central government policymaking processes. New Zealand is a developed country of 5 million people, with a substantial Indigenous (Māori) population. New Zealanders have a long tradition of debating big questions about the role of policy in promoting social, environmental, and economic well-being. And increasingly, the country's bicultural governance foundations, as expressed in the Treaty of Waitangi of 1840, are finding expression in the form, substance, and conduct of public affairs.

With this social and political background, it is perhaps natural that New Zealand should be a locus for developing policy practice about the multiple dimensions of, and perspectives on, well-being. The chapter contributes to the literature by focusing on the issues involved in translating well-being thinking into actual policy practice. There appears to be less documentation of practical experience in the well-being policy field, compared to the literature on conceptual definitions and measurement of well-being. This situation probably reflects that the practice itself is still emerging (Durand 2018; Exton and Shinwell 2018; Durand and Exton 2019).

The well-being framework with associated measures we look at is the New Zealand Treasury's Living Standards Framework (LSF). This framework features a "dashboard" of indicators and data, as well as tools and heuristics to support their use in producing policy advice. The primary users are Treasury analysts, who are part of the civil service in a parliamentary democracy. The framework and measures support and make more systematic their function, which is to provide policy advice to support stability and strong longer-term economic and social performance.

The framework and its tools were applied explicitly by the New Zealand Government as a core part of its "Wellbeing Budget" in 2019. The New Zealand

Government and the Treasury intend both to develop the framework and to broaden and deepen its application over coming years, to cover a range of other government policy processes (Robertson 2019; The Treasury 2018d).

The rest of the chapter proceeds as follows. The next section looks at the motivations for, and influences on, the development of the LSF. The following section briefly summarizes the framework and its associated tools. Then the next section discusses applications and impacts to date, particularly the 2019 Wellbeing Budget. The following section discusses the limits and challenges faced thus far and learnings for the further development and application of the framework, and the last section concludes.

Motivations: The Strategic Context in New Zealand

The Treasury's work on living standards has been influenced by many strands of thinking related to well-being, as well as changing economic and social circumstances. The work emerged against the background of vigorous debate about the role of public policy in promoting economic growth and well-being, following a major economic disruption and subsequent far-reaching reforms to government administration in New Zealand several decades ago. More recently, the Treasury has drawn ideas from academic literature, among other sources, that seek to reframe or reconfirm public policy's ultimate purpose in terms of a multifaceted conception of human well-being or flourishing (e.g., Fleurbaey 2009; Stiglitz, Sen, and Fitoussi 2009). Finally, the work is a practical response to critiques that traditional policy approaches are insufficient to confront complex contemporary challenges, such as rapid technological change, growing social disconnection and disparities, environmental degradation and climate change (e.g., Briassoulis 2004; Candel and Biesbroek 2016; Howlett and Vince 2017).

In the mid-1980s, New Zealand experienced a macroeconomic and political crisis. The response to the crisis included market-oriented structural, monetary, fiscal, and administrative reforms, which were implemented over roughly a decade (Evans et al. 1996; Dalziel 2002). The merits of the reforms in terms of their impact on economic performance and social conditions continue to be debated, while the broad principles of the reforms have been maintained by successive governments.

The reform period punctuated, and possibly invigorated, an ongoing debate in New Zealand about the appropriate mix of market-oriented and administrative approaches to public policy. This debate was stimulated by extensive public consultations as part of a Royal Commission report on Social Security in New Zealand in 1972 and a Royal Commission on Social Policy in 1988 (Barnes and Harris 2011).

Against this background, the New Zealand government has sought over the years to bring measurement to this debate. Various indicator sets have been produced, measuring social and environmental conditions, to complement conventional measures of economic performance based on market activity. In a report on the relevance of the experience of the Nova Scotia Genuine Progress Index to New Zealand, Colman (2004) reviewed over a hundred indicator projects for various countries and international organizations and suggested that in the early 2000s New Zealand was "far ahead of most countries in measuring social wellbeing" (150).

The Treasury was among the government agencies contributing to this thinking during that period (for example, see Jacobsen et al. 2002). Since then, it has conducted a range of work to develop practical tools to give life to the concept of living standards and to connect the relevant measures to its analysts' day-to-day work. An ongoing challenge is to provide sufficiently rich tools to support the breadth of the Treasury's work. This work includes advice on the quality and impact of government spending and regulation; budget management and prioritization; and working with other agencies to develop policy responses to economic, social, or environmental issues.

At the heart of this strategy remains the principle that high living standards depend on strong economic performance. Market-oriented economic policies can powerfully lift living standards by enabling people to participate in labour markets, earn higher incomes for their households, and apply those incomes towards whatever well-being means for them. Well-crafted education, labour, and goods market policies, for example, have driven the strong association between incomes and well-being evident across the ages (Senik 2014). Development and maintenance of such policies will always be an important core government function.

While higher market incomes are a very powerful means to the end of higher well-being, they are nevertheless only a means. Being explicit about the ultimate well-being objectives of policy promotes clarity about the channels and markets through which potential interventions are expected to work and about the expected impacts on the various well-being dimensions.

For complex policy problems in particular, such clarity can reveal sharp tradeoffs and interdependencies across the impacts. These linked effects may be especially relevant in markets where the trajectories of production and consumption raise concerns about environmental and social sustainability or acceptability. Examples may include contention over the development of wilderness for farmland or housing, or deregulation of markets that may create new jobs at the expense of old ones, with attendant concerns about social dislocation. Problems like this raise questions about whether or how to improve existing market mechanisms (including with new markets), whether or how to compensate for the undesired effects of market mechanisms administratively (for example, with redistributive monetary transfers), and what the appropriate mix of responses across these choices in any particular case may be.

While formal well-being frameworks and measures can help keep track of multiple impacts associated with such different intervention options, they are of course not a panacea. They cannot in themselves resolve difficult tradeoffs across competing objectives. That will always require governments to exercise human judgment and to apply (contested) values. But by promoting more systematic and transparent consideration of those competing objectives by human actors, the frameworks can support a broader and longer-run orientation in deliberations.

Overview of the LSF

In the early 2010s the Treasury brought several elements of this thinking together under a single work program, the LSF. The framework drew on a wide range of expert sources for its conceptual underpinnings (Gleisner et al. 2012). Later more formal theoretical work aimed to integrate these different strands (Karacaoglu 2015). This formal treatment developed along with a focus on applicability to the needs and capabilities of Treasury analysts. These analysts have to deal with a wide range of policy problems and ministerial demands under time pressure, which puts a premium on heuristics and tools that are relatively simple and easy to use (see, e.g., Au and Karacaoglu 2015).

The LSF continues to develop as a high-level approach to measuring and analysing the fundamentals supporting the living standards or well-being of current and future generations. The framework uses the "stock and flow" approach from economics to cover several domains of current well-being (flows), the resources underpinning future well-being ("capitals" or stocks), and resilience (which can be seen as a property of the capitals in the face of risk). It also recognizes the salience for policy of the distribution and incidence of well-being outcomes and impacts across the population.

Figure 9.1 shows schematically the basic LSF concepts – twelve domains of current well-being, four capitals, risk/resilience, and distribution.

The LSF's measurement layer, the Dashboard, contains indicators for the current well-being domains and the four capitals, with demographic and spatial disaggregations. In the 2018 version, these indicators have been drawn mostly from a recently implemented broader set of well-being indicators – called Indicators Aotearoa New Zealand (StatsNZ n.d.), managed by New Zealand's official statistics agency, StatsNZ.

The 2018 version of the LSF closely resembles the taxonomy and indicator counterparts in the OECD's *Better Life Initiative*. This choice followed a survey (King, Huseynli, and MacGibbon 2018) of a range of international and New Zealand–specific "quality-of-life" frameworks, which found a high degree of similarity among the frameworks surveyed. The Treasury chose to draw mostly on the OECD's framework because it is oriented towards the needs of policy

Current Wellbeing

Civic engagement and governance
Cultural identity
Environment
Health
Housing
Knowledge and skills

Income and consumption
Jobs and earnings
Safety
Social connections
Subjective wellbeing
Time use

Distribution

Indicators of Future Wellbeing

Natural capital

Human capital

Social capital

Financial and Physical

Risk and resilience

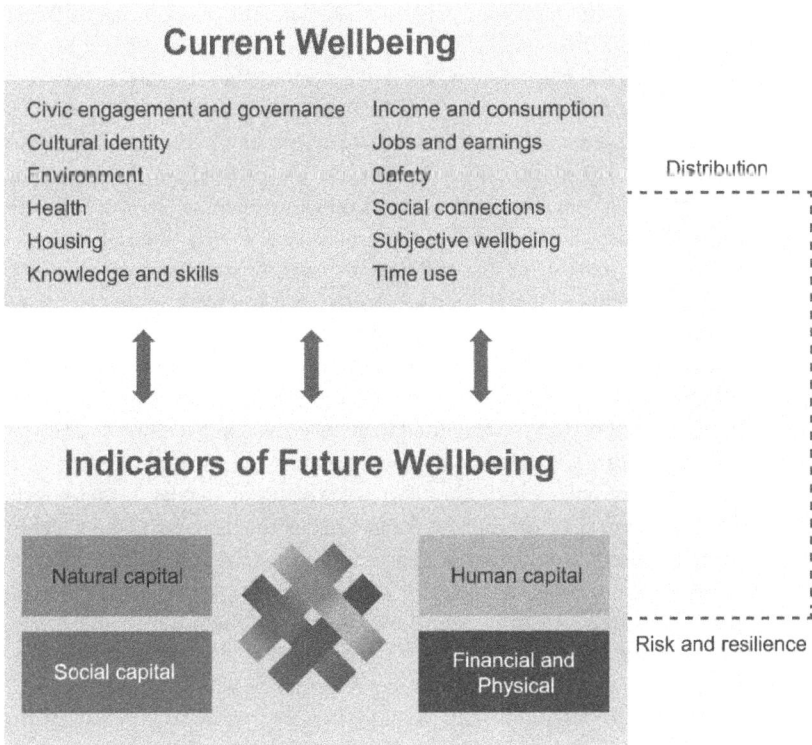

Figure 9.1. Wellbeing domains and key concepts in the 2018 Living Standards Framework

practitioners, including putting weight on international comparability in the choices of domains and indicators. Consultation with New Zealand experts followed with a view to ensuring applicability and fitness for the Treasury's needs.

As the Treasury is a New Zealand government agency, the concepts and domains needed to be broad enough to encompass the priorities, values, and philosophies of any future government the Treasury might expect to serve as an adviser. This meant adopting a multidimensional approach, rather than a single aggregate "index" measure – which would have required choosing relative weights for the domains, when these are contested and poorly identified. It also meant keeping the dashboard measures oriented towards medium-to-long-term national-level well-being outcomes. Finally, practical usability in the policy process was, as mentioned, a key objective across many of the design choices (Smith 2018; The Treasury 2018d).

In practice, the LSF and its associated tools are used primarily for diagnostic and proposal assessment purposes. The diagnostic use is in the development of advice about the most important economic, social, and environmental issues for the government's attention when setting its policy agenda. The use in proposal assessment is to help systematize advice about the impacts of different intervention options on the various well-being domains and capitals.

In the New Zealand government system, the Treasury leads the advice process on economic and fiscal policy and public-sector financial management (The Treasury 2018d). Other agencies lead on more specific "sectoral" policy areas (health, education, transport, environment, and so on). The LSF is therefore pitched at the "macro" or whole-economy level. It complements more disaggregated and granular sector-focused outcome frameworks maintained by the other public-sector agencies.

The framework and tools are, by design, not prescriptive or mechanistic about whether or how governments should intervene in response to any particular situation. Instead, they are intended to anchor fiscal and economic analysis to well-being outcomes, supported by the research evidence, and to guide analysts about the intervention logic they should be bringing to bear in their work. The ultimate success measure for the framework is the degree to which deliberation and decisions about spending and economic policy are more transparent, systematic, and targeted in terms of well-being objectives.

In this sense, the more explicit focus on intergenerational well-being means an enrichment, not a diminution, of the "traditional" finance ministry emphases on value for money, strong economic performance and productivity, fiscal prudence and macroeconomic stability. LSF concepts and measures augment the Treasury's relatively conventional and longstanding processes for macroeconomic forecasting and stabilization policy advice. System of National Accounts (i.e., GDP) concepts still have their place in macroeconomic analysis, as do generally accepted accounting principles (GAAP) in the reporting and analysis of government financial performance. The Treasury also administers and promotes the use of a range of social and non-monetary cost–benefit analysis processes founded on public economics disciplines (e.g., The Treasury 2015a, 2015b, 2018b).

The LSF brings together and organizes all these macro and micro analysis tools more consistently (The Treasury 2018e, 2018d) as part of the overall big task of identifying and prioritizing potential initiatives in a world of scarce resources. All the tools emphasize the use of clear assumptions that may be questioned and varied for better understanding the circumstances and choices the government faces. The approach can be understood as a way of promoting "policy coherence," or "harnessing synergies, managing trade-offs and policy conflicts, and addressing the potential ... intergenerational policy effects of domestic ... action" (OECD 2018, 3). The next section gives examples of how this was applied in the government's annual budget development and allocation process for 2019.

Impacts

As part of the process of developing the LSF, the Treasury has been road-testing various elements of it as it has evolved, in a range of work. It functions primarily as a heuristic device to help Treasury staff in their day-to-day work as they assess and advise on the well-being implications of economic, social, and environmental circumstances and on potential policy responses. More recently the framework has been used to support strategic economic and fiscal ("value for money") assessment work. In 2013, as part of the process of briefing the incoming government, the Treasury's assessment of the medium-term challenges and opportunities for New Zealand's economic performance, *Holding On and Letting Go*, used prosperity, inclusion and sustainability as organizing concepts and referred to the key elements of the LSF (The Treasury 2014). In 2016's *Statement on the Long-Term Fiscal Position*, the four capitals were used to organize discussion of the condition of, and outlook for, the economic, social, human, and environmental resource stocks in New Zealand. This approach reflected the role of the capitals in supporting productivity, economic performance and hence long-term fiscal sustainability (The Treasury 2016). Most recently, the 2018 *Investment Statement*, which reported on the state of the government's balance sheet and issues in public asset management, used the framework to extend the assessment beyond traditional metrics of the government's financial position and performance (the debt and deficit position) and considered as well the contribution of the government balance sheet and asset management to living standards (The Treasury 2018c).

The Treasury's regular assessment tools and guidance for public-sector financial management have also been adapted to incorporate LSF concepts. These tools include "Better Business Cases" guidance (The Treasury 2015a), a *Guide to Social Cost-Benefit Analysis* (The Treasury 2015b), and an associated spreadsheet model, "CBAx." The CBAx model helps analysts to quantify expected monetary and non-monetary impacts of spending proposals, projected over a horizon of up to fifty years. The user can monetize non-monetary impacts using a standardized lookup table of monetary values linked to evidence, if the user believes that would be informative to the analysis (The Treasury 2018b).

The Treasury used this tool in its business case analysis of a proposal to invest in the regeneration of a deprived neighbourhood, eastern Porirua in Wellington (Little 2019). Parts of Porirua are very deprived, with substantial quantities of aging public state houses, a significant gang presence, high levels of crime and very poor health and education outcomes. The business case identified a wide range of fiscal, economic, and well-being impacts of the investment proposal and quantified and monetized these benefits (to the government and to eastern Porirua residents), drawing on independent evidence about the monetized values. Quantified impacts (which did not include all identified impacts) included reduced hospitalizations from better housing and associated benefits from increased productivity and higher earnings from better education.

These tools and guidance instruments have been in place for some years. CBAx, for example, was used in two budgets before the 2019 Wellbeing Budget. Their alignment with LSF concepts has occurred progressively. They are practical examples of how well-being measures and concepts can be incorporated as a "common language" into analysts' day-to-day work and into public policy discourses. The intent is that they thereby become more familiar and drive uptake of well-being evidence into the policy process.

A common empirical language about well-being, including impact valuations, offers two main benefits. First, the improved consistency and transparency from the common language and concepts can help departments with different mandates and objectives work together better towards the common cause of improved national well-being. Second, it should facilitate comparison across competing initiatives for the purposes of prioritization and allocation of government effort and resources.

The broad scope of the language should also prompt analysts to take longer-term and richer views of the impacts of initiatives. The CBAx model, for example, encourages users to project costs and benefits out over a long horizon of fifty years. This long-term framing should, for some initiatives, bring into play impacts that might materialize only in the longer term but be nevertheless substantial. Or impacts may be considered that are beyond an agency's normal purview – "breaking down the silos," a goal often aspired to by scholars and practitioners of public policy. Such long-term and remote impacts might not be considered by an analyst in developing an initiative, were it not for the template or process encouraging such consideration. Examples might be longer-term mental health benefits that could arise from effective early education programs, or community engagement and resilience benefits derived from quality housing amenities.

Thinking of the framework's value as a heuristic applies equally to the use of monetization. Some audiences are hostile to monetization on the grounds that it encourages commodification of "priceless" aspects of life. The benefit of monetization is that it provides a common unit (for example, NZ dollars) with which outcomes on well-being dimensions that are typically measured in different units (say, level of education and years of healthy life expectancy) can be compared. Of course, this is not to diminish the contentious moral questions about whether it is appropriate to compare across some dimensions at all (e.g., where certain rights to safety and security are involved). Users also need to be conscious of the scientific limits to how reliably some impacts can be monetized. Because of these issues, the CBAx guidance urges pragmatism and caution in the use of monetization (The Treasury 2015b, 2018b).

Supporting the New Zealand Government's 2019 Well-Being Budget

In 2017 the work on the LSF, and especially its practical application, sharply accelerated as a result of the incoming government's announced intention not only to develop and use broader "measures of success" but also to embed well-being as an organizing principle throughout its policy program (Ardern 2017). The government was formed through a coalition agreement between the New Zealand Labour Party and the New Zealand First Party, and a confidence and supply agreement between the New Zealand Labour Party and the Green Party of Aotearoa New Zealand.

The new government stated that it would

> be a government of inclusion. All who live in this country are entitled to respect and dignity; all are entitled to live meaningful lives; all are entitled to care and compassion. Everyone should have a roof over their head and be warm in winter. Everyone should have food and a table to put it on … [the government] will lift up those who have been forgotten or neglected, it will take action on child poverty and homelessness, it will restore funding to education and the health systems to allow access for all, it will protect the environment and take action on climate change, and it will build a truly prosperous nation and a fair society, together. (Ardern 2017)

The government's description of its orientation and values could be mapped straightforwardly onto the LSF, which probably facilitated the connection of its policy program to key LSF dimensions, such as sustainability, an intergenerational orientation, and distribution.

The role of government agencies working more coherently together to address the thematic issues the parties in government had identified on the campaign trail was subsequently elaborated by the minister of finance (Robertson 2019). The government's intended reforms in this area constitute an extensive, multi-year program. They include legislative change to government and official reporting requirements about well-being (via the Public Finance Act), governance arrangements for the state sector (via the State Sector Act), and changes in the processes by which government agencies develop policy advice and deliver government services (Robertson 2019). In response to the government's intention to use the LSF in its well-being-oriented policy agenda and particularly the 2019 budget process, the Treasury released a number of discussion papers elaborating on the LSF thinking and concepts. It also developed the Dashboard for use in the budget policy process, and subsequently released the Dashboard publicly at the end of 2018 (The Treasury 2018d).

The 2019 Wellbeing Budget used the LSF and its measures explicitly in diagnosis and proposal assessment. First, LSF analysis was used as part of the government's setting of priorities and themes for the budget. These priorities and themes framed the guidance given to government agencies at the start of the initiative development process. Second, as proposed spending initiatives were developed and submitted by agencies, the LSF was used as part of the process of assessing and ranking them for the purposes of final budget allocations (New Zealand Government 2019).

The final budget priorities were decided based on information from the LSF Dashboard along with other expert evidence and input from government agencies. The five priorities, discussed below, were set out in the *Budget Policy Statement* (Robertson 2018), a high-level strategic document that the Public Finance Act requires the government to publish several months ahead of the budget itself. They were also incorporated into guidance issued to agencies setting out the process and parameters for developing initiatives, which also stated the criteria against which they would be assessed (The Treasury 2018a). This guidance was issued about eight months before the budget release itself in May 2019. While this length of lead time is not atypical of budget processes in New Zealand, one impact of using the LSF as a framing device early in the guidance stage was that it supported and gave focus to the government's desire for a more collaborative and well-being outcome–focused development of the priorities by ministers. This contributed to greater coherence in the eventual packages of initiatives and a clearer line of sight from the packages to the priorities (New Zealand Government 2019).

The priorities were reiterated in slightly modified form in the Wellbeing Budget (Table 9.1; New Zealand Government 2019, 6). The assessment of well-being circumstances and prospects using the LSF measures and other evidence to support the prioritization process was also described in a new chapter in the budget document, the "Wellbeing Outlook," which was expressly intended to supplement the macroeconomic and fiscal outlooks that typically feature in budget papers.

When agencies submitted their proposed initiatives for assessment, they were required to link the claimed impacts of their initiatives to LSF concepts where applicable. Agencies were also required to describe how they had collaborated with related agencies in the development of their initiatives. These elements were new for Budget 2019 and supplemented existing information requirements for initiative bids. Agencies are typically required to set out the underlying intervention logic, analysis of options for intervention, evidence supporting the claimed impacts, and how the initiatives would be implemented and evaluated. The intent of adding the new elements was to reinforce the budget's emphasis on an approach transcending agency boundaries and to promote comprehensive, balanced, and comparable assessments of intergenerational well-being implications across the proposed initiatives.

Table 9.1. 2019 Wellbeing budget priorities

Taking Mental Health Seriously – Supporting mental wellbeing for all New Zealanders, with a special focus on under 24-year-olds
Improving Child Wellbeing – Reducing child poverty and improving child wellbeing, including addressing family violence
Supporting Māori and Pasifika Aspirations – Lifting Māori and Pacific incomes, skills and opportunities
Building a Productive Nation – Supporting a thriving nation in the digital age through innovation, social and economic opportunities
Transforming the Economy – Creating opportunities for productive businesses, regions, iwi [Indigenous Māori tribes] and others to transition to a sustainable and low-emissions economy

Through the Wellbeing Budget process, the government decided on packages of initiatives (both spending and non-spending) corresponding to each of the five priorities. The packages for 2019 grouped operating and capital initiatives from a range of agencies and sectors under each priority, illustrating the government's use of the multidimensional approach and the requirement for agencies and ministers to collaborate on the development of packages. Some packages were highlighted with a "Wellbeing Approach in Action" narrative describing this approach (for example, packages targeting improved mental health, reduced family and sexual violence, and improved land-use practices).

The package responding to the priority relating to reduced child poverty and improved child well-being was perhaps the most notable example of the government's intentions to use intergenerational well-being principles in designing its intervention strategies, with new legislative accountability and reporting requirements. Under these new requirements, each budget appropriation bill must include a report discussing progress made in reducing child poverty, measured against short- and medium-term targets the government must set and publish. The government must also report the impact of the budget measures on child poverty. The Wellbeing Budget documentation accordingly included such reporting, including modelling of the impacts of earlier tax and transfer system initiatives, some new income support initiatives in Budget 2019, and qualitative discussion of other measures it viewed as relevant to the reduction of child poverty.

Reflections, Learnings, and Issues

As has been discussed above, the Treasury's (2018d) overarching aim for the LSF is to improve the policy advice process, and ultimately policy decisions, by strengthening the use of well-being evidence and by increasing transparency and coherence about how well-being considerations have informed the advice. The government's Wellbeing Budget 2019 process and documentation, and prior to that the strategic documents produced by the Treasury, show the progressive use of explicit well-being outcomes and (in the case of the Wellbeing Budget) measures derived from the framework. The government changed the production process for the Wellbeing Budget to enable well-being evidence to inform various stages of its development and provided an extensive narrative linking budget funding decisions and packages of initiatives to well-being priorities. The Budget 2019 process also highlighted how the framework can assist with prioritization and comparison of the relative value of initiatives by promoting more consistency and transparency about the meaning of "value for money" in a government context.

There has thus been a clear impact from the framework and measures on the process of decision-making, at least. The extent to which these process changes led to actual better decisions themselves is an empirical question requiring time for the relevant evidence to accumulate. More-thorough analysis is needed that controls for the effects of other factors influencing decision-making and outcomes. More time is also needed to develop and embed the underlying science in the evidence and policy system. More experience will improve understanding of how these advances can have the greatest chance of substantially and durably improving decisions by governments pursuing higher intergenerational well-being for New Zealanders.

The framework and its use thus far were evaluated as part of the OECD's member country survey process in 2019 (OECD 2019), which provided some insights into how the framework might evolve to have greater impact on the quality of policy decisions in terms of well-being. The OECD emphasized a number of conceptual and data gaps. The Treasury intends to address these in connection with the development of StatsNZ's Indicators Aotearoa New Zealand. The survey also suggested work on developing the framework together with other parts of the New Zealand public sector and stakeholders more widely. This was seen as necessary to strengthen support in the sector and greater coherence across outcomes frameworks used by agencies, broadening the ownership of the common well-being language. This work should also improve the public sector's collective understanding of the impact of the range of government policy levers on well-being outcomes.

The OECD also suggested that the roles and purposes of different indicators and government agency frameworks needed to be addressed to make the New Zealand well-being policy system itself more coherent. As noted above, the LSF and Dashboard are intended to support Treasury analysis of medium- to longer-term strategic issues pertaining to economic performance, and fiscal management for higher living standards. The sorts of well-being outcome measures appearing in the LSF thus tend to be relatively slow moving and subject to a range of diffuse influences, not all of which are under the precise control of governments. But in addition to these measures, governments generally also want indicators to hold themselves to account for delivery and with which to report their activities and success, which will generally be rather different in character. Accountability-focused indicators will tend to be closer to output or intermediate outcome measures, such as those defining child poverty for the purposes of the Child Poverty Reduction Act (CPRA), which are likely to be under the direct influence of government policy. In each case, selecting indicators to be fit for purpose, and choosing the right organ of the state to do the reporting, are important to for public understanding and buy-in to the overall system.

The heuristic approach and use of models such as CBAx have helped to bring well-being thinking to Treasury analysts' assessment of proposals and spending initiatives and thereby to influence the policy-development process in the wider New Zealand government system. However, there are reasons to be humble in some areas. The practical usability of the tools is perhaps the key element of strengthening the role of well-being in policymaking. This is because usability is essential for broad uptake across the thousands (in New Zealand's case) of analytical staff carrying out the day-to-day business of policy development and analysis in governments.

A recent external review (Hogan, Clough, and Yeabsley 2018) of the CBAx tool found that it had improved the quality of analysis in terms of better problem definitions, explicit consideration of broad impacts and outcomes, greater use of quantitative analysis, and transparency in explanations of assumptions. This finding is encouraging in terms of the LSF's aim to promote a common language and systematic comparison across initiatives in terms of well-being outcomes.

However, the review also noted the limits to quantification and monetization as approaches to evaluating certain social and environmental outcomes, and evidence gaps more generally, in our understanding of what makes the most difference to well-being. The review recommended further work to support agencies on the quality of inputs and sensitivity analysis. It also urged realism about the uncertainties attached to results where causal evidence may be weak, or where it may be less credible to claim an ability to robustly compare quite different outcome areas against each other. These findings chime with Connell and Kubisch's (1995) review of experience from a wide range of social programs. That review suggested that identifying long-term outcomes (e.g., "robust physical and mental health") is relatively easy, whereas linking them causally to intermediate outcomes (e.g., physiological and psychological states) and then to avenues and options for government action (e.g., primary vs. acute care vs. education system policies) is more difficult. The difficulty reflects the complexity of the human systems at work, the plethora of statistically confounding factors, and an incomplete evidence base.

Increased uptake and impact on the policy process of well-being measures and tools also depend, of course, on the incentives facing relevant actors in the policy system. As noted, government agencies and their analysts typically face resourcing and capability constraints. If an analyst is uncertain about whether a proposal that is quite speculative will be approved, the analyst may be disinclined to explore the evidence and options in the long term and broad manner hoped for, especially for relatively complex public-policy issues. Simply counting the direct fiscal cost in dollars or evaluating impacts in terms of relatively well-characterized outcomes, such as incomes and jobs (i.e., the traditional fiscal analysis approach), may be the easier – but less potentially insightful – path.

Moreover, there are challenges for government agencies in considering impacts outside their own sector where other agencies have primary responsibility, and where the full range of relevant data and expertise may be distributed widely across the government system (as is typical). Overcoming this issue of achieving more coherent and efficient cross-agency policy processes is hardly a new conundrum (see, e.g., Arnaboldi, Lapsley, and Steccolini 2015; Diefenbach 2009). As the experience with the Wellbeing Budget and broader narrative of the current New Zealand government has shown, strong support from the prime minister and other senior ministers can substantially strengthen the impetus for greater sophistication and better results.

Consistent with the thrust of these findings and reflections, the Treasury has throughout the development of the LSF continued to emphasize the needs and circumstances of users, whether they be Treasury analysts, colleagues in the broader public sector, or government ministers. A focus on users helps ensure that the development and embedding of any framework is not impeded by lack of customers. In many cases engagement with users can also elicit valuable information about methodological, valuation, and other content choices (Bleys and Whitby 2015). The principle of user responsiveness has guided the evolution of the System of National Accounts and GAAP, and its value is evident in the durability and continued development of those measurement systems. Those experiences also offer the lesson that full maturation of major policy-oriented measurement systems generally takes decades because that is how long it takes for a system to adapt to feedback and experience from users.

Conclusion

This chapter has reviewed and discussed New Zealand's application of a multidimensional well-being outcomes framework, the LSF, in its development from concepts and measures to application in core government policy processes, including prioritization and the development, appraisal, and comparison of potential initiatives.

In its function as the economic and fiscal policy adviser to the government, the Treasury has focused on the practical usability of the framework, learning through usage itself. The framework continues to develop primarily as an internal Treasury policy toolkit. Most recently it has been applied to support the far-reaching intentions of the New Zealand government to reorient policy processes towards intergenerational well-being. The development of the measurement framework and indicators has certainly been an important part of this effort, and they have been necessary to provide empirical colour and specificity to the concepts in policy practice. But at least as much attention has been given to designing the framework and associated tools with the needs of users at the forefront.

The experience of using the LSF as part of the budget-management process suggests some scientific and institutional challenges to be overcome in the maturation of well-being policy practice. The LSF is at a relatively early stage of development, and potential enhancements will no doubt emerge as scientific knowledge about well-being and its measurement increases and as practical experience accumulates.

NOTE

1   The Treasury, New Zealand. This chapter does not represent policy advice. The views, opinions, findings, and conclusions or recommendations expressed in the chapter are strictly those of the author. They do not necessarily reflect the views of the New Zealand Treasury or the New Zealand government. The New Zealand Treasury and the New Zealand government take no responsibility for any errors or omissions in, or for the correctness of, the information contained in the chapter.

REFERENCES

Ardern, Jacinda. 2017. *Speech from the Throne*. New Zealand Government, 8 November 2017. https://www.beehive.govt.nz/speech/speech-throne-2017.

Arnaboldi, Michela, Irvine Lapsley, and Ileana Steccolini. 2015. "Performance Management in the Public Sector: The Ultimate Challenge." *Financial Accountability & Management* 31, no. 1: 1–22.

Au, J., and Girol Karacaoglu. 2015. "Using the Living Standards Framework: Update and Policy Examples." *New Zealand Sociology* 30, no. 3: 27–40.

Barnes, Jo, and Paul Harris. 2011. "Still Kicking? The Royal Commission on Social Policy, 20 Years On." *Social Policy Journal of New Zealand* Issue 37.

Bleys, Brent, and Alistair Whitby. 2015. "Barriers and Opportunities for Alternative Measures of Economic Welfare." *Ecological Economics* 117: 162–72.

Briassoulis, Helen. 2004. *Policy Integration for Complex Policy Problems: What, Why and How*. Paper for the 2004 Berlin Conference "Greening of Policies: Interlinkages and Policy Integration."

Candel, Jeroen, and Robbert Biesbroek. 2016. "Toward a Processual Understanding of Policy Integration." *Policy Sciences* 49: 211–31.

Colman, Ronald. 2004. *The Nova Scotia Genuine Progress Index: Insights for New Zealand*. Working Paper 08/04, Centre for Social Research and Evaluation, Ministry for Social Development.

Coryn, Chris L.S., Lindsay A. Noakes, Carl D. Westine, and Daniela C. Schroeter. 2011. "A Systematic Review of Theory-Driven Evaluation Practice From 1990 to 2009." *American Journal of Evaluation* 32, no. 2: 199–226.

Dalziel, Paul. 2002. "New Zealand's Economic Reforms: An Assessment." *Review of Political Economy* 14, no. 1: 31–46.

Diefenbach, Thomas. 2009. "New Public Management in Public Sector Organisations: The Dark Sides of Managerialistic 'Enlightenment'." *Public Administration* 87, no. 4: 892–909.

Durand, Martine. 2018. "Countries' Experiences with Wellbeing and Happiness Metrics." In *Global Happiness Report*. New York: Global Happiness Council.

Durand, Martine, and Carrie Exton. 2019. "Adopting a Wellbeing Approach in Central Government: Policy Mechanisms and Practical Tools." In *Global Happiness and Wellbeing Policy Report*. New York: Global Happiness Council.

Evans, Lewis, Arthur Grimes, Bryce Wilkinson, and David Teece. 1996. "Economic Reform in New Zealand 1984–95: The Pursuit of Efficiency." *Journal of Economic Literature* 34, no. 4: 1856–902.

Exton, Carrie, and Michal Shinwell. 2018. *Policy Use of Well-Being Metrics: Describing Countries' Experiences*. OECD: SDD Working Paper No. 94.

Fleurbaey, Marc. 2009. "Beyond GDP: The Quest for a Measure of Social Welfare." *Journal of Economic Literature* 47, no. 4: 1029–75.

Gleisner, Ben, Fiona McAlister, Margaret Galt, and Joe Beaglehole. 2012. "A Living Standards Approach to Public Policy Making." *New Zealand Economic Papers* 46, no. 3: 211–38.

Hogan, Sarah, Peter Clough, and John Yeabsley. 2018. *Review of CBA Advice to Support Budget Initiatives: The Impact of CBAx and Lessons for Future Budget Processes*. Wellington: NZIER.

Howlett, Michael, and Joanna Zofia Vince, and Pablo Del Rio. 2017. "Policy Integration and Multi-Level Governance: Dealing with the Vertical Dimension of Policy Mix Designs." *Politics and Governance* 5, no. 2: 2183–463.

Jacobsen, Veronica, Nicholas Mays, Ron Crawford, Barbara Annesley, Paul Christoffel, Grant Johnston, and Sid Durbin. 2002. *Investing in Well-Being: An Analytical Framework*. New Zealand Treasury Working Paper 02/23.

Karacaoglu, Girol. 2015. *The New Zealand Treasury's Living Standards Framework – Exploring a Stylised Model*. Treasury Working Paper 15/12, September.

King, Anita, Gulnara Huseynli, and Nairn MacGibbon. 2018. *Wellbeing Frameworks for the Treasury*. Living Standards Series: Discussion Paper 18/01.

Kuipers, Ben S., Malcolm Higgs, Walter Kickert, Lars Tummers, Jolien Grandia, and Joris Van der Voet. 2014. "The Management of Change in Public Organizations: A Literature Review." *Public Administration* 92, no. 1: 1–20.

Kurtz, C.F., and D.J. Snowden. 2003. "The New Dynamics of Strategy: Sense-Making in a Complex and Complicated World." *IBM Systems Journal* 42(3): 462–483.

Lange, Glenn-Marie, Quentin Wodon, and Kevin Carey, eds. 2018. *The Changing Wealth of Nations 2018: Building a Sustainable Future*. Washington, DC: World Bank Group.

Little, Struan. 2019. *What the Treasury's Living Standards Framework Means for the Public Sector*. Speech to the IPANZ Deloitte Public Sector Conference, 15 August 2019.

New Zealand Government. 2019. *Budget 2019: The Wellbeing Budget*. 30 May 2019.

OECD. 2019. *OECD Economic Surveys: New Zealand 2019*. 25 June 2019.

– 2018. *Policy Coherence for Sustainable Development 2018: Towards Sustainable and Resilient Societies*. OECD.

Robertson, Grant. 2018. *Budget Policy Statement*. December 2018.

– 2019. *Minister of Finance Wellbeing Budget Speech*. 30 May 2019.

Senik, Claudia. 2014. "Wealth and Happiness." *Oxford Review of Economic Policy* 30, no. 1: 92–108.

Smith, Conal. 2018. *Treasury Living Standards Dashboard: Monitoring Intergenerational Wellbeing*. June 2018.

StatsNZ. n.d. *Ngā Tūtohu Aotearoa: Indicators Aotearoa New Zealand*. https://wellbeingindicators.stats.govt.nz/.

Stiglitz, Joseph, Amartya Sen, and Jean-Paul Fitoussi. 2009. *Report by the Commission on the Measurement of Economic Performance and Social Progress*. September 2009.

The Treasury. 2014. *Holding On and Letting Go: Opportunities and Challenges for New Zealand's Economic Performance*. Wellington: New Zealand Treasury.

– 2015a. *Better Business Cases: Guide to Developing the Detailed Business Case*. 30 September 2015. Wellington: New Zealand Treasury.

– 2015b. *Guide to Social Cost Benefit Analysis*. July 2015. Wellington: New Zealand Treasury.

– 2016. *He Tirohanga Mokopuna: 2016 Statement on the Long-Term Fiscal Position*. Wellington: New Zealand Treasury.

– 2018a. *Budget 2019: Guidance for Agencies*. 19 September 2018. Wellington: New Zealand Treasury.

– 2018b. *CBAx Tool User Guidance: Guide for departments and agencies using Treasury's CBAx tool for cost benefit analysis*. September 2018. Wellington: New Zealand Treasury.

– 2018c. *He Puna Hao Pātiki: 2018 Investment Statement: Investing for Wellbeing*. Wellington: New Zealand Treasury.

– 2018d. *Our People, Our Country, Our Future: Living Standards Framework: Background and Future Work*. 4 December 2018.

– 2018e. *The Treasury Approach to the Living Standards Framework*. February 2018.

Weiss, Carol H. 1995. "Nothing as Practical as Good Theory: Exploring Theory-based Evaluation for Comprehensive Community Initiatives for Children and Families." In *New Approaches to Evaluating Community Initiatives*, Volume 1: *Concepts, Methods, and Contexts*, edited by J.P. Connell, A.C. Kubisch, L.B. Schorr, and C.H. Weiss. Washington, DC: The Aspen Institute.

Westley, Frances, and Nino Antadze. 2010. "Making a Difference: Strategies for Scaling Social Innovation for Greater Impact." *The Public Sector Innovation Journal* 15, no. 2: article 2.

PART THREE

Canadian Experiences and Perspectives

10 Beyond Dollars and Cents: The Canadian Index of Wellbeing and Nova Scotia Quality of Life Initiative

CLAY DASILVA AND ANDERS HAYDEN

Introduction

One of the main initiatives in Canada's beyond-GDP story is the Canadian Index of Wellbeing (CIW). Building on pioneering contributions from Canadian researchers and practitioners, work on the CIW began a decade before the Stiglitz-Sen-Fitoussi (2009) Commission's landmark international report and later attracted international attention as one potential model for similar initiatives. More recently, the CIW has been part of one of the most significant provincial well-being measurement efforts, the Quality of Life Initiative in Nova Scotia – a province with a rich recent history of non-governmental, beyond-GDP activity.

This chapter provides a brief overview of the CIW framework, its development and applications, before a more detailed examination of its use in the Nova Scotia Quality of Life Initiative. A section on background and motivations puts the Initiative in the context of the province's perceived status as an economic laggard, recent efforts to unite Nova Scotians around a renewed drive for economic growth, and parallel attempts to broaden the understanding of success in a way that recognizes Nova Scotia's quality-of-life advantages while engaging people in reshaping the province. Two main products of the Initiative are discussed, the 2018 Nova Scotia Quality of Life Index and the 2019 Quality of Life Survey, including plans to turn the findings into actions that improve quality of life. An initial assessment of impacts and prospects is provided, followed by consideration of obstacles on the path, including the vast differentials in power and influence within "one Nova Scotia."

The chapter builds on an earlier analysis of the CIW and other Canadian beyond-GDP efforts (Hayden and Wilson 2016). It draws on semi-structured interviews and personal communication with leading participants in the CIW and Quality of Life Initiative and some observers of them, as well as analysis of publicly available documents and related media reports.[1]

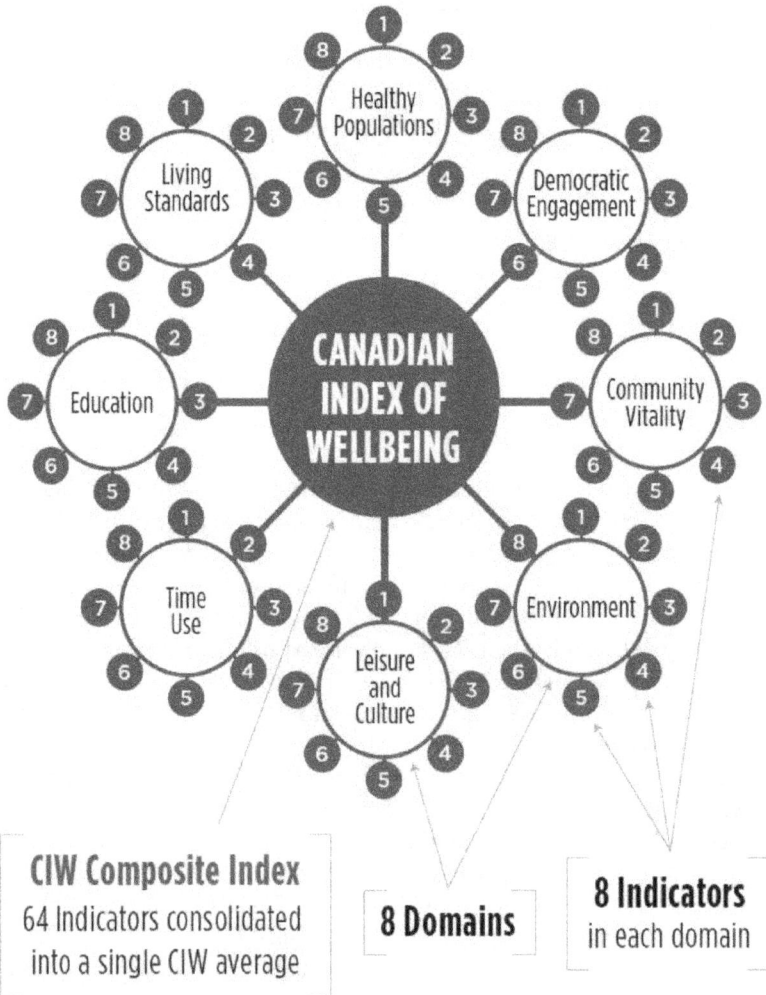

Figure 10.1. The Canadian Index of Wellbeing Framework

Source: Canadian Index of Wellbeing[3]

Canadian Index of Wellbeing

The CIW, produced by a team at the University of Waterloo led by Bryan Smale, is a composite index that aggregates sixty-four indicators[2] within eight domains. The CIW's working definition of well-being, which incorporates those domains, is the "presence of the highest possible quality of life in its full breadth of expression focused on but not necessarily exclusive to: good living standards, robust health, a sustainable environment, vital communities, an educated populace, balanced time use, high levels of democratic participation, and access to and participation in leisure and culture" (Smale, Gao, and Jiang 2020, 13).

The CIW was developed with input from many of Canada's leading thinkers in well-being and beyond-GDP measurement, with support from the Atkinson Charitable Foundation. In addition to drawing on expert and practitioner advice, multiple rounds of public consultation with Canadians about what they considered important to their quality of life and how to measure it, starting in 2000 (CPRN 2001), were central to developing the CIW's domains and selecting indicators.

To answer the question "How are Canadians *Really* Doing?" the CIW released national reports in 2011, 2012, and 2016, with another planned for 2022, as well as provincial reports in Ontario in 2014, Nova Scotia in 2018, and Saskatchewan in 2019 (see, e.g., CIW 2016; Engage and CIW 2018). A main finding has been that well-being, as measured by the Index, has not kept pace with GDP. Critics question the basis for such a comparison,[4] but Smale sees it mainly as a "conversation starter." The goal is to "engage people's curiosity and then we can expand on it and move to the dashboard and the particular indicators. ... The indicators are the things that people see as being more actionable."[5]

Earlier research found considerable disappointment among contributors to the development of the CIW, which had not lived up to hopes that it would "change the conversation around the water coolers of the nation" and be used by governments to measure progress and design policy (Hayden and Wilson 2016). Smale confesses that he was among those in the beyond-GDP movement guilty to some extent of the "indicators fantasy" that producing new well-being indicators – and having the CIW's prominent spokespeople promote them[6] – would inevitably lead governments to take notice and act on the information (see Hayden and Wilson, this volume). However, he now sees renewed grounds for optimism.[7]

As a general indicator of change, Smale says that when speaking to groups he no longer finds a need to convince them that GDP is an inadequate measure of social progress: "Everybody is on board. ... They're looking for the alternative already."[8] In addition, the CIW has seen particular growth in its community well-being work, having conducted well-being profiles and survey research for several municipalities and regions across the country, such as Oxford County, Ontario, which has used the CIW's community well-being survey to help measure progress on its community sustainability plan, and the Yukon government which is gathering well-being data across its territory. Meanwhile, the Ontario Trillium Foundation, a provincial government agency that distributes some $110 million annually, has used the CIW framework in its strategic plan and to inform grant-allocation decisions. The Alliance for Healthier Communities, an Ontario network of community-governed health care organizations, has also employed the CIW framework to guide its work, including expanding its focus from primary care to promoting a broader understanding of well-being and its social determinants (AOHC 2014). Finally, Smale has had discussions with federal government officials interested in how the CIW framework could inform investments in a well-being budget.

The CIW's community-level work has become, according to Smale, its most effective way of generating government interest. Rather than actively advocating government use of its framework, as in its early years, the CIW has recently had greater success through a "grassroots trickle-up effect," as federal interest in the CIW framework has followed hearing about its uses in communities across the country, as well as at the provincial level.[9]

The Nova Scotia Quality of Life Initiative

One of the CIW framework's main applications has been through the Nova Scotia Quality of Life Initiative, a multiyear collaborative project "focused on improving our understanding of our wellbeing and the actions that will improve it" (Engage 2020b, 2). The Initiative reflects the spirit of many other beyond-GDP efforts: "Traditionally, much of the information we use to make decisions that affect our daily lives is based on economic data. Those data are not wrong – they are just incomplete. With this Initiative, we are working to advance a comprehensive framework for measuring and improving the daily lives of all Nova Scotians" (Engage and CIW 2018, 3). The Initiative is led by Engage Nova Scotia, a non-profit organization, in conjunction with the CIW and a range of community partners, including the provincial and local governments, businesses, universities and colleges, and non-governmental organizations. It has included many public workshops and outreach events, the 2018 publication of the Nova Scotia Quality of Life Index (Engage and CIW 2018), and a large-scale Nova Scotia Quality of Life Survey in 2019 (Smale, Gao, and Jiang 2020).

Participation of local communities is a core element of the project, based on a philosophy and theory of change that recognizes the self-efficacy of individuals and their communities. The premise is that Nova Scotians actively *want* to "participate in making their province a better place to live," and often simply desire "more information and better tools to be effective." As such, the Quality of Life Initiative is designed to be collaborative and create a "middle space" where diverse actors come together to build a shared understanding of challenges and opportunities, while providing a "third way" that connects top-down and bottom-up approaches to social change.[10]

Background and Motivations

Considered a "have-not" province, Nova Scotia has long had a per-capita GDP well below the Canadian average, one of the country's highest poverty rates, a provincial budget heavily reliant on equalization payments and other federal transfers, an aging population, and difficulties retaining young people and attracting newcomers. Back in 2002, then opposition leader Stephen Harper linked Atlantic Canada's economic challenges to a "culture of defeat" – an idea that many Nova Scotians did not appreciate, but variations on the theme persisted in the province's political discourse. In addition, the province has long been marked by substantial inequalities, related to economic class, geographic region, and marginalization of Indigenous (mainly Mi'kmaq) and African Nova Scotian populations.

Despite all this, one study concluded that Nova Scotians were Canada's happiest people (Sharpe and Capeluck 2012). Other research showed that Atlantic Canada was the region with the highest life satisfaction, as non-economic factors – such as a stronger sense of community and provincial belonging, and trust in neighbours – more than compensated for lower incomes (Helliwell and Barrington-Leigh 2010).[11]

Against this backdrop, what would become Engage NS was initiated in mid-2012 by "a disparate group of social entrepreneurs, change-agents, business leaders, and advocates [who shared] an aspiration to help create a more vibrant, inclusive and resilient Nova Scotia."[12] Engage's (2020b, 4) mission came to be "to cultivate engagement, contribute to an evolving provincial narrative, and catalyze actions aimed at strengthening social cohesion and improving the quality of life for all Nova Scotians." Engage (2020c) is an "independent, non-profit" organization with its own governance board. That said, it has closer ties to government than most non-profits, making it something of a hybrid organization. It has benefitted from substantial funding from the province (among other sources) and secondment of government staff (Gorman 2015). While Engage is non-partisan, the Nova Scotia Liberal Party's former leader, Danny Graham, came to lead the organization as its chief engagement officer. Nancy Watson, previously with the province's Office of Policy and Priorities, became Engage's managing director.

Shortly after Engage began, Darrell Dexter's New Democratic Party government launched a conversation about the province's future. The Nova Scotia Commission on Building Our New Economy, chaired by Acadia University President Ray Ivany, began its work in fall 2012, with consultations on "the economic development opportunities and challenges facing the province" (Ivany et al. 2014, 2). By the time it delivered its report in 2014, Stephen McNeil's Liberal government, which continued to support the Commission's work, was in power.

The Ivany report's stark message began with its title: "Now or Never: An Urgent Call to Action for Nova Scotians." Its "core message" was that "Nova Scotia is today in the early stages of what may be a *prolonged period* of *accelerating population loss* and *economic decline*. These negative prospects are *not*, however, *inevitable or irreversible*" (Ivany et al. 2014, 3, emphasis in original). The report emphasized the imperative of uniting around the drive for economic growth, stating that "the single most significant impediment to change and renewal is the lack of a shared vision and commitment to economic growth and renewal across our province and among our key institutions and stakeholder communities" (vii). The agenda that it outlined combined many conventional neoliberal elements – e.g., private sector–led expansion, an orientation towards exports and competing globally, celebration of a culture of entrepreneurship, and restrained government spending to reduce the debt-to-GDP ratio – with progressive attitudinal changes to increase openness to immigration and reduce barriers facing First Nations and African Nova Scotians. The report mentioned "innovation" (or close variations) forty-one times, "attitude" thirty-seven times, "collaboration" thirty-seven times, and "inequality" not once (Bousquet 2017).

The OneNS dashboard was created to measure progress towards the commission's nineteen goals, with indicators for inter-provincial migration, international immigration, business start-ups, export value, labour-force participation, employment rate of First Nations and African Nova Scotians, venture capital, tourism expansion, net debt to GDP, among others.[13] This could be considered a beyond-GDP dashboard only in the narrowest sense: it includes many indicators other than GDP, but all of them – even those that many would consider important ends in themselves – are in this context a means towards the overriding goal of economic growth.

While Engage did play a role in continuing public engagement to support the Ivany Commission's work after it released its report (Gorman 2015), it came into being before the Commission and is a distinct entity. Engage has echoed some aspects of Ivany's call for change, notably attitudinal change, but the emphasis it places on key themes has differed from the Commission in some respects. Watson saw a need to "complement and expand" the Ivany report's incomplete message: "there was something missing" in its "totally economically oriented approach to fixing what was wrong with us."[14] Meanwhile, Graham referred to the Ivany report as a "seminal turning point for Nova Scotians" in becoming conscious of the need to find solutions to the province's longstanding issues but noted that disagreement remains about the exact strategies for moving forward. He stated that Engage's approach "builds upon where they have gone, but focuses greater attention on the need for 'inclusive economies' that are centred on leaving fewer people behind."[15]

Engage also put forward a more hopeful message about the province's strengths. Watson explained that in conversations with Nova Scotians, "We heard again and again that there was something distinct about this place and the people that perhaps wasn't being captured in the traditional narrative of a poor performing, hard-done-by province that had not lived up to its potential."[16] Or, borrowing a line from a well-known Scotiabank advertisement, "perhaps we're richer than we think" (Graham 2016; Watson 2018). Both Watson and Graham emphasized that some of Nova Scotia's strengths, which are not captured by conventional measures, are increasingly sought after today and worth protecting and promoting, such as strong social connections, connection to nature, work-time flexibility, and family time. "There are demonstrable advantages that exist in Nova Scotia that ... make it an attractive place," says Graham, who sees a quality-of-life emphasis as a way to attract both residents and investors.[17]

Engage's distinct approach was also evident in its submission to the Ivany Commission, which emphasized that "economic growth should not become a proxy for social progress or the advancement of wellbeing generally" – words included in Ivany's interim report, but not the final version (One Nova Scotia 2013; see also Graham 2016).[18]

In taking this position, Engage built on earlier efforts in Nova Scotia to look beyond GDP. Starting in 1997, GPI Atlantic produced a series of innovative reports calculating the true costs and benefits of economic and social activity (see Colman this volume; GPI Atlantic n.d.). Its work also included a community GPI survey, an initial effort to gather detailed quality-of-life data. This trail-blazing work increased awareness in the province of the limits of GDP and created a foundation for further beyond-GDP efforts.[19]

Through survey research in 2015, Engage found that Nova Scotians favoured looking beyond economic growth when tracking progress. When asked if "we should measure Nova Scotia's success by the growth in our economy," 68 per cent of respondents answered 7 or above on a 10-point scale. In contrast, 81 per cent gave a 7 or above to measuring success "by the improvement in our quality of life" (Engage 2015, 23). To do so, Engage opted to work with the CIW, attracted by a framework with a "broader, more comprehensive measure of success that didn't discount the importance of economic measures, but which included things that were more closely connected to people's daily lives and [that] we were hearing that people valued."[20]

Engage's work with the CIW has been "a matter of trying to expand the lens that we use to make decisions and to evaluate success," says Watson. With a more complete picture, "we'll be better equipped to make decisions that help everyone live a good life" (Graham, quoted in Vibert 2019). Engage hopes that the data gathering will result in "a substantial body of information that will help us all – at the local, regional and provincial level – work together with more up-to-date data to set priorities, build strategies and coordinate approaches to the opportunities identified" (Engage and CIW 2018, 16). Speaking more in terms of personal than organizational motivations, Graham stated that "I think it's clearer than ever that many of the beliefs that we had that drove our economy, that wrecked our environments, that created inequality need to be fixed, full stop. And the only way for us to do that well is to understand our challenges and our advantages and our opportunities at a richer level and to engage people more fully in the questions of our time" (quoted in Jess 2020).

Nova Scotia Quality of Life Index

One key product of the Initiative was *The Nova Scotia Quality of Life Index 1994–2014*, with twenty-one years of data on sixty of the CIW's sixty-four indicators, allowing an assessment of trends over time as well as comparisons between Nova Scotia and Canadian averages (Engage and CIW 2018). The report provided further evidence of some of the province's strengths and challenges. Domains in which Nova Scotia experienced more positive *trends* than Canada overall were the environment (due to improvements such as significant greenhouse gas reduction); time use (with favourable trends in the availability of flexible and regular work hours, commuting times, and feelings of time pressure), living standards (with positives including a larger decline in poverty and smaller increase in inequality than the rest of Canada), and leisure and culture (with declining provincial participation in arts, culture, social leisure, and volunteering, but an even steeper decline nationally).

Among the challenges evident in the data: regional disparities (with larger centres, notably Halifax, faring better economically), child poverty (affecting one in five children), youth retention (albeit with some initial indication of a recent reversal of the outflow of young people), mental health (30 per cent of Nova Scotians did not rate their mental health as "very good" or "excellent"), childcare (lack of progress in creating regulated daycare spaces), and personal relationships (declining numbers of people with five or more close friends).

Although some findings reinforced common perceptions, others revealed surprises, such as housing affordability. While Vancouver's and Toronto's stratospheric housing costs capture headlines, as of 2014, Nova Scotians spent "a higher proportion of their available incomes on rent, utilities, transportation, taxes and other shelter costs than anywhere else in the country" (Engage and CIW 2018, 13, 25).

Compared to the CIW's national reports, the Nova Scotia report put much less emphasis on the composite index than the underlying indicator dashboard (Engage and CIW 2018, 15). Nova Scotia's report did include a composite quality-of-life index – which rose 8.5 per cent from 1994 to 2014, compared to 9 per cent nationally – but relegated it to an appendix (Engage and CIW 2018, 65). Watson explained that Engage "shifted the emphasis away from the index approach." Although they understood that showing that the Index was not keeping pace with GDP could be effective in gaining attention, they had questions about the comparison's validity and, above all, "we wanted information that we could dive into, pull apart, and work with at a community or provincial level."[21]

Nova Scotia Quality of Life Survey

To get more fine-grained information, going beyond aggregate provincial figures to show variation within Nova Scotia, Engage and the CIW developed the Quality of Life Survey. Compared to the 2018 Index report, the survey had more emphasis on subjective levels of satisfaction with various aspects of well-being and with life in general. Engage invited 80,000 (one in five) Nova Scotian households to participate in the survey in May–June 2019. The response rate was high, at 16 per cent, with nearly 13,000 respondents completing the 230 questions, making it "the largest data-set of its kind in Canada" (Smale, Gao, and Jiang 2020, iii).

Initial results, released in March 2020, provided summary, descriptive statistics that illustrate geographic variation within the province. Overall, Nova Scotians report fairly high satisfaction with life in general (a mean, M, of 7.68 on a 10-point scale), with the Halifax Regional Municipality slightly below the mean despite higher average incomes in the province's largest city ($M = 7.61$) (Smale, Gao, and Jiang 2020, 279, see also 30). The Antigonish-Guysborough region had the highest life satisfaction ($M = 7.95$), which appeared to be linked to factors such as the lowest reported feelings of social isolation, highest percentage reporting good to excellent mental health, volunteering levels well above the provincial average (66.9 per cent vs. 52.1 per cent), and highest sense of belonging to one's community, although more statistical analysis is needed to confirm relationships among variables (Smale, Gao, and Jiang 2020, 44, 49, 68, 91).

Overall, three-quarters of Nova Scotians "are satisfied with their neighbourhood or community as a place to live (75.5%) and with its environmental quality (74.3%)" (Smale, Gao, and Jiang 2020, 12). Indeed, of the CIW's eight domains, "Nova Scotians are most satisfied with the Environment ($M = 5.33$ on a 7-point scale) and Community Vitality ($M = 4.83$)" (12). Very high numbers (88 per cent) agree that "there are plenty of opportunities to enjoy nature in the community where they live" (6). Among the positives in the community vitality domain are high levels of social connections and support, with Nova Scotians reporting an average of 5.84 close relatives, 4.86 close friends, and 4.17 neighbours from whom they could ask a favour (3); such forms of non-material wealth are known to have strong impacts on overall life satisfaction (e.g., Helliwell and Barrington-Leigh 2010).

Nova Scotians were least satisfied in the "democratic engagement" domain ($M = 3.88$ on a 7-point scale); for example, there was high agreement with the statement that "I do not think public officials care much what people like me think" ($M = 4.24$) (Smale, Gao, and Jiang 2020, 12, 109). Other challenges include: low percentages who rate the quality (19.5 per cent) and accessibility (13.3 per cent) of health care services in their community as very good or excellent (Smale, Gao, and Jiang 2020, 5); low levels of self-reported "work-life balance" ($M = 3.36$ on 7-point scale; Smale, Gao, and Jiang 2020, 10), running counter to the idea of a less stressed lifestyle in the province; serious issues of poverty and economic insecurity for a large minority of the population;[22] and a high percentage (40.7 per cent) expressing concern over inadequate supply of elder care services in their community (Smale, Gao, and Jiang 2020, 11).

One key question is what to make of all the data, only a small selection of which has been discussed above. Another is how to translate it into provincial and local government policies and actions by others in the community that improve quality of life. As Graham emphasizes, "This isn't a measurement exercise. This is a change exercise."[23]

Engage's efforts to interpret the data with its community partners and develop responses to it are informed by Otto Sharmer's Theory U (Scharmer 2009), explains Watson. Theory U "warns against the dangers of a group with a lot of raw information jumping too quickly 'across the U' to the point of crafting and implementing solutions. Instead, it encourages a long journey 'down the U' to deeply understand, consider, experiment with and perceive the information from multiple perspectives – a process that is rewarded with higher quality, better-aligned, longer-lasting outcomes."[24]

To avoid another report that "collects dust," local teams led by the Nova Scotia Community College have been established to analyse data in each of the province's ten regions, meet with local stakeholders and the public, and begin to set priorities for quality of life–boosting actions (Engage 2020a; Smale, Gao, and Jiang 2020, 2). Subsequent analysis identified six "critical issues" that the teams were concerned about exploring more deeply: social isolation, sense of community, feelings of trust, experience of discrimination, poverty, and health.[25] Smale noted that digging further into the data revealed some correlations that might have been expected – e.g., those most at risk of mental health problems, social isolation, or lack of access to health care tend to have lower incomes. Other findings were more surprising; while social isolation among older adults is a widespread concern, the survey found that a much higher proportion of those under forty feel socially isolated.[26]

Initial Impacts and Prospects

The Initiative's impacts will, of course, become clearer with time, but some initial observations are possible.

Watson argues that the Initiative's design – its process and structure – has been a success. The Initiative has sparked conversations in many communities involving individuals working in government, business, non-profits, academia, and the general public about shared challenges and opportunities. "The process itself is a core deliverable," she says, adding that it reflects values for "the kind of society and system of organizing ourselves that we were working towards": collaborative, iterative, diverse, inclusive, and decentralized.[27]

Beyond the process itself, it is still early to see impacts on policy choices, as the initiative has yet to advance far enough to be able to inform the various steps of policy development.[28] Nevertheless, signs of government interest are evident. In addition to the provincial government's funding of the work, it has been keen on departments gaining access to the data,[29] reflecting a wider interest within the provincial bureaucracy in measurement of results.

The province's Office of Strategy Management (OSM) has been engaged and interested in the Initiative's work.[30] The OSM "is responsible for communicating and managing priority objectives and working across departments to advance government's policy agenda. … It works closely with departments and agencies to translate government's priorities into policies, plans, programs, and initiatives intended to produce measurable results" (Nova Scotia 2019, 2, 3). Its role includes measuring and reporting back to Executive Council (Cabinet) on the achievement of government objectives. It has 130 different measures that departments report on – such as the percentage of the province with access to the Internet at an acceptable standard or student PISA scores in reading, math, and science – some of which have long existed, others were developed to support the current government's strategy, and some were informed by the Quality of Life Initiative or other well-being measures.[31]

That said, the relative importance of quality-of-life data compared to more conventional economic measurements needs to be put in perspective. Although the OSM tracks a wide range of indicators, the ones explicitly emphasized in its mandate to date are not those associated with the Quality of Life Initiative but with the Ivany report, whose growth-oriented goals are "at the forefront of the Office's mandate" (Nova Scotia 2019, 2).[32]

Looking ahead, many policy applications of the initiative's data are possible. One that stands out is place-based policy. Data on the varying strengths and challenges in the province's different regions could be used to develop regionally targeted policies and programs, rather than a single province-wide approach.[33]

While direct impacts on policy (or "instrumental use," as explained in the introductory chapter) are not yet evident, based on the experience of other cases (e.g., Hayden and Wilson 2018), "political use" will likely become more evident with time, i.e., actors in political debates using the evidence provided by new measurements as "ammunition" to assert or defend policy positions.

Meanwhile, some observers already point to changes in perceptions and frameworks of thought ("conceptual use"). The conversation about the province's goals and how to achieve them has shifted, according to a senior public servant, who attributes much of this shift to Engage Nova Scotia's work and the conversations that have resulted. Whether the issue is aging well, early childhood education, or innovation-driven entrepreneurship, "we're all having conversations where our measure of success is not more jobs created, or GDP contribution made. There's a greater level of layering and complexity of what people understand successes in policy to be." He added that, within government, "At the deputy minister and senior management level, it's almost now the orthodoxy that GDP is not the way to measure progress and success, it is one of many indicators."[34]

That said, the degree to which government departments look beyond GDP varies, with those working more directly with people – e.g., Community Services, Health and Wellness, and Education and Early Childhood Development – having a deep understanding of the need to look beyond GDP to measure progress, a senior public servant noted. Other departments, such as Transportation and Infrastructure Renewal, have less policy focus on such questions. Meanwhile, looking beyond GDP and accepting a quality-of-life orientation to governance is a greater challenge for finance departments, given their responsibility in ensuring that governments have the revenues needed to pay for expenses.[35]

The language of an "inclusive economy," which reflects one part of Engage's quality-of-life vision, is increasingly used by deputy ministers (top-level bureaucrats), says Graham, who, based on meetings with them, sees it is "a significant focus of theirs."[36] "Inclusive economic growth" has in fact been recognized as one of four pillars of the government's strategy; however, its exact meaning, the policies to achieve it, and how to measure it remain a work in progress.[37]

Looking beyond the provincial to municipal level, Graham sees initial signs of impact from involvement in the Quality of Life Initiative in the District of Guysborough, one of the Initiative's community partners. The district began a pilot project in June 2020 giving core municipal employees the option of working the same hours over a condensed four-day work week, allowing it to increase service hours while giving employees more family time by eliminating one daily commute per week (Yarr 2020). Graham sees this as "just one of many examples of how we think things will change as more and more people are exploring this work."[38]

Other observers remained unconvinced that the Initiative was having a substantial impact. While fully supporting beyond-GDP measurement – whether to show "who's sharing in the wealth … or the environmental destruction that comes with continual economic growth" – one interviewee active in the province's progressive movement saw no change in the McNeil government's neoliberal approach.[39] She saw more promising developments in New Zealand, where a well-being focus had been linked to new budget priorities (Ng, this volume). As for a broader change in the public conversation, she remained similarly unconvinced, pointing to the province's difficulty in moving beyond outdated approaches pitting jobs versus the environment to an "alternative vision of economic development" that allows for a "sustainable environment and decent jobs."[40] Ultimately, to convince sceptics, the Initiative will have to show that the data and conversations it is generating are helping to point towards and deliver on a vision that can resolve such challenges.

Obstacles

There are, as Graham notes, "tons of challenges" facing such an initiative.[41] We highlight some obstacles that stand out – to the interviewees and to us – as particularly significant.

Related to the challenge of getting finance departments to look beyond GDP, discussed above, is the training and ways of thinking that come with economics as a discipline. While a senior public servant noted that there were many good conversations within the public service about looking beyond GDP, conventional economic training is a factor that hinders a full embrace of a quality-of-life approach to governance.[42]

The biggest obstacle holding government back from embracing a wider set of quality-of-life measurements, according to a senior public servant, is the reluctance to create standards by which they will be measured and judged politically. The political risk of articulating a new measurement framework is that opposition parties and other critics would use any shortcomings on key indicators to attack the government for its apparent failings.[43]

Ensuring the process is inclusive and gives voice to under-represented communities has been a priority for Engage.[44] Nevertheless, "it continues to be a challenge to have voices that are less frequently heard as fully included as we would want them to be. As much outreach as has been done to the African Nova Scotian community, the Mi'kmaq community, the LGBTQ community, etc., there is still lots of work there," says Watson. She also points to a lack of people with the skills to take well-being data and work with it in communities to create change, bridging the gap between research and the grassroots.[45]

A broader obstacle awaits anyone with transformative hopes for the initiative. Many Nova Scotians appear to understand that they are not all equal in the process of reshaping the province – as seen in the high agreement with the statement, discussed above, that "I do not think public officials care much what people like me think." Whose opinions do public officials care about? Full examination of that question is beyond the scope of this chapter, but clearly some voices carry more weight than others.[46] When asked about the province's most powerful people, one investigative journalist pointed to wealthy individuals and families with names like Irving, Sobey, Risley, and Bragg, among others in the "who's who" of the province's power elite.[47] As another investigative journalist put it in a conversation with Graham, in Nova Scotia, those who are "in" are "very in" (Bousquet 2017, 19:45). Many aspects of the Quality of Life Initiative pose no threat to their interests, including having more data that helps to use limited public funds more effectively or the proposal to market the province as a high-quality-of-life jurisdiction to attract employees and investors. However, if people in communities across the province were to call for more redistributive social spending and/or higher wages to give substance to the slogan "inclusive economy" and address problems evident in the data – such as poverty, economic insecurity, and inadequate access to health, child, and elder care – would the province's most influential people go along without opposition? Alternatively, what would the response be if an emphasis on quality of life and environmental quality were to lead to more explicit demands to move beyond a growth-oriented economy?

Such questions have not been tested by events, at least so far. "We are currently managing to advance this in a way where there is not in fact resistance. That's not to say that there may not be, as choices need to be made," says Graham. He maintains that the Initiative would have been seen as more of a threat fifteen, ten, or even five years ago to "an orthodox ideology" based on "a belief that the market is the omnipotent corrector and provider of well-being" – an ideology he considers mistaken and no longer as dominant. He says the business community "see the potential of [the Initiative] for Nova Scotia," adding that "they do care ... about whether people are being left behind or falling between the cracks." That said, he acknowledges that "the path of getting to greater economic equality is where the rubber hits the road, and we're really in the early stages of testing what that looks like, and what the policy choices are ... Once the tough choices around what that means comes to light, however, it could get tricky."[48]

Conclusion

To conclude, we provide some reflections on the CIW and Nova Scotia Quality of Life Initiative, as they relate to questions facing the broader beyond-GDP movement.

The CIW was an early example of a measurement framework developed not only with expert input but also considerable public consultation. A participatory ethos is equally if not more evident in the Quality of Life Initiative. There is considerable value – which is increasingly recognized in the literature (e.g., McGregor 2015; Rodgers and Trebeck, this volume) – in participatory processes that bring people into conversations about what matters most, how to measure it, and how to act on those measurements. That said, actors have differing levels of power to shape outcomes; a risk of disillusionment exists if people become engaged in a process about what matters most to them, only to find that those with greater power are able to keep the focus on other priorities.

When the CIW first emerged, its promise was largely as a composite index that could rival, or at least complement, GDP as an overarching measure of progress (Hayden and Wilson 2016). It is noteworthy that the composite index has been downplayed in Nova Scotia, with greater emphasis on the indicator dashboard behind it – which reflects the fact that specific indicators have greater value for those seeking to act on the data, and also in line with a general shift in the debate towards dashboards of multiple measures (e.g., Stiglitz, Sen, and Fitoussi 2009).

The CIW-based indicator dashboard, combined with the survey data, offers a great deal of information about societal conditions in Nova Scotia. It remains to be seen how this information will be used over time, but based on an initial assessment, one valuable aspect is the revelation of some surprises, such as Nova Scotia's "number one" ranking in unaffordable housing or the greater problems of social isolation among those under forty than the elderly. Such examples highlight the value of an indicator dashboard that can help identify the emergence of such problems before they reach crisis levels. That said, to fulfil that role, it would be helpful to have more resources to produce data of this kind more frequently, so that problems evident, for example, in the 2014 data used in the Quality of Life Index report do not wait until a 2018 publication to be revealed.

This case also highlights the importance of being attentive to what any measurement framework can and cannot tell you. Caution is warranted, for instance, regarding the incomplete picture of Nova Scotia's environmental record. The 2018 Index showed strong improvements in the environmental domain, reflecting some real progress, notably GHG reduction (Engage and CIW 2018, 46–9). However, it did not tell you that, despite improvement, Nova Scotia remained a high-carbon jurisdiction, still burning coal for about half its electricity,[49] with the fourth-highest per-capita GHG emissions among provinces in 2018 (surpassed only by the three main oil producers)[50] and very high by international comparison (e.g., only one of twenty-eight EU countries, ultra-rich Luxembourg, emitted more per person).[51] Similarly, survey data showing high satisfaction with local environmental quality reflected one important aspect of life in a stunningly beautiful province by the sea but did not show the globally unsustainable impacts from production and consumption in the province (which indicators like per-capita carbon, material, or ecological footprints, for example, could help show).[52] Nor did the framework provide data on Nova Scotia–specific issues, e.g., whether fishery and forest resources were managed sustainably.[53]

Awareness has grown in the beyond-GDP community of the need to go beyond producing new measurements to ensuring their use in decision-making. Such awareness is evident in the Nova Scotia Quality of Life Initiative. Time will tell if the approach succeeds in driving change, but considerable effort has clearly gone into putting together local teams to examine the data and develop priorities for actions that respond to it. Nova Scotia also offers an interesting example of embedding the management, measurement, and reporting of key indicators into the mandates of top-level bodies within the public service. Unfortunately for those seeking a greater emphasis on quality of life and sustainability, the indicators prioritized in the Office of Strategy Management's mandate are those of the OneNS dashboard that grew out of the Ivany report and its conventional growth orientation. A similar integration of quality-of-life and sustainability indicators into the mandate of the Office, and/or the mandate letters for departments, would be one way to signal a new well-being orientation, but no sign exists yet of high-level political commitment of that kind.

The Quality of Life Initiative has put forward a compelling narrative in which "success is about more than just dollars and cents" (Watson 2018). A number of interviewees expressed confidence that this idea, and the more general importance of looking beyond GDP, has made considerable inroads, although sceptics will want to see more in the way of actual policy and social change before proclaiming success. Shifting frameworks of thought may be a necessary first step towards such change, but it remains to be seen if the climate of thought has changed enough to enable the breakthroughs that eluded similar efforts in the past.

Post-script: Shortly after replacing Stephen McNeil as Nova Scotia's Liberal leader and premier, Iain Rankin (2021), proclaimed that there is "a better way to measure success and define progress … by shifting our focus from purely economic measures to well-being and quality of life." Noting that "the pandemic accelerated the thinking around measuring success of societies, making us realize that … GDP is just one of several important measurements," Rankin announced a "Recovery Review" of government programs to assess not only their affordability but also "whether they enhance our lives and livelihoods, and whether they sustain or harm the environment." Rankin's adoption of the Quality of Life Initiative's language signalled a further advance for beyond-GDP thinking; however, his subsequent defeat by Tim Houston, who campaigned as a "progressive" conservative, added to the questions about whether the Initiative would lead to any substantive and lasting policy change.

NOTES

1 After a first draft was written, interviewees had the opportunity to review and, if necessary, revise points drawn from their interviews.

2 The full list of indicators is available at https://uwaterloo.ca/canadian-index-wellbeing /what-we-do/domains-and-indicators

3 Figure 10.1 used with permission of Bryan Smale, CIW.

4 As with any composite index, questions arise about whether the indicators selected accurately measure the concepts they aim to represent and about the weighting of each indicator. With the CIW, each indicator has an equal weight, suggesting equal importance to well-being – an idea that critics have objected to (see, e.g., Barrington-Leigh, this volume). Questions have also been raised about the theoretical basis for comparing CIW and GDP growth rates and assuming that the former should grow as much as the latter; any increase in the CIW – even if it trails GDP growth – could be interpreted as a positive sign that well-being is increasing.

5 Interview, Bryan Smale, CIW director, 29 June 2020.

6 Former Saskatchewan Premier Roy Romanow and former federal Health Minister Monique Bégin were the CIW's political champions in its early days.

7 Interview, Smale.

8 Interview, Smale.

9 Interview, Smale.

10 Personal communication, Nancy Watson, former managing director, Engage Nova Scotia, June 2020.

11 Since then, life satisfaction trends have been less favourable in Nova Scotia than other Atlantic provinces, with Nova Scotia no longer standing out among the highest-ranking provinces (Barrington-Leigh 2021). Like the rest of Canada, it nevertheless continues to rank highly when compared internationally (Conference Board of Canada 2021).

12 Personal communication, Watson.

13 The full OneNS dashboard is available at https://www.onens.ca/.

14 Interview, Watson, 23 June 2020.

15 Interview, Danny Graham, 22 June 2020.

16 Interview, Watson.

17 Interview, Graham, 22 June.

18 Interview, Graham, 22 June.

19 One interviewee referred to GPI Atlantic's "amazing time-use surveys," which were particularly valuable for a gender analysis of time use. Interview, Christine Saulnier, Nova Scotia director, Canadian Centre for Policy Alternatives, 6 July 2020.

20 Interview, Watson.

21 Interview, Watson.

22 25.6 per cent of respondents could not pay their bills on time at least once in the past year, and 18.4 per cent ate less due to a lack of food or money for food at least once in the past year (10).

23 Interview, Graham, 22 June.

24 Personal communication, Watson.

25 Interview, Smale; Smale and Gao (2020).

26 Interview, Smale; Smale and Gao (2020).

27 Interview, Watson.

28 Interview, senior public servant, 2 July 2020.

29 Interviews, Watson and Smale.

30 Interview, senior public servant.

31 Interview, senior public servant.

32 The Office's core activities include "work[ing] with the One Nova Scotia Collective to manage, measure and publicly report on collective progress toward the 19 goals set out by The Nova Scotia Commission on Building our New Economy." In addition, the OSM "participates in regular reports on the progress of One Nova Scotia through the OneNS dashboard" (Nova Scotia 2019, 2, 4).

33 Interview, senior public servant.

34 Interview, senior public servant.

35 Interview, senior public servant.

36 Interview, Graham, 25 June 2020.

37 Interview, senior public servant. See also Nova Scotia (2019, 1, 2).

38 Interview, Graham, 22 June.

39 Interview, Saulnier.

40 Interview, Saulnier.

41 Interview, Graham, 25 June.

42 Interview, senior public servant.

43 Interview, senior public servant. Similar point raised by another anonymous interviewee.

44 Interviews, Graham, 25 June, and Watson.

45 Interview, Watson.

46 Part of this greater influence can be traced to the ability of wealthy individuals to use donations to political parties, as well as their personal connections and lobbying capacity, to ensure their concerns are heard. Even more fundamental is the structural power of capital (e.g., Culpepper 2015), i.e., the need for government leaders to give high priority to the business community's concerns for a profitable business environment; otherwise investment may be withheld or shift to other jurisdictions, while tax revenues and employment – and the government's re-election hopes – shrink.

47 Personal communication with Linda Pannozzo of the *Halifax Examiner*. She adds that considerable power also resides with heads of major law firms and whoever chairs Nova Scotia Power's board.

48 Interview, Graham, 22 June.

49 52 per cent in 2018, according to Nova Scotia Power's figures.

50 Nova Scotia's per-capita emissions were 17.7 tonnes per capita in 2018. Calculations based on total emissions data from the federal government (https://www.canada.ca/en/environment-climate-change/services/climate-change/greenhouse-gas-emissions/sources-sinks-executive-summary-2020.html) and 2018

population figures from Statistics Canada (https://www150.statcan.gc.ca/t1/tbl1
/en/tv.action?pid=1710000501&pickMembers%5B0%5D=1.4&pickMembers%5
B1%5D=2.1). Looking ahead, Nova Scotia has committed to relatively ambitious
GHG reductions compared to other provinces: 53 per cent below 2005 levels by
2030.
51 2018 data from Eurostat: https://ec.europa.eu/eurostat/databrowser/view
/t2020_rd300/default/table?lang=en.
52 National CIW reports include the ecological footprint, but Nova Scotia data was
not available.
53 This is one of many criticisms of the approach that are raised by Ron Colman of
GPI Atlantic (personal communication).

REFERENCES

AOHC. 2014. "Measuring What Matters: How the Canadian Index of
Wellbeing Can Improve Quality of Life in Ontario." Toronto: Association of
Ontario Health Centres. https://issuu.com/aohc_acso/docs/2014-02-13
_-_discussion-paper-final.
Barrington-Leigh, Christopher P. 2021. "Trends." Life Satisfaction in Canada:
Resources from the Happiness Economics Group at McGill University. https://
lifesatisfaction.ca/trends/.
Bousquet, Tim. 2017. "Interview with Danny Graham." Examiner Radio. https://
www.halifaxexaminer.ca/featured/examineradio-137-danny-graham-is-engaged/.
CIW. 2016. "How Are Canadians Really Doing?" Waterloo, ON: Canadian Index of
Wellbeing and University of Waterloo.
Conference Board of Canada. 2021. "Life Satisfaction." How Canada Performs.
https://www.conferenceboard.ca/hcp/provincial/society/life-satisfaction.aspx?Asp
xAutoDetectCookieSupport=1.
CPRN. 2001. "Indicators of Quality of Life in Canada : A Citizens' Prototype:
Summary of Results of Public Dialogue Sessions and Prototype of National
Indicators." Ottawa: Canadian Policy Research Networks. https://uwaterloo.ca
/canadian-index-wellbeing/sites/ca.canadian-index-wellbeing/files/uploads/files
/Indicators_of_Quality_of_Life_in_Canada.sflb__0.pdf.
Culpepper, Pepper D. 2015. "Structural Power and Political Science in the Post-Crisis
Era." Business and Politics 17, no. 3: 391–409.
Engage. 2015. "Cultural Levers for Change Research Study." Halifax: Engage Nova
Scotia. https://static1.squarespace.com/static/5d388a67fad33f0001679229/t/5e62978
806bd1f796db86b55/1583519639061/eng001-1000_engage_ns_report.final_-1.pdf.
– 2020a. "About the Survey." Halifax: Engage Nova Scotia. https://engagenovascotia
.ca/aboutsurvey.
– 2020b. "Annual Report 2019/20." Halifax: Engage Nova Scotia. https://static1
.squarespace.com/static/5d388a67fad33f0001679229/t/5f0722c486d3d37ee40
61f70/1594303179269/Engage+Annual+Report+2019-2020.pdf.

– 2020c. "Our Story." Halifax: Engage Nova Scotia. https://engagenovascotia.ca
/our-story.

Engage, and CIW. 2018. "Nova Scotia Quality of Life Index: 1994–2014." Halifax:
Engage Nova Scotia/Canadian Index of Wellbeing.

Gorman, Michael. 2015. "Public to Prompt Ivany-Style Goals; Engage Nova Scotia
Gets up to $400,000 to Involve Nova Scotians in Projects Tied to Economic
Report." 14 February 2015.

GPI Atlantic. n.d. "A New Measure of Progress." Glen Haven, NS: Genuine Progress
Index Atlantic. http://www.gpiatlantic.org/.

Graham, Danny. 2016. "Engage Nova Scotia Survey Shows We Value Life Quality
over Economic Growth." *CBC News*, 2 May 2016. https://www.cbc.ca/news/canada
/nova-scotia/engage-nova-scotia-survey-shows-novascotians-value-quality-of
-life-1.3562273.

Hayden, Anders, and Jeffrey Wilson. 2016. "Is It What You Measure That Really
Matters? The Struggle to Move beyond GDP in Canada." *Sustainability* 8, no. 7:
623.

– 2018. "Taking the First Steps beyond GDP: Maryland's Experience in Measuring
'Genuine Progress.'" *Sustainability* 10, no. 2: 462.

Helliwell, John F., and Christopher P. Barrington-Leigh. 2010. "Measuring and
Understanding Subjective Well-Being." Working Paper 15887. Cambridge, MA:
National Bureau of Economic Research. http://www.nber.org/papers/w15887.

Ivany, Ray, Irene D'Entremont, Dan Christmas, Susanna Fuller, and John Bragg.
2014. "Now or Never: An Urgent Call to Action for All Nova Scotians: The Report
of the Nova Scotia Commission on Building Our New Economy." Halifax: One
Nova Scotia.

Jess, Amanda. 2020. "Former Liberal Leader Working to Help Those His Generation
Left Behind." *The Chronicle Herald*, 27 February 2020. https://www.thechronicle
herald.ca/news/now-atlantic/former-liberal-leader-working-to-help-those-his
-generation-left-behind-416717/.

McGregor, J. Allister. 2015. "Global Initiatives in Measuring Human Wellbeing:
Convergence and Divergence." CWiPP Working Paper Series No. 2. Sheffield, UK:
Centre for Wellbeing in Public Policy, University of Sheffield. https://www
.sheffield.ac.uk/polopoly_fs/1.522118!/file/CWiPP_WP_201502_McGregor.pdf.

Nova Scotia. 2019. "Business Plan 2019–20: Department of Business." Halifax:
Province of Nova Scotia.

One Nova Scotia. 2013. "Interim Report of the Nova Scotia Commission on Building
Our New Economy." Halifax: Nova Scotia Commission on Building Our New
Economy. https://documents.pub/document/interim-report-of-the-nova-scotia
-commission-on-building-our-new-economy.html.

Rankin, Iain. 2021. "Faring Well in Nova Scotia — a Re-Evaluation of Our Wealth &
Health." *Chronicle-Herald*, 11 March 2021. https://www.thechronicleherald.ca
/opinion/local-perspectives/iain-rankin-faring-well-in-nova-scotia-a
-re-evaluation-of-our-wealth-health-562404/.

Scharmer, Otto. 2009. *Theory U: Learning from the Future as It Emerges*. San Francisco: Berrett-Koehler Publishers.

Sharpe, Andrew, and Evan Capeluck. 2012. "Canadians Are Happy and Getting Happier: An Overview of Life Satisfaction in Canada, 2003–2011." Ottawa: Centre for the Study of Living Standards.

Smale, Bryan, and Mingjie Gao. 2020. "A Closer Look: The Nova Scotia Quality of Life Survey Based on the CIW Community Wellbeing Survey." Waterloo, ON: Canadian Index of Wellbeing and University of Waterloo. https://engagenovascotia.ca/s/NS-QoL_Supplementary-Analysis-Slides_Final-ys5d.pptx.

Smale, Bryan, Mingjie Gao, and Kai Jiang. 2020. "An Exploration of Wellbeing in Nova Scotia: A Summary of Results from the Nova Scotia Quality of Life Survey." Waterloo, ON: Canadian Index of Wellbeing and University of Waterloo. https://static1.squarespace.com/static/5d388a67fad33f0001679229/t/5e71250812d3805459021b82/1584473359939/NSQofLifeSurvey-AnExplorationOfWellbeing-March2020+%281%29.pdf.

Stiglitz, Joseph E., Amartya Sen, and Jean-Paul Fitoussi. 2009. "Report by the Commission on the Measurement of Economic Performance and Social Progress." Paris: Commission on the Measurement of Economic Performance and Social Progress. https://ec.europa.eu/eurostat/documents/8131721/8131772/Stiglitz-Sen-Fitoussi-Commission-report.pdf.

Vibert, Jim. 2019. "Quality of Life Focus of Engage Nova Scotia's Survey." *The Chronicle Herald*, 13 May 2019. http://www.thechronicleherald.ca/opinion/jim-vibert-quality-of-life-focus-of-engage-nova-scotias-survey-310991/.

Watson, Nancy M. 2018. "A Better Way than Dollars and Cents to Measure Success." *The Chronicle Herald*, 26 June 2018. https://uwaterloo.ca/canadian-index-wellbeing/news/better-way-dollars-and-cents-measure-success.

Yarr, Kevin. 2020. "How a 4-Day Work Week Is Going in Guysborough, N.S." *CBC News*, 25 June 2020. https://www.cbc.ca/news/canada/prince-edward-island/pei-4-day-work-week-guysborough-1.5626663.

11 Building an Epidemiology of Happiness

JOHN F. HELLIWELL, DAVID GYARMATI, CRAIG JOYCE, AND HEATHER ORPANA

Introduction

The title of this chapter, and the pre-2020 examples, were chosen before COVID-19 changed the world. Starting with the assumption that improving well-being is a central consideration for public policies, we aim to show how subjective well-being research can help, and already is helping, to choose public policies based on their consequences for all aspects of life. The arrival of COVID-19, and the attendant attempts to slow or stop its pace, made even more obvious the need for a broader epidemiology – one that considers not just the sources and physical consequences of disease but of all the sources and consequences of healthy and happy lives. When deciding how and when to establish lockdowns and other mitigation strategies, and how to plan low-risk ways to restore mobility, governments all over the world aimed to save lives and maintain essential services while minimizing the costs to the economy and the social fabric. The three main pillars of happier lives – physical and mental health, jobs and incomes, and a supportive social structure (Helliwell el al. 2020) – were all hit by COVID-19, requiring policy choices that consider all three types of consequence comparably. Our focus on well-being rather than illness involves a deliberate shift in the caring sciences from a problem-solving to a building mode, from the investigation and curing of disease to the creation of happier and healthier physical and social environments.

Epidemiology, the "study of the distribution and determinants of health-related states or events in specified populations, and the application of this study to the control of health problems" (Last et al. 2001, 62) has its origins in infectious diseases. In the mid-twentieth century, epidemiology expanded its focus to include chronic diseases and risk factors, followed by injuries and violence, and more recently the social determinants of health (Berkman et al. 2014; Pickett and Wilkinson 2015; and Kawachi and Subramanian 2018) and even loneliness (Holt-Lunstad 2017). Most recently, epidemiology has begun to include positive states of health (VanderWeele et al. 2020), and to supplement risk factors with protective and salutogenic factors (Orpana et al. 2016).

Happiness, which we are using here to cover life evaluations (cognitive measures of how happy people are with their lives as a whole) as well as positive and negative emotions, monitors how well things are going and not just whether disease and other problems are absent. The techniques of epidemiology are as well suited to study the origins and consequences of happiness as they are to trace the sources of disease. Such extended applications of epidemiology can be seen as a natural step in implementing a broader definition of health to include not just the absence of hardship and disease but also the creation of better lives from any starting point. This larger mandate was already in the founding constitution of the World Health Organization (1948), viz: "Health is a state of complete physical, mental and social well-being and not merely the absence of disease or infirmity."

Over the past forty years there has been increasing interest in refocusing government policies with the explicit aim of increasing equitable and sustainable human well-being. This change in policy perspective has been decades in the making, built on a growing dissatisfaction with using GDP per capita as a sufficient measure of human progress (Stiglitz, Sen, and Fitoussi 2009), inspired by the Bhutanese choice more than forty years ago to make happiness a national objective and fuelled by decades of research aimed at creating a transdisciplinary science of happiness. The High Level Meeting on Well-Being and Happiness, convened by Jigme Y. Thinley, prime minister of Bhutan, at the United Nations on 2 April 2012, was supported by the first *World Happiness Report* (Helliwell, Layard, and Sachs 2012), which assembled the available global data on national happiness and reviewed the related evidence from the emerging science of happiness. That evidence, which built on many other reviews of the science of well-being, provided strong support for the conclusion that the quality of people's lives can be coherently and reliably assessed by a variety of subjective well-being measures, collectively referred to in this chapter as "happiness." It also built upon, as did the UN meeting itself, the UK launch of a well-being initiative in November 2010, still unique in combining engagement at the highest level from the political, administrative, and data-gathering pillars of government. The initial constellation of these three supporting pillars was probably crucial in establishing widespread data-gathering and discussions in the United Kingdom (Allin 2021). Once started, these data and discussions fuelled a broad swath of innovations in firms and communities, and a variety of within-government and cross-pillar organizations, that have continued to deliver research and applications even without being a central feature of the political environment (Bache, this volume).

Progress before 2020

This chapter, which is part of a volume largely focused on a variety of ways of moving beyond GDP as a measure of national and community well-being, was intended to show that government researchers and policymakers have already moved beyond general discussions about alternative measures of human progress to a stage where the science of well-being can now be harnessed (as argued in Helliwell 2021 and Barrington-Leigh in this volume) to enable research based on subjective well-being to be used to design and rank policy options.

There is a growing range of government policies intended to improve happiness in many policy areas. At the broadest level, the Organisation for Economic Co-operation and Development (OECD) has recommended that countries adopt a whole-of-government approach to improving well-being, supported by broader and more systematic collection of well-being data, and the development and application of policy tools that use subjective well-being as the objective and as the means for comparing monetary and non-monetary costs and outcomes (Durand and Exton 2019). Within health care, using the happiness lens to evaluate different treatment alternatives has been advocated as a means of producing better health and more happiness with less drain on scarce resources (Peasgood, Foster, and Dolan 2019). Within Canada, the increasing importance attached to this sort of analysis was apparent in the prime minister's mandate letter of late 2019 directing the new associate minister of finance to "lead work within the Department of Finance (and in other ministries) … to better incorporate quality of life measurements into government decision-making and budgeting, drawing on lessons from other jurisdictions such as New Zealand and Scotland."[1]

There have been two global happiness and well-being policy reports (Global Happiness Council 2018 and 2019), each intended to draw together best practice examples from around the world in several key policy areas, including health, education, cities, workplaces, and the community. Subsequently, in October 2019 the OECD held an international workshop on putting well-being metrics into policy action, drawing participants from many local and national governments. Both New Zealand and Scotland, mentioned above, had high-level delegations, and there was widespread interest in using well-being metrics in the policymaking process. Both Scotland and New Zealand had gone further than most national governments in making well-being the official focus for policy design. New Zealand has had since 2015 an extended cost benefit tool (The Treasury 2019) to explicitly attach monetary values to intangible social outcomes, while the United Kingdom has gone furthest in the development and application of policy assessment tools that explicitly use subjective well-being research to support policy choices (Layard and O'Donnell 2015; Frijters and Krekel 2019).

There was no representation from Canadian federal policymaking departments at the 2019 OECD workshop, probably reflecting the fact that until recently there has been little explicit use of well-being as a central organizing principle in as public a way as has been the case for New Zealand and Scotland. Thus there is perhaps less recognition in Canada that subjective well-being research has in fact been used for several years to support cost–benefit analysis of just the sort that has been advocated for use by governments (Layard and O'Donnell 2015; Frijters et al. 2020) who wish to make well-being a central focus for their policy choices. Doing cost–benefit analysis using the lens of subjective well-being requires a large base of data and research to enable the estimation of the relative importance of various policy outcomes. Fortunately, Statistics Canada has been in the forefront internationally, being the first among the OECD countries (as reported by Durand and Smith 2013) to measure subjective well-being in mainline surveys. Life satisfaction is now measured regularly in the General Social Survey, the Canadian Community Health Survey (CCHS), and other household surveys, making possible the use of combined samples from different surveys (Bonikowska et al. 2014). This has permitted a large range of studies estimating the relative well-being effects, in the Canadian context, of many aspects of life, including income, unemployment, social trust (Helliwell and Wang 2011), and workplace trust (Helliwell and Huang 2011). These large geo-coded samples have also enabled comparisons of life satisfaction in cities and neighbourhoods (Helliwell, Shiplett, and Barrington-Leigh 2019), to assess why some places are happier than others and to show that immigrant life satisfaction converges to the average in the region where they live (Helliwell, Shiplett, and Bonikowska 2020).

The above studies are generally based on the use of other data in the same surveys in which the life satisfaction is measured. This permits analysis using individual-level observations, essential for discovering the relative importance of different sources of well-being. It has also been possible for health researchers to obtain agreement from individual respondents to the CCHS to link their life satisfaction with their use of health resources over the following six years (Goel et al. 2019) and to estimate a dose-response relation between life satisfaction and subsequent morbidity and mortality, even after adjusting for a large array of life circumstances and pre-existing medical conditions (Rosella et al. 2018). This type of study only becomes possible when there are large representative samples of individual life satisfaction observations to use as a basis for linkage with other records.

Another important component for increasing the pace and range of policy applications is the widespread understanding that life satisfaction, and other measures of how well life is going, are important health statistics, adding substance to the 1948 WHO declaration that good health is about the creation of positive states of health and mind, and not just the absence of disease and infirmity. Since measurement is a pre-condition for evidence-based policy analysis, the adoption of life satisfaction as a key national health statistic has the potential to bring the positive focus more fully into policy evaluations. The Public Health Agency of Canada has adopted a positive mental health surveillance framework in which life satisfaction is one of five key outcomes now part of regular, national health surveillance and reporting (Orpana et al. 2016). This framework has helped inform both subnational (Ontario Ministry of Health and Long-Term Care 2018) and international (BMC Proceedings 2020) surveillance activities, expanding the inclusion of well-being into surveillance in other jurisdictions. This important innovation marks Canada as one of the few countries to establish life satisfaction as a key national health statistic. Because life satisfaction, along with other measures of well-being, are monitored on a regular basis, this provides additional incentive to study the epidemiology of happiness, tracing its impacts on other aspects of physical health, as in the studies described above, and also to search for better understanding of how life satisfaction is created and spread.

The existence of a solid base of life satisfaction research enables policy evaluations to bring important intangible items directly into the analysis, making use of their estimated contributions to overall life evaluations. Bringing these intangibles up from the footnotes into central positions in project proposals changes the whole nature of policy evaluation, often leading to important differences in the ranking of alternative policies. It also becomes easier to compare policies coming to central agencies from departments with differing objectives and often competing claims on public financial resources. Within applied policy domains, there are signs that subjective well-being research has already begun to influence how policy evaluation is done. Two federal department studies have used well-being research to better understand the value of investments in health promotion and encouraging participation in sport and cultural activities. Both uncovered significant well-being impacts. In the health promotion example, the authors monetized a set of health behaviours often targeted by federally funded programs, valuing increased physical activity at $631 per week, increased fruit and vegetable consumption at $115 per week, and smoking cessation at $563 per week. These figures are intended to allow a comparison of the results of health promoting programs to the program costs themselves and demonstrate value for money in an area of policy where it is not always obvious (Shi et al. 2019). In the case of the study on participation in sport and cultural activities, the monetized value of the well-being outcomes exceeded the costs of the programs used to achieve them (Lemyre, Mader, and Ambarde 2018).

There has been a general strengthening over the past twenty-five years in the demand for better evidence to support policy decisions and to evaluate policy outcomes. The Social Research and Demonstration Corporation (SRDC) was founded in 1991 as an independent non-profit research organization created specifically by the federal government to develop, field test, and rigorously evaluate new policies and programs. SRDC conducts its research at a scale sufficient to provide significant results, often employing field experiments to test programs in real-world settings. The initial years saw the implementation of several large-scale social policy experiments on behalf of the federal government. Over the past twenty years the range of clients has grown to include many provincial governments, industry associations, foundations, and community partners as well as covering a much broader set of policy areas beyond employment and workforce development, including education and health. Over these same years, the range of outcomes considered in much of SRDC's research has expanded to include a rich set of psychosocial variables, including trust, social capital, and life satisfaction. In particular, subjective well-being research has been undertaken more frequently not only as part of impact analysis but also to enhance cost-benefit studies by monetizing many intangible impacts of policy interventions that were previously excluded. On many levels, this has been transformative for comparative policy analysis, as it allows for the valuation of a full range of economic and social impacts and for the comparison of these across policy interventions.

One such example, the Community Employment Innovation Project (CEIP), was a jointly sponsored initiative of Human Resources and Social Development Canada (HRSDC) and the Nova Scotia Department of Community Services. It tested an active re-employment strategy for unemployed individuals who volunteered to work on locally developed community projects in areas hit by chronic unemployment. In exchange for foregoing their Employment Insurance (EI) or Social Assistance (SA) benefits, CEIP offered participants wages to work on community projects for up to three years, giving them a significant period of stable income as well as an opportunity to gain work experience, acquire new skills, and expand their network of contacts. Beyond fulfilling the need for immediate employment, CEIP hoped to influence participants' longer-term employability by helping them preserve and possibly improve their human and social capital. At the same time, CEIP aimed to facilitate community development by supporting the "third sector" and encouraging activities that are meaningful for both the participant and the community.

SRDC was responsible for the design and implementation of the project, which started in 1999 and released its final report in 2008 (Gyarmati et al. 2008). This policy evaluation was the first of its kind to rigorously measure how community-designed and -managed projects could positively impact the levels of social capital and trust among not only participants but also in their communities, and to use subjective well-being to estimate the monetary value of these social impacts. This was one of the earliest and most comprehensive applications of subjective well-being in experimental policy analysis. Indeed, these were substantial, significantly improving the resulting analysis of the program's cost effectiveness. For instance, when only considering financial impacts of the program on outcomes such as earnings, the analysis showed that for every dollar in net cost to the government there were combined net benefits for society of $1.39. However, by incorporating subjective well-being into the analysis and monetizing even a small number of the intangible benefits of the program (e.g., social capital and trust), this improved the cost effectiveness substantially to $1.61 in combined net benefits for every dollar in cost to the government (Gyarmati et. al. 2008, 117–18). Without the inclusion of measures of subjective well-being, cost–benefit analyses such as these will significantly under-estimate the cost-effectiveness of programs.

A second example from SRDC's research is a more recent study, UPSKILL, a large-scale demonstration project that measured the impacts of literacy and essential skills (LES) training in the workplace (Gyarmati et al. 2014). The project used a random assignment design to provide the most reliable measures of the impacts of workplace training on skills, job performance, and a range of other social and financial outcomes of workers and firms. Over 100 firms and 1,500 workers in the accommodations sector participated across the country in 8 provinces.

The project involved the direct collaboration of many institutional and industry partners in the design and delivery of the program, and measures of social capital, trust, and life satisfaction were central to the analysis. The depth of collaboration increased the power and relevance of the findings. Although the skills being built and assessed were of basic literacy and numeracy, and hence were transferable, not tied to a particular job, the results were assessed using measures of success actually employed in the accommodations sector. This included industry-developed certification assessments to measure worker performance and a number of business indicators related to guest satisfaction, revenues, and productivity measures. The results could thus be assessed from the perspective of hotel operators, employees, customers, and society as a whole.

The findings indicated that workplace literacy training does, indeed, have large positive impacts on workers' skills and job performance, plus a wide range of social and financial outcomes of workers and firms. The cost–benefit analysis also revealed a significant positive return on investment for all stakeholders – including employers – of 23 per cent in the first year alone. Importantly, the study also used subjective well-being to monetize the positive impacts on social and psychological capital, permitting their inclusion in an extended cost–benefit analysis. Strikingly, results illustrate that the inclusion of a modest number of social impacts increases the cost-effectiveness of the program by over 80 per cent (Gyarmati et al. 2014, 117–20).

Furthermore, the measurement of trust and life satisfaction before, during, and after the project provided key insights not initially foreseen, thereby deepening understanding of how and when workplace training will generate positive impacts. For example, while the overall results were found to be significant for the sample as a whole, a more detailed subgroup analysis showed that many of the gains were concentrated in hotels with high levels of mutual trust (Gyarmati et al. 2014, 133). High levels of workplace trust have been shown to deliver happier lives for employees (Helliwell and Huang 2011), but this result goes further, showing that innovations in workplace practices and employee training are more effective for all participants where trust levels are high.

These examples all show the importance of having large samples of population-representative data on subjective well-being, of undertaking research using these data to obtain estimates of the relative values of tangible and intangible outcomes, and of using policy experiments to monitor the impacts on subjective well-being and its key determinants. To put these essential components to work in the service of a broader epidemiology of happiness requires that policy analysts are convinced of the need to monitor diverse sources and outcomes in a consistent manner. They also need enough exposure and training to put these pieces together, and a policy environment that welcomes evaluations of this breadth. This is likely to be accelerated where there is a whole-of-government commitment to well-being-based policymaking (Durand and Exton 2019). There are also some advantages, as shown by examples from both Canada and the UK, in having a solid background of data and research, along with a cadre of trained analysts able to deliver useful results when the demand for them arises.

The Epidemiology of Happiness in the COVID-19 Pandemic

Although the case for a broader epidemiology of happiness has existed for decades, its necessity is made even more urgent by COVID-19. The scope and scale of the COVID-19 pandemic and the response by governments around the world have been of proportions not seen in the past century. Policies that stop population movements and close down most activities that bring people physically close have been adopted to varying degrees in almost all countries. While serving a primary purpose of reducing the amount of sickness and death, they have also been intended to slow transmission by enough to avoid overloading health care systems by minimizing the number of COVID-19 patients requiring hospitalization, ICU admission, and ventilator support, while waiting for the development of a vaccine or effective treatments. Conventional epidemiology has been brought to the centre of the policy stage by identifying cases, tracking contacts, and modelling transmission rates under alternative mitigation policies, all while what is known about the novel virus evolves rapidly.

The centre-stage role taken by public health officers has been critical in helping to convince populations that severe disruption of their lives, on a scale never experienced before, can save enough lives and suffering to justify the measures taken. Given the risks of health care systems being overwhelmed, as shown by the early experiences in Wuhan and Lombardy, dedicated critical-care capacity was increased in a variety of ways, including delaying many other forms of medical diagnosis and treatment. As infection curves became flatter in many countries, and the pressures on critical care capacity became less likely, the need for a broader epidemiology became more obvious. What strategies provide the most well-being benefits relative to their contributions to keeping infections low while waiting for a vaccine or treatments? Mainline epidemiology remains in a central position in any broader analysis, since identifying cases, tracking contacts, learning in more detail about the transmission process, establishing the current and past prevalence of infection, and estimating the degree of population or herd immunity are all key requirements for subsequent stages of pandemic management. To be effective, these studies need to be set in the particular circumstances of regions, communities, living arrangements, institutions, and occupations.

One broader form of epidemiology, although not as broad as we propose, uses life-years saved as the key objective to help set priorities for the pace and scale of resuming other forms of medical treatment. For example, survival chances for patients with many forms of cancer depend on timely surgery, and many such surgeries were postponed or cancelled during the first stages of pandemic response. It has been possible to model life-years saved by restarting different types of cancer surgery (Sud et al. 2020), thereby inviting a broader analysis of the costs and benefits of alternative use patterns for existing medical resources during the second and later stages of pandemic management.

A further broadening, still using life years as the objective, might include the effects on self-harm and violence, and transport injuries, ranking eleventh and twelfth respectively in terms of global number of deaths in 2017 (http://ihmeuw.org/4srx). Lockdowns and physical-distancing measures kept people off the roads and at home, in some cases alone and possibly lonely. This simple description would suggest a decrease in traffic fatalities and an increase in suicides. Reality might be more complicated, as people drive faster on empty roads, and speed kills. As for suicide, Japan had suicide rates in April 2020, during lockdown, that were significantly lower than normal.[2] Durkheim's (1897) still magisterial early statistical analysis found that suicide rates were lower among population groups facing other risks to their existence and that suicide rates in countries farther from the equator have peaks in the summer, when people are having active social lives, leaving those left out more likely to have their hopes turn into hopelessness. Aggregate data for excess deaths, such as those provided by EuroMOMO (https://www.euromomo.eu) and Statistics

Canada (2020) can help, as they accumulate over the years, to show the number of excess deaths that include the combined effects of COVID-19, delayed surgeries, traffic fatalities, suicide, and other stress-related deaths. For some, lockdown meant a reduction of commuting and office stress, permitting more family time, some in person and the rest virtual. For them, life at home with the family became calmer and happier as it became less frenetic. Others were not so fortunate.

Social connections with family and friends have been found to be crucial supports for happiness, especially contacts with face-to-face rather than online friends (Helliwell and Huang 2013). The COVID-19 physical-distancing measures combined with lockdowns in many countries to remove most possibilities for close encounters with friends and family, so the existing evidence would suggest a very large hit to well-being. But in the absence of face-to-face possibilities, people shifted from in-person to electronic visits with friends and colleagues near and far. The extent to which this enabled individuals and families to maintain supportive and nurturing relationships, and hence happiness, under physical distancing is still being assessed.

How broad must epidemiology be to enable a proper balancing of the costs and benefits of alternative strategies for pandemic management? Useful examples are provided by two recent studies in the United Kingdom, one assessing the well-being costs of the pandemic, and the second, more ambitiously, providing an illustrative calculation of the costs and benefits of alternative dates for exiting from general lockdown. The costs study (Fujiwara et al. 2020) uses survey data from during the pandemic to estimate the well-being costs of lockdown, using matched samples of official national data for April 2019 as a baseline. They estimate a 13 per cent loss in life satisfaction implicitly due to COVID-19 and attribute more than half of this to the costs of social distancing. No account is taken of the costs of COVID-related deaths beyond bereavement effects. What is needed for an overall well-being assessment of COVID-19?

The Happiness Research Institute (2020) and Layard et al. (2020) both advocate using Well-being Adjusted Life Years (denoted WALYs in the former case and WELLBYs in the latter). In both cases, this involved an extension to the more usual well-being focus, which concentrates on the well-being of those still living, which has been shown to depend importantly on the average length of healthy life. But when a disease or other fatality-causing event takes place, and there are alternative ways of mitigating its effects, it is essential to attach a well-being benefit to life-years saved. Layard et al. (2020) apply this to the COVID-19 situation, using pre-COVID-19 research to set values for life-years saved, as well as the well-being consequences of the COVID-19-related effects on unemployment, income, mental health, confidence in government, schooling, road fatalities, COVID-19 deaths, commuting time, carbon dioxide emissions, and air quality. They calculate these effects for alternative dates of lockdown release. Approximate data are used to estimate the lives saved by a longer lockdown, with assumed monthly savings diminishing over time and eventually overshadowed by the reductions in income and employment and reductions in mental health, all of which are assumed to grow with a longer lockdown. Confidence in government handling is assumed to fall as the length of the lockdown increases. Setting the declining benefits against the rising costs leads to their conclusion that the net gain from lockdown diminishes as time passes. The authors were careful to say that they were illustrating the importance of bringing these diverse factors into play, rather than arguing that their calculations were supported by strong evidence. More complete application of well-being analysis requires more explicit analysis of different ways to release restrictive measures and broaden the range of safer activities, while keeping infection rates to zero (within COVID-19-free bubbles) and at minimal and carefully tracked and traced levels where transmission is more likely.

Looking Ahead

The pandemic has changed the policy environment in many ways. At a fundamental level, it has exposed the need for flexibility and resilience. The pandemic has shown the benefits of greater diversity of supply lines, adding another element to be included when choosing among policy options. But at a deeper human level individuals, families, and firms have been seeing life in new ways, some painful and others so positive as to incite pledges to maintain the social closeness created as a by-product of physical distancing, including the cooking, games, and laughter within the physically distanced family plus extended electronic social networks not previously used to such good purpose. The opportunities and preferences for different forms of work, entertainment, family life, and vacations may have changed not just during the stages of the pandemic but also for the longer term.

COVID-19 also dramatically altered the distribution of well-being. The direct costs of the disease have been much higher for those in exposed occupations or in elder-care or other forms of housing where outbreaks have occurred or where physical distancing is harder to achieve. The concentration of infection among the homeless and those with insecure housing, food, and employment, and the digital divide combine to suggest that the net effect is likely an increase in the inequality of well-being, which itself has been shown to decrease average well-being by more than does income inequality (Goff et al, 2018; Helliwell et al. 2020). This is exemplified by evidence of higher COVID-19 incidence and severity among those who were already disadvantaged, whether by race, health, income, or housing.[3]

Trust also deserves special mention. Differences among countries and communities in the extent to which people trust each other, and the related extent to which they reach out to help each other, have big effects on the well-being consequences of COVID-19, just as they have been shown to do in the face of other crises (Helliwell, Huang, and Wang 2014). Similarly, the extent to which people have confidence in their political and health systems are likely to influence how highly people evaluate their own lives under COVID-19 and how fully and happily they follow the advice or directives they receive. Research has already shown that individuals who live where they have trust in each other and in their shared public institutions are substantially buffered against the well-being costs of adversities including unemployment, fear, discrimination, low income, and ill health (Helliwell et al. 2020). Since COVID-19 has, to varying degrees, inflicted all these negative effects on at least some members of all societies, those living in high-trust communities and nations are likely in consequence to have life evaluations that fell less and recovered faster during the first stages of COVID-19. Research is increasingly showing that a virus-suppression strategy, with zero community transmission as the benchmark, has been the best, and perhaps only, way to avoid direct and indirect COVID-19 deaths while minimizing collateral damage to social cohesion, population health, incomes, and employment. High levels of social and institutional trust have been shown to increase the chances of this strategy being chosen, both within and among nations (Helliwell et al. 2021).

An epidemiology that aims to support the overall self-assessed quality of life will take all these factors into account, both during and after the pandemic. Never have the opportunities and need for such an overarching analysis been greater. The same sea changes affecting all walks and ways of life have by the same token made the analysis more difficult. In the pursuit of this overarching goal in a rapidly changing environment, the best should not be made the enemy of the good; responses need to be sure-footed but rapid. These circumstances require that policies be tailored to local circumstances and risks. The attendant uncertainties invite responses that are measured, examined carefully for their lessons, and altered in response to what is being learned. The same flexibility and diversity that has been seen as an asset to families, firms, and communities coping with COVID-19 are also likely to be features of the policies most likely to support well-being.

We have argued in this chapter that public policies should be designed to consider their overall effects on well-being and evaluated with this goal in mind. Research in subjective well-being has come far enough over the past quarter-century to have tangible implications for the setting and ranking of policy priorities, evaluating the results of policy interventions, and enhancing the manner in which cost–benefit analysis is done to understand policy impacts in a more holistic way than previously possible. We have illustrated the general case by specific examples from epidemiology, which has gradually been broadening its scope and techniques to consider positive measures of overall well-being. The arrival of COVID-19 has strengthened the need for such broadening, since the policy decisions being faced by governments dealing with the pandemic required an approach much broader than provided by more typical policy evaluations in all disciplines. We have described how such a broader approach to policy design and choice is fully consistent with the underlying aims of epidemiology. We could equally well argue that well-being analysis of the sort we propose offers similar gains in other policy disciplines. In particular, it could restore to economics the breadth of purpose and methods it had two centuries ago, when happiness was considered the appropriate goal for private actions and public policies.

Acknowledgments

The authors are grateful for helpful comments and suggestions from Aneta Bonikowska, Ceo Gaudet, Anders Hayden, Bev Holmes, Aziz Mulay-Shah, Grant Schellenberg, Meik Wiking, and Jeff Wilson.

NOTES

1   https://pm.gc.ca/en/mandate-letters/minister-middle-class-prosperity-and-associate
    -minister-finance-mandate-letter.
2   https://www.theguardian.com/world/2020/may/14/japan-suicides-fall-sharply
    -as-covid-19-lockdown-causes-shift-in-stress-factors.
3   This has been exemplified by outbreaks and deaths in elder-care facilities, prisons, and camps for migrant workers. On differing incidence by race in the United States, see Hooper, Nápoles, and Pérez-Stable (2020).

REFERENCES

Allin, Paul. 2021. "Reflections on the Introduction and Use of Official Measures of Subjective Well-Being in the UK." In *Measuring Well-Being: Interdisciplinary Perspectives from the Social Sciences and the Humanities*, edited by Matthew Lee, Laura Kubzansky, and Tyler VanderWeele. New York: Oxford University.

Berkman, Lisa F., Ichirō Kawachi, and M. Maria Glymour, eds. 2014. *Social Epidemiology*. Oxford: Oxford University Press.

BMC Proceedings. 2020. "Proceedings of the International Workshop 'Integration of International Expertise in the Development of a Mental Health Surveillance System in Germany.'" *BMC Proc* 14, 4. https://doi.org/10.1186 /s12919-020-00186-0.

Bonikowska, Aneta, John F. Helliwell, Frank Hou, and Grant Schellenberg. 2014. "An Assessment of Life Satisfaction Responses on Recent Statistics Canada Surveys." *Social Indicators Research* 118, no. 2: 617–43.

Durand, Martine, and Carrie Exton. 2019. "Adopting a Well-being Approach in Central Government: Policy Mechanisms and Practical Tools." In *Global Happiness and Wellbeing Policy Report 2019*, 140–62. New York: Global Happiness Council.

Durand, Martine, and Conal Smith. 2013. "The OECD Approach to Measuring Subjective Well-Being." In *World Happiness Report 2013*, edited by John F. Helliwell, Richard Layard, and Jeffrey D. Sachs, 112–37. New York: UN Sustainable Development Solutions Network.

Durkheim, Émile. 1897. *Le suicide: étude de sociologie*. Paris: Alcan.

Frijters, Paul, Andrew Clark, Chris Krekel, and Richard Layard. 2020. "A Happy Choice: Wellbeing as the Goal of Government." *Behavioural Public Policy*, 4, no. 2: 126–65. doi:10.1017/bpp.2019.39.

Frijters, Paul, and Chris Krekel. 2019. *A Handbook for Wellbeing Policy-Making in the UK: History, Measurement, Theory, Implementation, and Examples*. Oxford: Oxford University Press.

Fujiwara, Daniel, Paul Dolan, Ricky Lawton, Fatemeh Behzadnejad, Augustin Lagarde, Cem Maxwell, and Sebastien Peytrignet. 2020. *The Well-Being Costs of COVID-19 in the UK*. https://www.jacobs.com/sites/default/files/2020-05/jacobs-wellbeing-costs-of-covid-19-uk.pdf.

Global Happiness Council. 2018. *Global Happiness and Wellbeing Policy Report 2018*. New York: Sustainable Development Solutions Network.

– 2019. *Global Happiness and Wellbeing Policy Report 2019*. New York: Sustainable Development Solutions Network.

Goel, Vivek, Laura C. Rosella, Longdi Fu, and Amanda Alberga. 2018. "The Relationship between Life Satisfaction and Healthcare Utilization: A Longitudinal Study." *AmericanJjournal of Preventive Medicine* 55, no. 2: 142–50.

Goff, Leonard, John F. Helliwell, and Guy Mayraz. 2018. "Inequality of Subjective Well-Being as a Comprehensive Measure of Inequality." *Economic Inquiry* 56, no. 4: 2177–94.

Gyarmati, David, Shawn de Raaf, Boris Palameta, Claudia Nicholson, and Taylor Shek-Wai Hui. 2008. *Encouraging Work and Supporting Communities: Final Results of the Community Employment Innovation Project*. Ottawa: Social Research and Demonstration Corporation. http://www.srdc.org/media/8508/CEIP_finalrpt_ENG.pdf.

Gyarmati, David, Norm Leckie, Michael Dowie, Boris Palameta, Taylor Shek-Wai Hui, Elizabeth Dunn, and Sophie Hébert. 2014. *UPSKILL: A Credible Test of Workplace Literacy and Essential Skills Training*. Ottawa: Social Research and Demonstration Corporation. http://www.srdc.org/media/199774/upskill-technical-report-en.pdf.

Happiness Institute and Leaps by Bayer. 2020. *Wellbeing Adjusted Life Years: A Universal Metric to Quantify the Happiness Return on Investment*. Berlin: Happiness Institute and Leaps by Bayer.

Helliwell, John F. 2019. "How to Open Doors to Happiness." *Global Happiness and Wellbeing Policy Report 2019*, 8–25. New York: Global Happiness Council. https://s3.amazonaws.com/ghwbpr-2019/UAE/GH19_Ch2.pdf.

– 2021. "Measuring and Using Happiness to Support Public Policies." In *Measuring Well-Being: Interdisciplinary Perspectives from the Social Sciences and the Humanities*, edited by Matthew Lee, Laura Kubzansky, and Tyler VanderWeele. New York: Oxford University. Previously (No. w26529). National Bureau of Economic Research Working Paper 26529.

Helliwell, John F., and Lara B. Aknin. 2018. "Expanding the Social Science of Happiness." *Nature Human Behaviour* 2, no. 4: 248–52.

Helliwell, John F., and Haifang Huang. 2011. "Well-Being and Trust in the Workplace." *Journal of Happiness Studies* 12, no. 5: 747–67.

– 2013. "Comparing the Happiness Effects of Real and On-Line Friends." *PLoS ONE* 8, no. 9: e72754.

Helliwell, John F., Haifang Huang, and Shun Wang. 2014. "Social Capital and Well-Being in Times of Crisis." *Journal of Happiness Studies* 15, no. 1: 145–62.

Helliwell, John F., Haifang Huang, Shun Wang, and Max Norton. 2020. "Social Environments for World Happiness." In *World Happiness Report 2020*, edited by John F. Helliwell, Richard Layard, Jeffrey D. Sachs, and Jan-Emmanuel De Neve. New York: UN Sustainable Development Solutions Network.

– 2021. "Happiness, Trust and Deaths under COVID-19." In *World Happiness Report 2021*, edited by John F. Helliwell, Richard Layard, Jeffrey D. Sachs, Jan-Emmanuel De Neve, Lara Aknin and Shun Wang. New York: UN Sustainable Development Solutions Network.

Helliwell, John F., Richard Layard, and Jeffrey Sachs. 2012. *World Happiness Report*. New York: UN Sustainable Development Solutions Network. http://worldhappiness.report/download/.

Helliwell, John F., Hugh Shiplett, and Christopher P. Barrington-Leigh. 2019. "How Happy Are Your Neighbours? Variation in Life Satisfaction among 1200 Canadian Neighbourhoods and Communities." *PloS ONE* 14, no. 1. https://doi.org/10.1371/journal.pone.0210091.

Helliwell, John F., Hugh Shiplett, and Aneta Bonikowska. 2020. "Migration as a Test of the Happiness Set Point Hypothesis: Evidence from Immigration to Canada and the United Kingdom." *Canadian Journal of Economics* 53, no. 4: 1618–41. https://onlinelibrary.wiley.com/doi/pdf/10.1111/caje.12474.

Helliwell, John F., and Shun Wang. 2011. "Trust and Wellbeing." *International Journal of Wellbeing* 1, no. 1. doi:10.5502/ijw.v1i1.3.

Holt-Lunstad, Julianne. 2017. "The Potential Public Health Relevance of Social Isolation and Loneliness: Prevalence, Epidemiology, and Risk Factors." *Public Policy & Aging Report* 27, no. 4: 127–30.

Hooper, Monica Webb, Anna María Nápoles, and Eliseo J. Pérez-Stable. 2020. "COVID-19 and Racial/Ethnic Disparities." *JAMA* 323, no. 24: 2466–67. https://doi.org/10.1001/jama.2020.8598.

Kawachi, Ichiro, and S.V. Subramanian. 2018. "Social Epidemiology for the 21st Century." *Social Science & Medicine* 196: 240–5.

Last, John, Susan Harris, Michel Thuriaux, and Robert Spasoff. 2001. *A Dictionary of Epidemiology*. Chicago: International Epidemiological Association, Inc.

Layard, Richard, Andrew Clark, Jan-Emmanuel De Neve, Chris Krekel, Daisy Fancourt, Nancy Hey, and Gus O'Donnell. 2020. *When to Release the Lockdown? A Wellbeing Framework for Analysing Costs and Benefits.* (No. 13186). IZA Discussion Papers.

Layard, Richard, and Gus O'Donnell. 2015. "How to Make Policy when Happiness Is the Goal." *World Happiness Report 2015*, 76–87. https://worldhappiness.report /ed/2015/.

Lemyre, Xavier, Joelle Mader, and Marke Ambard. 2018. *Quantifying and Valuing the Wellbeing Impacts of Arts, Culture and Sports in Canada*. Ottawa: Heritage Canada. https://cudo.carleton.ca/system/files/dli_training/4330/wellbeing -impacts-arts-culture-and-sports-canada-final.pdf.

OECD. 2013. *OECD Guidelines on Measuring Subjective Well-Being*. Paris: OECD Publishing. http://www.oecd.org/statistics/Guidelines%20on%20Measuring%20 Subjective%20Well-being.pdf.

– 2019. *Putting Well-Being Metrics into Policy Action*. Report of meeting held 3–4 October 2019. Paris: OECD. http://www.oecd.org/statistics/putting-well-being -metrics-into-policy-action.htm.

Ontario Ministry of Long-Term Care. 2018. *Mental Health Promotion Guideline 2018*. http://health.gov.on.ca/en/pro/programs/publichealth/oph_standards/docs /protocols_guidelines/Mental_Health_Promotion_Guideline_2018.pdf.

Orpana, Heather, Julie Vachon, Jen Dykxhoorn, Louise McRae, and Gayatri Jayaraman. 2016. "Monitoring Positive Mental Health and Its Determinants in Canada: The Development of the Positive Mental Health Surveillance Indicator Framework." *Health Promotion and Chronic Disease Prevention in Canada: Research, Policy and Practice* 36, no. 1: 1.

Peasgood, Tessa, Derek Foster, and Paul Dolan. 2019. "Priority Setting in Healthcare through the Lens of Happiness." In *Global Happiness and Wellbeing Policy Report 2019*, 27–52. New York: Global Happiness Council. https://s3.amazonaws.com /ghwbpr-2019/UAE/GH19_Ch3.pdf.

Pickett, Kate E., and Richard G. Wilkinson. 2015. "Income Inequality and Health: A Causal Review." *Social Science & Medicine* 128: 316–26.

Rosella, Laura C., Longdi Fu, Emmalin Buajitti, and Vivek Goel. 2019. "Death and Chronic Disease Risk Associated with Poor Life Satisfaction: A Population-based Cohort Study." *American Journal of Epidemiology* 188, no. 2: 323–31.

Shi, Yipu, Craig Joyce, Ron Wall, Heather Orpana, and Christina Bancej. 2019. "A Life Satisfaction Approach to Valuing the Impact of Health Behaviours on Subjective Well-Being." *BMC Public Health* 19, no. 1: 1547.

Statistics Canada. 2020. "Provisional Death Counts and Excess Mortality, January to March 2019 and January to March 2020." *The Daily*, 13 May 2020. https:// www150.statcan.gc.ca/n1/daily-quotidien/200513/dq200513d-eng.htm.

Stiglitz, Joseph E., Amartya Sen, and Jean-Paul Fitoussi. 2009. *The Measurement of Economic Performance and Social Progress Revisited: Reflections and Overview.* Paris: Commission on the Measurement of Economic Performance and Social Progress.

Sud, Amit, Michael Jones, John Broggio, Chey Loveday, and Clare Turnbull. 2020. "Collateral Damage: The Impact on Outcomes from Cancer Surgery of the COVID-19 Pandemic." *Annals of Oncology.* doi:https://doi.org/10.1016/j.annonc.2020.05.009.

The Treasury. 2019. "CBAx Tool User Guidance: Guide for Departments and Agencies Using Treasury's CBAx Tool for Cost Benefit Analysis." Wellington: Treasury of New Zealand. https://treasury.govt.nz/sites/default/files/2019-09/cbax-guide-sep19.pdf.

VanderWeele, Tyler J., Ying Chen, Katelyn Long, Eric S. Kim, Claudia Trudel-Fitzgerald, and Laura D. Kubzansky. 2020. "Positive Epidemiology?" *Epidemiology* 31, no. 2: 189–93.

World Health Organization. 1948. "Preamble to the Constitution of WHO as Adopted by the International Health Conference, New York, 19 June–22 July 1946; Signed on 22 July 1946 by the Representatives of 61 States (Official Records of WHO, no. 2, p. 100) and Entered into Force on 7 April 1948." Geneva: World Health Organization.

12 Well-Being, Sustainability, and Progress: A Framework for Public and Policy Discourse and for Quantitative Decision-Making Using the Life Satisfaction Approach[1]

CHRISTOPHER P. BARRINGTON-LEIGH

1. Introduction and Context

The effort to modernize metrics for progress and social-economic success is still often framed as moving "beyond GDP." Not only have statistical agencies, policymakers, and societies as a whole largely failed to realize the call to converge on a broader and more appropriate measure of human well-being, but ironically the "de-growth" movement, which associates GDP with environmental harm, has served as part of the same chorus as growth-centric development economists. That is, advocating for growth and advocating for de-growth both keep the focus on GDP. Instead, to truly move beyond GDP, the time has come and the tools are at hand to measure what matters more directly – both to gauge human well-being and to gauge impacts on the environment.

This chapter explores a strong version of this vision, in which these measures are distinct and policy is accountable to them in distinct ways. It is premised on the existence of an indicator for human well-being that is meaningful enough to be a quantitative guide to decision-making in government. Life satisfaction – a transparent, compelling, comprehensive, and sensitive measure – appears to be such an indicator.

Life satisfaction contradicts GDP in a number of ways when interpreted as a measure of progress. For instance, life-satisfaction data have shown that a population might not become happier as it becomes richer, that an extra dollar of income going to a wealthy family has a measurably small impact on life satisfaction compared to when it goes to a low-income family, and that the quality of relationships in a workplace matter more, on average, than does income. Life-satisfaction data give us a way to value, quantitatively, the importance of feelings like community trust and a sense of belonging, the effect that a trustworthy government has on overall life quality, and the emotional cost of being unemployed, which is much greater than the financial disruption alone. Life-satisfaction data enable us to evaluate the relative benefits of addressing mental health problems as compared with other medical interventions, the lifelong non-monetary value of protecting children from adverse circumstances, the benefit of teaching social and emotional skills to people of all ages, and so much more.

On the other hand, based on what is known about the determinants of life satisfaction, it seems feasible to imagine a society with high life satisfaction but which is running down the resources left for future generations. While a government decision-maker can, if equipped with sufficient information, choose policies to nurture high life satisfaction in the near and medium term, there are limits to the scope of decisions that can be treated in such a well-being-driven framework. In particular, when future circumstances are outside the scope of past experience, or uncertainty is too high to carry out calculations and optimizations, or consequences from today run too far into the future, a well-being framework for policymaking is likely to fail to provide sufficient confidence for decision-making.

A second danger looms. There is a tendency to create indices of progress or well-being which combine multiple, disparate outcomes with entirely arbitrary weights, leaving them indefensible upon scrutiny, often after attracting initial public and political attention. Worse, such indices often conflate, i.e., add together, measures related to human experience with measures related to ecological limits. An example is the single (scalar) index created to track the highly influential UN Sustainable Development Goals (SDGs). It is a sum of one hundred numbers, all treated as equally important, which cover the disparate ideas captured by the SDGs. De Neve and Sachs (2020) note that indices for SDG goals 12 (responsible consumption and production) and 13 (climate action) have a negative relationship with well-being. They conclude that "policymakers may find pursuing [these] more difficult" as a result. Conflating measures of quality of life with those of ecological outcomes acts, like a focus on GDP, to buttress fears of a tension between progress and sustainability. Instead, these objectives must be rhetorically and conceptually separated to make sustainable development politically feasible.

The following complementary approaches address this challenge: (1) a system of constraints, particularly on material use and waste generation, acts to simplify decision-making about the far future, especially when the far future is characterized by high uncertainty; (2) within such constraints, government decisions can be informed by the best evidence on what makes for good current and medium-term future lives.

Several institutions, described in this chapter, will be necessary to realize this ideal. While the overall scenario of happiness-maximizing policy subject to physical limits represents a transformative change, most of the pieces are already in place, at least in an embryonic state. The sections below describe the following existing institutions:

1. the ongoing monitoring of happiness by government statistical agencies;
2. public databases of "happiness coefficients" which encapsulate knowledge about how much a particular change or difference in life circumstances is likely to improve or reduce an individual's quality of life;
3. government planning models of how events at one point in someone's life affect their behaviour, productivity, and need for government services later on in life; and
4. monitoring, accounting, and enforcement systems for implementing conservation constraints on the use of resources and emission of waste products.

With some further development of these institutions, they could together guide governments in making trade-offs between competing needs, while limiting long-run risks that may be said to define many of our sustainability threats.

2. What Is "Happiness"?

As is common in the economics of happiness literature, a number of possible distinctions (OECD 2013) within the domain of subjective well-being (SWB) are glossed over in this chapter. In this context, each of the following terms can be taken to mean respondents' quantitative answers to the satisfaction with life (SWL) question: life satisfaction, happiness, SWB, and even well-being. An international standard version of the SWL question in English is: "The following question asks how satisfied you feel, on a scale from 0 to 10. Zero means you feel "not at all satisfied" and 10 means you feel "completely satisfied". Overall, how satisfied are you with life as a whole these days?" (OECD 2013). The life-satisfaction approach relies on individual respondents to report their overall experience, taking into account everything together, in the right proportions. Then, statistical methods are used to unravel the importance of different contributions to a good life. Individually, respondents are not experts on how hypothetical changes to their lives would affect their life satisfaction, but they are sole experts on how good their own lived circumstances feel. Collectively, many respondents living a variety of different circumstances can inform us of which conditions foster the best lives.

3. Measuring Well-Being of Society

Even with all the evidence on the psychological and economic validity of life satisfaction as a metric (e.g., Frijters et al. 2020), using life satisfaction as a headline indicator for human progress is of course ultimately an ethical or philosophical choice. Nevertheless, it has strong rationale (e.g., Barrington-Leigh 2016a, 2016b; Barrington-Leigh and Escande 2018; Barrington-Leigh and Wollenberg 2019; Dolan, Layard, and Metcalfe 2011; Global Happiness Council 2018, 2019; Hall, Barrington-Leigh, and Helliwell 2011).

One way to think about SWL is as a headline indicator which may accompany a dashboard of other, more objective indicators. Reported in its raw form, SWL communicates the overall intent of an indicator system. Its subjective nature makes clear the primacy given to the lived experience of a target population.

Going a step further, SWL can be used to derive statistical evidence about the relative importance to well-being of each objective indicator. Although the process is not completely devoid of judgment, these statistical calculations, typically linear regressions, are open to scrutiny and subject to revision in light of further evidence.

Thus, life satisfaction can provide accountability to the choice of an entire dashboard of indicators, avoiding the need for the dashboard designers to impose judgment about which policies, government departments, or domains of life define well-being.

Taking another logical step, a scalar index (i.e., one number summarizing a whole set of indicators) of well-being can be constructed from a dashboard of objective measures. The same statistical inference used to determine the importance of each objective indicator can be used to provide weights to aggregate those indicators into a single number. In this way one can avoid assuming arbitrarily that all components of an index are equally important (Barrington-Leigh and Escande 2018), as do numerous indices like the UN Human Development Index or attempts to rank SDG performance (De Neve and Sachs 2020; Miola and Schiltz 2019).

By extension, SWL data can also suggest which indicators to drop entirely from an index or dashboard. If an indicator is included in a summary "well-being" dashboard or index, it should be because it is found to be important in statistical models of well-being, i.e., because it is useful in differentiating between those experiencing high quality of life and those experiencing low quality of life, overall. In this way, a hierarchy of indicators, or an overall index, organized around SWL has an intrinsic legitimacy in its conception and design. The value it embodies is clear, and the idea that policy should be targeted and accountable to improve such a measure is compelling. Its quantitative and transparent nature allows others both to understand and reproduce it.

In summary, SWL has a natural role both as a headline indicator in its raw measured form, and as an organizing concept, based on transparent and falsifiable evidence, for a broader array of (more) objective indicators. Below, in section 5, these objective indicators will represent intermediate policy objectives.

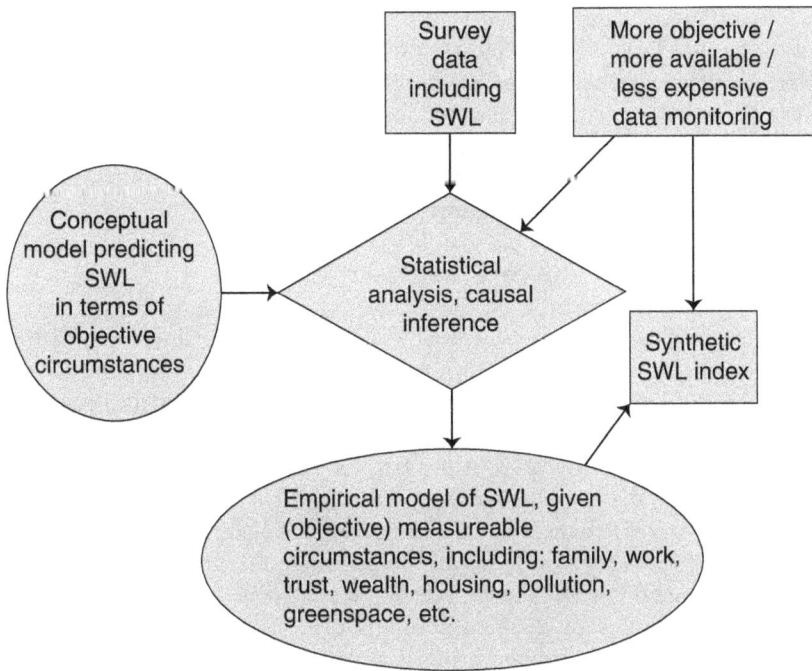

Figure 12.1. Measurement of life satisfaction (SWL) and generation of empirical weights for a well-being index

Being able to build an index out of objective measures has other advantages. Running surveys is always expensive, and life-satisfaction data require particularly large sample sizes because life satisfaction varies in response to so many factors. Objective and community-level conditions tend in this sense to be less noisy and therefore less expensive to measure, so they can be measured more frequently or with more demographic or geographic detail than the SWL that is needed to estimate weights.

Figure 12.1 presents a conceptual depiction of how a "synthetic SWL" index (lower-right rectangle) can be constructed and published using the weights from accumulated knowledge about the determinants of SWL (lower oval). The key element is the survey measurement of actual life-satisfaction reports (top-left rectangle), typically as part of a questionnaire which also assesses numerous other life conditions experienced by each respondent. The top-right grey box represents these other life conditions, along with any other measurable life circumstances applying to an individual or her geographic region.

Many national statistical agencies are already measuring the life satisfaction of their populations. For example, Statistics Canada poses the question to more than 90,000 residents each year as part of comprehensive health and social surveys. At least seven countries include the question in national panel surveys. The World Values Survey and the Gallup World Poll include overall life evaluation questions in their international surveys, which are in Gallup's case annual and cover most of the world's countries.

4. The Database of Happiness Coefficients

This wealth of data on people's lives in a wide variety of circumstances within and among countries, including respondents undergoing a diversity of changes and life events, and subject to a variety of public policies and policy changes, has provided a rich base of knowledge about what makes life good.

This academic knowledge is in the form of a large body of published statistical analyses over several decades. Recently, it has begun to be collected into a summary database (Frijters and Krekel 2021; What Works Centre for Wellbeing 2018; Barrington-Leigh and Lemermeyer 2021) in a form that could help governments evaluate the impacts of prospective policy.

This Database of Happiness Coefficients (DoHC) contains the same weights, or "coefficients," described above in the context of a dashboard of objective indicators. They tell us how happy someone, or some community, is likely to be given an objective description of their current life. In Figure 12.1, the lower oval depicts the DoHC.

Two key steps are needed to ensure that governments have access to a reputable database of these coefficients. First, internationally and possibly within each country or jurisdiction, it is incumbent on analysts to debate and distil knowledge about the relationship between policy-influenced variables and human experience, in an accountable and ongoing process.

The second key to the construction of a consensus model of the determinants of happiness is to increase the contribution of policy experiments and policy evaluations towards the evidence on life satisfaction. This means expanding the measurement and monitoring of happiness and its social supports. Exceptional effort should be made when a policy changes, or where a policy roll-out affects only a subset of the population or reaches different groups at different times. In this way more policy changes can be turned into policy experiments, typically through partnership with academia, by cleverly varying or randomizing who is initially impacted.

These elements can give rise to an accountable, open database growing in both confidence and scope, differentiated by country as needed or desired, which gives the best available estimates and confidence intervals for the effects of individual, social, and collective life circumstances on human life satisfaction.

The curation task of the DoHC should, at least initially, be up to the scientific community and civil society, rather than government. Happily, precisely those appointed groups have already taken up the task.

5. Investments over the Life Course

Coefficients in a DoHC can be used to predict the difference in happiness of employees in workplaces with different levels of trust, or the difference in happiness between people with stable and safe childhood environments and those without.

However, when it comes to policy, a government cannot directly change citizens' trust of coworkers, nor change the childhood experience of adults. Instead, a government interested in happiness considers making investments now to affect the future outcome of trust or the future burden of carried traumas. The question thus arises: how will intermediate outcomes evolve in the future, given the implementation of a particular policy rule, the provision of a particular public service, or the collective investment in a particular resource? Answering these questions more or less explicitly is already the task of each government department within their particular domain.

When government agencies justify specific expenditures on education, public health, rehabilitation, other social supports, or indeed on any civic infrastructure, it is based on a belief about how benefits will accrue in the future from those investments. Calculations of future outcomes based on models of such dynamics are used all the time to choose between alternative uses of public resources, even if those models are sometimes quite simplistic.

As a result of the availability of longitudinal, linked, citizen-based data, such government models are becoming more sophisticated. In recent years, for instance, New Zealand has revamped a number of its social spending programs to use the best evidence on how social service investments in an individual lead to savings over several decades. These calculations are focused primarily on achieving "a positive long-term financial impact for the social sector." That is, investing in human capital now saves the government money in the future. However, as the government notes, this investment approach "also has non-financial benefit as people experience longer lives, lived in better health and independence, with greater educational achievement and with dignity. As a specific funding mechanism, 'investment funding' gives providers an incentive to focus on these long-term impacts and value them alongside immediate, short-term gains" (Minister of Health 2016, 6). A rich DoHC is the ideal tool to evaluate these kinds of benefits in human terms. Ultimately, both financial costs and benefits can be expressed in terms of their well-being implications through use of a DoHC since government expenditures translate into increased taxes and livelihoods in predictable amounts, and these circumstances have implications for happiness.

Understanding investments over the life course of an individual requires coordination of efforts across multiple government departments. Moreover, expressing the benefit stream over time in overall quality-of-life terms, using the DoHC, puts into commensurable terms the cost effectiveness of spending across all government agencies. Thus, not only does the task require coordination and foster integrative policies, but it allows one department to value benefits of its services which normally accrue within the domain of another department – i.e., to properly value complementarities and synergies across offices, ministries, and jurisdictions. Ultimately, a common metric of performance can also facilitate happiness-based budgeting at the highest level.

6. Sustainability Is Different from Future Happiness

Many long-run government investments can feasibly be handled by the methods described above. Such spending will naturally include many environmental investments. There is already a large set of studies within the subjective well-being literature that quantifies the impact of environmental goods on life satisfaction. Therefore, a number of environmental exposure variables will naturally end up in the DoHC, and our understanding of how policy can affect those exposures in the future will inform certain environmental policies. For instance, exposure to noise, pollution, and green space appear to have an immediate, quantifiable, and sustained effect on life satisfaction (Maddison, Rehdanz, and Welsch 2020). Reduction of exposure to lead, or ensuring the viability of a fishery, may be predicted to affect other life conditions, listed in the DoHC, over a generation.

When the Calculus Fails

However, some future outcomes are too complex to predict well. How might gradual topsoil erosion, land-use change, groundwater depletion, or fossil-fuel extraction be incorporated into a government decision-making framework? One untenable option is as follows. Abiding by some variant of the Brundtland et al. (1987) definition of sustainability, or by the logic of "weak sustainability" articulated by Solow (1991), we would ensure that, overall, the well-being of those in the future is at least as high as our own. We would project how current policy options would affect objective outcomes in the future, coupled with a DoHC to calculate the corresponding impacts on overall life quality. The goal would be to calculate the optimal level and kinds of consumption to maximize current well-being while ensuring that, taking into account the numerous other gifts we bequeath to our descendants, future generations would still have good lives overall.

That plan is a mirage. For long-run, unfamiliar, unpredictable, complex, and uncertain dynamics, these calculations are not feasible. For such cases, it is not possible to choose an optimum based on accumulated knowledge about returns to investment (section 5) and the DoHC. Thus, the well-being approach fails in these cases and, one might say, the domain of "sustainability" considerations begins.[2]

For instance, reflecting on the contribution of academic economics to the question of how to manage greenhouse gases, it seems that two decades were squandered theorizing about the right discount rate and preference parameters which, if known, would point to a particular optimal combination of mitigating climate change versus adapting to it. Instead, if society had been equipped already with norms and institutions for an alternative, precautionary approach, we could more easily have recognized that this question could not yet be settled based on quantitative arguments about well-being.

An Approach to Long-Run Risk

How, then, are we to incorporate a concern for long-run risk or conservation into a framework which privileges human well-being?

Above all, the answer is to be willing to separate them (Neumayer 1999; Stiglitz, Sen, and Fitoussi 2009). There needs to be a second rationale, besides accountability to predicted changes in human well-being, that society accepts to justify limits. A sensible approach is to address long-run problems through physical constraints, rather than optimization of well-being, when they are too complex or risky to treat through a system of prediction and quantitative balancing of human outcomes.

For example, in the case of greenhouse gases, a plan to stop the expansion of emissions could have been put in place in the late twentieth century while further studies sought better precision on the future risks.[3] More generally, our extraction of material resources from the earth and our addition of material pollutants to natural reservoirs could be subject to controls, sometimes in the form of explicit limits, justified not by calculable future well-being but by a principle of conservation.

The approach can be applied to governments at all levels with enforcement authority: a city may decide to limit the growth of its footprint; a regional government in charge of mining may put an annual quota on both extraction rates and surface damage; and a national government may limit use of each ocean resource. In each case, a quota could be designed at first to halt further expansion of the rate of material extraction or effluent release, in ignorance of an "optimal" rate. The quota may subsequently be decreased, year over year, or otherwise adjusted based on arguments about the stability of the resource, as ecological evidence is available.

Key features of a system of sustainability constraints are that (1) the constraints are not calculated with regard to human well-being or benefits, but rather to objective physical measures (directly or indirectly) and (2) that the physical measures are particular to each resource or waste stream, rather than being aggregated into an overall measure of environmental status or damage.[4]

For the purposes of making a distinction between well-being-driven policies and those justified by conservation considerations, there is no need to proceed into the details of how physical limits are implemented. The feasibility of building a democratic consensus for a particular level of emissions or rate of emissions cuts, the feasibility of solving collective action problems across multiple governments, and the problem of mechanism design for implementing controls, all lie beyond the scope of this chapter. The focus is instead on protecting a life-satisfaction approach from being burdened by non-commensurable objectives that it cannot accommodate. It is for this reason that society must have a complementary principle by which to manage certain long-run risks. That principle relates to controlling change, especially in natural resources, when future implications of current consumption are unclear.

In the greenhouse gas case, for example, carbon neutrality has become a principled goal for firms, regions, and nations. Early action could have been to institute a steadily and predictably rising price of emissions, without initial knowledge of how high it should end up. A price instrument can adjust over time to meet a more quantity-based decarbonization rule, with the principle remaining one of sustainability rather than optimization of well-being. Carbon neutrality does not relate to any particular level of human well-being; in this sense it is arbitrary. Acceptance of conservation constraints and tolerance of uncertainty about the long-run costs to well-being are key to this policy framing.

Within the space defined by such constraints, policy can continue to optimize human well-being using the life-satisfaction approach. Thus, a number of constraints protect the depletion of natural stocks of many kinds, but within those constraints society is generally directed to improve human satisfaction according to the best available knowledge.

Figure 12.2 depicts the combined institutions. The "ecological constraints" box represents sustainability-related constraints to policy, and the "Systems Knowledge" oval represents the content of section 5, that is, the translation of prospective policies today into objective outcomes in the future. The DoHC in turn translates these into a population distribution of expected human experience, upon which policy choices can be based.

To reiterate the nature of the present proposal, let me point out that there is no description in this diagram of how to choose the stringency of conservation, such as the rate of convergence to zero for non-renewable extraction or pollution flows. The enormous literature on this subject remains relevant

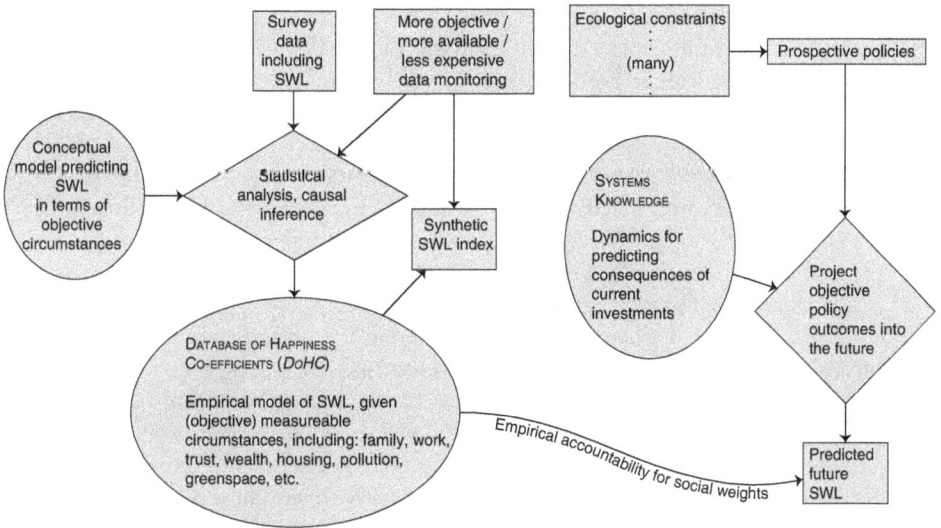

Figure 12.2. Components of a well-being-oriented policymaking process

in the context of the "constraints" box in Figure 12.2 and is not addressed here. Instead, my point of advocacy is to avoid casting all conservation considerations as components of well-being. This mistake can be avoided if public discourse admits a second principle for policy, using a conservation or precautionary rationale to justify the stabilization of ecological (or other) systems.

Three Critiques

A FALSE DICHOTOMY BETWEEN WELL-BEING AND SUSTAINABILITY?

Like most dichotomies, this one is not rigid. Material limits are most likely to be considered and introduced when there is a perceived risk to future human well-being. Later, when relevant natural and social science becomes sufficiently well understood that a calculus of future well-being can be applied, the material limit designed for ecological sustainability may be replaced by one fine-tuned for long-run well-being.

Conversely, every prospective policy comes with some risk, i.e., an imperfect prediction of its future consequences to human well-being. Predictions are, technically speaking, distributions of probabilities over different possible outcomes. For instance, a government model of human life course development may recognize some uncertainty in life expectancy of current generations and in future immigration flows; these possibilities will be reflected in a range of expected policy outcomes expressed in terms of well-being.

For this reason, among others, there will always remain room for democratic will and political preference in policy, even in an environment where the population expects justification in terms of, and accountability to, a quality-of-life measure. The difference between this uncertainty in future well-being and that which motivates a physically denominated limit to conserve some resource is in principle only a matter of degree; however, practically speaking, two separate rationales – human well-being and principled conservation – are easier to understand and, I suggest, to institutionalize.

The dichotomy also has some internal coherence. Stabilizing natural systems and shifting to a reliance on sustainable resources may help to reduce uncertainty about the structure of life in future decades, thereby facilitating the kind of projections needed for a well-being approach to other policies. Conversely, focusing on an optimistic, quality of life–oriented discourse within the context of some material constraints should make the principled imposition of those constraints more palatable for all involved.

Lastly, in some contexts, a commitment to conservation principles is likely to buttress social cohesion and identity, and in turn life satisfaction. Indeed, an important support for life satisfaction is the degree to which people feel a connection to a meaningful social identity and a sense of cultural continuity (Chandler and Lalonde 1998). Similarly, the opportunity to act in support of others is a powerful promoter of individual well-being (Aknin et al. 2013). While the cultural benefits of embracing a principled conservation policy may be as difficult to calculate as the anthropocentric environmental benefits, they may be considerable. One might speculate that the promise of separating policy rationale about individual and collective happiness from stories about conservation may open the door to more narrative approaches, maybe akin to those Indigenous peoples have used for millennia, for explaining the imposition of resource-limiting rules. That is, allowing conservation constraints to be portrayed as part of a people's identity rather than subject to arguments about well-being may have some immediate benefits for people's well-being.

UNBOUNDED COSTS TO CONSERVATION?
Another critique is that the costs to well-being of an unnecessary or overly conservative constraint may be just as high as the potential damage of not imposing controls. There are two important premises which may make the physical-limits approach compelling in the face of this concern.

The first relevant premise is one of the major insights from life-satisfaction research. It is that the scope for improving, or indeed diminishing, life experience through non-material changes to society is enormous, while the scope for changing lives through material means is relatively limited (Barrington-Leigh

2016b). This is generally counter-intuitive in the context of developing economies; nevertheless, the evidence spans all levels of development. Projections based on past development suggest that changes in GDP per capita and healthy life expectancy between now and 2050 are unlikely to change world average life satisfaction by even one point on the eleven-point scale (Barrington-Leigh and Galbraith 2019). By contrast, different feasible trajectories of a few non-material variables by 2050 account for a variation of nearly 3.5 points on the same scale, with the optimistic end leaving the average country as happy as today's Belgium and Costa Rica (Figure 12.3). One interpretation is that the scope for improving lives may be surprisingly undiminished under the imposition of some material constraints.

The second proposition in defence of precautionary constraints is that on moderate time scales, innovation partly compensates for supply limitations. When material constraints are transparent and predictable, markets respond appropriately through innovation and substitution. The idea that such constraints can spur innovation so strongly as to be beneficial even in the short term (Porter and Van der Linde 1995) has support in a variety of contexts, although it will not apply universally. Nevertheless, the innovation bred by transparent constraints on a given material flow will always increase efficiency in the use or production of the constrained material and will always mitigate the reduction in consumption benefit that would otherwise be experienced. We can be certain, for instance, that had oil become expensive one hundred years ago, wind and solar power technology and electric transportation infrastructure would have advanced much earlier than it has. Policy should therefore focus on optimizing human well-being within a set of ecologically motivated constraints, rather than giving undue focus to opportunity lost to those constraints.

SUSTAINABILITY PROBLEMS NOT SOLVED?
Another possible objection to the proposal of this section is the opposite of the previous one. It is that constraining resource extraction or pollution does not necessarily entail constraining it sufficiently. While true, this critique is more relevant to specific approaches to instituting consumption constraints, rather than to the general idea of imposing them.

Different environmental-control instruments are appropriate in different situations. In instituting such protections, there are plenty of problems to do with free riding across jurisdictions, intermingled with those to do with public will. However, these are likely either ameliorated or unaffected by implementing the ideas in this chapter, which emphasizes separating a physical or ecological rationale for policy from one based on the science of well-being. If a public accepts a well-being-subject-to-limits approach, and if the institutions to enforce limits are in place, then updating limits in light of new ecological

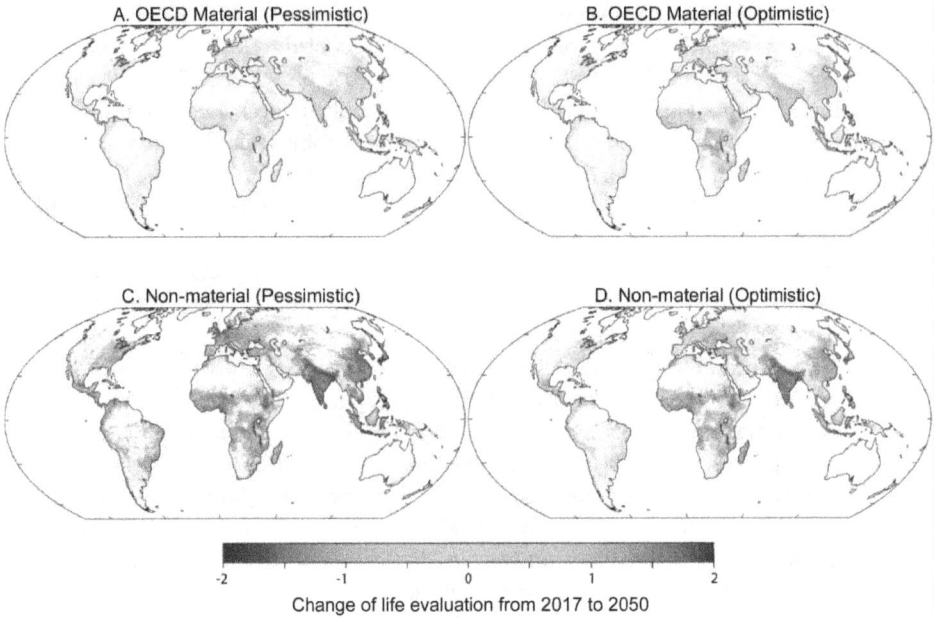

Figure 12.3. Optimistic and pessimistic scenarios in which only material outcomes change (A, B) or only non-material outcomes change (C, D). Based on Barrington-Leigh and Galbraith (2019).

science, for instance, may be easier than debating the social costs and benefits of running down a natural stock.

Precedents for Physical Limits

Fortunately, as with the institutions described in earlier sections, the institutions for limiting physical throughput are neither completely novel in concept nor in practice.

For instance, water-extraction quantities, SO_2 emissions, fishery catches, forestry-cut volumes, urban-development perimeters, and CO_2 emissions are examples of material flows subject to caps, often allocated by auctions of tradeable quotas or other material controls.

Pigouvian taxes, i.e., taxes on environmental externalities, also have a long pedigree. In many situations the optimal instrument provides price certainty in the short run but is adjusted to meet physical-constraint objectives in the long run. An example is the Western Climate Initiative's carbon-pricing approach for Quebec and California.[5]

In practice, international competition and political pressures will limit how stringent governments are willing to be in imposing controls. Nevertheless, expanding institutions and social acceptance for self-imposed limits expressed in physical and ecological terms, rather than those justified by projected human benefits, is an important complement to well-being-based policymaking.

7. Conclusion

For brevity, and because further work is needed on some topics, this chapter does not discuss a staged transition for implementing a well-being budgeting framework, the complexity of policymaking in hierarchical institutions, the pitfalls of alternative approaches, monitoring and enforcement costs for material constraints, the challenges raised by international trade and non-cooperation, or the additional complexities of distributional issues or temporal discounting. However, each of these aspects is already under consideration in the context of well-being-driven policy or being actively worked on (e.g., Frijters and Krekel 2020; Global Happiness Council 2019; Happiness Research Institute 2020) or will remain relatively unchanged by a transition to a well-being-led framework.

The intent here is, first, to convey the sense that the science and economics of happiness is mature enough to support a global reorientation of policymaking; second, to fill in the missing piece of how such a world can approach sustainability questions that are not yet sufficiently amenable to the life-satisfaction approach; and third, to explain the role of an institutional layer dealing with "medium-term" dynamics between policy decisions and the known determinants of life satisfaction. Overall, the point is that each of the necessary institutions already exists at least embryonically, allowing for an incrementalist transition to embracing a new, well-being-centred policy approach. The task of transforming governments towards accountability to more human-centred measures of well-being cannot take place as a sudden revolution but as a mutually reinforcing evolution of public expectation and government practice.

Life satisfaction can act as an organizing concept for measuring human-centred outcomes and their distribution and can provide empirical accountability both to the selection of a broader dashboard of objective indicators and to important parts of the policy development and selection process. However, designing policy to maximize human well-being of this sort is entirely insufficient to achieve sustainability, so a complementary approach for long-term risk is described in this chapter. Indeed, in "moving beyond GDP," it appears to be as important to properly situate ecological concerns as it is to choose a sensible measure of life quality. The common mistake of assigning extra, rather than less, meaning to GDP by targeting a slow-down and the even more common mistake (e.g., Bleys 2008; Talberth, Cobb, and Slattery 2006) of anthropomorphizing the environment by trying to integrate its health into indices of the well-being of humans (Neumayer 1999) are both unproductive in the long run. Moreover, they go nowhere near far enough in strength or specificity of protection for ecological integrity.

Two ideological transformations are thus needed in public discourse. First, a reorientation of social and economic policy towards the subjective experience of humans and its evidence base, and second, an acceptance of ecological limits without an explicit justification in terms of human well-being, but which are instead denominated in ecological terms. Fundamental to my optimism that populations will embrace the second rationale is a belief that the first reorientation will reap large benefits to well-being through non-material domains of life, thereby coming to understand that ecological limits do not pose a strong threat to such well-being. However, an embrace of physical limits may also come about more directly, through gaining familiarity with carbon neutrality policies, for instance, even as support for them is driven by fear of threats to human well-being.

In line with the widespread desire for more compelling measures of progress, the public will increasingly look to life satisfaction as a prominent, or headline, indicator of the state of society, and as a measure of the differences between subgroups in overall experience. Also, with access to the same independently curated DoHC on which the government relies, civil society will be able to evaluate the government's rationalization of its policies using a common language and a sensible objective. Whether this revised objective leads to subtle or transformative changes over the long run remains to be seen; I would gamble on transformative.

For those concerned with the decoupling of growth and environmental impacts as an impossible challenge, any economic growth under the beyond-GDP institutions described here would by construction be entirely decoupled from material flows under constant or decreasing caps. Happily, under a system with an explicit objective to improve life satisfaction, there may be very little public attention on the growth or contraction of GDP because data on more compelling and relevant measures would be at hand.

While providing a new level of accountability to policy, this framework accommodates plenty of breadth for creativity and diversity in policies and political platforms. This is due to two factors. The first is the complexity of ideas about how economic and social outcomes of policy will evolve over time, e.g., the dynamics of investment into humans over their life course, which in principle may encompass much of the social sciences (section 5). The second is the existence of normative debates about how to deal with distributional issues, i.e., inequality, in well-being or in other intermediate outcomes.

I conclude that the key institutions described in this chapter already have real-life precedents. The practical successes and lessons from existing subnational implementations of material caps are valuable in designing a more comprehensive system of such constraints, but ultimately any transition rests on new institutions becoming accepted and expected by the public. Due to the convergence of a maturation of happiness research, wide concern about global climate change, and a global health crisis requiring reflection about institutional norms and about core trade-offs in the drivers of well-being, the time may be at hand.

NOTES

1   This chapter is an abridged and adapted version of the following published paper: Christopher P. Barrington-Leigh, "Life Satisfaction and Sustainability: A Policy Framework," SN Social Sciences 1, no. 176 (2021). DOI:10.1007 /s43545-021-00185-8.

2   I am not proposing to define sustainability, and I refer to conservation, sustainability, and precautionary principle loosely and interchangeably in this section. The important distinction is between well-being optimization and another, complementary, principled rationale, which I suggest should be conservationist.

3   If the greenhouse-gas example sounds somewhat far-fetched, it is likely because there is an additional challenge in the case of global public goods. The resulting collective action problem confounds the present discussion on government policymaking because national governments cannot enforce global decisions. In fact, the lack of international enforcement and coordination will also complicate placing limits on extracting raw materials which are traded or which are embedded in traded goods.

4   Thus, it is useful to control the amount of bauxite mined each year, but not to limit the total amount of economic activity, nor to trade off bauxite mining for, say, groundwater conservation by combining the two in an integrated ecological index of some kind and imposing a limit in terms of that index.

5   The greenhouse-gas case has shown us, again, that social costs are not only a subject of endless calculation; they can also be easily and radically manipulated, such as when the US Environmental Protection Agency's (EPA) value dropped by one to two orders of magnitude in 2017. A principled approach committing to carbon reduction in physical terms is subject to political and public debate and leadership, but less subject to complex calculations like the EPA's.

REFERENCES

Aknin, Lara B., Christopher P. Barrington-Leigh, Elizabeth W. Dunn, John F. Helliwell, Justine Burns, Robert Biswas-Diener, Imedla Kemeza, Paul Nyende, Claire E. Ashton-James, and Michael I. Norton. 2013. "Prosocial Spending and Well-Being: Cross-Cultural Evidence for a Psychological Universal." *Journal of Personality and Social Psychology* (US) 104, no. 4: 635–52. doi:10.1037/a0031578.

Barrington-Leigh, Christopher. 2016a. "The Role of Subjective Well-Being as an Organizing Concept for Community Indicators." In *Community Quality of Life and Wellbeing: Best Cases VII*, edited by Rhonda Phillips, Meg Holden, and Chantal Stevens, 19–34. Community Quality-of-Life Indicators. New York: Springer.

– 2016b. "Sustainability and Well-Being: A Happy Synergy." *Development* 59, no. 3: 292–8. https://doi. org/10.1057/s41301–017–0113-x.

Barrington-Leigh, Christopher, and Alice Escande. 2018. "Measuring Progress and Well-Being: A Comparative Review of Indicators." *Social Indicators Research* 135, no. 3: 893–925. http://dx.doi.org/10.1007/s11205-016-1505-0.

Barrington-Leigh, Christopher, and Eric Galbraith. 2019. "Feasible Future Global Scenarios for Human Life Evaluations." *Nature Communications* 10, no. 1: 161. doi:10.1038/s41467-018-08002-2.

Barrington-Leigh, Christopher, and Ekaterina Lemermeyer. 2021. "Canadian Database of Happiness Coefficients." http://lifesatisfaction.ca/dohc.

Barrington-Leigh, Christopher, and Jan Wollenberg. 2019. "Informing Policy Priorities Using Inference from Life Satisfaction Responses in a Large Community Survey." *Applied Research Quality Life* 14, no. 4: 911–24. doi:10.1007/s11482-018-9629-9.

Bleys, Brent. 2008. "Proposed Changes to the Index of Sustainable Economic Welfare: An Application to Belgium." *Ecological Economics* 64, no. 4: 741–51. doi:10.1016/j.ecolecon.2007.10.013.

Brundtland Commission. 1987. *Our Common Future*. New York: World Commission on Environment and Development.

Chandler, Michael J., and Christopher Lalonde. 1998. "Cultural Continuity as a Hedge against Suicide in Canada's First Nations." *Transcultural Psychiatry* 35, no. 2: 191–219.

De Neve, Jan-Emmanuel, and Jeffrey D. Sachs. 2020. "Sustainable Development and Well-Being." In *World Happiness Report 2020*, edited by by John Helliwell, Richard Layard, Jeffrey D. Sachs, and Jan-Emmanuel De Neve, 113–28. New York: Sustainable Development Solutions Network. http://worldhappiness.report /ed/2020/.

Dolan, Paul, Richard Layard, and Robert Metcalfe. 2011. "Measuring Subjective Well-Being for Public Policy." Office for National Statistics paper.

Frijters, Paul, and Christian Krekel. 2021. *A Handbook for Wellbeing Policy-Making in the UK: History, Measurement, Theory, Implementation, and Examples*. Oxford: Oxford University Press.

Frijters, Paul, Andrew E. Clark, Christian Krekel, and Richard Layard. 2020. "A Happy Choice: Wellbeing as the Goal of Government." *Behavioural Public Policy* 4, no. 2: 126–65.

Global Happiness Council. 2018. *Global Happiness Policy Report*. New York: Global Happiness Council. https://www.worldgovernmentsummit.org/api/publications /document?id=304a8bc4-e97c-6578-b2f8-ff0000a7ddb6.

– 2019. *Global Happiness Policy Report*. New York: Global Happiness Council. https://s3.amazonaws.com/ghwbpr-2019/UAE/GHWPR19.pdf.

Hall, Jon, Christopher Barrington-Leigh, and John Helliwell. 2011. "Cutting through the Clutter: Searching for an Over-Arching Measure of Well-Being." *DICE Report* 8, no. 4: 8–12.

Happiness Research Institute. 2020. *Wellbeing Adjusted Life Years: A Universal Metric to Quantify the Happiness Return on Investment*. Berlin: Happiness Research Institute.

Maddison, David, Katrin Rehdanz, and Heinz Welsch, eds. 2020. *Handbook on Well-Being, Happiness, and the Environment*. Cheltenham, UK: Edward Elgar.

Minister of Health. 2016. *New Zealand Health Strategy: Future Direction*. Wellington: Minister of Health.

Miola, Apollonia, and Fritz Schiltz. 2019. "Measuring Sustainable Development Goals Performance: How to Monitor Policy Action in the 2030 Agenda Implementation?" *Ecological Economics* 164: 106373. https://doi.org/10.1016 /j.ecolecon.2019.106373.

Neumayer, Eric. 1999. "The ISEW – Not an Index of Sustainable Economic Welfare." *Social Indicators Research* 48, no. 1: 77–101. doi:10.1023/A:1006914023227.

OECD. 2013. *OECD Guidelines on Measuring Subjective Well-Being*. Paris: OECD Publishing. doi:10.1787/9789264191655-en.

Porter, Michael E., and Claas Van der Linde. 1995. "Toward a New Conception of the Environment-Competitiveness Relationship." *Journal of Economic Perspectives* 9, no. 4: 97–118.

Solow, Robert M. 1991. "Sustainability: An Economist's Perspective." Marine Policy Center (Woods Hole Oceanographic Institution, Massachussetts).

Stiglitz, Joseph E., Amartya Sen, and Jean-Paul Fitoussi. 2009. "Report by the Commission on the Measurement of Economic Performance and Social Progress." Paris: Commission on the Measurement of Economic Performance and Social Progress. http://www.stiglitz-sen-fitoussi.fr.

Talberth, John, Clifford Cobb, and Noah Slattery. 2006. *The Genuine Progress Indicator*. Oakland, CA: Redefining Progress.

What Works Centre for Wellbeing. 2018. "Wellbeing in Policy Analysis." http:// whatworkswellbeing. org/wp-content/uploads/2018/03/Overview-incorporating -wellbeing-in-policy-analysis-vMarch2018.pdf.

13 Measuring Comprehensive Wealth in Canada

ROB SMITH, KIERAN MCDOUGAL, AND LIVIA BIZIKOVA

Introduction

Recent decades have seen significant concern expressed around the use of conventional indicators, notably GDP, to assess the progress of nations. GDP and other short-term indicators can lead decision-makers to favour policies with benefits today over those that may be better aligned with long-term sustainability. Even if quarterly GDP growth is positive for a country, that growth may not be sustainable if is predicated on policies that undermine the future.

Globally, there are significant and ongoing efforts to assess progress beyond GDP. A recent boost to such efforts has come from Sustainable Development Goal (SDG) target 17.19, which calls for countries to build on existing initiatives to develop new measures of progress. Similarly, G7 leaders at their 2018 summit called for new indicators of prosperity and well-being, noting that GDP alone is not enough to measure success.[1] In addition, the UN Secretary General called in 2021 for countries to move beyond GDP, stressing the need for nations to find new measures that focus on inclusive and sustainable growth and prosperity (UN Secretary-General, 2021).

Among the many beyond-GDP initiatives, the World Bank (2011, 2018, and 2021), the United Nations (UNU–IHDP and UNEP 2012), and others promote a paradigm in which sustainable development is defined as managing a portfolio of capital stocks in ways that either preserve or enhance it in order to maintain the nation's ability to provide well-being to its citizens over time. The central measure in this paradigm is known as *comprehensive wealth*.

Comprehensive wealth (CW) is defined as the value of all the assets a nation has at its disposal. It includes produced capital in the form of buildings, machinery, and other manufactured assets; financial capital like stocks and bonds; natural capital, such as forests and mineral deposits; human capital in the form of an educated and productive workforce; and, finally, social capital in the form of effective systems of cooperation (Box 1).[2]

CW is a nearly theoretically ideal[3] measure of the sustainability of intergenerational well-being when defined as the *per-capita* stock of wealth, providing a clear, coherent, and systematic framework for assessing sustainability that offers a conceptually sound complement to GDP (Arrow et al. 2012; Polasky et al. 2015; see also Dasgupta 2001, 2009, 2012, and 2014; Managi and Kumar 2018; UNU–IHDP and UNEP 2012; World Bank 2011 and 2018; Dasgupta 2021).

Several global reports have called for measures of comprehensive wealth, including:

- the report of the French Commission on the Measurement of Economic Performance and Social Progress (the so-called Stiglitz Commission; Stiglitz, Sen, and Fitoussi 2009) and its follow-up (Stiglitz et al. 2018)
- the report of the UN Economic Commission for Europe (UNECE) on statistics for sustainable development (UNECE et al. 2009)
- the Dasgupta Review on the Economics of Biodiversity (Dasgupta 2021)

Efforts to implement the concept of comprehensive wealth include the series of reports from the United Nations Environment Programme (UNEP) (UNU–IHDP and UNEP 2012 and 2014; Managi and Kumar 2018) that explore the concept in detail and provide data for 140 countries.[4] As part of its Index of Economic Well-Being, the Ottawa-based Centre for the Study of Living Standards was the first to publish estimates of comprehensive wealth for Canada (Osberg and Sharpe 2011).

The International Institute for Sustainable Development has released two in-depth studies on the topic for Canada (IISD 2016 and 2018). Below we discuss the way in which IISD has measured CW for Canada, using what we call the *National Comprehensive Wealth Index* (NCWI) and an accompanying suite of non-monetary indicators. We discuss the methodological approach and its limitations in the next section and the trends in the overall index, as well as trends in each of its components, and the non-monetary indicators and their implications for decision-making in the following section. We conclude with recommendations to increase the use of CW measures in Canada and suggestions for improvements in the index to improve its utility for decision-making.

Methodological Approach

We refer to the stock of comprehensive wealth *per capita* as the National Comprehensive Wealth Index (NCWI). Following economic theory (Dasgupta 2001, 2014, and 2021; Dasgupta and Mäler 2000; Hamilton and Clemens 1999), an increasing NCWI means that development is likely sustainable[5] since the basis for well-being (that is, the production of goods and services for consumption) is growing faster than price and population levels. If the NCWI is falling over time, development is unsustainable and well-being is either declining or will fall at some point in the future.[6]

Though the assets that comprise CW can, in principle, be measured in physical units, they are for all practical purposes most usefully measured in monetary units. The main advantage of monetary values is that nearly all assets, both tangible and intangible, can be measured using them. A further advantage is the ability to "add up" assets of different sorts. The value of a forest can be added to the value of a pulp mill to come up with an overall value for natural and produced capital owned by a forest company. Further, since prices reflect relative values, monetary valuation, in theory, automatically weights different assets according to their contribution to well-being. However, not all assets can be easily measured in this way, as they are not traded in markets (for example, ecosystems) and measurement in physical units is needed to account for their importance. The challenges of valuation are taken up further in the discussion of limitations below.

BOX 13.1. THE ELEMENTS OF THE COMPREHENSIVE WEALTH PORTFOLIO

Comprehensive wealth measures the five types of assets a nation has at its disposal.

- Produced capital includes roads, railways, ports, houses, machinery, and the wide variety of other manufactured assets found in the economy.
- Financial capital covers stocks, bonds, and other forms of financial assets. Investments by governments, businesses, and households are often aimed at building up stocks of produced and financial capital.
- Natural capital includes market natural resources, such as timber, minerals, oil, and gas. It also includes ecosystems of all kinds; for example, wetlands that help create clean drinking water and forests that act as carbon storehouses. Ecosystems are not only important for supporting life – they are also economically valuable, though their value is rarely realized through the market.
- The collective knowledge, skills, and capabilities of the labour force make up human capital – the result of lifelong learning in both formal and informal settings. Formal education is an important source of human capital but on-the-job learning and what we learn from our families and peers are equally important. Education helps make individuals more productive, which in turn

can increase the productivity of their coworkers. Education also helps people contribute more fully to society as a whole. Human capital is the largest source of wealth in most countries and in developed countries in particular.

- Social capital – the norms and behaviours that define interactions between members of society – is another broad component of the comprehensive wealth portfolio. Systems of laws and governance shape society and the economy. Cultural norms play an important role at home and in the work-place. Social ties and networks provide support for people trying to get ahead or overcome hard times. The norms and behaviours that define social capital dictate the use, distribution, and value of the other capital assets and therefore play an important role in creating wealth. Some nonetheless consider social capital to be an enabling factor that contributes to the value of the other forms of capital rather than a distinct form of capital itself (UNU–IHDP and UNEP 2012).

Calculating the NCWI

The NCWI was calculated as a chained volume index of per-capita produced, natural, human, and financial capital stocks. Specifically, the NCWI is a chained Törnqvist volume index in which the elements of the index – the individual quantities of produced, natural, human, and financial assets – are aggregated using their relative monetary values as weights.

The data necessary to compile it were obtained from Statistics Canada, either from officially published statistics (produced, natural, and financial assets) or from research studies (human capital; Gu and Wong 2010). Data on financial assets were available only in nominal terms and were, therefore, adjusted for inflation before use in the index. This was done using Statistics Canada's implicit price index for final domestic demand as the price deflator. Conversion of nominal asset values to per capita terms was accomplished simply by dividing by Statistics Canada's national population estimates. The nominal per capita values so calculated were then used as weights for the asset volumes in the index.

Challenges and Limitations in Calculating the NCWI

The main practical limitations of the NCWI are:

- its exclusion of social capital, which cannot be included because the concepts, methods, and data sources required to value it are not yet available

- its exclusion of so-called critical assets, which must be measured in the context of CW using non-monetary indicators and, therefore, cannot be included in the NCWI

The above limitations would apply to the NCWI no matter what country it was measured for. In addition, its application to Canada excluded several market natural assets that could not be valued due to data and methodological gaps (notably, commercial fish stocks and surface and groundwater resources) as well as liabilities associated with natural capital, which cannot be measured with existing data.[7]

Because social capital cannot be valued in monetary terms (as noted in the above, values are required as weights in the volume index), it must be measured for now using a suite of non-monetary indicators outside the NCWI (see Annex 1). Research is underway that shows promise for the valuation of social capital, however, so it may be possible in the foreseeable future to have an NCWI that includes social capital (Hamilton et al. 2017).

While, in theory, the monetary value of any asset can be assessed, assets that are *critical* to human well-being should not be expressed in monetary terms. Any degradation of these assets imposes direct costs on well-being, and prices are, therefore, not relevant. For this reason, separate physical measures of critical assets are required to complement the index and a full assessment of the sustainability of well-being rests on review of both the NCWI and the physical measures of critical assets.

The question of which assets are critical to well-being is not easily answered, and there is considerable uncertainty in the literature on the issue (Ekins 2014; Ekins et al. 2003). The concept is related to the precautionary notion that ecological thresholds must not be crossed if potentially large and unpredictable losses in ecological benefits are to be avoided, a view that dates back to the work of Ciriacy-Wantrup (1952) on "safe minimum standards" for use of the environment's goods and services. As Ekins et al. (2003) note, "with the present uncertain state of knowledge about ecosystems, and environmental functions generally, it is very difficult to judge which [natural assets] are critical and which are not." This is, of course, because both thresholds and the current distance from them are difficult to assess empirically.

In assessing Canada's CW, we took the view that both ecosystems and the climate system could be considered critical to well-being on the grounds that both of these provide goods and services that are not readily replaced and that empirical evidence suggests both are either close to or beyond the thresholds where large and unpredictable losses might occur. We acknowledge, however, that this approach was simply an expedient application of the precautionary principle (when in doubt, assume that an ecological system is critical) and that further research would be required to identify those natural assets that are truly critical to Canadians' well-being. It also reflected the fact that monetary measures of ecosystem assets remain, today, difficult to develop due to shortcomings in both data and methods, so inclusion of ecosystem assets in the NCWI would have been challenging had we wished to pursue it.

We refer to non-critical natural assets (such as minerals, fossil fuels, timber, and land) as "market" natural capital and ecosystems and the climate as "non-market" natural capital. The former we include in the NCWI and the latter we measure using a suite of non-monetary indicators (see Annex 1). While not ideal (as it complicates the assessment of sustainability using CW), this mixed approach of combining measures of semi-comprehensive wealth with a set of non-monetary metrics capturing aspects of wealth that are not appropriate for inclusion in CW indexes nonetheless "seems to provide a sensible approach to providing a set of signals of whether society is proceeding along a sustainable development trajectory" (Polasky et al. 2017, 462).

Our hope is that researchers' capacities to measure CW will improve with time and that the semi-comprehensive measures possible for Canada today will become more comprehensive with time. Filling the gaps related to marine and water resources would be a significant step forward, and we encourage Statistics Canada to devote resources to this. So too would further research to identify which ecosystems are truly critical (that is, close to thresholds) and which are far enough from thresholds to be considered for inclusion in the NCWI. Research could then focus on valuation of those ecosystems, with the remaining close-to-threshold ecosystems reserved for measurement using non-monetary metrics.

In spite of the challenges in measuring CW in Canada today, we believe the approach provides an essential complement to GDP and should be part of tools available to decision-makers in the country today. We believe that many of the limitations will be overcome as data availability and methods improve, making what is already a useful tool even more valuable as a guide to policy and prioritization of investments.

Results

We consider first the results in the NCWI and then the trends in the various non-monetary indicators used to complement the NCWI.

Trends in the NCWI for Canada

The NCWI grew 8.4 per cent in total over the thirty-five years from 1980 to 2015. In 1980 the NCWI stood at $647,000 per Canadian (chained 2007 dollars).[8] By 2015 it had risen to $701,000, for an annual average growth rate of 0.23 per cent. Growth over the period was not constant, however. We find two periods when Canadian development was on an unambiguously unsustainable path: first

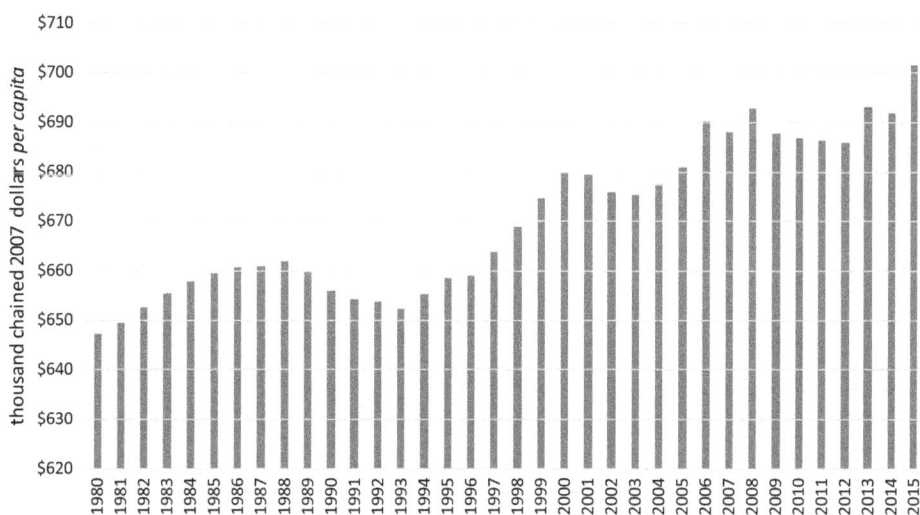

Figure 13.1. National Comprehensive Wealth Index, Canada, 1980–2015 (scale adjusted for emphasis)

Source: IISD, 2018.

from 1988 to 1992 and again from 2008 to 2012.[9] The NCWI declined steadily during both of these periods (Figure 13.1). During the first period (1988–92), all elements of the NCWI showed declines or stagnation. The decline in the second period was concentrated in the areas of natural, human, and financial capital, with produced capital growing (though slowly) during that period. The second period of decline may well have continued beyond 2012 to 2015 (and further) had it not been for unprecedented growth in one element of Canada's comprehensive portfolio – financial capital – that began in 2013. This growth was the result of historically strong gains in Canadians' foreign stock holdings – most notably US equities – and declines in the value of the Canadian dollar. It was not, it should be noted, the result of increased Canadian foreign investment, which was negative in net terms from 2008 to 2015 (and since).[10] The question whether Canada's economic development could have been considered sustainable in the years between 1980 and 2015 other than these two periods of decline in the NCWI cannot be determined on the basis of it alone, as was noted above and is discussed further below.

Trends in the Individual Elements of the NCWI

Looking at the individual elements of the NCWI, **human capital** – the largest component of Canada's wealth by far – was nearly flat over the period. The

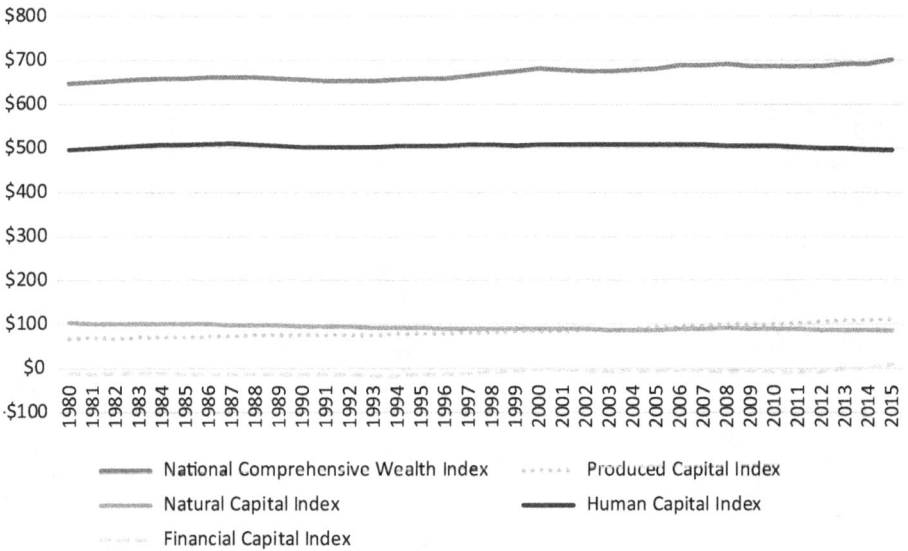

Figure 13.2. National Comprehensive Wealth Index and component sub-indexes, Canada, 1980–2015

Source: IISD, 2018.

average Canadian held just slightly less human capital in 2015 ($496,000) than in 1980 ($498,000) (Figure 13.2). The decline in Canada's human capital, even if slight, occurred in the context of substantial increases in the share of Canadians obtaining some kind of formal education certificate, diploma, or degree. From 1986 to 2016, the share of the population aged fifteen and older with a bachelor's degree or higher increased from 10 per cent to 23 per cent, according to Statistics Canada.

On average, human capital for younger workers (aged 15–34) grew at a rate of 0.25 per cent annually from 1980 to 2015 (total growth of 9 per cent). In contrast, human capital for prime age (35–54) and older (55–74) workers grew on average by 0.62 per cent and 1.1 per cent annually respectively (total growth of 25 per cent and 46 per cent). This suggests that younger workers had greater difficulty translating their increased investments in education into returns in the workforce.

The reasons for the lack of growth in human capital are complex. One simple factor is at play, however: the aging of the population. As the average Canadian worker gets older, his/her remaining years in the workforce drops. Fewer years left to work translates into less lifetime income and, other things equal, less human capital, according to the lifetime-income approach used by Gu and Wong (2010). Other factors could be that increased education spending

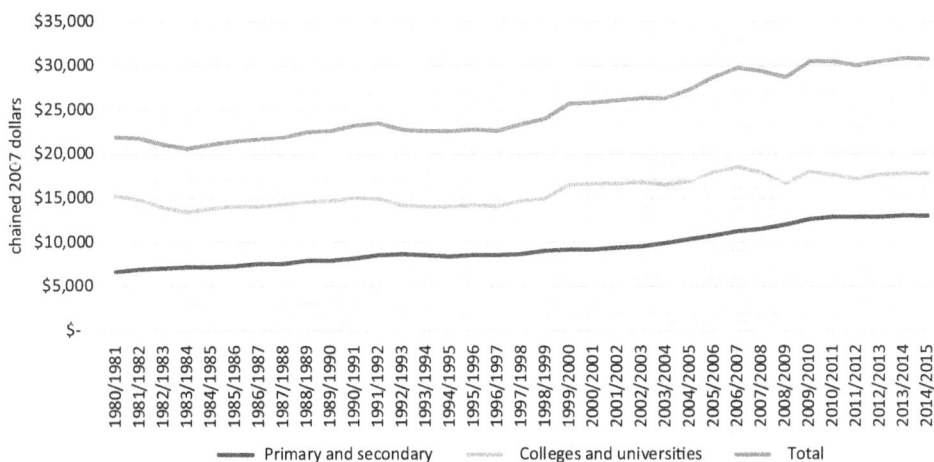

Figure 13.3. Education spending, Canada, 1980/1–2014/15

Source: IISD, 2018.

is necessary just to maintain a given level of human capital in today's competitive global economy. In Canada, real spending on education per student did increase substantially over the period, rising from $21,950 to $30,740, for an average annual growth rate of 0.97 per cent, according to Statistics Canada. It is worth noting, however, that this growth rate lagged that of real net national income per capita (1.28 per cent). It is also worth noting that the majority of the increase in spending occurred at the primary/secondary level rather than the university level (Figure 13.3).

Turning to the trend in **market natural capital**, it declined at a relatively steady rate of 0.50 per cent annually, from $103,000 to $86,000 per capita, for a total decline of 16.5 per cent over the period. The rate of decline was steady over the period, with the exception of the mid-2000s, when additions to physical reserves of oil sands and, to a lesser extent, potash drove the value temporarily upward.[11]

The downward trend in Canada's market natural capital was the result of pressure on the index from declines in physical quantities of most commercial natural assets. Only per-capita stocks of bituminous coal, gold, oil sands, and potash increased in physical terms between 1980 and 2015 (Table 13.1). Per-capita quantities of all other commercial natural assets declined. Lead reserves were less than 1 per cent of their 1980 level in 2015. Reserves of zinc, molybdenum, and silver per capita had all fallen to less than one-eighth of their 1980 extents by 2015. Nickel, copper, natural gas liquids, uranium, and conventional crude oil reserves were all below half their 1980 per-capita amounts.

Table 13.1. Index of per-capita physical quantities of market
natural assets, Canada, 2015 (1980=1)

Lead	0.6
Zinc	7.4
Silver	10.8
Molybdenum	12.5
Nickel	23.3
Copper	40.4
Natural gas liquids	42
Uranium	48.5
Conventional crude oil	49.5
Commercial timber	59.4
Natural gas	59.5
Agricultural land	65.4
Iron	68.4
Sub-bituminous coal and lignite*	70.9
Built-up land	92.2
Gold	164.3
Bituminous coal	122.7
Potash	294.7
Crude bitumen (oil sand)	782.7

Note: Bituminous coal index is for 2000 rather than 2015 due
to the confidentiality of coal statistics after 2000.
Source: IISD, 2018.

The downward pressure on market natural capital was offset somewhat by
large increases in the physical quantities and relative prices of oil sands and
potash. Without oil sands and potash, market natural capital would have fallen
considerably more than it did. The index, excluding oil sands and potash, fell
from $103,000 in 1980 to $79,000 in 2015 (an annual average decline of 0.75
per cent compared to the 0.5 per cent annual decline in natural wealth including all assets).

The above shines a light on how much Canada's market natural capital wealth
is tied to trends in just two assets, potash and oil sands, with the latter facing
an uncertain future due to concerns over pipeline expansions, environmental
impacts, and competition from other fossil fuel and renewable energy sources.
Statistics Canada reports that the value of Canada's oil and gas assets fell by 83

per cent in 2015 on the heels of the drop in oil prices. While oil prices are noto-riously volatile, current trends in global energy markets suggest oil prices are likely to trend downward in the long term, raising the risk of stranding some of Canada's oil sands assets.

An unknown with respect to Canada's market natural capital is what will hap-pen to it as the climate changes. Since climate is considered a critical asset here, it was assessed using non-monetary indicators and, therefore, not included in the NCWI. See the discussion below for further details.

Produced capital, for its part, increased at an average annual rate of 1.47 per cent, from $67,200 to $112,000 per capita (a total increase of 66.7 per cent), making produced capital the bright spot in the evolution of Canada's compre-hensive wealth. This otherwise positive trend was tempered, however, by the fact that the growth in fixed capital was heavily concentrated in just two assets: housing and oil and gas extraction infrastructure. As a result, Canada's fixed capital became more concentrated over the period. The share of residential structures and oil and gas extraction infrastructure in fixed capital grew from 45 per cent in 1980 to 60 per cent in 2015. Rather than contributing to the diversification of Canada's economy, then, investments in fixed capital over the period tended towards putting "more eggs in one basket." There are several reasons for concern about this.

With respect to housing, the large investments over the period obviously benefited homeowners' wealth (growing debt burdens notwithstanding) but did little to increase the overall productive capacity of the economy. Invest-ments in housing also crowded out household investment in financial assets, leaving the rest of the economy with reduced domestic investment. With respect to oil and gas infrastructure, the concern is partly that so much of the business sector's fixed capital – fully one quarter – is tied up in just one industry and partly that this infrastructure is tied to Canada's oil and gas assets, which are facing considerable uncertainty themselves. The risk of stranding some of this fixed capital if oil and gas assets do not recover the value they have lost in recent years is not negligible.

Financial capital increased sharply over the period, rising from −$11,600 to $9,000, as measured by Statistics Canada's international investment position (IIP). For most of its history, Canada's IIP has been negative, meaning that non-residents have typically owned more Canadian financial assets than Canadians have owned foreign financial assets. The trend beginning in 2013 was generally towards a diminishing gap between the two, however; that is, towards the net balance of foreign financial asset ownership being in Canada's favour. In 2014 the IIP moved into positive territory, with Canadians owning more foreign financial assets than non-residents owned Canadian assets. In real per-capita terms, Canadians owned about $9,000 in net foreign financial assets in 2015 compared with net foreign liabilities of about $11,600 in 1980.

In spite of this positive trend, Canada's financial capital remained fragile in 2015. Its upward movement was not, in fact, the result of increased acquisition of foreign financial assets by Canadians. Rather, it resulted from favourable stock and currency market conditions that drove holding gains in the value of Canada's net foreign assets. Such gains are vulnerable to changes in market conditions. Another concern is the use of debt by households to fund spending above sustainable levels since the late 1990s.

Trends in Other Elements of the CW Portfolio

As discussed above, not all forms of capital can or should be included in the NCWI. Trends in climate and ecosystems were considered outside the NCWI here on the grounds that both are close to or beyond thresholds where large and unpredictable losses in well-being might be associated with their continued use, meaning that they must be tracked separately from other forms of capital. In addition, ecosystems are not easily measured in monetary terms today due to shortcomings in data and methods, so their inclusion in the NCWI would have been difficult even had we wished to do so. This was the case for social capital, as well, so it, too, was tracked using non-monetary indicators.

TRENDS IN CLIMATE AND ECOSYSTEMS

Based on a suite of physical indicators drawn from Statistics Canada, Canada's climate was found to be changing in ways consistent with the predictions of the scientific community (Collins et al. 2013):

- **Precipitation**, measured as the annual departure from the 1961–90 normal, generally increased in Canada between 1948 and 2015, with the greatest increases coming in the north. The national trend suggests that precipitation increased by 18 per cent on average compared with the normal between 1948 and 2015. The trend in the north showed an even greater departure from normal (39 per cent).
- **Temperature**, as measured by annual departures from the 1961–90 normal, showed a trend similar to that of precipitation, with an overall increase nationally from 1948 to 2015 and the greatest increases coming in the north. At the national level, the temperature trend suggests a 1.8 degree Celsius average departure from normal from 1948 to 2015.
- In spite of increased precipitation, annual average **snow cover** declined across the country from 1972 to 2015 in the months of May and June (the data for the month of April do not show a statistically significant trend). The trend for May suggests an average reduction in snow cover of 0.86 million km² over the period, and the trend for June suggests a reduction of 1.67 million km².

- The **mass of selected glaciers** in the Western Cordillera and High Arctic declined from 1960 to 2015, as measured by the cumulative loss in mass over the period. All six glaciers studied lost significant mass, with those in the Western Cordillera (southern Alberta and BC) losing more than those in the High Arctic.
- **Water yield** – an estimate of the annual renewal of Canada's freshwater resources – showed no statistically significant trend from 1971 to 2014.
- The **extent of sea ice**, as measured by average area covered by sea ice during the summer, declined from 1968 to 2015 in all regions studied.

Similarly, Canada's key ecosystems were found to have declined in extent and quality (assessed in terms of their degree of development[12]), though the data time series available to assess them was much shorter than for other forms of capital:

- **Forests** declined slightly in area between 2000 and 2011, mainly due to losses from pest infestations and fires. Despite the extent of Canada's forests, about 40 per cent of them were considered "developed" in 2011.
- **Wetlands** also declined in most parts of the country, other than the Maritimes and the north. These losses, while relatively small, came on top of much larger declines in wetlands in earlier periods of the nation's development. Cumulatively, Canada has lost a large (but unknown) share of its original wetlands since European settlement. With most of the country's remaining wetlands found in northern regions, only about one-fifth (21 per cent) of those remaining were considered developed in 2011.
- Some 20 per cent of **surface water** areas were considered developed nationally in 2011. Regionally, about 40 per cent of surface water areas were considered developed in Newfoundland and Labrador, New Brunswick, Nova Scotia, PEI, Alberta, and British Columbia.
- **Grasslands** saw small declines in area from 2000 to 2011. As with wetlands, these declines came on top of large historical losses. Unlike wetlands, however, remaining grasslands are significantly threatened by further development. An estimated 95 per cent of remaining grasslands in Alberta and Manitoba were considered developed in 2011. In Saskatchewan, the corresponding figure was about 77 per cent.

TRENDS IN SOCIAL CAPITAL

Canada's **social capital**, which cannot yet be valued in monetary terms and therefore could not be included in the NCWI, appears to be stable but not growing on the basis of a series of non-monetary indicators (see Annex 1). Diversity in social networks and trust in institutions showed steady increases,

Table 13.2. Summary of trends in the elements of the comprehensive wealth portfolio, Canada, 1980–2015

Indicator	Per-capital level in 1980	Per-capita level in 2015	Annual growth rate 1980–2015
	Chained 2007 dollars		
National Comprehensive Wealth Index	$647,000	$701,000	0.23 per cent
Produced Capital Index	$67,200	$112,000	1.47 per cent
Market Natural Capital Index	$103,000	$86,000	minus 0.50 per cent
Financial Capital Index	–$11,600	$9,000	N/A
Human Capital Index	$496,000	$495,000	minus 0.01 per cent
Non-market Natural Capital	N/A	N/A	Unknown, but available non-monetary indicators suggest declines in key ecosystems and the climate system
Social Capital	N/A	N/A	Unknown, but available non-monetary indicators suggest stability

Source: IISD, 2018.

while voter turnout in federal elections generally declined (rebounding somewhat after 2008). Other social capital indicators showed little change in either direction over the period.

Summary of Trends in Canadian CW

Table 13.2 summarizes the trends in both the NCWI and the elements of the CW portfolio assessed with non-monetary indicators.

Other Countries Are Managing Their Wealth Better than Canada

Canada is fortunate to be wealthy compared with its peers. In a 2018 global study on comprehensive wealth (based on methods broadly consistent with

Table 13.3. United Nations' estimates of comprehensive wealth for G7 countries, 1990–2014

Country	Real comprehensive wealth per capita*							Annual growth rate 1990–2014	
	1990	1995	2000	2005	2010	2014	Rank (2014)	Per cent	Rank (2014)
Canada	348	342	343	346	351	328	1	minus 0.25 per cent	7
France	161	174	186	199	213	222	5	1.35 per cent	2
Germany	225	237	251	261	274	285	2	0.99 per cent	5
Italy	147	159	171	185	195	196	7	1.21 per cent	4
Japan	212	236	255	267	277	284	3	1.23 per cent	3
United Kingdom	145	155	170	183	194	201	6	1.37 per cent	1
United States	219	225	240	257	270	276	4	0.97 per cent%	6

*All values expressed in thousand constant US dollars
Source: Managi and Kumar 2018.

those used in the NCWI), the UN ranked Canada first among G7 nations in terms of *the level* of comprehensive wealth per capita. Its position at the top of this list was due largely to its reserves of natural capital, an advantage that puts the country in a position of clear strength vis-à-vis its peers. Canada had nearly four times more natural capital than the next closest G7 country in 2014 (the United States). At the same time – and consistent with the trend in the NCWI – the UN ranked Canada last among G7 members in terms of *the growth* in comprehensive wealth. By the UN's estimates, Canada's comprehensive wealth actually fell between 1990 and 2014 (by 0.25 per cent annually on average), whereas that of every other G7 nation grew substantially (Table 13.3).

Clearly, other countries are doing better than Canada in growing their comprehensive wealth portfolios – and catching up to Canada's level as a result. In 1990 the average comprehensive wealth in other G7 countries was 53 per cent of Canada's; by 2014 this share had climbed to 74 per cent. At current rates of growth, the UN's findings suggest Canada will lose its first-place position to Japan in 2024 and will fall to fifth place in less than a generation (by 2039).

Conclusions and Recommendations

The sustainability of Canadian development can be characterized – at best – as fragile since the 2008 global financial crisis, with atypical trends in financial markets accounting for most of the growth in comprehensive wealth from 2009 to 2015. More recent data suggest that development remained fragile and/or unsustainable after 2015. This view contrasts with the robust view of Canada's development offered by GDP.

It is a particular concern that human capital did not grow at all in Canada from 1980 to 2015. The reasons for this are not fully clear. It is partly due to the aging of the population, but also to weak human capital among young workers. More study is required to understand the reasons for Canada's poor performance.

Also of concern is the substantial concentration of Canada's market natural capital and produced capital. In the former case, Canada's asset mix moved away from a broad suite of minerals and conventional oil, gas, and coal assets towards a focus on oil sands and potash. In terms of produced capital, Canada's asset mix moved heavily towards houses and oil and gas extraction infrastructure.

In terms of financial capital, a principal concern is in how Canadian households have changed their saving behaviours. Since 1997 the sector has routinely spent all of its disposable income, leaving the majority of lending in Canada to come from non-residents. Excessive borrowing from foreign lenders lowers CW, other things being equal.

Social capital is the most complex and least understood element of the comprehensive wealth portfolio, yet the need to measure social capital has never been greater. While Statistics Canada already measures some of its elements, its data are infrequent and incomplete. Based on what is available, social capital appears stable.

Finally, climate change – one of the most serious threats to Canada's well-being – appears to be unfolding as predicted by scientists, while ecosystems are declining (albeit slowly) in extent and growing more developed over time.

Dealing with the challenges faced by Canada's comprehensive wealth portfolio is, it goes without saying, complex. It is not made any easier by the fact that data on comprehensive wealth are not regularly reported in Canada (or anywhere, for that matter). In contrast, GDP – which tells a different and more positive story about progress – is published regularly. We believe Statistics Canada must begin doing the same for comprehensive wealth, regularly publishing it alongside GDP so decision-makers are given a balanced perspective on the country's development.

At the same time, research is needed to address the practical shortcomings in CW measures. Statistics Canada's data on market natural capital must be completed by adding missing marine and water assets. Researchers should consider which ecosystem assets are truly critical in Canada, so those that are not can be valued and incorporated in the NCWI. Statistics Canada's experimental measures of human capital should be regularized as official statistics, and its occasional measures of social capital should be published more regularly. Nascent research on the valuation of social capital should be pursued so that it may eventually be included in the NCWI as well.

Annex 1: Non-monetary Indicators of Climate, Ecosystems, and Social Capital

Non-monetary indicators of climate, ecosystems	
Ecosystems (non-monetary)	Forest extent
	Wetland extent
	Surface water extent
	Grassland extent
Climate (non-monetary)	Precipitation
	Temperature
	Snow cover
	Glacier mass
	Water yield
	Sea ice extent
Social capital	
Civic engagement	Participation in group activities
	Volunteering
	Diversity in social networks
	Control over public decisions
	Voter turnout
Trust and cooperative norms	Generalized trust
	Trust in neighbours and strangers
	Trust that a lost wallet will be returned
	Trust in institutions

Source: IISD (2018).

Annex 2: Note on Data Quality

Statistical reliability of the CW indicators was assessed qualitatively on the basis of the authors' knowledge of data sources and conceptual and methodological soundness. Indicators were rated as "very reliable," "reliable," or "acceptable." Indicators were considered very reliable when they were characterized by source data that were mainly derived from highly reliable sources like Statistics Canada surveys or from other sources that were considered highly reliable and by concepts and methods that were based on accepted environmental, economic, or statistical theory and that did not require arbitrary or subjective decisions regarding important parameters. Indicators that met all but one of the above criteria were deemed reliable. Those that failed to meet two or more of the criteria were deemed acceptable.

All the main CW indicators were considered very reliable or reliable. Only one sub-indicator of the Human Capital Index (the Education Spending Index) was considered acceptable.

Annex 3: Measuring Human Capital

Three approaches are commonly used to measure human capital (UNECE 2016): the indicator approach, the cost-based approach (Schultz 1960 and 1961; Kendrick 1976), and the lifetime-income approach developed by Jorgenson and Fraumeni (1989, 1992a, and 1992b). The cost-based approach measures the value of investments in the creation of human capital, especially the cost of education and training. The lifetime-income approach measures human capital as the discounted value of the future income individuals expect to earn throughout their lifetime. It sees income as the return on investment in human capital.

Human capital was measured in the study using the lifetime-income approach, which we believe is the approach most closely aligned with economic theory. The theory of capital services suggests that an asset's market value will be determined by what buyers are willing to pay today for the future flow of services they will obtain through ownership and use of the asset; in other words, an asset's value is equal to the discounted value of the future stream of income earned by using the asset in a production process. The lifetime income approach to human capital valuation is consistent with this theory. It says that the value of an individual's skills, capacities, and knowledge (i.e., her human capital) is equal to the discounted value of the future earnings she will gain from selling her labour (i.e., the service rendered by her human capital) in the market. While it is reasonable to expect that the income she earns off her human capital will increase or at least stabilize as she ages, the inescapable fact is that she also has fewer years of life ahead of her to earn those higher wages as time goes by. So, while the rental rate of her capital goes up as time goes by, the total value of that capital to her, sadly, declines as she approaches the end of her working life.

NOTES

1 http://www.g7.utoronto.ca/summit/2018charlevoix/communique.html.
2 As Hamilton and Clemens (1999), Dasgupta and Mäler (2000), and Dasgupta (2021) demonstrate, taking the capital assets the economy inherited from the past as the determinants of intergenerational well-being, a criterion for sustainable development can be reduced to tracking the change in a weighted sum of the stocks of those assets, with the weights being the marginal contributions of the

stocks to intergenerational well-being. These weights are the known as the assets' "shadow prices," and the weighted sum is the economy's CW.

3 It falls short of the theoretical ideal because some well-being is derived from sources, such as pure spirituality, that cannot reasonably be construed as flowing from identifiable assets.

4 UNEP refers to comprehensive wealth as "inclusive wealth."

5 Growing real per-capita wealth is not a guarantee of increased well-being in the future since those in the future may squander their inheritance and reduce their well-being in spite of being provided with the basis for increased well-being from those that came before them.

6 For formal proof of this see, for example, the appendix in Dasgupta (2001) and the very thorough exposition in Dasgupta (2021).

7 For example, the liabilities associated with decommissioning of mine sites or oil rigs or the climate liability associated with the eventual combustion of fossil fuel reserves. Though some data on environmental liabilities are available in Canada (see, for example, IISD [2017]), they are not comprehensive. They ignore, for example, the value of liabilities recognized by corporations and municipalities.

8 All figures are quoted in real – that is, inflation-adjusted – per-capita terms using chained 2007 dollars as the unit of measure, unless otherwise indicated.

9 There may have been other periods of unsustainability that were not picked up in our analysis because of gaps in the NCWI.

10 Clearly, growth in the NCWI predicated on holding and currency gains in stock markets is a shakier foundation for long-term well-being than would be actual net increases in foreign investment holdings.

11 Note that "reserves" refers to known and actively exploited deposits of resources. Reserves may increase even as they are being exploited, if the rate of discovery of new resources is greater than the rate of depletion of existing reserves or if new technologies (such as fracking) allow previously un-extractable deposits to be exploited.

12 Ecosystems were considered "developed" if they were located within one kilometre of a linear feature like a road or a pipeline or within ten kilometres of other types of human land uses (for example, mines, dams, or inhabited areas).

REFERENCES

Arrow, Kenneth J., Partha Dasgupta, Lawrence H. Goulder, Kevin J. Mumford, and Kirsten Oleson. 2012. "Sustainability and the Measurement of Wealth." *Environment and Development Economics* 17, no. 3: 317–53.

Ciriacy-Wantrup, S.V. 1952. *Resource Conservation: Economics and Policies.* Berkeley: University of California Press.

Collins, Matthew, Reto Knutti, Julie Arblaster, Jean-Louis Dufresne, Thierry Fichefet, Pierre Friedlingstein, Xuejie Gao, et al. 2013. "Long-term Climate Change: Projections, Commitments and Irreversibility." In *Climate Change 2013:*

The Physical Science Basis. Contribution of Working Group I to the Fifth Assessment Report of the Intergovernmental Panel on Climate Change, edited by Thomas F. Stocker, Dahe Qin, Gian-Kasper Plattner, Melinda M.B. Tignor, Simon K. Allen, Judith Boschung, Alexander Nauels, Yu Xia, Vincent Bex, and Pauline M. Midgley, 1029–136. Cambridge: Cambridge University Press.

Dasgupta, Partha. 2001. *Human Well-Being and the Natural Environment*. Oxford: Oxford University Press.

– 2009. "The Welfare Economic Theory of Green National Accounts." *Environmental Resource Economics* 42, no. 1: 3–38.

– 2012. "Natural Capital as Economic Assets: A Review." In *Inclusive Wealth Report 2012*, edited by UNU–IHDP and UNEP, 121–42. Cambridge: Cambridge University Press.

– 2014. "Measuring the Wealth of Nations." *Annual Review of Resource Economics* 6: 17–31.

– 2021. *The Economics of Biodiversity: The Dasgupta Review*. London: HM Treasury.

Dasgupta, Partha, and Karl-Göran Mäler. 2000. "Net National Product, Wealth, and Social Well-being." *Environment and Development Economics* 5, no. 1: 69–93.

Ekins, Paul. 2014. "Strong Sustainability and Critical Natural Capital." In *Handbook of Sustainable Development*, edited by Giles Atkinson, Simon Dietz, Eric Neumayer, and Matthew Agarwala, 55–71. Cheltenham, UK: Edward Elgar Publishing.

Ekins, Paul, Sandrine Simon, Lisa Deutsch, Carl Folke, and Rudolf De Groot. 2003. "A Framework for the Practical Application of the Concepts of Critical Natural Capital and Strong Sustainability." *Ecological Economics* 44: 165–85.

Fenichel, Eli P., and Joshua K. Abbott. 2014. "Natural Capital: From Metaphor to Measurement." *Journal of the Association of Environmental and Resource Economists* 1, nos. 1/2: 1–27.

Jorgenson, Dale W., and Barbara M. Fraumeni. 1989. "The Accumulation of Human and Non-human Capital, 1948–1984." In *The Measurement of Saving, Investment, and Wealth*, edited by Robert E. Lipsey and Helen Stone Tice, 227–82. Chicago: University of Chicago Press. https://www.nber.org/system/files/chapters/c8121/c8121.pdf.

– 1992a. "Investment in Education and U.S. Economic Growth." *Scandinavian Journal of Economics* 94, Suppl.: S51–S70. https://scholar.harvard.edu/jorgenson/publications/investment-education-and-us-economic-growth.

– 1992b. "The Output of the Education Sector." In *Output Measurement in the Service Sectors*, edited by Zvi Griliches, 303–41. Chicago: University of Chicago Press. https://www.nber.org/system/files/chapters/c7238/c7238.pdf.

Gu, Wulong, and Ambrose Wong. 2010. *Estimates of Human Capital in Canada: The Lifetime Income Approach (Economic Analysis Research Paper Series, No. 62)*. Ottawa: Statistics Canada.

Hamilton, Kirk, and Michael Clemens. 1999. "Genuine Savings Rates in Developing Countries." *World Bank Economic Review* 13, no. 2: 333–56.

Hamiltion, Kirk, John F. Helliwell, and Michael Woolcock. 2017. "Social Capital, Trust, and Well-being in the Evaluation of Wealth." In *National Wealth: What Is Missing, Why It Matters*, edited by Kirk Hamilton and Cameron Hepburn, 275–94. Oxford: Oxford University Press.

Insurance Bureau of Canada. n.d. *Facts of the Property and Casualty Insurance Industry.* http://www.ibc.ca/ns/resources/ industry-resources/insurance -fact-book.

International Institute for Sustainable Development (IISD). 2016. *Comprehensive Wealth in Canada – Measuring What Matters in the Long Run.* Winnipeg: IISD.

– 2018. *Comprehensive Wealth in Canada 2018 – Measuring What Matters in the Long Term.* Winnipeg: IISD.

Kendrick, John W. 1976. *The Formation and Stocks of Total Capital.* New York: Columbia University Press.

Kumar, Pushpam, and Shunsuke Managi. 2018. *Inclusive Wealth Report 2018.* London: Routledge.

OECD. 2001. *Productivity Measurement with Changing-Weight Indices of Outputs and Inputs.* Paris: OECD.

Osberg, Lars, and Andrew Sharpe. 2011. *Beyond GDP: Measuring Economic Well-Being in Canada and the Provinces, 1981–2010.* Ottawa: Centre for the Study of Living Standards.

Polasky, Stephen, Benjamin Bryant, Peter Hawthorne, Justin Johnson, Bonnie Keeler, and Derric Pennington. 2015. "Inclusive Wealth as a Metric of Sustainable Development." *Annual Review of Environment and Resources* 40, no. 1: 445–66.

Schultz, Theodore W. 1960. "Capital Formation by Education." *Journal of Political Economy* 68: 571–83.

– 1961. "Investment in Human Capital." *American Economic Review* 51, no. 1: 1–17.

Stiglitz, Joseph E., Amartya Sen, and Jean-Paul Fitoussi. 2009. *Report by the Commission on the Measurement of Economic Performance and Social Progress.* Paris: Commission on the Measurement of Economic Performance and Social Progress.

Stiglitz, Joseph E., Jean-Paul Fitoussi, and Martine Durand. 2018. *For Good Measure: Advancing Research on Well-Being Metrics Beyond GDP.* Paris: OECD Publishing.

UN Economic Commission for Europe (UNECE). 2009. *Measuring Sustainable Development.* Geneva: United Nations.

– 2016. *Guide on Measuring Human Capital* (ECE/CES/STAT/2016/6). Prepared by the Task Force on Measuring Human Capital. https://www.unece.org/fileadmin /DAM/stats/publications/2016/ECECESSTAT20166_E.pdf.

UN Secretary-General. 2021. *Our Common Agenda: Report of the Secretary-General.* New York: United Nations. https://www.un.org/en/content/common-agenda -report/assets/pdf/Common_Agenda_Report_English.pdf.

UNU–IHDP, and UNEP. 2012. *Inclusive Wealth Report 2012 – Measuring Progress Toward Sustainability*. Cambridge: Cambridge University Press.
– 2014. *Inclusive Wealth Report 2014 – Measuring Progress Toward Sustainability*. Cambridge: Cambridge University Press.
World Bank. 2011. *The Changing Wealth of Nations: Measuring Sustainable Development in the New Millennium*. Washington, DC: The World Bank.
– 2018. *The Changing Wealth of Nations 2018: Building a Sustainable Future*. Washington, DC: The World Bank.
– 2021. *The Changing Wealth of Nations 2021: Managing Assets for the Future*. Washington, DC: World Bank. https://www.worldbank.org/en/publication/changing-wealth-of-nations.

14 Time for a Reality Check: Lessons from Bhutan, Canada, and New Zealand

RONALD COLMAN

When I began work on new measures of progress a quarter-century ago, I was convinced of the power of truth and good evidence to influence policy.

I wasn't the only measurement person to hold this belief. In fact, I can't think of a single colleague involved in the field in the 1990s and early 2000s who didn't share the view that strong, new evidence would shine the spotlight on hitherto neglected environmental and social issues excluded from core progress measures and thereby inevitably elicit much-needed policy action.[1] Regularly, we trumpeted the slogan "If you don't count it, it won't get attention." So we did count what matters, and we presented that evidence over and over again to seemingly receptive policy audiences.

In fact, what brought many of us to this work was our belief that governments were making such bad decisions on environmental, social, health, education, and other key constituents of well-being largely because they weren't getting the full story. They were being deceived by the dominant GDP-based measures that equate how well we are doing as a society with economic growth.

Those same GDP-based measures were sending policymakers misleading messages on ecological well-being (counting natural resource depletion and fossil fuel use as growth, for example), on health (counting sickness costs and cigarette and junk food sales as growth), on security (counting costs of war and crime as growth), and more. They concealed growing inequities and they devalued all unpaid work, including volunteerism and most women's work.

All we had to do, my colleagues and I naively believed, was tell the whole truth and governments would see the necessity of urgent action to improve societal well-being and – without being overly dramatic – to save humanity.

We knew our work was truly urgent. By the early to mid-1990s all the evidence was in that humanity was headed for a disastrous collision with planetary limits. We knew time was running out. Looking at the existing trend lines, the evidence showed we had maybe a fifteen-year window to turn things around before it was too late.

And the very existence of that evidence, interestingly, was also the good news that fired up us measurement fanatics.

For the first time in history we actually had the strong, reliable evidence necessary to tell the truth. Due to new scientific and epidemiological evidence, innovative statistical surveys and analyses, and pioneering work in fields like ecological economics and natural resource accounting, we had, by the mid-1990s, good greenhouse gas, forest, fisheries and other inventories, reliable population health, time use and social capital surveys, and even full-cost accounts that, for example, tracked the true economic costs of driving, energy use, pollution, and other actions.

At last we had all the raw materials necessary to produce strong, rigorously sound, comprehensive measures of well-being and progress, and full-cost accounts showing the economic, social, and ecological benefits and costs of economic activity.

If we could do that work meticulously, using the best available evidence and methodologies, and if we could thereby shine a light on key factors of well-being and survival hitherto ignored in the conventional economic accounts, how could policymakers ignore the truth?

We Were Wrong!

Twenty-five years later, after copious rigorous, detailed research, after countless reports and presentations by outstanding researchers, after press conferences and good media coverage, after working closely with governments in three countries and with dedicated non-profits, and after high hopes and apparent possibilities were continually disappointed, I have to conclude that our new progress measures have failed to make a significant dent in the policy arena or to shift policy in any fundamentally transformative or meaningful way.

In 2012, with participation from the UN secretary-general, the president of Costa Rica, Prince Charles, and 800 government ministers, diplomats, Nobel Prize winners, scholars, religious leaders, and non-governmental leaders, the government of Bhutan even took the initiative for a new economic paradigm based on sustainability, equity, and well-being to the United Nations. In strong support, the UN secretary-general (2012) declared: "The old model is broken. We need to create a new one."

In the heady atmosphere of hope, enthusiasm, and potential, we then assembled a global expert team of seventy top-notch economists, scientists, and other scholars to craft a possible framework for that new economy for endorsement at the following year's UN General Assembly. Recalling the pivotal 1944 Bretton Woods gathering that laid the foundation and created the institutions of the present global economic system, we dared to say we were crafting a "new Bretton Woods."

All of that and much more fell apart. There's no need now to dwell in the past, to go back over the gory details, to blame or recriminate about where we went wrong or what we might have done better. In fact, different well-being and indicator folk tried so many different approaches and methods on so many fronts that we can't really fault any particular strategy.

The truth remains that our hard evidence has not shifted policy in any significant way. On the contrary, the economic growth imperative at huge (and now well-documented) ecological and social costs, is more dominant and powerful than ever.

In fact, the proof that truth, evidence, and hard facts and figures do not talk or influence policy when they run counter to the dominant economic paradigm and its powerful vested interests goes far beyond our measurement work. Scientists are just as frustrated. For example, thirty years ago, when we still had a narrow window of opportunity, we already had all the evidence we needed for urgent action on climate change.

At the end of December 2015 – the hottest and wettest December in the hottest year on record to that date – Myles Allen, head of climate research at Oxford University, commented: "As scientists, it's a little humbling that we've been saying this for 20 years now, and it's not until people notice daffodils coming out in December that they start to say, 'Maybe they're right'" (quoted in Gillis 2015).

So what's important for us measurement folk now is first of all to stop pretending that ever more reports, documents, scholarly articles, navel-gazing conferences (with large carbon footprints) where we preach to the converted, are going to make any substantial difference. And that includes all the grand, annual OECD conferences with titles that may mistakenly imply a transformative policy shift to sustainable and equitable well-being that the OECD has hitherto shown no intention of putting into practice – titles like "Putting Well-Being Metrics into Policy Action" and "Metrics that Make a Difference: International Conference on the Policy Uses of Well-being and Sustainable Development Indicators" (October 2019).

For many years, we've been there, done that, and have nothing much to show for it. If, instead, we can stop kidding ourselves and look our failure squarely in the face, we can take a more daring second step – namely, to ruthlessly analyse and understand the actual resistance and dominant forces that have derailed all our best-intentioned efforts, dug in their heels more firmly than ever, and driven humanity onto a now seemingly inexorable path to self-destruction.

If we can do that honestly, we might even take a third step to discover an entirely new way forward. In short, the purpose of calling a spade a spade is not to sink into despair at past failures. On the contrary, it's to keep telling the truth, as we determined to do three decades ago, to recognize that this truth now includes our own failure, and to keep the faith that the truth will win!

Why Did We Fail?

In venturing here into that second analytical step, I can only report what I have observed and learned from the experience of the last twenty-five years working on new measures with governments in Canada, Bhutan, and New Zealand.[2]

First and foremost, we well-being measurement folk have subtly and unwittingly bought into the widely prevalent democratic myth that it is the arena of government and policymaking that primarily determines our lives and future. What we discovered the hard way, which our democratic blinders had concealed, was the extent to which elected politicians are beholden to powerful economic forces with a vested interest in "business as usual" and to bureaucracies that thrive on maintenance rather than change.

Dare We Name the Elephant in the Room?

In fact, to go a step further, I believe the resistance to our challenges to the doctrine of limitless growth springs not just from "powerful economic forces" but from the very nature and inner structure of a capitalist system reliant on continued growth for its very survival. We now know that our full-cost accounting work and its holistic *long-term* approach threatens the *short-term* business bottom lines and immediate shareholder interests that largely run our lives, control the political arena, and determine our future.

We saw that graphically and in technicolour in the massive bailouts and economic stimulus packages of the 2008–9 global financial crisis and Great Recession when political party differences faded into insignificance and when climate change and environmental conservation fell completely off the policy agenda in the frenzy to get the economy growing again.

Naming "capitalism" as the greatest and possibly insuperable obstacle to the adoption of new progress measures and of a new economic paradigm remains the silent elephant in the room in all our measurement work, in scholarly articles and reports, and at OECD and other conferences.

But if we genuinely want to understand our failures and move forward, we now have to put the question squarely on the table: Is market capitalism compatible with environmental sustainability? Does our concern to maximize income and consumption and the concomitant desire of business to maximize sales and profits prevent any genuine transition to sustainability?

This question in turn leads to deeper questions about the very nature of our dominant economic system. For example: is limitless growth (and hence ever-expanding resource and energy consumption) a capitalist imperative? Can a capitalist enterprise survive by marking time, stabilizing production levels, and contenting itself with a given revenue stream? Or will it thereby cede market share to enterprises that continue to expand and improve their competitive advantage through growing economies of scale? And if such ongoing growth is necessary for the survival of enterprises in a capitalist economy, what are the implications for climate change and for the survival of much of the living world?

And the troubling questions go on: Since economic competitiveness requires limiting production costs, can enterprises afford to invest in stringent and costly measures to safeguard the environment, or will they move to places with looser environmental and safety regulations? Similarly, is it possible to conceive of "fair distribution" as a pillar of a new economic paradigm, when enterprises reduce production costs and market their products more competitively by relying on cheap labour and moving their factories to where labour is cheapest? Have we not simply exported dirty industries, waste, deadly pollution, resource depletion, and cheap labour from London and Los Angeles to Delhi, Beijing, and Dhaka?

Conversely, therefore, the question must be asked: Does not a "new economic paradigm" based on ecological sustainability, fair distribution, and efficient resource use challenge the very foundations of the capitalist system itself? If so, how will the necessary transition happen? Can powerful business interests possibly be persuaded to cooperate in actions that threaten their own survival? If not, what kind of system and what forms of ownership, production, and distribution could replace present capitalist structures?

And How Complicit Are We Ourselves?

Perhaps the most difficult question of all that we dare not look in the face is: are all of us, including our jet-setting well-being scholars, policy wonks, and high carbon-footprint OECD conference participants, complicit in this dominant system? Let's take just one example: On 24th April 2013, the Rana Plaza factory complex in the industrial suburb of Savar in Dhaka, Bangla Desh, collapsed, killing 1,130 people and injuring 2,500 in the deadliest disaster in garment industry history. Eight months later, *The New York Times* reported that many leading brand-name manufacturers were refusing to take any responsibility for the disaster, even though their "brands depend on factories in developing countries like Bangladesh, where wages are very low and the pressure to work faster and cheaper has spawned familiar problems: unsafe buildings, substandard work conditions and repeated wage and labor violations. Consumers know little about these factories." (Yardley 2013) How many of us acknowledge that our bargain-hunting for the lowest-cost jeans encourages factory owners to persist in maintaining the deplorable conditions under which those jeans are produced? Dare we take such personal responsibility for the Rana Plaza collapse?

There are many other well-known examples. For instance, how willing are the rich countries and the elites of all countries, including their scholars, to acknowledge that our own excess fossil fuel use and greenhouse gas emissions are contributing to flooding in Bangladesh and forcing Tuvalu residents to flee their sinking nation (Allen 2004)? And how willing are we ourselves to walk the talk in reducing our consumption, energy use, airplane and automobile travel, and overall greenhouse gas emissions by, say, 50 per cent or more?

Because the above analysis makes no claims to be the whole story, the preceding section is deliberately phrased as questions rather than definitive answers. Thus, I have read and heard impressive analyses that see the core reasons for the domination and persistence of our present untenable and unsustainable system not in the structure of capitalism but in Judeo-Christian values, in the consequent and supposedly inherent flaws of human nature (e.g., greed, selfishness, and aggression), in the nature of the dominant technology, and in the inability of the West to come to terms with its declining global influence (e.g., Holland 2019; Mahbubani 2018; Malhotra 2011).

So I don't ask here that the above analysis be accepted at face value, only that these questions be openly asked, forthrightly put on the table, and assiduously and urgently examined. And thus, one last set of questions:

What Can Scholars and Analysts Do to Move Forward?

If we first openly acknowledge that in three decades we have failed to shift policy, and then as a second step examine honestly *why* we have failed, might we then move to a third step that looks at genuine and essential ways forward? Urgent though that third step has become with the future of humanity and countless other species hanging in the balance, we won't begin to shift direction without daring to ask questions like those above. Therefore, scholars might consider, probe, and experiment in the following ways: Will the OECD or any respectable government or leading university dare to organize a conference to address the above questions squarely, fearlessly, and without hesitation? Will scholars, scientists, and measurement aficionados themselves expand the focus of their research and publish peer-reviewed articles to include such questions? Will the media (largely corporate-owned) dare to report their findings? And if all the above actually happens, might consumers even be persuaded to temper the materialist desires that fuel capitalism and its ever-expanding production? And if scholars, economists, policy analysts, and journalists won't take the lead in asking these questions, why not? Is it because they are afraid that the only alternative to capitalism is Soviet-,

Chinese-, or Cambodian-style authoritarianism so that any challenge to capitalism per se is akin to treason? Or might they actually study Karl Marx dispassionately and put aside such fears by recognizing that the Soviet, Chinese, and Cambodian experiments have nothing to do with the "communism" he advocated?

Even more to the point, can we researchers put aside our fears of "no alternative" and simply acknowledge that Marx could not possibly know in the mid-nineteenth century about planetary limits, climate change, resource depletion, and species extinction? Even in more modern times could the economists and policymakers who at Bretton Woods in 1944 fashioned our present global economic system know those ecological realities? Rather than blame past ignorance and short-sightedness, might we instead simply acknowledge that we now know much better and therefore no longer have an excuse to keep buying into utterly outmoded economic structures that now threaten our very survival?

And if so, might we dare to acknowledge that, while Marx's critique of the inner structure and workings of capitalism may still be brilliant, insightful, and highly relevant today, we now need to build an entirely new economic system based on principles of sustainability, equity, and efficient resource use?

The good news in all this is that we actually possess the knowledge, expertise, technology, and working models to create such an entirely new economic system to replace our present growth-driven capitalist structures. But we won't begin to move those models from the fringe to the mainstream unless we dare ask the big, core questions that go to the root of our present malaise.

Concomitant Reasons for Failure

If there is any truth to Marx's economic analysis, then the structure of the dominant economic system also powerfully influences the nature of the accompanying political system, ideology, values, and culture. And if so, then no wonder we measurement folk were deluded in thinking that governments and policymakers were our target audience and had the power to turn our evidence into policy.

But capitalism's powerful influence on other social institutions, dominant values, academia, and the non-profit sector, virtually all of which have vested interests in "business as usual," helps explain other concomitant reasons for our failure to move the new progress measures from the fringe to the mainstream in any significant or transformative way. Here are just three of many examples I personally encountered again and again over the last quarter century.

The Pressure for Maintenance vs. Change

Bureaucracies, whether government, academic, or corporate, thrive on maintenance and are threatened by any fundamental change to the existing system. Habitual patterns – collective as well as individual – are hard to break! Proposals get mired in bureaucracies that, by their nature, are threatened by change, and typically function to maintain the status quo and fend off anything that rocks the boat.

Witnessing these bureaucratic realities close up has taught me something about the limits of political power, even of a head of state with a strong parliamentary majority. In many years working in the Himalayan Kingdom of Bhutan, former Prime Minister Jigmi Y. Thinley struck me as an exceptional leader with remarkable intelligence, genuine vision, and deep concern for nature and for the world.

But he could not do what he wanted alone. The prime minister once confessed to me that he was already seen as being too much of a micromanager, with ministries subtly rebelling against his interventions on matters of detail. Without the bureaucracy fully on his side, even a head of state simply could not get his ministries to carry out the major changes he wanted to initiate.

One of those major changes was Bhutan's call for "a new Bretton Woods," which met resistance from powerful institutions like the World Bank (created at the 1944 Bretton Woods Conference). Bhutan's large and powerful neighbour (India) resisted Bhutan's "new economic paradigm" initiative that, among other things, called for a major shift to renewable energy from the fossil fuels that power India's economy. And Bhutan's own Foreign Ministry bureaucrats, under pressure from external allies, watered down and eviscerated the prime minister's initiative.

Bhutan's Agriculture Ministry, wedded to its newly adopted synthetic fertilizer-dependent "high-yield seeds," subtly undermined the prime minister's call for Bhutan to become the world's first fully organic country. And Bhutan's Education Ministry bureaucrats did not want the extra burden of redoing the country's entire school curriculum in line with the integrated ecologically sustainable, socially equitable, and culturally appropriate values of Bhutan's supposed "Gross National Happiness" development policy (see Kim and MacKenzie, this volume).

On numerous occasions, I observed officials, having mastered the art of telling the prime minister what they knew he wanted to hear in line with his vision, quietly acting otherwise in their daily work. Too often, I saw, the prime minister believed and accepted what he was being told as reality, when in fact many of his directives were being stalled and sidelined.

I witnessed a similar underlying pressure for "maintenance" and resistance to real change in my work in Canada. Time and again, temporary bursts of inspiration and potential change were stymied by the simple weight of existing systems and infrastructure. Two examples among many will suffice here: GPI full-cost accounting studies on the massive hidden costs of driving and obesity produced detailed recommendations on economically efficient ways to reduce vehicular use and greenhouse gas emissions and to promote mass transit, good nutrition, and physical activity (e.g., Savelson, Colman, and Martin 2008; Colman 2000). In practice, however, rapid ex-urban development with its car-dependent shopping malls and massive parking lots, lack of public transportation, highway construction, and reliance on vehicular commuting defied all efforts to promote integrated land use and transportation planning and other measures to reduce vehicular use. Similarly on the health front, earnest and well-meaning efforts to promote nutritious food, including by government agencies, were consistently overwhelmed by the massive corporate junk food advertising budget aimed at children. This pressure for maintenance and resistance to change is mirrored globally. In 2011 the International Energy Agency (IEA 2011) warned that by 2017, without drastic immediate action, high levels of CO_2 emissions will be so "locked in" by existing infrastructure, such as power plants, factories, buildings, and highways, that "rising fossil-fuel energy use will lead to irreversible and potentially catastrophic climate change." The action didn't happen, the IEA's due date passed, and greenhouse gas emissions continued to increase globally.

The examples are endless, but the point is the same: existing economic structures are so deeply embedded in our built infrastructure, bureaucracies, media, personal lifestyles, and values that pressure to maintain the existing system resists even the best-intentioned non-governmental and highest-level political initiatives for change.

"I Don't Want Your Hope!"

Greta Thunberg told the World Economic Forum in Davos in January 2019: "I want you to panic. I want you to feel the fear I feel every day, and then I want you to act. I want you to act as you would in a crisis. I want you to act as if our house is on fire. Because it is."

Drafting speeches, statements, and press releases, I've too often been party to raising hopes that fail to translate to action. For there is a subtle but dangerous trap that lurks in the fanfare that frequently accompanies well-intentioned governmental and high-level initiatives, conferences, and consultations.

Might it not create more harm than good to raise expectations and then disappoint them rather than not raise hopes at all? Raising hopes and disappointing them time and again eventually leads people to give up hope if not to anger them, and to stop believing that requests for participation and advice are genuine.

I've seen and participated in too many workshops, trainings, meetings, partnerships and impressive commitments and promises to adopt sustainable practices and more. But that, in truth, is the easy part. Putting something into practice is a whole other story, and I've also seen too many of those initiatives dissipate, fall apart, and quietly disappear.

The problem with initiatives that end in disappointment – as our team learned over and again from Nova Scotia to New Zealand[3] to Bhutan – is that they may dampen future efforts and discourage future investments of time and resources. Good intentions alone don't cut the mustard unless accompanied by a masterful implementation strategy, skilful means, deep personal commitment, and real perseverance and staying power.

Again, I believe the trap of hope that Greta so ruthlessly punctures is a function and by-product of our deeply entrenched economic structures that resist any efforts to turn words into action that may dent the existing system. In fact, the only real breaks we've given nature were when the economic system itself imploded in the Great Recession of 2008–9 and when COVID-19 led to a sharp drop in greenhouse gas emissions in many countries in 2020. Conversely, regardless of the hopes raised by the 2015 Paris Climate Accord and other international agreements, economic growth spurred a 1.6 per cent global increase in greenhouse gas emissions in 2017 and a 2.7 per cent increase in 2018.

In recent years, we've seen the OECD, the European Union, several governments (the United Kingdom, France, Japan, New Zealand, Bhutan, and more) adopt new frameworks for measuring progress, we've cheered the powerful Stiglitz-Sen-Fitoussi (2009) Commission recommendations, and we've seen a "green GDP" come and go in China (Li and Lang 2010). Yet all the while, we've seen ever more cars on the roads, a resurgence of coal use, and global greenhouse gas emissions hitting record highs. Ironically, as new progress measures have made inroads in mainstream institutions, we have yet to see any transformative impact towards greater sustainability, equity, and well-being.

Maybe it's time for us measurement folk to heed Liza Doolittle's words in *My Fair Lady*: "Words, words, words, I'm so sick of words.... Is that all you blighters can do? ... Don't say how much, show me ... show me now!" If words are truly sacred, as I believe they are, then we are surely misusing them when we mislead our audiences into assuming words portend appropriate action.

And yet, here I am writing again! Some rare words like Greta's do seem to inspire action. Mine, frankly, have not! For those like me, then, perhaps it's time to walk the talk and put a moratorium on more words, speeches, consultations, and conferences, at least until we put our previous ones into action.

Co-opting (and Eviscerating) the Truth

Most insidiously – and hardest to detect, expose, and thwart – noble initiatives are frequently co-opted, and thereby eviscerated and watered down. I witnessed this on many fronts at Bhutan's 2 April 2012 UN meeting to launch a "New Economic Paradigm" based on sustainability and equity.

Thus, the widely touted *World Happiness Report* (Helliwell, Layard, and Sachs 2012), which was born at that meeting, failed to include a single environmental dimension even though ecological conservation is one of the four core pillars of Bhutan's "Gross National Happiness" development policy. It thus ignored a fundamentally important truth: that human well-being depends on nature.[4]

At the same UN meeting, very many ambassadors and cabinet ministers from different countries, recognizing the popularity of Bhutan's initiative, clearly felt they had no choice but to ride its wave. So one after another took the microphone to make the right noises about the need for change, the importance of environment, and the inadequacy of GDP, while their actual remarks betrayed their lack of commitment and understanding.

Co-optation goes beyond such lack of commitment: It involves, for example, "mainstreaming" radical initiatives so that they conveniently fit existing parameters and assumptions and allow business as usual and untrammelled growth to continue under the guise of high-sounding labels like "sustainable development," "care for the environment," and "inclusion." And so, a number of Indian, Chinese, European, and other diplomats at the April 2012 UN meeting donned the mantle of Bhutan's proposed "new economic paradigm" with no intention of forsaking their growth agendas or reducing unrestrained consumption.

Cynical co-optation of noble intention has happened time and again through misuse of the word "sustainability." The Irving Company in eastern Canada called itself the "sustainable forest company" and trumpeted its "investment in a sustainable future" even as it continued to clear-cut forests at an increasing rate. Its narrow definition of "sustainability" meant replacing as much fibre as it extracted, even when it was replacing an old, diverse, multi-aged, multi-species forest with a single-age, single-species monoculture plantation. "Greenwashing" is another name for this strategy, and it has become a subspecialty of the advertising industry.

Co-opting principled initiatives can also happen much more subtly. Subversion of the intent of Bhutan's UN initiative was manifested in expressed "support" for a "new economic paradigm," sustainability, and poverty alleviation while at the same time dodging equity issues and failing to challenge the dominant growth syndrome or the excess consumption of the rich. That position skilfully uses progressive language to avoid touching any politically sensitive hot potato.

In Canada I witnessed Nova Scotia's New Democratic Party cynically co-opt our Genuine Progress Index (GPI) language as a convenient political tool to bash the government while in opposition, only to quickly abandon it as soon as it came to power in 2009. Bits and pieces of the GPI, such as our work on health promotion and the avoidable costs of common health risk factors (Colman 2002; GPI Atlantic n.d.), have been adopted at various times to further particular agendas. But the GPI as a whole speaks too many inconvenient truths to be swallowed whole.

I've had similar debates with former colleagues who have compromised the integrity of their work by settling for flawed conventional indicators in place of important evidence that is more difficult to chew. For a decade I've not gone public with such criticisms in the interests of maintaining a façade of harmony and unity within our alternative indicator community. But the deteriorating state of our world and the demonstrable failure of our new measures to change humankind's self-destructive trajectory show we can no longer delay the time for honest reckoning and reality check.

Co-optation is often more difficult to overcome than straightforward opposition from vested interests because it is more difficult to spot. When noble ideas are co-opted, subtly watered down, or adopted only in part, the language sounds right, the appearance and intention seem worthy, and the real danger comes in the guise of a friend and ally. I don't know that there is one solution to this conundrum that fits all cases. Increasingly, my own inclination is to speak up about such co-optation and evisceration when it's identified, but of course that may risk alienating potential allies and leaving one isolated.

What Now?

Because this essay focuses on the failure of our improved progress measures to shift policy, readers may feel it is unduly negative and pessimistic. But that's not so. I simply argue that without acknowledging past failures and deeply analysing their causes, we will be incapable of setting a constructive path forward. Maybe a bucket of cold water is necessary now to wake us from our dreams when we keep sleeping through the alarms.

But that has nothing to do with revelling in failure or giving up in despair. On the contrary, as this short conclusion clarifies, that cold water is simply intended to suggest how our measurement work might be more useful in the future. So, this conclusion will briefly outline the strong foundation that now exists and then suggest three steps – as a profession, as individuals, and in the audience we address – that might move us forward more effectively.

First, nothing I've said here disparages the excellent work of the past, only the delusion that this work has fundamentally changed policy or turned things around in any significant way as many in our measurement community had originally assumed would happen.

As a measurement community we've now gathered copious good data, refined methodologies, and constructed convincing, comprehensive progress measures. None of that would have been possible without the outstanding work of natural resource accountants, ecological economists, epidemiologists, meteorologists, statisticians, and more. Nor would our new measures point a convincing way forward without the innovative work of renewable energy pioneers, organic farmers, sustainable foresters, appropriate technology designers, and more.

Nor has the fundamental goal that many of us alternative measurement folk share changed. While some may differ on minor details, my colleagues and I are still fundamentally united around both the vision and practicalities of a new economy that functions sustainably within planetary limits and ensures fair distribution and efficient use of limited resources. Please see the appendix for the outline we collectively prepared with the government of Bhutan for the April 2012 UN meeting. It is more relevant and necessary now, a decade later, than it ever was.

In short, neither the value of past measurement work nor the integrity of the vision many of us share is in dispute here. All we want is to use the former effectively to realize the latter. And that's where we've failed. So, it's addressing that missing link that is the purpose of this essay. Recognizing that, here are three possible steps we might take.

First, as a research community, we can shift the focus of our work to a much broader, deeper, and more systematic analysis of the *resistances* we have faced in influencing policy. I've asked a series of questions above that I'd like to see seriously addressed in research studies, conference presentations, and then public and media releases. For example, instead of presenting statistics and calling vaguely for urgent action, let's probe seriously why that action is not forthcoming.

The questions above are not comprehensive nor definitive, but they point to the kind of analysis urgently required and hitherto in seriously short supply. Suffice it here to say that, as a research community, we'll continue to tread water and preach to the converted unless we come to terms with our own inefficacy and dare to confront the resistances we've faced.

It's been said that genuine pursuit of the truth requires only two key ingredients: It must not be afraid of its own conclusions nor of conflict with the powers that be. The sad reality of both our own research and of initiatives like Bhutan's "new economic paradigm" has been a hurried retreat both from its own conclusions and from conflict with the powers that be. The conclusions were just too radical – considerably more than originally conceived by most – and the powers that be just too powerful.

So, we researchers need to be a lot braver. Instead of just delicately churning out ever more numbers and shying away from where those numbers point, let's be explicit that our results and conclusions deeply challenge existing structures and business as usual and inevitably point to a radically new and different economic system that adjusts production and consumption to the finite limits of our planet and distributes resources fairly and efficiently.

Second, as individuals, it's no longer enough to confine ourselves to words, papers, and presentations. As Greta has shown us, we need to start walking the talk. We are not just research aficionados. We are also human beings with a direct stake in the survival of this planet and in our children's future. Can we set an example by joining our professional and personal lives with integrity?

Research shows that ecological footprint expands in direct proportion to educational attainment (Pannozzo et al. 2008, 309–10), and so most of us researchers and scholars have enormous carbon and resource use footprints. We fly to too many conferences, take part in too many consultations, and deliver too many papers that end up making no real difference.

This second step is the direct consequence of the first: If we do find the nature and structure of capitalism to be at the heart of resistance to our efforts and to attempts to stabilize the atmosphere and stop destructive resource depletion, pollution, and species extinctions, how can we effectively challenge that system at its core and move beyond it? For too long, so-called radicals have thought they were doing that by finger-pointing and blaming multinational corporations and politicians. And their efforts have been utterly futile.

To survive, however, capitalism requires both supply *and* demand, production *and* consumption. We forget the latter and thus conveniently avoid examining how our own lifestyles and desires feed and sustain the very system we pretend to criticize. We may not be able to affect the supply and production side directly, but the demand and consumption side is entirely up to us.

We can boycott, and thereby disrupt the system that is leading us to certain disaster, sharply reduce our own complicity in it, and present that action as an integral part of our writings, talks, and research findings. If we can sharply cut demand and consumption, capitalism will become unhinged.

So, can we as individuals start by taking a vow to cut our own consumption, ecological footprints, and greenhouse gas emissions by 50 per cent, even if that means cancelling a few international conferences and European vacations, boycotting air-freighted mangos in winter, and sharply simplifying our lives? If we study, research, write, speak, and walk that talk in our own lives, might we even contribute to a movement with the power to forge the new system through its own steam and determination – bypassing and short-circuiting the politicians we've tried so long, hard, and fruitlessly to persuade?

Third, in direct line with the above, I suggest we researchers sharply change the intended audience of all our work. So far, we've directed our work to other experts and scholars, to policy audiences, and to a lesser extent to nongovernmental organizations. In terms of shifting policy priorities, that hasn't gotten us far.

Instead, I suggest we now aim our studies and results far more intently at the real agents of change at the grassroots level and especially to youth. They urgently need our results and our evidence both to educate themselves and to ensure real credibility in their efforts to effect fundamental change. They have far less stake in the existing system – and why should they have when this is the system that's destroyed their future? They are far more fully and genuinely open to what we have to say than any of our past scholarly or policy audiences, and they have a direct and personal stake in the new sustainability and equity-based system we are advocating.

Thus, Greta Thunberg has openly recognized the need for a complete paradigm shift remarkably along the lines of the new economic paradigm that Bhutan and many in the beyond-GDP community tried to promote: "[T]here are no solutions within our current systems. We need a whole new way of thinking. The political system that you have created is all about competition.... That must come to an end. We need to start cooperating and sharing the remaining resources of this planet in a fair way" (Thunberg 2019; see also Carrington 2019; Hertsgaard 2019). Here, I would suggest, is our new audience. And unlike policymakers who consistently sow seeds of doubt in good science and who ignore and side-line hard evidence, Greta repeatedly says: "Listen to the scientists." She and those like her want our facts, and they will use them to create the new world.

This is far from a negative, pessimistic, or despairing conclusion. But all these three suggested steps require a big leap for us researchers and scholars. Do we dare step up to the plate? Rather than point fingers and put the burden of change on policy and business actors with powerful stakes in "business as usual," are we ourselves brave enough to cut our own usual business and radically shift tracks? If we are, and if we act quickly, we can reverse past failures and be the agents of change we've always wanted our work to generate.

Appendix 14.1: A New Economic Paradigm

The following outline of the central principles that might guide a new economic paradigm is drawn from work I did with the Royal Government of Bhutan and with the co-founder of ecological economics, Robert Costanza, and his colleagues in preparation for the meeting Bhutan hosted for 800 distinguished delegates at UN headquarters in New York on 2 April 2012.

A new economic paradigm can be built on the following principles, understandings, and actions:

1) The new economy recognizes our interdependence with nature and with each other.
2) It requires a healthy balance among thriving natural, human, social, cultural, and built assets.

These assets, which overlap and interact in complex ways to produce all benefits, are generally defined as follows:

Natural capital: The natural environment, its biodiversity, and the ecosystem goods and services they provide. These goods and services are essential to basic needs, such as survival, climate regulation, habitat for other species, water supply, food, fibre, fuel, recreation, cultural amenities, and the raw materials required for all economic production.

Social and cultural capital: The web of interpersonal connections, social networks, cultural heritage, traditional knowledge, trust, and the institutional arrangements, rules, norms, and values that facilitate human interactions and cooperation between people. These contribute to social cohesion; strong, vibrant, and secure communities; and good governance, and they help to fulfil basic human needs, such as participation, affection, and a sense of belonging.

Human capital: Human beings and their attributes, including physical and mental health, knowledge, and other capacities that enable people to be productive members of society. This involves the balanced use of time to fulfil basic human needs, such as employment, spirituality, understanding, skills development, creativity, and freedom.

Built capital: Buildings, machinery, transportation infrastructure, and all other human artefacts and services that fulfil basic human needs, such as shelter, subsistence, mobility, and communications.

3) These assets depend on the natural world, whose functions can generally not be replaced by human activity. Sustainability therefore requires that we live off the interest generated by natural capital without depleting the capital itself.
4) Balancing and investing in all those dimensions of our wealth requires that:
   a) We live sustainably within the capacity of our finite planet to provide the resources needed for this and all future generations;
   b) These resources are distributed fairly within this generation, between generations, and between humans and other species;
   c) We use these resources as efficiently and effectively as possible;
   d) We respect and strengthen the cultural, community, health, knowledge, and spiritual foundations of our world to produce sustainable well-being and harmony among all life forms.

5) We have never had greater global capacity, understanding, material abundance, and opportunities to achieve these objectives. This includes scientific knowledge, communications, technology, resources, productive potential, higher education, and ability to feed everyone on earth. We have many inspiring and successful examples of legislation, initiatives, and best practices at multiple scales on which we can build.

6) However, human society is moving in a destructive direction at an increasing rate. For example, global greenhouse gas emissions continue to grow, humanity is using resources much faster than nature can regenerate them, biodiversity is diminishing rapidly, global ecosystem services are in decline, inequality is growing, more and greater conflicts and disasters are in the making, producing more refugees than at any time since the Second World War, and political will is lacking.

7) "Business as usual" threatens the survival of humans and other species and is no longer an option. On a finite planet, excessive consumption by high-income groups leaves less for others, increases social exclusion, and undermines well-being.

8) Many of these dangerous trends are a result of our current, unsustainable, growth-based economic paradigm, which rests on flawed measures of progress. These measures largely ignore the value of natural and social capital and the distribution of wealth and income. They misleadingly count natural capital depletion and many human and social costs as economic gain. The architects of gross domestic product (GDP) themselves counselled that GDP should never be used as a measure of welfare, as it incorrectly is today. The European Union, OECD, the Sarkozy-Stiglitz Commission, Japan, and many others have therefore recognized the need to find viable alternatives.

9) Unless we change the current economic paradigm, which is a fundamental cause of the current crises, we will never realize the world we all want. That paradigm, institutionalized at Bretton Woods in 1944, was devised prior to widespread understanding of finite global resource limits and scientific knowledge about climate change. We need a new Bretton Woods.

10) To move onto a sustainable and beneficial path will require:
   - A fundamental change of world view to one which recognizes that we live on a finite planet;
   - Replacing the present pursuit of limitless growth and increasing consumption with goals of material sufficiency, equitable distribution, and sustainable well-being;
   - A redesign of the world economy that preserves natural systems essential to life and well-being, and balances natural, social, human, and built assets;

- Reclaiming the broad definition and goals of economics as the science, management, and well-being of our global household.

11) In order to realize the future we all want, we must build on prior work to develop the new economy in the following areas, among others, by actions like:

Ecological sustainability

- Establishing a system for effective and equitable governance and management of the natural commons, including the atmosphere, oceans, freshwater systems, and biodiversity;
- Investing in sustainable infrastructure, such as renewable clean energy, energy efficiency, public transit, watershed protection measures, green public spaces, clean technology, and support for green businesses;
- Creating mechanisms such as taxes, cap and auction systems, and common asset trusts to reduce resource depletion, pollution, and greenhouse gas emissions and to stay within basic planetary boundaries and resource limits;
- Dismantling incentives towards excessive materialistic consumption by, for example, banning advertising to children and instead educating for sustainability;
- Moving towards sustainable agriculture to feed the earth's population without destroying its biodiversity;
- Developing linked policies to balance population and consumption with the earth's natural, social, and economic capacity.

Fair Distribution

- Reducing systemic inequalities, both internationally and within nations, by improving the living standards of the poor, providing an adequate social safety net, limiting excess consumption and unearned income, and preventing private capture of the common wealth;
- Supporting, promoting, and providing incentives for local economies and systems of cooperative ownership and management of enterprises;
- Instituting fair trade systems that promote sustainable production methods and fair returns to producers;
- Transferring technology to enable lower-income nations to shift rapidly to sustainable production methods and suffer no loss of competitive advantage as they transition to a sustainable economy;

- Establishing a system for effective and equitable governance and management of the social commons, including cultural inheritance, financial systems, and information systems;
- Creating fulfilling employment for all, which contributes to the common good, achieves better work–life balance, and nurtures healthy workplace relations.

Efficient Use of Resources

- Using full-cost accounting measures to internalize externalities, value non-market assets and services, reform national accounting systems, and ensure that prices reflect actual social and environmental costs of production and distribution;
- Instituting fiscal reforms that reward equitable, sustainable, and well-being-enhancing actions and penalize unsustainable behaviours that diminish collective well-being. Examples include elimination of perverse subsidies to the fossil fuel industry, incentives for renewable energy, and ecological tax reforms with compensating mechanisms that avoid additional burdens on low-income groups;
- Implementing systems of cooperative investment in stewardship and payment for ecosystem services;
- Increasing financial and fiscal prudence by reducing speculation, ensuring equitable access to and responsible use of credit, and requiring that financial instruments and practices contribute to the public good;
- Ensuring access to and sharing of the information required to move to a sustainable economy.

NOTES

1   From the founders of the new field of ecological economics, like Herman Daly (Daly and Cobb 1989) and Robert Constanza (Costanza et al. 2009), to the architects of ecological footprint accounting, like William Rees and Mathis Wackernagel (1996), that view was expressed in one form or another by virtually all those engaged in constructing alternative progress measures.
2   For a more detailed account of this experience, see Colman (2021).
3   The vulnerability of these initiatives to political change was demonstrated when New Zealand's National Party government (2008–17) largely overturned or discontinued the leading-edge sustainability and well-being reporting efforts initiated by the previous Labour Party government under Prime Minister Helen

Clark (1999–2008). Though the focus on well-being has been revived by the present Labour government under Jacinda Ardern (Ng, this volume), it is too early to judge its staying power in the face of political change.
4   Possibilities exist for proponents of happiness measurement to integrate the dependence of human well-being on nature into their frameworks; see Barrington-Leigh (this volume) for one potential approach.

REFERENCES

Allen, Leslie. 2004. "Will Tuvalu Disappear Beneath the Sea?" *Smithsonian Magazine*, August 2004. https://www.smithsonianmag.com/science-nature/will-tuvalu-disappear-beneath-the-sea-180940704/.
Carrington, Damian. 2019. "School Climate Strikes: 1.4 Million People Took Part, Say Campaigners." *The Guardian*, 19 March 2019. https://www.theguardian.com/environment/2019/mar/19/school-climate-strikes-more-than-1-million-took-part-say-campaigners-greta-thunberg.
Colman, Ronald. 2000. "The Cost of Obesity in Nova Scotia." Glen Haven, NS: GPI Atlantic. http://www.gpiatlantic.org/pdf/health/obesity/ns-obesity.pdf.
– 2021. *What Really Counts: The Case for a Sustainable and Equitable Economy*. New York: Columbia University Press.
– 2002. "The Cost of Chronic Disease in Nova Scotia." Glen Haven, NS: GPI Atlantic. http://www.gpiatlantic.org/pdf/health/chronic.pdf.
Costanza, Robert, Maureen Hart, Stephen Posner, and John Talberth. 2009. "Beyond GDP: The Need for New Measures of Progress." Pardee Papers 4. Boston: Frederick S. Pardee Center for the Study of the Longer-Range Future, Boston University. http://www.oecd.org/site/progresskorea/globalproject/42613423.pdf.
Daly, Herman E., and John B. Cobb. 1989. *For the Common Good: Redirecting the Economy toward Community, the Environment, and a Sustainable Future*. Boston: Beacon Press.
Gillis, Justin. 2015. "Climate Chaos, across the Map." *The New York Times*, 30 December 2015. https://www.nytimes.com/2015/12/31/science/climate-chaos-across-the-map.html.
GPI Atlantic. n.d. "Population Health Publications." http://www.gpiatlantic.org/publications/health.htm.
Helliwell, John, Richard Layard, and Jeffrey Sachs. 2012. "World Happiness Report." New York: Earth Institute, Columbia University.
Hertsgaard, Mark. 2019. "The Climate Kids Are Coming." *The Nation*, 28 January 2019. https://www.thenation.com/article/archive/greta-thunberg-climate-change-davos/.
Holland, Tom. 2019. *Dominion: The Making of the Western Mind*. London: Little, Brown.
IEA. 2011. "World Energy Outlook 2011." Paris: International Energy Agency. https://www.iea.org/publications/freepublications/publication/WEO2011_WEB.pdf.

Li, Vic, and Graeme Lang. 2010. "China's 'Green GDP' Experiment and the Struggle for Ecological Modernisation." *Journal of Contemporary Asia* 40, no. 1: 44–62. https://doi.org/10.1080/00472330903270346.

Mahbubani, Kishore. 2018. *Has the West Lost It? A Provocation*. London: Allen Lane.

Malhotra, Rajiv. 2011. *Being Different: An Indian Challenge to Western Universalism*. New Delhi: Harper Collins India

Pannozzo, Linda, Ronald Colman, Nathan Ayer, Tony Charles, Chris Burbidge, David Sawyer, Seton Stiebert, Aviva Savelson, and Colin Dodds. 2008. "The 2008 Nova Scotia GPI Accounts: Indicators of Genuine Progress." Glen Haven, NS: GPI Atlantic. http://www.gpiatlantic.org/pdf/integrated/gpi2008.pdf.

Savelson, Aviva, Ronald Colman, and William Martin. 2008. "The GPI Transportation Accounts: Sustainable Transportation in Halifax Regional Municipality." Glen Haven, NS: GPI Atlantic. http://www.gpiatlantic.org/pdf /transportation/hrmtransportation.pdf.

Stiglitz, Joseph E., Amartya Sen, and Jean-Paul Fitoussi. 2009. "Report by the Commission on the Measurement of Economic Performance and Social Progress." Paris: Commission on the Measurement of Economic Performance and Social Progress. http://www.stiglitz-sen-fitoussi.fr/documents/rapport_anglais.pdf.

Thunberg, Greta. 2019. "'Our House Is on Fire': Greta Thunberg, 16, Urges Leaders to Act on Climate." *The Guardian*, 25 January 2019. https://www.theguardian.com /environment/2019/jan/25/our-house-is-on-fire-greta-thunberg16-urges-leaders -to-act-on-climate.

UN Secretary-General. 2012. "Secretary-General's Remarks to High-Level Thematic Debate on 'The State of the World Economy and Finance and Its Impact on Development.'" https://www.un.org/sg/en/content/sg/statement/2012-05-17 /secretary-generals-remarks-high-level-thematic-debate-state-world.

Wackernagel, Mathis, and William E. Rees. 1996. *Our Ecological Footprint: Reducing Human Impact on the Earth*. Gabriola Island, BC: New Society Publishers.

Yardley, Jim. 2013. "Clothing Brands Sidestep Blame for Safety Lapses." *The New York Times*, 30 December 2013. https://www.nytimes.com/2013/12/31/world/asia /garment-makers-stumble-on-call-for-accountability.html.

Conclusion: Towards Sustainable Well-Being

ANDERS HAYDEN, CÉOFRIDE GAUDET, AND JEFFREY WILSON

The contributions to this volume grow out of and expand upon ideas generated at a workshop we hosted at Dalhousie University on the theme of "Beyond GDP: International Experiences, Canada's Options." They illustrate the breadth of innovative thinking that has characterized the beyond-GDP movement worldwide in its quest to respond to the limitations of GDP when misused for purposes that it was not intended to fulfil and for which it is poorly suited: as an overarching indicator of a society's success or level of well-being. GDP remains a useful indicator in certain limited respects; there are still reasons to calculate it, or something similar, to serve those purposes.[1] However, a range of alternatives is now available that can provide more direct measures of well-being, as well as options to measure a key issue that GDP ignores: sustainability.

In this concluding chapter, we review the answers and often competing perspectives the contributors provide in response to the questions that gave rise to this book,[2] starting with the impacts of beyond-GDP measurement initiatives to date and their promising possibilities and applications. We then review and offer some observations on competing measurement frameworks and the difficulties of finding a consensus choice among them. This is followed by consideration of complementary measures and related policy tools that can help ensure that new measurements are taken into account in policymaking, along with barriers to introducing beyond-GDP metrics and using them in decision-making, which range from practical challenges to more fundamental obstacles to the most ambitious hopes. The chapter concludes with contrasting views on next steps, drawing on the distinction, introduced in the opening chapter, between reformist and transformative visions for beyond-GDP measurement and suggesting possibilities for some common ground between them.

Still Limited Impacts, Promising Possibilities

One key impact of beyond-GDP initiatives to date has been the increasingly broad acceptance – or "mainstreaming" – of the idea that GDP is not an adequate measure of well-being or national success, along with a related desire for alternatives. Without conducting a study of changes in beliefs over time, one cannot precisely show the degree to which such a shift has taken place. However, one can point to a range of indications, such as statements from proponents of alternative metrics who say they no longer find it necessary to make the case for a need to move beyond GDP as people are "looking for the alternative already," or from a senior public servant about the increasing prevalence within government of conversations in which measures of success are multilayered and more complex than simply looking at the contribution to GDP (quoted in Dasilva and Hayden). Whether at OECD conferences on well-being measurement that gather thousands of participants or our own more modestly scaled workshop, levels of interest and participation are very high. The many years of work by people in this field, including key contributions from Canadians, appear to be having some impact in reshaping frameworks of thought and mental models, or "conceptual use" as explained in the introductory chapter, with potentially significant long-term effects.

However, direct impacts on policy, or "instrumental use," have – with some notable exceptions – been modest so far, with contributors to the volume depicting the situation in contrasting ways. Some chapters point to the limited impacts of the beyond-GDP initiatives or approaches they examined (Bache; Bleys and Thiry; Berik; Hayden and Wilson) or indeed the beyond-GDP movement more generally (Colman). In Britain, for example, well-being has yet to supplant conventional economic concerns and become a core state priority, although a well-being perspective has informed some policy initiatives and innovations, and there are grounds for optimism about further advances (Bache).

Although many hopes for beyond-GDP measurement have yet to be fulfilled – particularly transformative hopes of moving beyond a growth-centred economy – those who see a glass half full can point to a growing number of examples of policy uses. The most striking case remains Bhutan's use of its Gross National Happiness (GNH) Policy Screening Tool (Kim and MacKenzie), which led it to decide not to pursue World Trade Organization membership in 2008. More recent initiatives include New Zealand's use of its Living Standards Framework for a variety of purposes, most notably informing a "well-being budget," while also providing a new "common language" of well-being that can help break down policy silos and enable different departments to work towards shared goals (Ng). A number of European jurisdictions have also used well-being measurements to inform budgeting, albeit with varying "degrees of sincerity" (Laurent) – while Canada took initial steps in 2021 in assessing how budget measures affect indicators in its draft quality-of-life framework (Department of Finance 2021a, 414). Several other examples of use throughout the policy cycle are noted by Durand and Mira d'Ercole.

Among many promising possibilities, not all of which can be reviewed here, the idea of gearing economic policy towards goals other than GDP growth has taken a partial step forward with the commitment by some pioneering governments to a "wellbeing economy" (Bache; Hayden and Wilson; Rodgers and Trebeck) – a key idea we return to near the end of this chapter. Similarly, beyond-GDP measurement has the potential to support a new narrative of prosperity and well-being in which "success is about more than just dollars and cents" (Watson 2018, cited in Dasilva and Hayden). Appraisal and evaluation of policy and spending initiatives in new ways that account for a wider range of costs and benefits has made headway, as discussed below. The many possibilities for using beyond-GDP measurement to generate better, evidence-based policies outlined in the Introduction include their use in identifying issues requiring government attention (Dasilva and Hayden; Kim and MacKenzie; Ng), such as gaps in well-being among different segments of the population, with related possibilities to develop targeted or place-based policies to address well-being disparities.

Meanwhile, Helliwell et al. (this volume) highlight the promise of an emerging "epidemiology of happiness," which can inform many policy decisions, based on the understanding of the causes and consequences of healthy and happy lives that has grown in tandem with advances in well-being measurement. The COVID-19 crisis highlights the importance of such an approach – and indeed a well-being orientation more generally. Although more time will be needed for a full account of successes and failures in national COVID-19 responses, it appears to be no coincidence that, at the time of writing, countries standing out for effectively prioritizing protection of human lives include beyond-GDP and well-being-economy leaders, with Bhutan (#1), New Zealand (#2), and Iceland (#6) topping the Lowy Institute's (2021) Covid Performance Index.[3]

Which Measurement Framework?

The wide range of beyond-GDP measurement options reflects the great interest in finding better ways to measure prosperity and well-being but also creates a considerable challenge in finding consensus on a way forward (Hoekstra 2019). In our more ambitious moments, we entertained thoughts of finding such a consensus at the workshop that preceded this book, but sharply differing perspectives remain among contributors to this volume and within the beyond-GDP movement generally (and occasionally among ourselves as editors). Without aiming to provide definitive conclusions, we offer some observations on the major alternatives covered in the book, while inviting readers to develop their own judgments about the measurement options in light of the cases made by their proponents in the preceding chapters.

Over the years, much beyond-GDP work has centred on developing a single measure to rival and potentially dethrone GDP from its dominant position. This is understandable given the communication advantages of a single number that summarizes a complex reality and allows for a comparison with GDP. However, we find ourselves in agreement with the OECD High-Level Expert Group's first key conclusion: "No single metric will ever provide a good measure of the health of a country" (Durand and Mira D'Ercole, this volume; see also Stiglitz, Fitoussi, and Durand 2018). Well-being is a multidimensional concept, while sustainability requires its own separate measurements. One can combine multiple measures into a single composite index, but that raises seemingly intractable problems of how to weight each component – a problem that cannot be escaped by weighting all components equally, as that implicitly and unrealistically assumes each component's equal importance to well-being.[4] Problems also arise when conceptually distinct matters of well-being and sustainability are aggregated into a single overall number whose meaning is unclear – akin, as Stiglitz, Sen, and Fitoussi (2009, 17) argued, to combining a car's speed and fuel-tank readings into one value.

Criticisms of this kind apply to many beyond-GDP alternatives, including one of Canada's most prominent measures, the Canadian Index of Wellbeing (CIW). However, such criticisms do not negate the CIW's value. Its use in the Nova Scotia Quality of Life Initiative has seen less emphasis on the CIW as a composite index and more on the indicator dashboard behind it (as well as the related community survey), which provide more actionable data for users (Dasilva and Hayden). This change in emphasis is consistent with the shift in the broader debate towards dashboards of multiple measures, as reflected in the Stiglitz-Sen-Fitoussi (2009) report and the OECD's subsequent work (Durand and Mira D'Ercole). A dashboard, i.e., the Living Standards Framework, also informed one of the most prominent recent policy examples, New Zealand's wellbeing budget (Ng).

Momentum has also grown behind the measurement of subjective well-being (a.k.a. happiness), and specifically life satisfaction or life evaluations. Proponents of life-satisfaction measurement argue that it can serve as an overarching well-being indicator – and indeed have proposed that increasing happiness/life satisfaction serve as government's core goal (Frijters et al. 2020).[5] In their chapters, Helliwell et al. and Barrington-Leigh make a strong case for the use of life-satisfaction data, whose potential applications have grown, as noted above, with a growing base of data on life satisfaction over many years and evidence about its determinants, as well as advances in policy tools enabling its use in cost–benefit analysis.

A focus on life satisfaction as the key measurement and policy goal could certainly be an improvement on prioritizing GDP – as it is a more direct measure of well-being and a more defensible end goal than GDP growth, which at best ought to be considered one means among others to higher ends. From an environmental perspective, it could also increase attention to the many non-material ways of improving well-being – e.g., enhancing a sense of social belonging, mutual support, and trust – which, as Barrington-Leigh (this volume) points out, have greater potential to enhance well-being and are more environmentally sustainable than increased material consumption (see also Helliwell 2019). However, we have reservations about endorsing life satisfaction as the single overarching measure and public-policy objective.

Life satisfaction unquestionably provides valuable information about well-being, but focusing on it alone risks replacing one incomplete picture of how well society is doing – GDP – with an improved but still insufficient picture. Critics point to the possibility of people adapting to and accepting inequitable or problematic conditions (see, e.g., Berik, this volume). This issue comes up, for example, in Nova Scotia, where high life satisfaction may reflect strengths such as strong social connections, a sense of belonging, and access to natural beauty, but critics also see "low expectations" at play in a context of high levels of poverty, economic insecurity, and concern over insufficient access to public services (Dasilva and Hayden). Whatever the cause of high life satisfaction in this case, a more complete quality-of-life picture requires data on many other variables in addition to life satisfaction.

A single-minded focus on life satisfaction also cannot account for sustainability, either in what is measured or in offering normative guidance about how to think about responsibilities to future generations (Durand 2020). A real possibility exists of high life satisfaction today at the expense of people tomorrow. Acknowledging this concern, Barrington-Leigh highlights the need to establish conservation-oriented material constraints on activity to address environmental sustainability, within which life satisfaction could be maximized. While work remains to refine some details, such as how to determine those sustainability-related material constraints, this effort to link environmental sustainability to the life-satisfaction approach stands out as a fruitful avenue for future work.[6]

A case thus exists for life satisfaction as one indicator in a larger dashboard that includes other objective measures of social conditions and environmental sustainability. That, of course, still leaves major questions to resolve about the dashboard's other components and how large it should be. Many countries, Canada included, have been developing metrics to gauge progress towards the SDGs, with their 169 targets and 232 indicators. However, as Stiglitz, Fitoussi, and Durand (2018, 61) point out, a dashboard that large is unmanageable and must be narrowed to establish priorities (see also Durand and Exton 2019, 146). Nor is such a large dashboard likely to have the communicative power to capture political or public attention. One main option, advocated by Stiglitz, Sen, and Fitoussi (2009), is to identify a set of headline indicators, reflecting core priorities,[7] behind which a larger dataset exists.[8] For example, Scotland's National

Performance Framework identifies eleven priority national outcomes,[9] behind which is a larger dashboard of eighty-one indicators. Canadians can refer to such examples as possible models but should debate and determine their own priorities, renewing and expanding the discussions that occurred two decades ago leading to the CIW's creation.

Critics of dashboards remain, including Berik, who argues in her chapter that dashboards suffer from "too much information," cannot provide an assessment of changes in overall well-being over time, and – while they can help spotlight issues for policy attention – can provide only rough or imprecise guidance for budgeting and other policy decisions. Berik makes a case for the Genuine Progress Indicator (GPI), which includes some two dozen monetary adjustments – for factors including income inequality, environmental degradation, unpaid work, underemployment, and the loss of leisure from overwork – to the value of personal consumption, making it, in effect, "an externality-corrected GDP." In addition to GPI's incorporation of key contributors to and detractors from well-being that are ignored not only by GDP but also by some other beyond-GDP options, Berik emphasizes its value as a monetary measure to evaluate the welfare impact of policy proposals by enabling policy simulations and assessment of trade-offs.

The GPI has played a key role in the historical development of beyond-GDP measurement (Hayden and Wilson). It had considerable momentum behind it a few years ago, with a number of state-level initiatives in the United States (Hayden and Wilson 2018), among other international applications, and many observers saw it as a leading beyond-GDP alternative (e.g., Kubiszewski et al. 2013). Some setbacks to the GPI were political – e.g., changes of governor in Maryland, before GPI-related work could be fully applied to policymaking, and in Oregon, before a GPI initiative could get off the ground. Other questions have arisen about the GPI's theoretical foundation, given that it appears to mix the measurement of sustainability and well-being within a single number. Berik acknowledges that the GPI does not in fact measure sustainability – which was implied by its original formulation as the Index of Sustainable Economic Welfare – and instead points to recent efforts at a GPI reset, reformulating it as a measure of current welfare, as well as updating and standardizing the methodology. We welcome further work to refining the GPI and illustrating policy applications in light of the value of having a variety of different indicators, which can provide multiple perspectives and a richer overall picture of how a society is doing.

Berik also expresses concern that dashboards may not do enough to illustrate the costs of economic output and its growth. This is a valid concern considering examples of government "manipulation" of indicator selection to present their record in a good light (Laurent, this volume) and the limited perspective some indicator sets provide on environmental impacts, as in Nova Scotia

(Dasilva and Hayden). Indeed, it is a concern with the indicators being considered in Canada's preliminary work on a new quality-of-life dashboard (Department of Finance 2021b). That said, it all depends on which indicators are on the dashboard. These can include, for example, consumption-based indicators of ecological, carbon, or material footprints, which have been used to trace environmental impacts back to the high and growing consumption of wealthy nations, even if the production and pollution take place elsewhere. Meanwhile Raworth's (2017) growth-critical "doughnut economics" is based on a dashboard to track the degree to which planetary boundaries are respected and key social needs are met. A reformulated GPI itself might even serve as one element of a broader dashboard or, alternatively, individual GPI components (see Table 1 and Appendix, Berik, this volume) could serve as dashboard indicators, while the monetized satellite accounts associated with these indicators may yet find important applications.

The comprehensive wealth (CW) approach (Smith, McDougal, and Bizikova) similarly involves monetized estimates of the value of key assets that contribute to well-being – in this case produced, financial, natural, human, and social capital. This approach responds to calls for better sustainability measures and development of more comprehensive balance sheets (Durand and Mira D'Ercole, this volume; Stiglitz, Fitoussi, and Durand 2018). It faces challenges in providing accurate estimates of the value of the various forms of capital, particularly social capital, which currently cannot be calculated for inclusion in the index, and "critical assets," which require separate non-monetary indicators. Given such limitations, comprehensive wealth numbers should be interpreted cautiously. For example, the authors acknowledge that the increase in Canada's CW from 1980 to 2015 should not necessarily be interpreted as progress towards sustainability since the status of critical natural assets needs to be assessed separately. That said, such metrics can help to identify vulnerabilities, for example, by pointing to medium- or long-term financial risks in countries that are relying too heavily on a narrow set of natural resources or limited forms of produced capital. We thus welcome further work to refine this approach and address current limitations.

Debate on alternative options is likely to continue for some time, which is healthy in a democratic society given that different metrics reflect different political and normative commitments. For now, we believe that a dashboard including subjective well-being (life satisfaction), other objective well-being indicators, and sustainability measures – with a focused set of headline indicators behind which there is a larger dataset – stands out as an option around which it would be fruitful for government, with broad public input, to put further efforts. Indeed, after we first wrote those words, Canada's federal government signalled its intention to move in that direction with its draft quality-of-life measurement framework (Department of Finance 2021b).[10]

As discussed above, new well-being metrics can now be applied to policy-making in various ways (e.g., in well-being budgeting and new approaches to cost–benefit analysis), and it is time to make fuller use of these existing possibilities. That said, work remains to refine various measurement options, particularly with regard to sustainability, and to ensure that an adequate picture of a nation's environmental impacts is provided in any dashboard. Indeed, we are open to the possibility that, through further debate and growing experience in applying the options in the policy sphere, other approaches may emerge as dominant.

Apart from the question of which metrics governments choose to help inform policy choices, we see value in having multiple measurement perspectives – or "indicator pluralism" – within society more broadly. This can help generate a more complete picture of well-being and sustainability and allow various social actors to highlight data and related issues that they believe merit greater public attention. In addition, "triangulation" – i.e., referring to multiple measures of the same concept, from varying standpoints – can help gain a truer picture of complex ideas, such as well-being.[11]

Complementary Measures and Policy Tools

One cannot simply assume that production of new indicators will inevitably lead policymakers to take the information into account, resulting in changes in policies, or generate any particular response from the public. This assumption – the "indicators fantasy," introduced in chapter one – has affected many of those involved in the beyond-GDP movement (including at least one of this book's editors in earlier days). Although some may still suffer from it, there have been promising responses to the problem. Indeed, many of the positive examples earlier in this chapter reflect growing recognition of the need to go beyond producing new metrics to integrating them into the policy process (Durand and Mira D'Ercole, this volume; see also Durand and Exton 2019).

In his chapter, Laurent refers to the next step, now underway, of the "age of institutionalization" of alternative indicators. Related developments include advances in policy tools that can bring well-being data into decision-making processes – such as the integration of life satisfaction into cost–benefit analysis, which has seen applications in Britain (Bache) and Canada (Helliwell et al.), or New Zealand's CBAx tool that can convert non-monetary impacts on dashboard indicators into monetary units for use in cost–benefit analysis (Ng). Also important in expanding future possibilities for policy use are improvements in well-being statistics (Durand and Mira d'Ercole), and the growing evidence base on the determinants of well-being, which gives policymakers greater capacity to know which levers they can pull to generate well-being gains (Bache; Barrington-Leigh; Helliwell et al.).

Awareness of the need to go beyond simply producing new indicators and collecting data is evident in cases such as Nova Scotia's Quality of Life Initiative, which established local teams to analyse quality-of-life data and identify priority actions in response to it (Dasilva and Hayden). Meanwhile, in Bhutan, calculation of the GNH Index has never been the central element – indeed, it is a relatively recent addition – within a broader GNH development approach. In addition to policies aiming to promote environmentally sustainable and equitable development while preserving cultural traditions, as well as the aforementioned GNH Policy Screening Tool, Kim and MacKenzie point to other complementary actions that go "beyond numbers." These include engaging civil society in promoting GNH values at the grassroots level, promoting social entrepreneurship that incorporates those values into the economy, and an idea that academic discussions of pathways to change often leave out: inner transformation of mindsets and behaviours.[12]

A deeper embedding of well-being metrics into policymaking would involve moving beyond a siloed to a whole-of-government[13] approach to the pursuit of well-being (Durand and Mira D'Ercole, this volume; Durand and Exton 2019). In addition to use of well-being frameworks and indicators in shaping budget decisions, discussed above, Durand and Exton (2019) point to options such as legislation that requires the use of well-being approaches; for example, France's Sas Law[14] requires the government to regularly report on a set of well-being indicators, while Wales's Wellbeing of Future Generations Act requires public bodies to put seven well-being goals at the centre of decision-making. Other options include integrating well-being frameworks and indicators into strategic planning, capacity building and guidance for public servants in the use of well-being metrics, and creating new institutions. Examples of the latter include the Future Generations Commissioner in Wales with a role as a guardian of sustainable well-being, new ministries or departments to lead well-being efforts, and bodies that keep track of the growing evidence base on the determinants of well-being, such as the UK's What Works Centre for Wellbeing. Meanwhile in Canada, embedding the measurement and pursuit of sustainable well-being into departmental mandates is a key option, building on the prime minister's initial 2019 mandate to the Minister of Middle Class Prosperity and Associate Minister of Finance to lead work in this area, which has resulted in efforts to develop a new quality-of-life measurement framework (Department of Finance 2021b). Innovative measures that can bring a sustainable well-being lens into policymaking also include reviews of public spending and programs to assess whether they promote or hinder sustainability and well-being, as in Finland (Laurent) and proposed in Nova Scotia (Dasilva and Hayden; see also APP-GWE 2019), while New Zealand's well-being budget included an overall well-being outlook for New Zealand alongside a conventional economic and fiscal outlook (Ng).

Positive contributions can also come from participatory processes linked to beyond-GDP initiatives that generate public conversations about what matters most, how to measure it, and how to achieve it. Rodgers and Trebeck emphasize processes that allow the public, and especially the most disadvantaged, to be actively engaged in setting priorities and determining how to measure progress towards core goals, which can "prefigure" the shifts in power and deepening of democracy needed to achieve a well-being economy (see also Fioramonti 2017). A participatory ethos has also been evident in the Canadian Index of Wellbeing, which was developed through public consultation in tandem with expert input, and the Nova Scotia Quality of Life Initiative, with a process designed to be collaborative, diverse, inclusive, and decentralized, in line with the kind of society the Initiative is trying to promote. While these participatory approaches have considerable promise, we add two notes of caution. First, such approaches do not eliminate the need for expert input, for example, to ensure that any democratically determined indicators also have validity as measures of the concepts they aim to represent. Indeed, examples in the book involve a productive interplay between public participation and expertise. Second, the Nova Scotia case illustrates challenges in ensuring the participation of marginalized communities, along with considerable scepticism among people about whether governments care about "what people like me think" (Dasilva and Hayden, this volume; Smale, Gao, and Jiang 2020, 109). Significant inequalities of power and influence lead to questions about whether, in practice, such participatory processes will be able to provide equitable opportunities to shape not only measurement choices but, even more importantly, the policy responses to the data generated.

Barriers

The chapter authors identify numerous obstacles to the introduction of beyond-GDP metrics and their use in decision-making – as does the wider literature (e.g., Bleys and Whitby 2015; Hayden and Wilson 2017; Whitby et al. 2014). In this volume, the barriers identified range from practical challenges to more fundamental obstacles to the most ambitious beyond-GDP aspirations. Among the former are difficulties in producing beyond-GDP data on a timely basis (a product, in part, of the limited resources devoted to them), which limits their usefulness in highlighting issues requiring policy action (Dasilva and Hayden) and in evaluating possible interventions (Bleys and Thiry; see also Bleys and Whitby 2015). There are continued needs to address the limitations of proposed measurement options and refine their measurement (Berik; Smith et al.) or add complementary elements to them (Barrington-Leigh), as well as the dominance of conventional economic training within government departments and lack of familiarity with alternative, well-being-focused approaches (Dasilva and Hayden). Meanwhile, generation of evidence from new well-being measures offers no guarantee that governments will have the political will to act on the evidence (Bache; Hayden and Wilson); in the extreme, this problem takes the form of a "post-fact" or "post-truth" politics that poses a substantial obstacle, wherever it flares up, to any form of evidence-based policy.

Some barriers have generated responses and some progress in addressing them. The "indicators fantasy," that providing more complete and accurate information is all that is needed, has been an obstacle to achieving significant impacts (Colman; Hayden and Wilson), although some steps in addressing it have been taken, as discussed above. A need has existed for more evidence about policies that can generate greater well-being; that evidence base has been growing (Bache; Barrington-Leigh; Helliwell et al.). That said, work remains in developing an alternative theoretical framework for how policies can improve well-being in sustainable ways – one that can rival and supersede the economic theories in which GDP is embedded (Bleys and Thiry). Indicators have in the past been developed without enough consideration for the needs of users of those statistics (Bleys and Whitby 2015); awareness of the problem has led to a positive example, in the case of New Zealand's Living Standards Framework, of conscious efforts to emphasize the needs of users (Ng). Recognition of the limited frequency and availability of many key non-economic indicators has also led to recent investments to bolster Statistics Canada's capacity to measure quality of life (Department of Finance 2021a, 313; 2021b, 5). Meanwhile, the neoliberal ideological hegemony that not long ago represented a formidable obstacle has been – although not entirely overcome – substantially eroded, creating more openness to beyond-GDP alternatives (Dasilva and Hayden).

One persistent issue is the lack of consensus on important elements of the beyond-GDP agenda, which reflects the deep complexity of the issues (Bleys and Thiry). While there is a broadly shared critique of GDP, disagreement remains over how to define and measure the multidimensional concept of well-being (Bache; Bleys and Thiry), as the earlier section on different measurement frameworks illustrates. The multiple agendas and currents of thought within the beyond-GDP movement help to explain the wide interest across varied sectors of society, while posing challenges in developing a unified and coherent approach (Bleys and Thiry; Hayden and Wilson). For some participants in the debate, the continued pre-eminence of GDP and limited impact of beyond-GDP efforts is linked to the ever-growing number of disparate measurement initiatives; the priority from this perspective is to develop a unified approach to well-being and sustainability measurement that the beyond-GDP community rallies behind (Hoekstra 2019). In addition, Bleys and Thiry note the normative divisions between those who see new indicators as part of the project of building a radically new economy and supporters of new metrics who do not question the wider economic system – what we refer to as the transformative and reformist perspectives.

Those divisions also affect the starkly contrasting views, introduced in chapter one, on whether the beyond-GDP movement has arrived at a moment of breakthroughs or whether it is time to acknowledge failures, the existence of more profound obstacles, and the need to develop new strategies. The most critical assessment of the movement's progress comes from Colman, whose decades of work on alternative prosperity measurements has been linked to the goal of moving beyond a growth-centred economy. In his call for a "reality check," he argues that decades of beyond-GDP work have not shifted policies on any substantial scale and this, in turn, requires a clear-eyed assessment of the reasons for that failure. He highlights resistance to a new economic paradigm from powerful interests with a stake in business as usual (issues also raised by Berik, and Dasilva and Hayden), bureaucratic resistance to change, and capitalism's growth dependency, while also critiquing the cooptation of radical initiatives that are watered down as they are mainstreamed.

The most fundamental obstacles to a transformative, post-growth vision of moving beyond GDP have to do with those intertwined questions of capitalism and its growth dependency that Colman highlights. Indeed, one could consider GDP a reasonably good measure of success in achieving the norms and goals of neoliberal capitalism, as one anonymous reviewer pointed out, with the monetary value of economic output serving as a rough proxy for the availability of profit-making opportunities (while also being correlated with job opportunities and government revenues) even as it ignores key issues such as inequitable distribution and ecological degradation. The fact that the latter issues can no longer be ignored politically – as concern has intensified over rising inequalities and the climate crisis, making it increasingly clear that more GDP cannot be equated with societal progress – helps to explain the growing mainstream political interest in supplementing GDP with other indicators of economic and social performance, along with related goals of "inclusive" and "sustainable" growth. Yet such ideas still remain tied to the pursuit of GDP growth. Canada's preliminary moves towards a broader quality-of-life measurement framework, for example, come with the idea that increasing GDP remains "crucial" (Department of Finance 2021a, 410).

Efforts to dethrone GDP from its dominant place among indicators confront the perceived political imperative of economic growth – a particularly vexing problem for a transformative, post-growth vision. Given existing economic institutions and prevailing understandings of what is possible within them, it is not simply a matter of choosing another measurement to prioritize and then forgetting GDP and the level of economic output and growth it measures. A full examination of growth imperatives is beyond the scope of this book (see, e.g., Jackson 2020; Richters and Simoneit 2019; Wiedmann et al. 2020), but we can say briefly that changing the indicators does not, in itself, make society any less dependent on economic growth to solve problems such as unemployment (a problem that is highly destructive of well-being) or to generate the revenues governments need to finance public spending – much of which has important well-being benefits to the population, not to mention benefits to government leaders in enhancing their reelection prospects. In competitive conditions where profit-seeking businesses face intense pressures to increase efficiencies and reduce labour inputs and costs, resulting increases in labour productivity threaten rising unemployment, and with it a deterioration of government finances and risks of social instability – unless economic output expands at a rate sufficient to absorb those displaced by more productive methods as well as new entrants to labour markets. Challenges of that kind drive governments – even those known for their beyond-GDP indicators – to believe that they must keep the economy as measured by GDP growing. Possible responses to these challenges are discussed below.

Next Steps: Reformist and Transformative Paths Forward

For some participants in the debate, the next steps involve continuing to refine and apply the work done in this area, moving forward towards more substantial reforms and possible breakthroughs on the horizon. A reformist vision of this kind is evident in the recommendations of the OECD's High-Level Expert Group (Durand and Mira D'Ercole), who outline a number of useful steps to achieve the organization's motto of "better policies for better lives." These include continued work to improve well-being-related measures (including measures of inequality, trust, and other social norms) and develop better measures of sustainability, improved collection of subjective well-being data, assessing policies for their effects on people's economic insecurity, and, most significantly, using well-being metrics to inform all stages of the policy process. There is a related role for further refinement of and experimentation with new policy tools to show how new well-being and sustainability metrics can be applied to policy decisions, such as cost–benefit analysis innovations. Particularly important are ideas for a deeper embedding of well-being metrics into policymaking and moving beyond a siloed to a whole-of-government approach to the pursuit of well-being (Durand and Mira D'Ercole, this volume; Durand and Exton 2019), discussed under "complementary measures" above. Other contributors offer ideas in a similar spirit, including continuing to build the evidence base on ways to improve well-being (Bache; Barrington-Leigh), further initiatives to integrate indicators into policymaking including budgeting (Laurent), and gaining further experience with applying methods to bring well-being indicator data into policy (Ng).

In Canada, release of *Toward a Quality of Life Strategy for Canada* (Department of Finance 2021b) illustrates federal government interest in moving in a direction broadly consistent with the OECD's well-being framework and dashboard approach, and goals of inclusive and sustainable growth.[15] Next steps for this work focus on completing, with further public input, the quality-of-life framework to define and measure success and "consider[ing] ways to better incorporate the framework – and quality of life data and evidence more broadly – into government decision-making" (24). In a federation as decentralized as Canada – with provinces often serving as policy-innovation laboratories and holding key powers in areas central to well-being and sustainability, such as health, education, and environment – provincial actions are equally important, with Nova Scotia standing out as one province potentially ripe for new well-being initiatives, while local government initiatives have also been shown to have important impacts (Dasilva and Hayden). Incorporating Indigenous perspectives on the meaning and measurement of well-being, addressing gaps in data on well-being in Indigenous communities (Department of Finance 2021b, 17), and – most significantly – strengthening policy action to address the stark well-being disparities between Indigenous and non-Indigenous communities also stand out as key priorities for Canada.

While some observers will see recent advances in Canada and elsewhere and the prospect of further advances as reason to stay the course, others see a need for a significant change in strategies. In their analysis of the "rise and fall" of the EU's beyond-GDP initiative, Bleys and Thiry note that initial hopes for transformative change after the 2008–9 economic crisis were soon followed by restoration of a conventional emphasis on economic growth, with beyond-GDP efforts limited to production of new statistics rather than shifts in policies and priorities. Looking ahead, they see greater potential in the rise of post-growth economics and ecological macroeconomics and moving beyond "Beyond GDP," i.e., focusing not on changing the dominant indicator but on a new policy agenda and accompanying social narrative that move "beyond growth." Meanwhile Colman calls on beyond-GDP researchers and practitioners to be more vocal about how the numbers they generate point to the need for a radically different economic system based on fair and efficient distribution within the limits of a finite planet and to aim to reach new audiences, particularly young leaders and grassroots activists.

These chapters calling for new strategies are among those in the transformative camp, seeking a new post-growth economy.[16] From this perspective, the steps forward discussed in this chapter – which are more in line with the reformist approach of using new measurements to improve policymaking without challenging the growth paradigm or other core features of the existing economy – can appear less than fully inspiring, as the motivation has been to achieve much more. Even Bhutan, the country seemingly most committed to beyond-GDP measurement, with GNH enshrined in its constitution and numerous related achievements (Kim and MacKenzie), can be seen to have fallen short of fully implementing a new post-growth economic paradigm based on sustainability, equity, and well-being (Colman).[17] Proponents of a new paradigm of that kind can point, for example, to the rapidly vanishing time available to address the climate emergency (IPCC 2018) – an emergency acknowledged in word by many government bodies, including Canada's House of Commons, but not yet sufficiently in deed – as evidence of the need for a major economic transformation.

A transformative vision that sees beyond-GDP measurement as part of a wider beyond-growth project faces some major challenges, as noted above. The possibility of managing a post-growth society on the basis of a very different indicator or set of indicators, with little[18] or no reference to GDP, would depend on disentangling society from its current dependence on economic growth. Some will reflect on that daunting task and turn back to hopes of making growth greener and more inclusive. However, given the lateness of the hour in dealing with urgent ecological challenges and the meagre results to date of green-growth efforts seeking to decouple GDP growth from environmental impacts (Haberl et al. 2020; Parrique et al. 2019; Wiedmann et al. 2020) – not to mention the possibility of a prolonged period of slow economic growth or secular stagnation largely for non-ecological reasons (Dorling 2020; Gordon 2015; Vollrath 2020) – work by ecological economists on how to manage an economy without growth is of great importance (e.g., Jackson 2017; Lange 2018; Victor 2019).[19] So, too, are debates over proposals such as work-time reduction, a job guarantee, basic income or universal basic services, and greater equity in asset ownership, which may offer possibilities to maintain employment and economic security even in a post-growth economy. Such issues are also being examined in connection with concepts such as Raworth's (2017) "doughnut economics," the new economy and "next system project" (e.g., Speth 2015), degrowth (e.g., Kallis et al. 2020), eco-socialism (e.g., Löwy 2020), sufficiency (e.g., Alexander 2019), and questioning of affluent overconsumption (e.g., Wiedmann et al. 2020). Meanwhile, in Britain, Jackson (2020) has called for a formal inquiry into reducing the UK economy's growth dependency to accompany the development of new measures of sustainable prosperity and a policy framework aiming to deliver societal well-being rather than GDP growth. As Colman notes in his chapter, a key question – one beyond the scope of this book – for further debate among those seeking a new post-growth economic paradigm is whether such changes require a move beyond capitalism.[20]

These transformative post-growth ideas raise a very challenging set of issues, from which most mainstream political actors tend to steer clear. As a result, it is also worth thinking about possibilities to find some productive common ground between reformist and transformative visions. Indeed, the boundaries between the two approaches can be blurred, and an ambitious reformist approach – building on ideas discussed above – may turn out to expand the possibilities for transformative efforts.

One interim step with potential to bridge the transformative–reformist divide is to work towards explicit commitments from governments to prioritize well-being or sustainable well-being as an overriding objective – in the spirit of what Danny Graham of Engage Nova Scotia refers to as bringing people together for the "next iteration of what's possible" (Dasilva and Hayden). The Wellbeing Economy Governments (WEGo) of New Zealand, Iceland, Scotland, Wales, and Finland illustrate that it is possible for countries to commit, as Scotland's first minister put it, to "redefining" what it means to be a "successful country" and "putting wellbeing at the heart of what we are doing" (Sturgeon 2020). This does not mean that such countries are abandoning either GDP measurement or pursuit of GDP growth – indeed, they clearly state they are not doing so[21] – but it does imply that GDP is no longer the primary measure of success, while GDP growth is seen as one means among others towards the end of well-being. A similar approach is evident in a recent report to the OECD on "Beyond Growth," which, while stopping short of rejecting growth as an objective, displaces it from its status as the primary goal in favour of four paramount objectives for economic policy: environmental sustainability, rising well-being, falling inequality, and system resilience (i.e., ability to withstand financial, environmental, and other shocks) (Secretary General's Advisory Group on a New Growth Narrative 2019; see also Bleys and Thiry, this volume).

We believe it would be of value for governments – at federal and provincial levels in Canada as well as in other countries – to signal such a shift in orientation, for example, by joining the Wellbeing Economy Governments,[22] which would involve a commitment to "collaborate in pursuit of innovative policy approaches to create wellbeing economies – sharing what works and what does not, to inform policymaking for change."[23] This recommendation comes with two caveats. First, a risk exists of such initiatives being too closely associated with individual politicians; if so a change of government or party leadership can result in such initiatives being quickly abandoned. It is thus valuable to build cross-party and wider societal support[24] (in addition to having strong political leadership from the top to ensure different government departments work together to achieve a shared vision). The second caveat is that such steps should not be limited to symbolic action. As noted in the introductory chapter, symbolic use of indicators involves giving "ritualistic assurances that those who make the decisions hold appropriate attitudes towards decision-making" (Hezri 2004, 366). Rather than simply signalling progressive/ecological values, it would be important for any proclamation of a well-being economy orientation to be backed by concrete initiatives, with well-being budgeting among the possibilities.

Those with transformative hopes to build a post-growth "new economy" will likely see the limits of such steps – and indeed be concerned, in line with Colman's analysis, that the transformative elements of a well-being economy agenda may be lost as it is mainstreamed. But another way to think about such steps, and the adoption of beyond-GDP measurement more generally, is as a *transitional* strategy to help create more favourable conditions for the pursuit of sustainability and equity. The dominance of conventional economic values disadvantages the efforts of all those working for environmental sustainability, equity, and other social values.[25] By putting greater weight on social and environmental considerations alongside economic values, beyond-GDP measurement could help level the playing field and open up "space in which more transformational possibilities can be cultivated" (Clarke 2014, 9).[26]

At the same time, political and social movement efforts to promote the importance of sustainable and equitable well-being are likely to support the use of new measurement frameworks. Citizen participation can support both reformist and transformative visions but is particularly important for the latter in building public and political support for a shift in societal priorities, such as the climate justice movement's efforts to galvanize action to address the climate emergency and crisis of inequality. As Colman argues, stronger connections between beyond-GDP researchers and such movements are needed if changes in measurement frameworks are to be linked to transformative political change.

While significant differences of perspective remain within the beyond-GDP community about the path ahead, we are encouraged by the growing number of international experiences and substantial Canadian contributions to build on, and see considerable promise for further advances, whether by using improved metrics to generate better policies or as one element of larger efforts to achieve more transformative change. As societies seek to rebuild better following the social and economic shock of the COVID-19 pandemic, redress a legacy of racial and other inequalities, accelerate efforts to decarbonize societies, and generate well-being within planetary boundaries – while other challenges, such as automation of growing numbers of jobs, await – the importance of the debate over the meaning of societal success, how to measure it, and how to act in response to those measurements is perhaps greater than ever.

NOTES

1 For example, GDP is correlated with tax revenues, and GDP forecasts are thus useful for government budgeting and related issues, such as debt management.

2 For the full wording of the questions, see preface, i–ii.

3 Figures from March 2021. Laurent (this volume) also highlights Finland's effective COVID-19 response. High social trust and confidence in public institutions, and

low income inequality, are among the variables associated with low COVID-19 death rates and also with high well-being (Helliwell et al. 2021).

4 In his chapter, Barrington-Leigh proposes weighting each component in proportion to its known contribution to increasing life satisfaction, which is a possible solution, although it requires acceptance of the overriding importance of life satisfaction as an end goal.

5 For a more detailed review of the debate on life satisfaction/happiness as the goal of government, see other articles responding to Frijters et al. (2020) in the same special issue.

6 Bhutan's GNH offers another way to link environmental conservation – one of four GNH pillars – to happiness; however, as Kim and MacKenzie (this volume) point out, Bhutan's Buddhist understanding of happiness is quite different from Western notions and incorporates an emphasis on responsibility, harmony with nature, and concern for the happiness of others.

7 These could shift over time with changing social needs and democratically determined political priorities.

8 The larger dataset could still be of value in identifying issues that deserve to move up the priority list or adding additional perspective on other indicators. For example, in Nova Scotia, the CIW-based dashboard of sixty indicators included valuable evidence of a surprising lack of housing affordability; however, additional environmental indicators not in the dashboard would provide a more complete picture of the province's mixed environmental record (Dasilva and Hayden, this volume).

9 These outcomes are related to children and young people, communities, culture, economy, education, environment, fair work and business, health, human rights, international matters, and poverty. For details, see https://nationalperformance.gov.scot/national-outcomes.

10 The proposed framework includes five main domains – prosperity, health, environment, society, and good governance – with nineteen headline indicators and eighty-three indicators in total, with plans to further refine the indicator set.

11 We might find, for example, that future governments look at well-being assessments from various sources, similar to the Canadian government's current use of multiple private-sector GDP forecasts, in addition to their own, to help counter the potential problem of overly rosy government assessments.

12 Despite differing assessments of Bhutan's experience, the chapter by Kim and MacKenzie and the contrasting analysis by Colman are noteworthy for both touching on the role of personal transformation – a seeming reflection of the Buddhist underpinnings of GNH.

13 "Whole of government" should be seen as an approximation rather than taken literally. New metrics and a broader sustainable well-being orientation can help break down departmental silos but may be less relevant for some government

activities, e.g., Canada's management of its relations with the United States and China.

14 In his chapter, Laurent (this volume) argues that such a law is useful but the French government's response to it was flawed, as it manipulated the process by selecting indicators that put its record in a favourable light.

15 The Department of Finance (2021b, 7–8, 12) acknowledges the OECD's beyond-GDP work as a major influence Canada's latest initiatives in this area. Canada was slow to develop a substantial response to the OECD's beyond-GDP work, which first emerged during the Conservative Harper government but now appears to be catching up with the majority of OECD countries that have quality-of-life or well-being initiatives in some form (Department of Finance 2021a, 411).

16 Other authors with transformative goals are somewhat more optimistic about the inroads and impacts so far. Laurent, for example, argues that "well-being indicators have already started to deliver progress. But more is needed."

17 Among Bhutan's successes are substantial poverty reduction, increases in life expectancy, a constitutionally enshrined commitment to maintain at least 60 per cent of land under forest cover, and net-negative GHG emissions (Kim and MacKenzie) – in addition to achievements in combatting COVID-19, discussed above. However, Bhutan has not fulfilled all the hopes of those seeking transformation beyond the growth paradigm. Colman notes that Bhutan failed to gain international support for a "new economic paradigm," some domestic GNH initiatives encountered bureaucratic resistance, and its more radical challenge to a GDP-growth-based economy faded with the end of Jigmi Thinley's prime ministership in 2013.

18 Even a society that deprioritizes economic growth could have reasons to track whatever annual variations in economic output occur to facilitate tasks such as government budgeting.

19 Keyßer and Lenzen (2021) show that scenarios to limit warming to 1.5°C in which economic output declines due to stringent climate mitigation ("degrowth") have much greater technological feasibility than conventional scenarios assuming continued GDP growth (i.e., they rely less on risky and unproven negative emissions technologies and do not require rates of new technology adoption well beyond historical norms), although they face political feasibility challenges.

20 For many observers a growth imperative is central to capitalism, making a post-growth or degrowth project inherently anti-capitalist (e.g., Hickel 2021); however, some ecological economists argue that a non-growing, steady-state capitalism is possible with substantial institutional reforms (e.g., Lawn 2011). Tim Jackson (2017; 2021), a prominent contributor to post-growth debates, has taken a more explicit stance on the need to move beyond capitalism in his latest book compared to previous work. See also Wiedmann et al. (2020) for a review of this debate.

21 See NZ Government (2019, 2, 5) and Sturgeon (2020).

22 While Canada is not a WEGo member, Department of Finance (2021b, 7) officials began participating in WEGo Policy Labs in summer 2020.

23 WEGo members also commit to: "progress toward the UN Sustainable Development Goals, in line with Goal 17, fostering partnership and cooperation to identify approaches to delivering wellbeing" and "address the pressing economic, social, and environmental challenges of our time." https://wellbeingeconomy.org /wego.

24 In Canada, it might be hard to envision the current federal Conservative Party signing on; however, one can imagine building support for a well-being orientation among the four other parties with seats in the House of Commons.

25 Interview, Stuart Clarke of the Town Creek Foundation. See Hayden and Wilson (2018).

26 Clarke's analysis had the GPI specifically in mind but can also apply to other beyond-GDP metrics.

REFERENCES

Alexander, Samuel. 2019. "What Would a Sufficiency Economy Look Like?" In *Just Enough*, edited by Matthew Ingleby and Samuel Randalls, 117–34. London: Palgrave Macmillan.

APPGWE. 2019. "A Spending Review to Increase Wellbeing." London: All-Party Parliamentary Group on Wellbeing Economics. https://wellbeingeconomics .co.uk/wp-content/uploads/2019/05/Spending-review-to-ncrease-wellbeing -APPG-2019.pdf.

Bleys, Brent, and Alistair Whitby. 2015. "Barriers and Opportunities for Alternative Measures of Economic Welfare." *Ecological Economics* 117 (September): 162–72. https://doi.org/10.1016/j.ecolecon.2015.06.021.

Clarke, Stuart. 2014. "Town Creek Foundation Stakeholder Meeting." Easton, MD: Town Creek Foundation. http://c.ymcdn.com/sites/abagrantmakers.site-ym.com /resource/resmgr/Communications/Town_Creek_Foundation_Stakeh.pdf.

Department of Finance. 2021a. "A Recovery Plan for Jobs, Growth, and Resilience: Budget 2021." Ottawa: Department of Finance Canada. https://www.budget .gc.ca/2021/home-accueil-en.html.

– 2021b. "Toward a Quality of Life Strategy for Canada." Ottawa: Department of Finance Canada.

Dorling, Danny. 2020. *Slowdown: The End of the Great Acceleration—and Why It's Good for the Planet, the Economy, and Our Lives.* New Haven, CT: Yale University Press.

Durand, Martine. 2020. "What Should Be the Goal of Public Policies?" *Behavioural Public Policy* 4, no. 2: 226–35. https://doi.org/10.1017/bpp.2019.45.

Durand, Martine, and Carrie Exton. 2019. "Adopting a Well-Being Approach in Central Government: Policy Mechanisms and Practical Tools." In *Global*

Happiness and Wellbeing Policy Report 2019, edited by Global Council for Happiness and Wellbeing, 140–62. New York: Sustainable Development Solutions Network.

Fioramonti, Lorenzo. 2017. *Wellbeing Economy: Success in a World without Growth.* Johannesburg: Pan Macmillan SA.

Frijters, Paul, Andrew E. Clark, Christian Krekel, and Richard Layard. 2020. "A Happy Choice: Wellbeing as the Goal of Government." *Behavioural Public Policy* 4, no. 2: 126–65. https://doi.org/10.1017/bpp.2019.39.

Gordon, Robert J. 2015. "Secular Stagnation: A Supply-Side View." *The American Economic Review* 105, no. 5: 54–9. https://doi.org/10.1257/aer.p20151102.

Haberl, Helmut, Dominik Wiedenhofer, Doris Virág, Gerald Kalt, Barbara Plank, Paul Brockway, Tomer Fishman, et al. 2020. "A Systematic Review of the Evidence on Decoupling of GDP, Resource Use and GHG Emissions, Part II: Synthesizing the Insights." *Environmental Research Letters* 15, no. 6: 065003. https://doi.org /10.1088/1748-9326/ab842a.

Hayden, Anders, and Jeffrey Wilson. 2017. "'Beyond GDP' Indicators: Changing the Economic Narrative for a Post-Consumerist Society?" In *Social Change and the Coming of Post-Consumer Society: Theoretical Advances and Policy Implications*, edited by Maurie J. Cohen, Halina S. Brown, and Philip J. Vergragt, 170–91. New York: Routledge.

– 2018. "Taking the First Steps beyond GDP: Maryland's Experience in Measuring 'Genuine Progress.'" *Sustainability* 10, no. 2: 462. https://doi.org/10.3390 /su10020462.

Helliwell, John. 2019. "Measuring and Using Happiness to Support Public Policies." NBER Working Paper No. 26529. Cambridge, MA: National Bureau of Economic Research.

Helliwell, John F., Richard Layard, Jeffrey Sachs, and Jan-Emmanuel De Neve, eds. 2021. *World Happiness Report 2021.* New York: Sustainable Development Solutions Network. https://worldhappiness.report/ed/2021/.

Hezri, Adnan A. 2004. "Sustainability Indicator System and Policy Processes in Malaysia: A Framework for Utilisation and Learning." *Journal of Environmental Management* 73, no. 4: 357–71. https://doi.org/10.1016/j.jenvman.2004.07.010.

Hickel, Jason. 2021. *Less Is More: How Degrowth Will Save the World.* Portsmouth, NH: William Heinemann.

Hoekstra, Rutger. 2019. *Replacing GDP by 2030.* Cambridge: Cambridge University Press.

IPCC. 2018. "Global Warming of 1.5°C: Summary for Policymakers." Geneva: Intergovernmental Panel on Climate Change.

Jackson, Tim. 2017. *Prosperity without Growth.* 2nd ed. Abingdon, UK: Routledge.

– 2020. "Wellbeing Matters—Tackling Growth Dependency." London: All-Party Parliamentary Group on Limits to Growth. https:///appg-briefing-no3/.

– 2021. *Post Growth: Life after Capitalism.* London: Polity.

Kallis, Giorgis, Susan Paulson, Giacomo D'Alisa, and Federico Demaria. 2020. *The Case for Degrowth*. Cambridge, UK: Polity.

Keyßer, Lorenz T., and Manfred Lenzen. 2021. "1.5 °C Degrowth Scenarios Suggest the Need for New Mitigation Pathways." *Nature Communications* 12, no. 1: 2676. https://doi.org/10.1038/s41467-021-22884-9.

Kubiszewski, Ida, Robert Costanza, Carol Franco, Philip Lawn, John Talberth, Tim Jackson, and Camille Aylmer. 2013. "Beyond GDP: Measuring and Achieving Global Genuine Progress." *Ecological Economics* 93 (September): 57–68. https://doi.org/10.1016/j.ecolecon.2013.04.019.

Lange, Steffen. 2018. *Macroeconomics without Growth*. Marburg, Germany: Metropolis-Verlag.

Lawn, Philip. 2011. "Is Steady-State Capitalism Viable? A Review of the Issues and an Answer in the Affirmative." *Annals of the New York Academy of Sciences* 1219, no. 1: 1–25.

Löwy, Michael. 2020. "Ecosocialism: A Radical Alternative." In *Reflections on Socialism in the Twenty-First Century*, edited by Claes Brundenius, 199–210. Cham, Switzerland: Springer. https://doi.org/10.1007/978-3-030-33920-3_10.

Lowy Institute. 2021. "Covid Performance Index." Lowy Institute, 13 March 2021. https://interactives.lowyinstitute.org/features/covid-performance/.

NZ Government. 2019. "The Wellbeing Budget." Wellington, NZ: New Zealand Government.

Parrique, Tim, Jonathan Barth, François Briens, Christian Kerschner, Alejo Kraus-Polk, Anna Kuokkanen, and Joachim Spangenberg. 2019. "Decoupling Debunked – Evidence and Arguments against Green Growth as a Sole Strategy for Sustainability." Brussels: European Environmental Bureau. https://mk0eeborgicuypctuf7e.kinstacdn.com/wp-content/uploads/2019/07/Decoupling-Debunked.pdf.

Raworth, Kate. 2017. *Doughnut Economics*. London: Random House.

Richters, Oliver, and Andreas Simoneit. 2019. "Growth Imperatives: Substantiating a Contested Concept." *Structural Change and Economic Dynamics* 51 (December): 126–37. https://doi.org/10.1016/j.strueco.2019.07.012.

Secretary General's Advisory Group on a New Growth Narrative. 2019. "Beyond Growth: Towards a New Economic Approach." Paris: OECD. https://www.oecd.org/naec/averting-systemic-collapse/SG-NAEC(2019)3_Beyond%20Growth.pdf.

Smale, Bryan, Mingjie Gao, and Kai Jiang. 2020. "An Exploration of Wellbeing in Nova Scotia: A Summary of Results from the Nova Scotia Quality of Life Survey." Waterloo, ON: Canadian Index of Wellbeing and University of Waterloo. https://static1.squarespace.com/static/5d388a67fad33f0001679229/t/5e71250812d3805459021b82/1584473359939/NSQofLifeSurvey-AnExplorationOfWellbeing-March2020+%281%29.pdf.

Speth, James Gustave. 2015. "Getting to the Next System: Guideposts on the Way to a New Political Economy." Washington, DC: The Next System Project. https://thenextsystem.org/gettowhatsnext.

Stiglitz, Joseph E., Jean-Paul Fitoussi, and Martine Durand. 2018. "Beyond GDP - Measuring What Counts for Economic and Social Performance." Paris: OECD. http://www.oecd.org/corruption/beyond-gdp-9789264307292-en.htm.

Stiglitz, Joseph E., Amartya Sen, and Jean-Paul Fitoussi. 2009. "Report by the Commission on the Measurement of Economic Performance and Social Progress." Paris: Commission on the Measurement of Economic Performance and Social Progress. http://www.stiglitz-sen-fitoussi.fr/documents/rapport_anglais.pdf.

Sturgeon, Nicola. 2020. "Wellbeing Economy Alliance Conference: First Minister's Speech." Keynote address, Edinburgh, 22 January 2020. https://www.gov.scot/publications/wellbeing-economy-alliance-conference/.

Victor, Peter A. 2019. *Managing without Growth: Slower by Design, Not Disaster.* 2nd ed. Cheltenham, UK: Edward Elgar.

Vollrath, Dietrich. 2020. *Fully Grown: Why a Stagnant Economy Is a Sign of Success.* Chicago: University of Chicago Press.

Watson, Nancy M. 2018. "A Better Way than Dollars and Cents to Measure Success." *The Chronicle Herald*, 26 June 2018. https://uwaterloo.ca/canadian-index-wellbeing/news/better-way-dollars-and-cents-measure-success.

Whitby, Alistair, et al. 2014. "BRAINPOoL Project Final Report: Beyond GDP - from Measurement to Politics and Policy." Hamburg: World Future Council. http://www.brainpoolproject.eu/wp-content/uploads/2014/05/BRAINPOoL-Project-Final-Report.pdf.

Wiedmann, Thomas, Manfred Lenzen, Lorenz T. Keyßer, and Julia K. Steinberger. 2020. "Scientists' Warning on Affluence." *Nature Communications* 11, no. 1: 1–10. https://doi.org/10.1038/s41467-020-16941-y.

Contributors

Ian Bache, professor, Department of Politics, co-director, Centre for Wellbeing in Public Policy, University of Sheffield

Christopher P. Barrington-Leigh, associate professor, Institute for Health and Social Policy and the Bieler School of Environment, McGill University

Günseli Berik, professor, Department of Economics, University of Utah

Livia Bizikova, director, Knowledge for Integrated Decisions, International Institute for Sustainable Development

Brent Bleys, associate professor, Department of Economics, Ghent University, Belgium

Ronald Colman, founding director, GPI Atlantic

Clay Dasilva, doctoral candidate, Balsillie School of International Affairs, University of Waterloo

Martine Durand, former (retired) OECD chief statistician and director of the OECD Statistics and Data Directorate

Céofride Gaudet, retired federal government economist and policy analyst, and former public servant in residence, School for Resource and Environmental Studies, Dalhousie University

David Gyarmati, president and CEO, Social Research and Demonstration Corporation

Anders Hayden, associate professor, Department of Political Science, Dalhousie University

John F. Helliwell, professor emeritus, Vancouver School of Economics, University of British Columbia; fellow of the Royal Society of Canada; officer of the Order of Canada.

Craig Joyce, senior analyst, Finance Canada

Julia C. Kim, program director, GNH Centre, Bhutan; Executive Committee member, the Club of Rome

Éloi Laurent, Centre for Economic Research (OFCE) and Paris School of International Affairs (PSIA), Sciences Po; Ponts Paris Tech; Stanford University

Amy MacKenzie, senior consultant, Group ATN Consulting Inc.

Kieran McDougal, associate, International Institute for Sustainable Development

Marco Mira d'Ercole, former (retired) head of household statistics, OECD Statistics and Data Directorate

Tim Ng, former deputy secretary, chief economic advisor, New Zealand Treasury

Heather Orpana, senior research scientist, Public Health Agency of Canada

Julia Rodgers, doctoral candidate, Department of Political Science, Dalhousie University

Rob Smith, senior associate, International Institute for Sustainable Development; Principal, Midsummer Analytics

Géraldine Thiry, associate professor, department of economics, ICHEC Brussels Management School, Brussels, Belgium

Katherine Trebeck, co-founder, Wellbeing Economy Alliance and WEAll Scotland

Jeffrey Wilson, assistant professor, School of Environment, Enterprise and Development (SEED), Faculty of Environment, University of Waterloo

Index

Note: Page numbers in *italics* indicate figures and tables.

www.ingramcontent.com/pod-product-compliance
Lightning Source LLC
Chambersburg PA
CBHW030235030426
42336CB00009B/106